THE ESSENTIAL STOIC

The Most Important Writings from the Masters of Stoicism

Marcus Aurelius
Epictetus
Seneca

ST. MARTIN'S ESSENTIALS
NEW YORK

Published in the United States by St. Martin's Essentials,
an imprint of St. Martin's Publishing Group

 For information, address St. Martin's Publishing Group, 120 Broadway, New York, NY 10271.

www.stmartins.com

The Library of Congress Cataloging-in-Publication Data is available upon request.

ISBN 978-1-250-32535-8 (trade paperback)
ISBN 978-1-250-32536-5 (ebook)

Our books may be purchased in bulk for promotional, educational, or business use. Please contact your local bookseller or the Macmillan Corporate and Premium Sales Department at 1-800-221-7945, extension 5442, or by email at MacmillanSpecialMarkets@macmillan.com.

First St. Martin's Essentials Edition: 2024

10 9 8 7 6 5 4 3 2 1

THE ESSENTIAL STOIC

CONTENTS

INTRODUCTION

Going through the most challenging and trying moments in our lives, we seek support. Sage advice, an inspiring quote, or a beautiful insight can give you direction when you are at a loss for where to go.

I was looking for support when I was an athlete at the Olympics. The pressure of performing weighs heavily, especially knowing how much energy it takes to get to the Games. My challenge was to maintain mental calm in the heat of the moment. I found the answers to my challenge in the texts bundled in this book. I found them in Seneca's wise counsel—he stood by me with his words like a good friend—and in Marcus Aurelius' deep musings on leadership and Epictetus' clear and strict principles.

My big dream was to become an Olympic champion. I could only achieve that goal if I stopped being distracted by the thought of gold and focused on my own character values. I needed the discipline to work hard and deliver quality. I needed the courage not to let the fear of failure consume me. I pursued justice and wisdom to make the right choices, respect my opponents, and pay attention to my colleagues and others around me.

The stoics say you should follow these character values in your life. I apply Stoic philosophy as a guide, a thought system to counterbalance inevitable setbacks and unpredictability in my life. It helps give direction to my dreams and ambitions and keeps me on the right track.

I would like to briefly highlight one example. I blamed my father for my parents' nasty divorce. I was especially angry with him and had no contact with him for years. Thanks to the teachings of Epictetus, I understood that my tendency to judge was the source of my anger. I learned that my anger was not caused by my father but by my conception of what a good father should be. That thought liberated me. I sought contact with him again and gradually my anger dissipated.

It is exactly what the stoics mean by finding peace of mind. In an important part of my life, I found peace instead of anger; it enriched my life and, in the process, enabled me to perform better as an athlete. A few months after reconnecting with my father, in 2010 I won the 1,500-meter gold medal at the speed skating event in Vancouver. And who cheered loudest of all in the stands? My father.

Since I stopped being a professional athlete, the stoic lessons have helped me in my many roles in life—as an entrepreneur, son, father, husband, friend, associate, or colleague. Marcus Aurelius taught me I should always keep my guiding principles in mind and that the autonomy I pursue will never lead to a worthwhile life if it is not accompanied by a deep human connection with others. Life is a team sport. Seneca taught me to be less strict with myself. He speaks beautifully and wisely to me as a writer and teaches me to guard myself against setbacks and the opinions of others. It gave me an anchor when, as an entrepreneur, I saw my business almost collapse during the coronavirus pandemic because of disrupted production chains.

With my performance drive, ambition, and my will to win, I may not naturally be a stoic. But that is precisely why I try to apply this mindset to my professional career. It allows me to find the right mental balance. Sharp and relaxed. Wanting to win gold but not focusing on gold. Every day we can choose to live a good life, be a good person, and do what is right. To achieve that, we should not sit back but act. We can chat about it, but actions are the real test of character. A good life must be lived, and lessons must be applied. This is why Stoic philosophy appeals to me so much. The stoics are not armchair philosophers. They are the people who test and adjust their ideas in the real world to pursue a better life for themselves and others.

Everyone deserves the lessons described in these timeless and unique works. They have been an important foundation of my happiness for over twenty years. They are the lessons I draw on daily; not life hacks or easy tricks but deep life lessons that require attention, reflection, and, above all, action to come to life. Day in, day out.

—Mark Tuitert

MARCUS AURELIUS

Meditations

Translated by George Long

Edited by Edwin Ginn

Contents

Preface

Perhaps some may question the wisdom of putting out the Thoughts of Marcus Aurelius Antoninus to be used as a Reader by children in the schools. It may appear to them better suited to the mature mind. The principle, however, that has governed us in selecting reading for the young has been to secure the best that we could find in all ages for grown-up people. The milk and water diet provided for "my dear children" is not especially complimentary to them. They like to be treated like little men and women, capable of appreciating a good thing. One finds in this royal philosopher a rare generosity, sweetness and humility, qualities alike suited to all ages.

Adopting the philosopher's robe at twelve, he remains a student all his life. The precepts that he would give for the government of others, he has practised upon himself. In his time, as in ours, there were good physicians for the mind and body, who could make wise prescriptions for the government of their neighbors, but were unable to apply them to themselves. The faults of our fellows are so numerous and so easy to cure that one is readily tempted to become the physician, while our own faults are so few and so unimportant that it is hardly worth while to give any attention to them. Hence we have a multitude of physicians for humanity in general, and a scarcity of individual healers.

It was the doctrine of Marcus Aurelius that most of the ills of life come to us from our own imagination, that it was not in the power of others seriously to interfere with the calm, temperate life of an individual, and that when a fellow being did anything to us that seemed unjust he was acting in ignorance, and that instead of stirring up anger within us it should stir our pity for him. Oftentimes by careful self-examination we should find that the fault was more our own than that of our fellow, and our sufferings were rather from our own opinions than from anything real. The circle of man's knowledge is very limited, and the largest circles do not wholly include the smallest. They are intersecting and the segment common to any two is very small. Whatever lies outside this space does not exist for both. Hence arise innumerable contests. The man having the largest intelligence ought to be very generous to the other. Being thankful that he has been blessed in so many ways, he should do all in his power to enlighten his less favored fellow, rather than be angry with him on account of his misfortune. Is he not sufficiently punished in being denied the light?

Assisting his uncle in the government of the great Roman Empire at seventeen, it was his aim constantly to restrain the power of the strong and to assist the weak. He studied the laws of his country, not for wisdom alone, but that he might make them more beneficial to his people. All his life he tried to bring his fellows to a higher level, and to think charitably of each other. Occupying himself a palace he lived simply, like other men. It was his greatest delight to retire to his country home and there, dwelling among his books, to meditate upon the great problems of life. He claimed that a man's life should be valued according to the value of the things to which he gave his attention. If his whole thought was given to clothing, feeding and housing himself comfortably, he should be valued like other well-housed and well-fed animals. He would, however, derive the greatest pleasure and benefit in this life by acting in accordance with reason, which demands of every human being that his highest faculties should govern all the rest, and that each should see to it that he treated his fellow kindly and generously and that if he could not assist him to a higher level he should at least not stand in his way. When he speaks of the shortness of time and the value of fame, riches and power, for which men strive in this world, he speaks not from the standpoint of one who would wish to obtain these things, but as a Roman emperor enjoying the highest honors that man might expect to attain in this world. He certainly was in a position to speak intelligently concerning these matters, and his opinions ought to have weight with the coming generations. Children may not prefer to read such thoughts; perhaps the majority of children do not prefer the Bible to other books. Still, we all think it is well for them to be obliged to read it. Perhaps requiring the use of such literature in the schools might be as valuable as the adding, subtracting, multiplying and dividing of interminable numbers, the memorizing of all the capes, bays and rivers in the world, and the dates of all the battles that have occurred since the creation of man. We should strive to stimulate the thinking powers of children, leading them to form wise judgments concerning the important things of life, without catering too much to their own wishes at an age when they cannot form an intelligent opinion of what is best for themselves.

At our first reading of the Thoughts of Marcus Aurelius Antoninus, we marked many sentences that appeared to us specially good; in the second, twice as many more. Where all is good it is hard to emphasize, but we will cite just one of his reflections, as illustrating the trend of his mind: "I have often wondered," he says, "how it is that every man loves himself more than all the rest of men, and yet sets less value on his own opinion of himself than on the opinion of others."

We have given Long's translation of the Thoughts complete, as published by Messrs. Little, Brown & Co., but we have omitted some unimportant portions of the biography and philosophy in the interest of space and economy. We have also given the philosophy in a supplement, thinking it better that it should come after the Thoughts themselves. We shall issue a pocket edition on very thin paper for the convenience of such as wish to make a special study of the work. We also propose to issue a similar edition of the writings of Epictetus.

—*Edwin Ginn*
January 20, 1893

Biographical Sketch of Marcus Aurelius Antoninus

M. Antoninus, the son of Annius Verus and Domitia Calvilla, was born at Rome, A.D. 121. The Emperor T. Antoninus Pius married Faustina, the sister of Annius Verus, and was consequently the uncle of M. Antoninus. When Hadrian adopted Antoninus Pius and declared him his successor in the empire, Antoninus Pius adopted both L. Ceionius Commodus and M. Antoninus, generally called M. Aurelius Antoninus.

The youth was most carefully brought up. He thanks the gods (I. 17) that he had good grandfathers, good parents, a good sister, good teachers, good associates, good kinsmen and friends, nearly everything good. He had the happy fortune to witness the example of his uncle and adoptive father, Antoninus Pius, and he has recorded in his work (I. 16; VI. 30) the virtues of this excellent man and prudent ruler. Like many young Romans he tried his hand at poetry and studied rhetoric. There are letters extant showing the great affection of the pupil for the master, and the master's great hopes of his industrious pupil.

When he was eleven years old he assumed the dress of philosophers, something plain and coarse, became a hard student, and lived a most laborious, abstemious life, even so far as to injure his health. He abandoned poetry and rhetoric for philosophy, and attached himself to the sect of the Stoics. But he did not neglect the study of law, which was a useful preparation for the high place which he was designed to fill. We must suppose that he learned the Roman discipline of arms, which was a necessary part of the education of a man who afterwards led his troops to battle against a warlike race.

Antoninus has recorded in his first book the names of his teachers, and the obligations which he owed to each of them. The way in which he speaks of what he learned from them might seem to savor of vanity or self-praise, if we look carelessly at the way in which he has expressed himself; but if anyone draws this conclusion, he will be mistaken. Antoninus means to commemorate the merits of his several teachers, what they taught, and what a pupil might learn from them. Besides, this book, like the eleven other books, was for his own use; and if we may trust the note at the end of the first book, it was written during one of M. Antoninus' campaigns against the Quadi, at a time when the commemoration of the virtues of his illustrious teachers might remind him of their lessons and the practical uses which he might derive from them.

Among his teachers of philosophy was Sextus of Chaeroneia, a grandson of Plutarch. What he learned from this excellent man is told by himself (I. 9). His favorite teacher was Rusticus (I. 7), a philosopher, and also a man of practical good sense in public affairs. Rusticus was the adviser of Antoninus after he became emperor. Young men who are destined for high places are not often fortunate in those who are about them, their companions and teachers; and I do not know any example of a young prince having had an education which can be compared with that of M. Antoninus. Such a body of teachers distinguished by their acquirements and their character will hardly be collected again; and as to the pupil, we have not had one like him since.

Hadrian died in July, A.D. 138, and was succeeded by Antoninus Pius. M. Antoninus married Faustina, his cousin, the daughter of Pius, probably about A.D. 146, for he had a daughter born in A.D. 147. He received from his adoptive father the title of Caesar, and was associated with him in the administration of the state. The father and the adopted son lived together in perfect friendship and confidence. Antoninus was a dutiful son, and the emperor Pius loved and esteemed him.

Antoninus Pius died in A.D. 161. The Senate, it is said, urged M. Antoninus to take the sole administration of the empire, but he associated with himself the other adopted son of Pius, L. Ceionius Commodus, who is generally called L. Verus. Thus Rome for the first time had two emperors. Verus was an indolent man of pleasure, and unworthy of his station. Antoninus however bore with him, and it is said that Verus had sense enough to pay to his colleague the respect due to his character. A virtuous emperor and a loose partner lived together in peace, and their alliance was strengthened by Antoninus giving to Verus for wife his daughter Lucilla.

The reign of Antoninus was first troubled by a Parthian war, in which Verus was sent to command; but he did nothing, and the success that was obtained by the Romans in Armenia and on the Euphrates and Tigris was due to his generals. This Parthian war ended in A.D. 165. Aurelius and Verus had a triumph

(A.D. 166) for the victories in the East. A pestilence followed, which carried off great numbers in Rome and Italy, and spread to the west of Europe.

The north of Italy was also threatened by the rude people beyond the Alps from the borders of Gallia to the eastern side of the Hadriatic. These barbarians attempted to break into Italy, as the Germanic nations had attempted near three hundred years before; and the rest of the life of Antoninus, with some intervals, was employed in driving back the invaders. In A.D. 169 Verus suddenly died, and Antoninus administered the state alone.

During the German wars Antoninus resided for three years on the Danube at Carnuntum. The Marcomanni were driven out of Pannonia and almost destroyed in their retreat across the Danube; and in A.D. 174 the emperor gained a great victory over the Quadi.

In A.D. 175, Avidius Cassius, a brave and skilful Roman commander who was at the head of the troops in Asia, revolted and declared himself Augustus. But Cassius was assassinated by some of his officers, and so the rebellion came to an end. Antoninus showed his humanity by his treatment of the family and the partisans of Cassius; and his letter to the Senate, in which he recommends mercy, is extant.

Antoninus set out for the East on hearing of Cassius' revolt. Though he appears to have returned to Rome in A.D. 174, he went back to prosecute the war against the Germans, and it is probable that he marched direct to the East from the German war. His wife Faustina, who accompanied him into Asia, died suddenly at the foot of the Taurus, to the great grief of her husband. Capitolinus, who has written the life of Antoninus, and also Dion Cassius accuse the empress of scandalous infidelity to her husband and of abominable lewdness. But Capitolinus says that Antoninus either knew it not or pretended not to know it. Nothing is so common as such malicious reports in all ages, and the history of imperial Rome is full of them. Antoninus loved his wife, and he says that she was "obedient, affectionate, and simple." The same scandal had been spread about Faustina's mother, the wife of Antoninus Pius, and yet he too was perfectly satisfied with his wife. Antoninus Pius says after her death in a letter to Fronto that he would rather have lived in exile with his wife than in his palace at Rome without her. There are not many men who would give their wives a better character than these two emperors. Capitolinus wrote in the time of Diocletian. He may have intended to tell the truth, but he is a poor, feeble biographer. Dion Cassius, the most malignant of historians, always reports and perhaps he believed any scandal against anybody.

Antoninus continued his journey to Syria and Egypt, and on his return to Italy through Athens he was initiated into the Eleusinian mysteries. It was the practice of the emperor to conform to the established rites of the age, and to perform religious ceremonies with due solemnity. We cannot conclude from this that he was a superstitious man, though we might perhaps do so if his book did not show that he was not. But this is only one among many instances that a ruler's public acts do not always prove his real opinions. A prudent governor will not roughly oppose even the superstitions of his people; and though he may wish that they were wiser, he will know that he cannot make them so by offending their prejudices.

Antoninus and his son Commodus entered Rome in triumph, perhaps for some German victories, in A.D. 176. In the following year Commodus was associated with his father in the empire, and took the name of Augustus. This year A.D. 177 is memorable in ecclesiastical history. Attalus and others were put to death at Lyon for their adherence to the Christian religion. The evidence of this persecution is a letter preserved by Eusebius. It contains a very particular description of the tortures inflicted on the Christians in Gallia, and it states that while the persecution was going on, Attalus, a Christian and a Roman citizen, was loudly demanded by the populace and brought into the amphitheatre; but the governor ordered him to be reserved, with the rest who were in prison, until he had received instructions from the emperor. Many had been tortured before the governor thought of applying to Antoninus. The imperial rescript, says the letter, was that the Christians should be punished, but if they would deny their faith, they must be released. On this the work began again. The Christians who were Roman citizens were beheaded; the rest were exposed to the wild beasts in the amphitheatre.

The war on the northern frontier appears to have been uninterrupted during the visit of Antoninus to the East, and on his return the emperor again left Rome to oppose the barbarians. The Germanic people were defeated in a great battle A.D. 179. During this campaign the emperor was seized with some contagious malady, of which he died in the camp, A.D. 180, in the fifty-ninth year of his age. His son Commodus was with him. The body, or the ashes probably, of the emperor were carried to Rome, and he received the honor of deification. Those who could afford it had his statue or bust; and when Capitolinus wrote, many people still had statues of Antoninus among the Dei Penates or household deities. He was in a manner made a saint. Commodus erected to the memory of his father the Antonine column which is now in the Piazza Colonna at Rome. The bassi rilievi which are placed in a spiral line round the shaft commemorate the victories of Antoninus over the Marcomanni and the Quadi, and the miraculous shower of rain which refreshed the Roman soldiers and discomfited their enemies. The statue of Antoninus was placed on the capital of the column, but it was removed at some time unknown, and a bronze statue of St. Paul was put in the place by Pope Sixtus the fifth.

In order to form a proper notion of the condition of the Christians under M. Antoninus we must go back to Trajan's time. When the younger Pliny was governor of Bithynia, the Christians were numerous in those parts, and the worshippers of the old religion were falling off. The temples were deserted, the festivals neglected, and there were no purchasers of victims for sacrifice. Those who were interested in the maintenance of the old religion thus found that their profits were in danger. Christians of both sexes and of all ages were brought before the governor, who did not know what to do with them. He could come to no other conclusion than this, that those who confessed to be Christians and persevered in their religion ought to be punished; if for nothing else, for their invincible obstinacy. He found no crimes proved against the Christians, and he could only characterize their religion as a depraved and extravagant superstition, which might be stopped if the people were allowed the opportunity of recanting. Pliny wrote this in a letter to Trajan. He asked for the emperor's directions, because he did not know what to do. He remarks that he had never been engaged in judicial inquiries about the Christians, and that accordingly he did not know what to inquire about or how far to inquire and punish. This proves that it was not a new thing to examine into a man's profession of Christianity and to punish him for it. Trajan's rescript is extant. He approved of the governor's judgment in the matter, but he said that no search must be made after the Christians; if a man was charged with the new religion and convicted, he must not be punished if he affirmed that he was not a Christian and confirmed his denial by showing his reverence to the heathen gods. He added that no notice must be taken of anonymous informations, for such things were of bad example. Trajan was a mild and sensible man; and both motives of mercy and policy probably also induced him to take as little notice of the Christians as he could, to let them live in quiet if it were possible. Trajan's rescript is the first legislative act of the head of the Roman state with reference to Christianity, which is known to us. It does not appear that the Christians were further disturbed under his reign.

In the time of Hadrian it was no longer possible for the Roman government to overlook the great increase of the Christians and the hostility of the common sort to them. If the governors in the provinces were willing to let them alone, they could not resist the fanaticism of the heathen community, who looked on the Christians as atheists. The Jews too, who were settled all over the Roman Empire, were as hostile to the Christians as the Gentiles were. With the time of Hadrian begin the Christian Apologies, which show plainly what the popular feeling towards the Christians then was. A rescript of Hadrian to Minucius Fundanus, the Proconsul of Asia, which stands at the end of Justin's first Apology, instructs the governor that innocent people must not be troubled, and false accusers must not be allowed to extort money from them; the charges against the Christians must be made in due form, and no attention must be paid to popular clamors; when Christians were regularly prosecuted and convicted of illegal acts, they must be punished according to their deserts; and false accusers also must be punished. Antoninus Pius is said to have published rescripts to the same effect. The terms of Hadrian's rescript seem very favorable to the Christians; but if we understand it in this sense, that they were only to be punished like other people for illegal acts, it would have had no meaning, for that could have been done without asking the emperor's advice. The real purpose of the rescript is that Christians must be punished if they persisted in their belief, and would not prove their renunciation of it by acknowledging the heathen religion.

In the time of M. Antoninus the opposition between the old and the new belief was still stronger, and the adherents of the heathen religion urged those in authority to a more regular resistance to the invasions of the Christian faith. Melito in his Apology to M. Antoninus represents the Christians of Asia as persecuted under new imperial orders. Shameless informers, he says, men who were greedy after the property of others, used these orders as a means of robbing those who were doing no harm. He doubts if a just emperor could have ordered anything so unjust; and if the last order was really not from the emperor, the Christians entreat him not to give them up to their enemies. We conclude from this that there were at least imperial rescripts or constitutions of M. Antoninus which were made the foundation of these persecutions. The fact of being a Christian was now a crime and punished, unless the accused denied their religion. Then come the persecutions at Smyrna, which some modern critics place in A.D. 167, ten years before the persecution of Lyon. The governors of the provinces under M. Antoninus might have found enough even in Trajan's rescript to warrant them in punishing Christians, and the fanaticism of the people would drive them to persecution, even if they were unwilling. But besides the fact of the Christians rejecting all the heathen ceremonies, we must not forget that they plainly maintained that all the heathen religions were false. The Christians thus declared war against the heathen rites, and it is hardly necessary to observe that this was a declaration of hostility against the Roman government, which tolerated all the various forms of superstition that existed in the empire, and could not consistently tolerate another religion, which declared that all the rest were false and all the splendid ceremonies of the empire only a worship of devils.

If we had a true ecclesiastical history, we should know how the Roman emperors attempted to check the new religion; how they enforced their principle of finally punishing Christians, simply as Christians, which Justin in his Apology affirms that they did, and I have no doubt that he tells the truth; how far popular clamor and riots went in this matter, and how far many fanatical and ignorant Christians—for there were many such—contributed to excite the fanaticism on the other side and to imbitter the quarrel between the Roman government and the new religion. Our extant ecclesiastical histories are manifestly falsified, and what truth they contain is grossly exaggerated; but the fact is certain that in the time of M. Antoninus the heathen populations were in open hostility to the Christians, and that under Antoninus' rule men were put to death because they were Christians. Eusebius, in the preface to his fifth book, remarks that in the seventeenth year of Antoninus' reign, in some parts of the world, the persecution of the Christians became more violent, and that it proceeded from the populace in the cities; and he adds, in his usual style of exaggeration, that we may infer from what took place in a single nation that myriads of martyrs were made in the habitable earth. The nation which he alludes to is Gallia; and he then proceeds to give the letter of the churches of Vienna and Lugdunum. It is probable that he has assigned the true cause of the persecutions, the fanaticism of the populace, and that both governors and emperor had a great deal of trouble with these disturbances. How far Marcus was cognizant of these cruel proceedings we do not know, for the historical records of his reign are very defective. He did not make the rule against the Christians, for Trajan did that; and if we admit that he would have been willing to let the Christians alone, we cannot affirm that it was in his power, for it would be a great mistake to suppose that

Antoninus had the unlimited authority which some modern sovereigns have had. His power was limited by certain constitutional forms, by the Senate, and by the precedents of his predecessors. We cannot admit that such a man was an active persecutor, for there is no evidence that he was, though it is certain that he had no good opinion of the Christians, as appears from his own words. But he knew nothing of them except their hostility to the Roman religion, and he probably thought that they were dangerous to the state, notwithstanding the professions false or true of some of the Apologists. So much I have said, because it would be unfair not to state all that can be urged against a man whom his contemporaries and subsequent ages venerated as a model of virtue and benevolence. If I admitted the genuineness of some documents, he would be altogether clear from the charge of even allowing any persecutions; but as I seek the truth and am sure that they are false, I leave him to bear whatever blame is his due. I add that it is quite certain that Antoninus did not derive any of his ethical principles from a religion of which he knew nothing.

There is no doubt that the Emperor's Reflections—or his Meditations, as they are generally named—is a genuine work. In the first book he speaks of himself, his family, and his teachers; and in other books he mentions himself.

It is plain that the emperor wrote down his thoughts or reflections as the occasions arose; and since they were intended for his own use, it is no improbable conjecture that he left a complete copy behind him written with his own hand; for it is not likely that so diligent a man would use the labor of a transcriber for such a purpose, and expose his most secret thoughts to any other eye. He may have also intended the book for his son Commodus, who however had no taste for his father's philosophy.

The last reflection of the Stoic philosophy that I have observed is in Simplicius' Commentary on the Enchiridion of Epictetus. Simplicius was not a Christian, and such a man was not likely to be converted at a time when Christianity was grossly corrupted. But he was a really religious man, and he concludes his commentary with a prayer to the Deity which no Christian could improve. From the time of Zeno to Simplicius, a period of about nine hundred years, the Stoic philosophy formed the characters of some of the best and greatest men. A man's greatness lies not in wealth and station, as the vulgar believe, nor yet in his intellectual capacity, which is often associated with the meanest moral character, the most abject servility to those in high places, and arrogance to the poor and lowly; but a man's true greatness lies in the consciousness of an honest purpose in life, founded on a just estimate of himself and everything else, on frequent self-examination, and a steady obedience to the rule which he knows to be right, without troubling himself, as the emperor says he should not, about what others may think or say, or whether they do or do not do that which he thinks and says and does.

The Thoughts of Marcus Aurelius Antoninus

I.

1. From my grandfather Verus [I learned] good morals and the government of my temper.
2. From the reputation and remembrance of my father, modesty and a manly character.
3. From my mother, piety and beneficence, and abstinence, not only from evil deeds, but even from evil thoughts; and further, simplicity in my way of living, far removed from the habits of the rich.
4. From my great-grandfather, not to have frequented public schools, and to have had good teachers at home, and to know that on such things a man should spend liberally.
5. From my governor, to be neither of the green nor of the blue party at the games in the Circus, nor a partisan either of the Parmularius or the Scutarius at the gladiators' fights; from him too I learned endurance of labor, and to want little, and to work with my own hands, and not to meddle with other people's affairs, and not to be ready to listen to slander.
6. From Diognetus, not to busy myself about trifling things, and not to give credit to what was said by miracle-workers and jugglers about incantations and the driving away of daemons and such things; and not to breed quails [for fighting], nor to give myself up passionately to such things; and to endure freedom of speech; and to have become intimate with philosophy; and to have been a hearer, first of Bacchius, then of Tandasis and Marcianus; and to have written dialogues in my youth; and to have desired a plank bed and skin, and whatever else of the kind belongs to the Grecian discipline.

7. From Rusticus I received the impression that my character required improvement and discipline; and from him I learned not to be led astray to sophistic emulation, nor to writing on speculative matters, nor to delivering little hortatory orations, nor to showing myself off as a man who practices much discipline, or does benevolent acts in order to make a display; and to abstain from rhetoric, and poetry, and fine writing; and not to walk about in the house in my outdoor dress, nor to do other things of the kind; and to write my letters with simplicity, like the letter which Rusticus wrote from Sinuessa to my mother; and with respect to those who have offended me by words, or done me wrong, to be easily disposed to be pacified and reconciled, as soon as they have shown a readiness to be reconciled; and to read carefully, and not to be satisfied with a superficial understanding of a book; nor hastily to give my assent to those who talk overmuch; and I am indebted to him for being acquainted with the discourses of Epictetus, which he communicated to me out of his own collection.

8. From Apollonius I learned freedom of will and undeviating steadiness of purpose; and to look to nothing else, not even for a moment, except to reason; and to be always the same, in sharp pains, on the occasion of the loss of a child, and in long illness; and to see clearly in a living example that the same man can be both most resolute and yielding, and not peevish in giving his instruction; and to have had before my eyes a man who clearly considered his experience and his skill in expounding philosophical principles as the smallest of his merits; and from him I learned how to receive from friends what are esteemed favors, without being either humbled by them or letting them pass unnoticed.

9. From Sextus, a benevolent disposition, and the example of a family governed in a fatherly manner, and the idea of living conformably to nature; and gravity without affectation, and to look carefully after the interests of friends, and to tolerate ignorant persons, and those who form opinions without consideration: he had the power of readily accommodating himself to all, so that intercourse with him was more agreeable than any flattery; and at the same time he was most highly venerated by those who associated with him; and he had the faculty both of discovering and ordering, in an intelligent and methodical way, the principles necessary for life; and he never showed anger or any other passion, but was entirely

free from passion, and also most affectionate; and he could express approbation without noisy display, and he possessed much knowledge without ostentation.

10. From Alexander the grammarian, to refrain from fault-finding, and not in a reproachful way to chide those who uttered any barbarous or solecistic or strange-sounding expression; but dexterously to introduce the very expression which ought to have been used, and in the way of answer or giving confirmation, or joining in an inquiry about the thing itself, not about the word, or by some other fit suggestion.

11. From Fronto I learned to observe what envy and duplicity and hypocrisy are in a tyrant, and that generally those among us who are called Patricians are rather deficient in paternal affection.

12. From Alexander the Platonic, not frequently nor without necessity to say to any one, or to write in a letter, that I have no leisure; nor continually to excuse the neglect of duties required by our relation to those with whom we live, by alleging urgent occupations.

13. From Catulus, not to be indifferent when a friend finds fault, even if he should find fault without reason, but to try to restore him to his usual disposition; and to be ready to speak well of teachers, as it is reported of Domitius and Athenodotus; and to love my children truly.

14. From my brother Severus, to love my kin, and to love truth, and to love justice; and through him I learned to know Thrasea, Helvidius, Cato, Dion, Brutus; and from him I received the idea of a polity in which there is the same law for all, a polity administered with regard to equal rights and equal freedom of speech, and the idea of a kingly government which respects most of all the freedom of the governed; I learned from him also consistency and undeviating steadiness in my regard for philosophy; and a disposition to do good, and to give to others readily, and to cherish good hopes, and to believe that I am loved by my friends; and in him I observed no concealment of his opinions with respect to those whom he condemned, and that his friends had no need to conjecture what he wished or did not wish, but it was quite plain.

15. From Maximus I learned self-government, and not to be led aside by anything; and cheerfulness in all circumstances, as well as in illness; and a just admixture in the moral character of sweetness and dignity, and to do what was set before me without complaining. I observed that everybody believed that he thought as he spoke, and that in all that he did he never had any bad intention; and he never showed amazement and surprise, and was never in a hurry, and never put off doing a thing, nor was perplexed nor dejected, nor did he ever laugh to disguise his vexation, nor, on the other hand, was he ever passionate or suspicious. He was accustomed to do acts of beneficence, and was ready to forgive, and was free from all falsehood; and he presented the appearance of a man who could not be diverted from right, rather than of a man who had been improved. I observed, too, that no man could ever think that he was despised by Maximus, or ever venture to think himself a better man. He had also the art of being humorous in an agreeable way.

16. In my father I observed mildness of temper, and unchangeable resolution in the things which he had determined after due deliberation; and no vain-glory in those things which men call honors; and a love of labor and perseverance; and a readiness to listen to those who had anything to propose for the common weal; and undeviating firmness in giving to every man according to his deserts; and a knowledge derived from experience of the occasions for vigorous action and for remission. And I observed that he had overcome all passion for boys; and he considered himself no more than any other citizen; and he released his friends from all obligation to sup with him or to attend him of necessity when he went abroad, and those who had failed to accompany him, by reason of any urgent circumstances, always found him the same. I observed, too, his habit of careful inquiry in all matters of deliberation, and his persistency, and that he never stopped his investigation through being satisfied with appearances which first present themselves; and that his disposition was to keep his friends, and not to be soon tired of them, nor yet to be extravagant in his affection; and to be satisfied on all occasions, and cheerful; and to foresee things a long way off, and to provide for the smallest without display; and to check immediately popular applause and all flattery; and to be ever watchful over the things which were necessary for the administration of the empire, and to be a good manager of the expenditure, and patiently to endure the blame which he got for such conduct; and he was neither superstitious with respect to the gods, nor did he court men by gifts or by trying to please them, or by flattering the populace; but he showed sobriety in all things and firmness, and never any mean thoughts or action, nor love of novelty. And the things which conduce in any way to the commodity of life, and of which fortune gives an abundant supply, he used without arrogance and without excusing himself; so that when he had them, he enjoyed them without affectation, and when he had them not, he did not want them. No one could ever say of him that he was either a sophist or a [home-bred] flippant slave or a pedant; but every one acknowledged him to be a man ripe, perfect, above flattery, able to manage his own and other men's affairs. Besides this, he honored those who were true philosophers, and he did not reproach those who pretended to be philosophers, nor yet was he easily led by them. He was also easy in conversation, and he made himself agreeable without any offensive affectation. He took a reasonable care of his body's health, not as one who was greatly attached to life, nor out of regard to personal appearance, nor yet in a careless way, but so that through his own attention he very seldom stood in need of the physician's art or of medicine or external applications. He was most ready to give without envy to those who possessed any particular faculty, such as that of eloquence or knowledge of the law or of morals, or of anything else; and he gave them his help, that each might enjoy reputation according to his deserts; and he always acted conformably to the institutions of his country, without showing any affectation of doing so. Further, he was not fond of change nor unsteady, but he loved to stay in the same places, and to employ himself about the same things; and after his paroxysms of headache he came immediately fresh and vigorous to his usual occupations. His secrets were not many, but very few and very rare, and these only about public matters; and he showed prudence and economy in the exhibition of the public spectacles and the construction of public buildings, his donations to the people, and in such things, for he was a man who looked to what ought to be done, not to the reputation which is got by a man's acts. He did not take the bath at unseasonable hours; he was not fond of building houses, nor curious about what he ate, nor about the texture and color of his clothes, nor about the beauty of his slaves.* His dress came from Lorium, his villa on the coast, and from Lanuvium generally.† We know how he behaved to the toll-collector at Tusculum who asked his pardon; and such was all his behavior. There

* This passage is corrupt, and the exact meaning is uncertain.

† Lorium was a villa on the coast north of Rome, and there Antoninus was brought up, and he died there. This also is corrupt.

was in him nothing harsh, nor implacable, nor violent, nor, as one may say, anything carried to the sweating point; but he examined all things severally, as if he had abundance of time, and without confusion, in an orderly way, vigorously and consistently. And that might be applied to him which is recorded of Socrates, that he was able both to abstain from, and to enjoy, those things which many are too weak to abstain from, and cannot enjoy without excess. But to be strong enough both to bear the one and to be sober in the other is the mark of a man who has a perfect and invincible soul, such as he showed in the illness of Maximus.

17. To the gods I am indebted for having good grandfathers, good parents, a good sister, good teachers, good associates, good kinsmen and friends, nearly everything good. Further, I owe it to the gods that I was not hurried into any offence against any of them, though I had a disposition which, if opportunity had offered, might have led me to do something of this kind; but, through their favor, there never was such a concurrence of circumstances as put me to the trial. Further, I am thankful to the gods that I was subjected to a ruler and a father who was able to take away all pride from me, and to bring me to the knowledge that it is possible for a man to live in a palace without wanting either guards or embroidered dresses, or torches and statues, and such-like show; but that it is in such a man's power to bring himself very near to the fashion of a private person, without being for this reason either meaner in thought, or more remiss in action, with respect to the things which must be done for the public interest in a manner that befits a ruler. I thank the gods for giving me such a brother, who was able by his moral character to rouse me to vigilance over myself, and who at the same time pleased me by his respect and affection; that my children have not been stupid nor deformed in body; that I did not make more proficiency in rhetoric, poetry, and the other studies, in which I should perhaps have been completely engaged, if I had seen that I was making progress in them; that I made haste to place those who brought me up in the station of honor, which they seemed to desire, without putting them off with hope of my doing it some other time after, because they were then still young; that I knew Apollonius, Rusticus, Maximus; that I received clear and frequent impressions about living according to nature, and what kind of a life that is, so that, so far as depended on the gods, and their gifts, and help, and inspirations, nothing hindered me from forthwith living according to nature, though

I still fall short of it through my own fault, and through not observing the admonitions of the gods, gifts, and help, and inspirations, nothing hindered me from forthwith living according to nature, though I still fall short of it through my own fault, and through not observing the admonitions of the gods, and, I may almost say, their direct instructions; that my body has held out so long in such a kind of life; that I never touched either Benedicta or Theodotus, and that, after having fallen into amatory passions, I was cured, and though I was often out of humor with Rusticus, I never did anything of which I had occasion to repent; that, though it was my mother's fate to die young, she spent the last years of her life with me; that, whenever I wished to help any man in his need, or on any other occasion, I was never told that I had not the means of doing it; and that to myself the same necessity never happened, to receive anything from another; that I have such a wife, so obedient, and so affectionate, and so simple; that I had abundance of good masters for my children; and that remedies have been shown to me by dreams, both others, and against bloodspitting and giddiness . . . ; and that, when I had an inclination to philosophy, I did not fall into the hands of any sophist, and that I did not waste my time on writers [of histories], or in the resolution of syllogisms, or occupy myself about the investigation of appearances in the heavens; for all these things require the help of the gods and fortune.

Among the Quadi at the Granua.*

II.

1. Begin the morning by saying to thyself, I shall meet with the busybody, the ungrateful, arrogant, deceitful, envious, unsocial. All these things happen to them by reason of their ignorance of what is good and evil. But I who have seen the nature of the good that it is beautiful, and of the bad that it is ugly, and the nature of him who does wrong, that it is akin to me, not [only] of the same blood or seed, but that it participates in [the same] intelligence and [the same] portion of the divinity, I can neither be injured by any of them, for no one can fix on me what is ugly, nor can I be angry with my kinsman, nor hate him. For we are made for co-operation, like

* This is corrupt.

feet, like hands, like eyelids, like the rows of the upper and lower teeth. To act against one another, then, is contrary to nature; and it is acting against one another to be vexed and to turn away.

2. Whatever this is that I am, it is a little flesh and breath, and the ruling part. Throw away thy books; no longer distract thyself: it is not allowed; but as if thou wast now dying, despise the flesh; it is blood and bones and a network, a contexture of nerves, veins, and arteries. See the breath also, what kind of a thing it is; air, and not always the same, but every moment sent out and again sucked in. The third, then, is the ruling part; consider thus: Thou art an old man; no longer let this be a slave, no longer be pulled by the strings like a puppet to unsocial movements, no longer be either dissatisfied with thy present lot, or shrink from the future.
3. All that is from the gods is full of providence. That which is from fortune is not separated from nature or without an interweaving and involution with the things which are ordered by providence. From thence all things flow; and there is besides necessity, and that which is for the advantage of the whole universe, of which thou art a part. But that is good for every part of nature which the nature of the whole brings, and what serves to maintain this nature. Now the universe is preserved, as by the changes of the elements so by the changes of things compounded of the elements. Let these principles be enough for thee; let them always be fixed opinions. But cast away the thirst after books, that thou mayest not die murmuring, but cheerfully, truly, and from thy heart thankful to the gods.
4. Remember how long thou hast been putting off these things, and how often thou hast received an opportunity from the gods, and yet dost not use it. Thou must now at last perceive of what universe thou art now a part, and of what administrator of the universe thy existence is an efflux, and that a limit of time is fixed for thee, which if thou dost not use for clearing away the clouds from thy mind, it will go and thou wilt go, and it will never return.
5. Every moment think steadily as a Roman and a man to do what thou hast in hand with perfect and simple dignity, and feeling of affection, and freedom, and justice, and to give thyself relief from all other thoughts. And thou wilt give thyself relief if thou dost every act of thy life as if it were the last, laying aside all carelessness and passionate aversion from the commands of reason, and all hypocrisy, and self-love, and discontent with the portion which has been given to thee. Thou seest how few the

things are, the which if a man lays hold of, he is able to live a life which flows in quiet, and is like the existence of the gods; for the gods on their part will require nothing more from him who observes these things.

6. Do wrong to thyself, do wrong to thyself, my soul; but thou wilt no longer have the opportunity of honoring thyself. Every man's life is sufficient. But thine is nearly finished, though thy soul reverences not itself, but places thy felicity in the souls of others.
7. Do the things external which fall upon thee distract thee? Give thyself time to learn something new and good, and cease to be whirled around. But then thou must also avoid being carried about the other way; for those too are triflers who have wearied themselves in life by their activity, and yet have no object to which to direct every movement, and, in a word, all their thoughts.
8. Through not observing what is in the mind of another a man has seldom been seen to be unhappy; but those who do not observe the movements of their own minds must of necessity be unhappy.
9. This thou must always bear in mind, what is the nature of the whole, and what is my nature, and how this is related to that, and what kind of a part it is of what kind of a whole, and that there is no one who hinders thee from always doing and saying the things which are according to the nature of which thou art a part.
10. Theophrastus, in his comparison of bad acts—such a comparison as one would make in accordance with the common notions of mankind—says, like a true philosopher, that the offences which are committed through desire are more blamable than those which are committed through anger. For he who is excited by anger seems to turn away from reason with a certain pain and unconscious contraction; but he who offends through desire, being overpowered by pleasure, seems to be in a manner more intemperate and more womanish in his offences. Rightly, then, and in a way worthy of philosophy, he said that the offence which is committed with pleasure is more blamable than that which is committed with pain; and on the whole the one is more like a person who has been first wronged and through pain is compelled to be angry; but the other is moved by his own impulse to do wrong, being carried towards doing something by desire.
11. Since it is possible that thou mayest depart from life this very moment, regulate every act and thought accordingly. But to go away from among

men, if there are gods, is not a thing to be afraid of, for the gods will not involve thee in evil; but if indeed they do not exist, or if they have no concern about human affairs, what is it to me to live in a universe devoid of gods or devoid of providence? But in truth they do exist, and they do care for human things, and they have put all the means in man's power to enable him not to fall into real evils. And as to the rest, if there was anything evil, they would have provided for this also, that it should be altogether in a man's power not to fall into it. Now that which does not make a man worse, how can it make a man's life worse? But neither through ignorance, nor having the knowledge but not the power to guard against or correct these things, is it possible that the nature of the universe has overlooked them; nor is it possible that it has made so great a mistake, either through want of power or want of skill, that good and evil should happen indiscriminately to the good and the bad. But death certainly, and life, honor and dishonor, pain and pleasure,—all these things equally happen to good men and bad, being things which make us neither better nor worse. Therefore they are neither good nor evil.

12. How quickly all things disappear,—in the universe the bodies themselves, but in time the remembrance of them. What is the nature of all sensible things, and particularly those which attract with the bait of pleasure or terrify by pain, or are noised abroad by vapory fame; how worthless, and contemptible, and sordid, and perishable, and dead they are,—all this it is the part of the intellectual faculty to observe. To observe too who these are whose opinions and voices give reputation; what death is, and the fact that, if a man looks at it in itself, and by the abstractive power of reflection resolves into their parts all the things which present themselves to the imagination in it, he will then consider it to be nothing else than an operation of nature; and if any one is afraid of an operation of nature, he is a child. This, however, is not only an operation of nature, but it is also a thing which conduces to the purposes of nature. To observe too how man comes near to the Deity, and by what part of him, and when this part of man is so disposed (VI. 28).

13. Nothing is more wretched than a man who traverses everything in a round, and pries into the things beneath the earth, as the poet says, and seeks by conjecture what is in the minds of his neighbors, without perceiving that it is sufficient to attend to the daemon within him, and to reverence it sincerely. And reverence of the daemon consists in keeping it pure from passion and thoughtlessness, and dissatisfaction with what comes from gods and men. For the things from the gods merit veneration for their excellence; and the things from men should be dear to us by reason of kinship; and sometimes even, in a manner, they move our pity by reason of men's ignorance of good and bad; this defect being not less than that which deprives us of the power of distinguishing things that are white and black.

14. Though thou shouldest be going to live three thousand years, and as many times ten thousand years, still remember that no man loses any other life than this which he now lives, nor lives any other than this which he now loses. The longest and shortest are thus brought to the same. For the present is the same to all, though that which perishes is not the same; and so that which is lost appears to be a mere moment. For a man cannot lose either the past or the future: for what a man has not, how can any one take this from him? These two things then thou must bear in mind; the one, that all things from eternity are of like forms and come round in a circle, and that it makes no difference whether a man shall see the same things during a hundred years, or two hundred, or an infinite time; and the second, that the longest liver and he who will die soonest lose just the same. For the present is the only thing of which a man can be deprived, if it is true that this is the only thing which he has, and that a man cannot lose a thing if he has it not.

15. Remember that all is opinion. For what was said by the Cynic Monimus is manifest; and manifest too is the use of what was said, if a man receives what may be got out of it as far as it is true.

16. The soul of man does violence to itself, first of all, when it becomes an abscess, and, as it were, a tumor on the universe, so far as it can. For to be vexed at anything which happens is a separation of ourselves from nature, in some part of which the natures of all other things are contained. In the next place, the soul does violence to itself when it turns away from any man, or even moves towards him with the intention of injuring, such as are the souls of those who are angry. In the third place, the soul does violence to itself when it is overpowered by pleasure or by pain. Fourthly, when it plays a part, and does or says anything insincerely and untruly. Fifthly, when it allows any act of its own and any movement to be without an aim, and does anything thoughtlessly and without considering what it is, it being right that even the smallest things be done with reference to an end; and the end of rational animals is to follow the reason and the law of the most ancient city and polity.

17. Of human life the time is a point, and the substance is in a flux, and the perception dull, and the composition of the whole body subject to putrefaction, and the soul a whirl, and fortune hard to divine, and fame a thing devoid of judgment. And, to say all in a word, everything which belongs to the body is a stream, and what belongs to the soul is a dream and vapor, and life is a warfare and a stranger's sojourn, and after-fame is oblivion. What then is that which is able to conduct a man? One thing, and only one, philosophy. But this consists in keeping the daemon within a man free from violence and unharmed, superior to pains and pleasures, doing nothing without a purpose, nor yet falsely and with hypocrisy, not feeling the need of another man's doing or not doing anything; and besides, accepting all that happens, and all that is allotted, as coming from thence, wherever it is, from whence he himself came; and, finally, waiting for death with a cheerful mind, as being nothing else than a dissolution of the elements of which every living being is compounded. But if there is no harm to the elements themselves in each continually changing into another, why should a man have any apprehension about the change and dissolution of all the elements? For it is according to nature, and nothing is evil which is according to nature.

18. This in Carnuntum.

III.

1. We ought to consider not only that our life is daily wasting away and a smaller part of it is left, but another thing also must be taken into the account, that if a man should live longer, it is quite uncertain whether the understanding will still continue sufficient for the comprehension of things, and retain the power of contemplation which strives to acquire the knowledge of the divine and the human. For if he shall begin to fall into dotage, perspiration and nutrition and imagination and appetite, and whatever else there is of the kind, will not fail; but the power of making use of ourselves, and filling up the measure of our duty, and clearly separating all appearances, and considering whether a man should now depart from life, and whatever else of the kind absolutely requires a disciplined reason,—all this is already extinguished. We must make haste, then, not only because we are daily nearer to death, but also because the conception of things and the understanding of them cease first.

2. We ought to observe also that even the things which follow after the things which are produced according to nature contain something pleasing and attractive. For instance, when bread is baked some parts are split at the surface, and these parts which thus open, and have a certain fashion contrary to the purpose of the baker's art, are beautiful in a manner, and in a peculiar way excite a desire for eating. And again, figs, when they are quite ripe, gape open; and in the ripe olives the very circumstance of their being near to rottenness adds a peculiar beauty to the fruit. And the ears of corn bending down, and the lion's eyebrows, and the foam which flows from the mouth of wild boars, and many other things,—though they are far from being beautiful if a man should examine them severally,—still, because they are consequent upon the things which are formed by nature, help to adorn them, and they please the mind; so that if a man should have a feeling and deeper insight with respect to the things which are produced in the universe, there is hardly one of those which follow by way of consequence which will not seem to him to be in a manner disposed so as to give pleasure. And so he will see even the real gaping jaws of wild beasts with no less pleasure than those which painters and sculptors show by imitation; and in an old woman and an old man he will be able to see a certain maturity and comeliness; and the attractive loveliness of young persons he will be able to look on with chaste eyes; and many such things will present themselves, not pleasing to every man, but to him only who has become truly familiar with Nature and her works.
3. Hippocrates, after curing many diseases, himself fell sick and died. The Chaldaei foretold the deaths of many, and then fate caught them too. Alexander and Pompeius and Caius Caesar, after so often completely destroying whole cities, and in battle cutting to pieces many ten thousands of cavalry and infantry, themselves too at last departed from life. Heraclitus, after so many speculations on the conflagration of the universe, was filled with water internally and died smeared all over with mud. And lice destroyed Democritus; and other lice killed Socrates. What means all this? Thou hast embarked, thou hast made the voyage, thou art come to shore; get out. If indeed to another life, there is no want of gods, not even there; but if to a state without sensation, thou wilt cease to be held

by pains and pleasures, and to be a slave to the vessel, which is as much inferior as that which serves it is superior: for the one is intelligence and deity; the other is earth and corruption.

4. Do not waste the remainder of thy life in thoughts about others, when thou dost not refer thy thoughts to some object of common utility. For thou losest the opportunity of doing something else when thou hast such thoughts as these,—What is such a person doing, and why, and what is he saying, and what is he thinking of, and what is he contriving, and whatever else of the kind makes us wander away from the observation of our own ruling power. We ought then to check in the series of our thoughts everything that is without a purpose and useless, but most of all the over-curious feeling and the malignant; and a man should use himself to think of those things only about which if one should suddenly ask, What hast thou now in thy thoughts? with perfect openness thou mightest immediately answer, This or That; so that from thy words it should be plain that everything in thee is simple and benevolent, and such as befits a social animal, and one that cares not for thoughts about pleasure or sensual enjoyments at all, nor has any rivalry or envy and suspicion, or anything else for which thou wouldst blush if thou shouldst say that thou hadst it in thy mind. For the man who is such, and no longer delays being among the number of the best, is like a priest and minister of the gods, using too the [deity] which is planted within him, which makes the man uncontaminated by pleasure, unharmed by any pain, untouched by any insult, feeling no wrong, a fighter in the noblest fight, one who cannot be overpowered by any passion, dyed deep with justice, accepting with all his soul everything which happens and is assigned to him as his portion; and not often, nor yet without great necessity and for the general interest, imagining what another says, or does, or thinks. For it is only what belongs to himself that he makes the matter for his activity; and he constantly thinks of that which is allotted to himself out of the sum total of things, and he makes his own acts fair, and he is persuaded that his own portion is good. For the lot which is assigned to each man is carried along with him and carries him along with. And he remembers also that every rational animal is his kinsman, and that to care for all men is according to man's nature; and a man should hold on to the opinion not of all, but of those only who confessedly live according to nature. But as to those who live not so, he always bears in mind what kind of men they are both at home and from home, both by night and by day, and what they are, and with what men they live an impure life. Accordingly, he does not value at all the praise which comes from such men, since they are not even satisfied with themselves.

5. Labor not unwillingly, not without regard to the common interest, nor without due consideration, nor with distraction; nor let studied ornament set off thy thoughts, and be not either a man of many words, or busy about too many things. And further, let the deity which is in thee be the guardian of a living being, manly and of ripe age, and engaged in matter political, and a Roman, and a ruler, who has taken his post like a man waiting for the signal which summons him from life, and ready to go, having need neither of oath nor of any man's testimony. Be cheerful also, and seek not external help nor the tranquillity which others give. A man then must stand erect, not be kept erect by others.
6. If thou findest in human life anything better than justice, truth, temperance, fortitude, and, in a word, anything better than thy own mind's self-satisfaction in the things which it enables thee to do according to right reason, and in the condition that is assigned to thee without thy own choice; if, I say, thou seest anything better than is, turn to it with all thy soul, and enjoy that which thou hast found to be the best. But if nothing appears to be better than the Deity which is planted in thee, which has subjected to itself all thy appetites, and carefully examines all the impressions, and, as Socrates said, has detached itself from the persuasions of sense, and has submitted itself to the gods, and cares for mankind; if thou findest everything else smaller and of less value than this, give place to nothing else, for if thou dost once diverge and incline to it, thou wilt no longer without distraction be able to give the preference to that good thing which is thy proper possession and thy own; for it is not right that anything of any other kind, such as praise from the many, or power, or enjoyment of pleasure, should come into competition with that which is rationally and politically [or practically] good. All these things, even though they may seem to adapt themselves [to the better things] in a small degree, obtain the superiority all at once, and carry us away. But do thou, I say, simply and freely choose the better, and hold to it.—But that which is useful is the better.—Well, then, if it is useful to thee as a rational being, keep to it; but if it is only useful to thee as an animal, say so, and maintain thy judgment without arrogance: only take care that thou makest the inquiry by a sure method.

7. Never value anything as profitable to thyself which shall compel thee to break thy promise, to lose thy self-respect, to hate any man, to suspect, to curse, to act the hypocrite, to desire anything which needs walls and curtains: for he who has preferred to everything else his own intelligence and daemon and the worship of its excellence, acts no tragic part, does not groan, will not need either solitude or much company; and, what is chief of all, he will live without either pursuing or flying from [death]; but whether for a longer or a shorter time he shall have the soul enclosed in the body, he cares not at all: for even if he must depart immediately, he will go as readily as if he were going to do anything else which can be done with decency and order; taking care of this only all through life, that his thoughts turn not away from anything which belongs to an intelligent animal and a member of a civil community.

8. In the mind of one who is chastened and purified thou wilt find no corrupt matter, nor impurity, nor any sore skinned over. Nor is his life incomplete when fate overtakes him, as one may say of an actor who leaves the stage before ending and finishing the play. Besides, there is in him nothing servile, nor affected, nor too closely bound [to other things], nor yet detached [from other things], nothing worthy of blame, nothing which seeks a hiding-place.

9. Reverence the faculty which produces opinion. On this faculty it entirely depends whether there shall exist in thy ruling part any opinion inconsistent with nature and the constitution of the rational animal. And this faculty promises freedom from hasty judgment, and friendship towards men, and obedience to the gods.

10. Throwing away then all things, hold to these only which are few; and besides, bear in mind that every man lives only this present time, which is an indivisible point, and that all the rest of his life is either past or it is uncertain. Short then is the time which every man lives, and small the nook of the earth where he lives; and short too the longest posthumous fame, and even this only continued by a succession of poor human beings, who will very soon die, and who know not even themselves, much less him who died long ago.

11. To the aids which have been mentioned let this one still be added: Make for thyself a definition or description of the thing which is presented to thee, so as to see distinctly what kind of a thing it is in its substance, in its nudity, in its complete entirety, and tell thyself its proper name, and the

names of the things of which it has been compounded, and into which it will be resolved. For nothing is so productive of elevation of mind as to be able to examine methodically and truly every object which is presented to thee in life, and always to look at things so as to see at the same time what kind of universe this is, and what kind of use everything performs in it, and what value everything has with reference to the whole, and what with reference to man, who is a citizen of the highest city, of which all other cities are like families; what each thing is, and of what it is composed, and how long it is the nature of this thing to endure which now makes an impression on me, and what virtue I have need of with respect to it, such as gentleness, manliness, truth, fidelity, simplicity, contentment, and the rest. Wherefore, on every occasion a man should say: This comes from god; and this is according to the apportionment and spinning of the thread of destiny, and such-like coincidence and chance; and this is from one of the same stock, and a kinsman and partner, one who knows not, however, what is according to his nature. But I know; for this reason I behave towards him according to the natural law of fellowship with benevolence and justice. At the same time, however, in things indifferent I attempt to ascertain the value of each.

12. If thou workest at that which is before thee, following right reason seriously, vigorously, calmly, without allowing anything else to distract thee, but keeping thy divine part pure, as if thou shouldst be bound to give it back immediately; if thou holdest to this, expecting nothing, fearing nothing, but satisfied with thy present activity according to nature, and with heroic truth in every word and sound which thou utterest, thou wilt live happy. And there is no man who is able to prevent this.

13. As physicians have always their instruments and knives ready for cases which suddenly require their skill, so do thou have principles ready for the understanding of things divine and human, and for doing everything, even the smallest, with a recollection of the bond which unites the divine and human to one another. For neither wilt thou do anything well which pertains to man without at the same time having a reference to things divine; nor the contrary.

14. No longer wander at hazard; for neither wilt thou read thy own memoirs, nor the acts of the ancient Romans and Hellenes, and the selections from books which thou wast reserving for thy old age. Hasten then to the end which thou hast before thee, and, throwing away idle hopes, come to thy own aid, if thou carest at all for thyself, while it is in thy power.

15. They know not how many things are signified by the words stealing, sowing, buying, keeping quiet, seeing what ought to be done; for this is not effected by the eyes, but by another kind of vision.

16. Body, soul, intelligence: to the body belong sensations, to the soul appetites, to the intelligence principles. To receive the impressions of forms by means of appearances belongs even to animals; to be pulled by the strings of desire belongs both to wild beasts and to men who have made themselves into women, and to a Phalaris and a Nero: and to have the intelligence that guides to the things which appear suitable belongs also to those who do not believe in the gods, and who betray their country, and do their impure deeds when they have shut the doors. If then everything else is common to all that I have mentioned, there remains that which is peculiar to the good man, to be pleased and content with what happens, and with the thread which is spun for him; and not to defile the divinity which is planted in his breast, nor disturb it by a crowd of images, but to preserve it tranquil, following it obediently as a god, neither saying anything contrary to the truth, nor doing anything contrary to justice. And if all men refuse to believe that he lives a simple, modest, and contented life, he is neither angry with any of them, nor does he deviate from the way which leads to the end of life, to which a man ought to come pure, tranquil, ready to depart, and without any compulsion perfectly reconciled to his lot.

IV.

1. That which rules within, when it is according to nature, is so affected with respect to the events which happen, that it always easily adapts itself to that which is possible and is presented to it. For it requires no definite material, but it moves towards its purpose, under certain conditions, however; and it makes a material for itself out of that which opposes it, as fire lays hold of what falls into it, by which a small light would have been extinguished: but when the fire is strong, it soon appropriates to itself the matter which is heaped on it, and consumes it, and rises higher by means of this very material.

2. Let no act be done without a purpose, nor otherwise than according to the perfect principles of art.
3. Men seek retreats for themselves, houses in the country, sea-shores, and mountains; and thou too art wont to desire such things very much. But this is altogether a mark of the most common sort of men, for it is in thy power whenever thou shalt choose to retire into thyself. For nowhere either with more quiet or more freedom from trouble does a man retire than into his own soul, particularly when he has within him such thoughts that by looking into them he is immediately in perfect tranquillity; and I affirm that tranquillity is nothing else than the good ordering of the mind. Constantly then give to thyself this retreat, and renew thyself; and let thy principles be brief and fundamental, which, as soon as thou shalt recur to them, will be sufficient to cleanse the soul completely, and to send thee back free from all discontent with the things to which thou returnest. For with what art thou discontented? With the badness of men? Recall to thy mind this conclusion, that rational animals exist for one another, and that to endure is a part of justice, and that men do wrong involuntarily; and consider how many already, after mutual enmity, suspicion, hatred, and fighting, have been stretched dead, reduced to ashes; and be quiet at last.—But perhaps thou art dissatisfied with that which is assigned to thee out of the universe.—Recall to thy recollection this alternative; either there is providence or atoms [fortuitous concurrence of things]; or remember the arguments by which it has been proved that the world is a kind of political community [and be quiet at last].—But perhaps corporeal things will still fasten upon thee.—Consider then further that the mind mingles not with the breath, whether moving gently or violently, when it has once drawn itself apart and discovered its own power, and think also of all that thou hast heard and assented to about pain and pleasure [and be quiet at last].—But perhaps the desire of the thing called fame will torment thee.—See how soon everything is forgotten, and look at the chaos of infinite time on each side of [the present], and the emptiness of applause, and the changeableness and want of judgment in those who pretend to give praise, and the narrowness of the space within which it is circumscribed [and be quiet at last]. For the whole earth is a point, and how small a nook in it is this thy dwelling, and how few are there in it, and what kind of people are they who will praise thee.

This then remains: Remember to retire into this little territory of thy own, and above all do not distract or strain thyself, but be free, and look at things as a man, as a human being, as a citizen, as a mortal. But among the things readiest to thy hand to which thou shalt turn, let there be these, which are two. One is that things do not touch the soul, for they are external and remain immovable; but our perturbations come only from the opinion which is within. The other is that all these things which thou seest, change immediately and will no longer be; and constantly bear in mind how many of these changes thou hast already witnessed. The universe is transformation: life is opinion.

4. If our intellectual part is common, the reason also, in respect of which we are rational beings, is common: if this is so, common also is the reason which commands us what to do, and what not to do; if this is so, there is a common law also; if this is so, we are fellow-citizens; if this is so, we are members of some political community; if this is so, the world is in a manner a state. For of what other common political community will any one say that the whole human race are members? And from thence, from this common political community comes also our very intellectual faculty and reasoning faculty and our capacity for law; or whence do they come? For as my earthly part is a portion given to me from certain earth, and that which is watery from another element, and that which is hot and fiery from some peculiar source (for nothing comes out of that which is nothing, as nothing also returns to non-existence), so also the intellectual part comes from some source.

5. Death is such as generation is, a mystery of nature; composition out of the same elements, and a decomposition into the same; and altogether not a thing of which any man should be ashamed, for it is not contrary to [the nature of] a reasonable animal, and not contrary to the reason of our constitution.

6. It is natural that these things should be done by such persons, it is a matter of necessity; and if a man will not have it so, he will not allow the fig-tree to have juice. But by all means bear this in mind, that within a very short time both thou and he will be dead; and soon not even your names will be left behind.

7. Take away thy opinion, and then there is taken away the complaint, "I have been harmed." Take away the complaint, "I have been harmed," and the harm is taken away.

8. That which does not make a man worse than he was, also does not make his life worse, nor does it harm him either from without or from within.
9. The nature of that which is [universally] useful has been compelled to do this.
10. Consider that everything which happens, happens justly, and if thou observest carefully, thou wilt find it to be so. I do not say only with respect to the continuity of the series of things, but with respect to what is just, and as if it were done by one who assigns to each thing its value. Observe then as thou hast begun; and whatever thou dost, do it in conjunction with this, the being good, and in the sense in which a man is properly understood to be good. Keep to this in every action.
11. Do not have such an opinion of things as he has who does thee wrong, or such as he wishes thee to have, but look at them as they are in truth.
12. A man should always have these two rules in readiness; the one to do only whatever the reason of the ruling and legislating faculty may suggest for the use of men; the other, to change thy opinion, if there is any one at hand who sets thee right and moves thee from any opinion. But this change of opinion must proceed only from a certain persuasion, as of what is just or of common advantage, and the like, not because it appears pleasant or brings reputation.
13. Hast thou reason? I have.—Why then dost not thou use it? For if this does its own work, what else dost thou wish?
14. Thou hast existed as a part. Thou shalt disappear in that which produced thee; but rather thou shalt be received back into its seminal principle by transmutation.
15. Many grains of frankincense on the same altar: one falls before, another falls after; but it makes no difference.
16. Within ten days thou wilt seem a god to those to whom thou art now a beast and an ape, if thou wilt return to thy principles and the worship of reason.
17. Do not act as if thou wert going to live ten thousand years. Death hangs over thee. While thou livest, while it is in thy power, be good.
18. How much trouble he avoids who does not look to see what his neighbor says or does or thinks, but only to what he does himself, that it may be just and pure; or, as Agathon says, look not round at the depraved morals of others, but run straight along the line without deviating from it.
19. He who has a vehement desire for posthumous fame does not consider

that every one of those who remember him will himself also die very soon; then again also they who have succeeded them, until the whole remembrance shall have been extinguished as it is transmitted through men who foolishly admire and perish. But suppose that those who will remember are even immortal, and that the remembrance will be immortal, what then is this to thee? And I say not what is it to the dead, but what is it to the living. What is praise, except indeed so far as it has a certain utility? For thou now rejectest unseasonably the gift of nature, clinging to something else. . . .

20. Everything which is in any way beautiful is beautiful in itself, and terminates in itself, not having praise as part of itself. Neither worse then nor better is a thing made by being praised. I affirm this also of the things which are called beautiful by the vulgar, for example, material things and works of art. That which is really beautiful has no need of anything; not more than law, not more than truth, not more than benevolence or modesty. Which of these things is beautiful because it is praised, or spoiled by being blamed? Is such a thing as an emerald made worse than it was, if it is not praised? or gold, ivory, purple, a lyre, a little knife, a flower, a shrub?

21. If souls continue to exist, how does the air contain them from eternity?—But how does the earth contain the bodies of those who have been buried from time so remote? For as here the mutation of these bodies after a certain continuance, whatever it may be, and their dissolution make room for other dead bodies, so the souls which are removed into the air after subsisting for some time are transmuted and diffused, and assume a fiery nature by being received into the seminal intelligence of the universe, and in this way make room for the fresh souls which come to dwell there. And this is the answer which a man might give on the hypothesis of souls continuing to exist. But we must not only think of the number of bodies which are thus buried, but also of the number of animals which are daily eaten by us and the other animals. For what a number is consumed, and thus in a manner buried in the bodies of those who feed on them! And nevertheless this earth receives them by reason of the changes [of these bodies] into blood, and the transformations into the aerial or the fiery element.

What is the investigation into the truth in this matter? The division into that which is material and that which is the cause of form [the formal].

22. Do not be whirled about, but in every movement have respect to justice, and on the occasion of every impression maintain the faculty of comprehension [or understanding].

23. Everything harmonizes with me, which is harmonious to thee, O Universe. Nothing for me is too early or too late, which is in due time for thee. Everything is fruit to me which thy seasons bring, O Nature: from thee are all things, in thee are all things, to thee all things return. The poet says, Dear city of Cecrops; and wilt not thou say, Dear city of Zeus?

24. Occupy thyself with few things, says the philosopher, if thou wouldst be tranquil.—But consider if it would not be better to say, Do what is necessary, and whatever the reason of the animal which is naturally social requires, and as it requires. For this brings not only the tranquillity which comes from doing well, but also that which comes from doing few things. For the greatest part of what we say and do being unnecessary, if a man takes this away, he will have more leisure and less uneasiness. Accordingly, on every occasion a man should ask himself, Is this one of the unnecessary things? Now a man should take away not only unnecessary acts, but also unnecessary thoughts, for thus superfluous acts will not follow after.

25. Try how the life of the good man suits thee, the life of him who is satisfied with his portion out of the whole, and satisfied with his own just acts and benevolent disposition.

26. Hast thou seen those things? Look also at these. Do not disturb thyself. Make thyself all simplicity. Does any one do wrong? It is to himself that he does the wrong. Has anything happened to thee? Well, out of the universe from the beginning everything which happens has been apportioned and spun out to thee. In a word, thy life is short. Thou must turn to profit the present by the aid of reason and justice. Be sober in thy relaxation.

27. Either it is a well-arranged universe* or a chaos huddled together, but still a universe. But can a certain order subsist in thee, and disorder in the All? And this too when all things are so separated and diffused and sympathetic.

28. A black character, a womanish character, a stubborn character, bestial, childish, animal, stupid, counterfeit, scurrilous, fraudulent, tyrannical.

* Antoninus here uses the word κόσμος both in the sense of the Universe and of Order, and it is difficult to express his meaning.

29. If he is a stranger to the universe who does not know what is in it, no less is he a stranger who does not know what is going on in it. He is a runaway, who flies from social reason; he is blind, who shuts the eyes of the understanding; he is poor, who has need of another, and has not from himself all things which are useful for life. He is an abscess on the universe who withdraws and separates himself from the reason of our common nature through being displeased with the things which happen, for the same nature produces this, and has produced thee too: he is a piece rent asunder from the state, who tears his own soul from that of reasonable animals, which is one.

30. The one is a philosopher without a tunic, and the other without a book: here is another half naked: Bread I have not, he says, and I abide by reason—and I do not get the means of living out of my learning, and I abide [by my reason].

31. Love the art, poor as it may be, which thou hast learned, and be content with it; and pass through the rest of life like one who has intrusted to the gods with his whole soul all that he has, making thyself neither the tyrant nor the slave of any man.

32. Consider for example, the times of Vespasian. Thou wilt see all these things, people marrying, bringing up children, sick, dying, warring, feasting, trafficking, cultivating the ground, flattering, obstinately arrogant, suspecting, plotting, wishing for some to die, grumbling about the present, loving, heaping up treasure, desiring consulship, kingly power. Well, then, that life of these people no longer exists at all. Again, remove to the times of Trajan. Again, all is the same. Their life too is gone. In like manner view also the other epochs of time and of whole nations, and see how many after great efforts soon fell and were resolved into the elements. But chiefly thou shouldst think of those whom thou hast thyself known distracting themselves about idle things, neglecting to do what was in accordance with their proper constitution, and to hold firmly to this and to be content with it. And herein it is necessary to remember that the attention given to everything has its proper value and proportion. For thus thou wilt not be dissatisfied, if thou appliest thyself to smaller matters no further than is fit.

33. The words which were formerly familiar are now antiquated: so also the names of those who were famed of old, are now in a manner antiquated, Camillus, Caeso, Volesus, Leonnatus, and a little after also Scipio and

Cato, then Augustus, then also Hadrianus and Antoninus. For all things soon pass away and become a mere tale, and complete oblivion soon buries them. And I say this of those who have shone in a wondrous way. For the rest, as soon as they have breathed out their breath, they are gone, and no man speaks of them. And, to conclude the matter, what is even an eternal remembrance? A mere nothing. What then is that about which we ought to employ our serious pains? This one thing, thoughts just, and acts social, and words which never lie, and a disposition which gladly accepts all that happens, as necessary, as usual, as flowing from a principle and source of the same kind.

34. Willingly give thyself up to Clotho [one of the fates], allowing her to spin thy thread into whatever thing she pleases.

35. Everything is only for a day, both that which remembers and that which is remembered.

36. Observe constantly that all things take place by change, and accustom thyself to consider that the nature of the universe loves nothing so much as to change the things which are and to make new things like them. For everything that exists is in a manner the seed of that which will be. But thou art thinking only of seeds which are cast into the earth or into a womb; but this is a very vulgar notion.

37. Thou wilt soon die, and thou art not yet simple, nor free from perturbations, nor without suspicion of being hurt by external things, nor kindly disposed towards all; nor dost thou yet place wisdom only in acting justly.

38. Examine men's ruling principles, even those of the wise, what kind of things they avoid, and what kind they pursue.

39. What is evil to thee does not subsist in the ruling principle of another; nor yet in any turning and mutation of thy corporeal covering. Where is it then? It is in that part of thee in which subsists the power of forming opinions about evils. Let this power then not form [such] opinions, and all is well. And if that which is nearest to it, the poor body, is cut, burnt, filled with matter and rottenness, nevertheless let the part which forms opinions about these things be quiet; that is, let it judge that nothing is either bad or good which can happen equally to the bad man and the good. For that which happens equally to him who lives contrary to nature and to him who lives according to nature, is neither according to nature nor contrary to nature.

40. Constantly regard the universe as one living being, having one substance and one soul; and observe how all things have reference to one perception,

the perception of this one living being; and how all things act with one movement; and how all things are the co-operating causes of all things which exist; observe too the continuous spinning of the thread and the contexture of the web.

41. Thou art a little soul bearing about a corpse, as Epictetus used to say (I. c. 19).

42. It is no evil for things to undergo change, and no good for things to subsist in consequence of change.

43. Time is like a river made up of the events which happen, and a violent stream; for as soon as a thing has been seen, it is carried away, and another comes in its place, and this will be carried away too.

44. Everything which happens is as familiar and well known as the rose in spring and the fruit in summer; for such is disease, and death, and calumny, and treachery, and whatever else delights fools or vexes them.

45. In the series of things, those which follow are always aptly fitted to those which have gone before; for this series is not like a mere enumeration of disjointed things, which has only a necessary sequence, but it is a rational connection; and as all existing things are arranged together harmoniously, so the things which come into existence exhibit no mere succession, but a certain wonderful relationship (VI. 38; VII. 9; VII. 75, note).

46. Always remember the saying of Heraclitus, that the death of earth is to become water, and the death of water is to become air, and the death of air is to become fire, and reversely. And think too of him who forgets whither the way leads, and that men quarrel with that with which they are most constantly in communion, the reason which governs the universe; and the things which they daily meet with seem to them strange: and consider that we ought not to act and speak as if we were asleep, for even in sleep we seem to act and speak; and that we ought not, like children who learn from their parents, simply to act and speak as we have been taught.

47. If any god told thee that thou shalt die to-morrow, or certainly on the day after to-morrow, thou wouldst not care much whether it was on the third day or on the morrow, unless thou wast in the highest degree mean-spirited; for how small is the difference. So think it no great thing to die after as many years as thou canst name rather than to-morrow.

48. Think continually how many physicians are dead after often contracting their eyebrows over the sick; and how many astrologers after predicting with great pretensions the deaths of others; and how many philosophers after endless discourses on death or immortality; how many heroes after killing thousands; and how many tyrants who have used their power over men's lives with terrible insolence, as if they were immortal; and how many cities are entirely dead, so to speak, Helice and Pompeii and Herculaneum, and others innumerable. Add to the reckoning all whom thou hast known, one after another. One man after burying another has been laid out dead, and another buries him; and all this in a short time. To conclude, always observe how ephemeral and worthless human things are, and what was yesterday a little mucus, to-morrow will be a mummy or ashes. Pass then through this little space of time conformably to nature, and end thy journey in content, just as an olive falls off when it is ripe, blessing nature who produced it, and thanking the tree on which it grew.

49. Be like the promontory against which the waves continually break, but it stands firm and tames the fury of the water around it.

Unhappy am I because this has happened to me? Not so, but happy am I, though this has happened to me, because I continue free from pain, neither crushed by the present nor fearing the future. For such a thing as this might have happened to every man; but every man would not have continued free from pain on such an occasion. Why then is that rather a misfortune than this a good fortune? And dost thou in all cases call that a man's misfortune which is not a deviation from man's nature? And does a thing seem to thee to be a deviation from man's nature, when it is not contrary to the will of man's nature? Well, thou knowest the will of nature. Will then this which has happened prevent thee from being just, magnanimous, temperate, prudent, secure against inconsiderate opinions and falsehood; will it prevent thee from having modesty, freedom, and everything else, by the presence of which man's nature obtains all that is its own? Remember too on every occasion which leads thee to vexation to apply this principle: not that this is a misfortune, but that to bear it nobly is good fortune.

50. It is a vulgar, but still a useful help towards contempt of death, to pass in review those who have tenaciously stuck to life. What more then have they gained than those who have died early? Certainly they lie in their tombs somewhere at last, Cadicianus, Fabius, Julianus, Lepidus, or any one else like them, who have carried out many to be buried, and then were carried out themselves. Altogether the interval is small [between birth and death]; and consider with how much trouble, and in company with what sort of people, and in what a feeble body this interval is laboriously passed. Do not then consider life a thing of any value. For look to the immensity of time behind thee, and to the time which is before thee, another boundless space. In this infinity then what is the difference between him who lives three days and him who lives three generations?

51. Always run to the short way; and the short way is the natural: accordingly say and do everything in conformity with the soundest reason. For such a purpose frees a man from trouble, and warfare, and all artifice and ostentatious display.

V.

1. In the morning when thou risest unwillingly, let this thought be present,—I am rising to the work of a human being. Why then am I dissatisfied if I am going to do the things for which I exist and for which I was brought into the world? Or have I been made for this, to lie in the bed-clothes and keep myself warm?—But this is more pleasant.—Dost thou exist then to take thy pleasure, and not at all for action or exertion? Dost thou not see the little plants, the little birds, the ants, the spiders, the bees working together to put in order their several parts of the universe? And art thou unwilling to do the work of a human being, and dost thou not make haste to do that which is according to thy nature?—But it is necessary to take rest also.—It is necessary. However, Nature has fixed bounds to this too: she has fixed bounds to eating and drinking, and yet thou goest beyond these bounds, beyond what is sufficient; yet in thy acts it is not so, but thou stoppest short of what thou canst do. So thou lovest not thyself, for if thou didst, thou wouldst love thy nature and her will. But those who love their several arts exhaust themselves in working at them unwashed and without food; but thou valuest thy own nature less than the turner values the turning art, or the dancer the dancing art, or the lover of money values his money, or the vainglorious man his little glory. And such men, when they have a violent affection to a thing, choose neither to eat nor to sleep rather than to perfect the things which they care for. But are the acts which concern society more vile in thy eyes and less worthy of thy labor?

2. How easy it is to repel and to wipe away every impression which is troublesome or unsuitable, and immediately to be in all tranquillity.

3. Judge every word and deed which are according to nature to be fit for thee; and be not diverted by the blame which follows from any people nor by their words, but if a thing is good to be done or said, do not consider it unworthy of thee. For those persons have their peculiar leading principle and follow their peculiar movement; which things do not thou regard, but go straight on, following thy own nature and the common nature; and the way of both is one.
4. I go through the things which happen according to nature until I shall fall and rest, breathing out my breath into that element out of which I daily draw it in, and falling upon that earth out of which my father collected the seed, and my mother the blood, and my nurse the milk; out of which during so many years I have been supplied with food and drink; which bears me when I tread on it and abuse it for so many purposes.
5. Thou sayest, Men cannot admire the sharpness of thy wits.—Be it so: but there are many other things of which thou canst not say, I am not formed for them by nature. Show those qualities then which are altogether in thy power, sincerity, gravity, endurance of labor, aversion to pleasure, contentment with thy portion and with few things, benevolence, frankness, no love of superfluity, freedom from trifling, magnanimity. Dost thou not see how many qualities thou art immediately able to exhibit, in which there is no excuse of natural incapacity and unfitness, and yet thou still remainest voluntarily below the mark? or art thou compelled through being defectively furnished by nature to murmur, and to be stingy, and to flatter, and to find fault with thy poor body, and to try to please men, and to make great display, and to be so restless in thy mind? No, by the gods; but thou mightest have been delivered from these things long ago. Only if in truth thou canst be charged with being rather slow and dull of comprehension, thou must exert thyself about this also, not neglecting it nor yet taking pleasure in thy dulness.
6. One man, when he has done a service to another, is ready to set it down to his account as a favor conferred. Another is not ready to do this, but still in his own mind he thinks of the man as his debtor, and he knows what he has done. A third in a manner does not even know what he has done, but he is like a vine which has produced grapes, and seeks for nothing more after it has once produced its proper fruit. As a horse when he has run, a dog when he has tracked the game, a bee when it has made the honey, so a man when he has done a good act, does not call out for others

to come and see, but he goes on to another act, as a vine goes on to produce again the grapes in season.—Must a man then be one of these, who in a manner act thus without observing it?—Yes.—But this very thing is necessary, the observation of what a man is doing: for, it may be said, it is characteristic of the social animal to perceive that he is working in a social manner, and indeed to wish that his social partner also should perceive it.—It is true what thou sayest, but thou dost not rightly understand what is now said: and for this reason thou wilt become one of those of whom I spoke before, for even they are misled by a certain show of reason. But if thou wilt choose to understand the meaning of what is said, do not fear that for this reason thou wilt omit any social act.

7. A prayer of the Athenians: Rain, rain, O dear Zeus, down on the ploughed fields of the Athenians and on the plains.—In truth we ought not to pray at all, or we ought to pray in this simple and noble fashion.

8. Just as we must understand when it is said, That Aesculapius prescribed to this man horse-exercise, or bathing in cold water, or going without shoes, so we must understand it when it is said, That the nature of the universe prescribed to this man disease, or mutilation, or loss, or anything else of the kind. For in the first case Prescribed means something like this: he prescribed this for this man as a thing adapted to procure health; and in the second case it means, That which happens to [or suits] every man is fixed in a manner for him suitably to his destiny. For this is what we mean when we say that things are suitable to us, as the workmen say of squared stones in walls or the pyramids, that they are suitable, when they fit them to one another in some kind of connection. For there is altogether one fitness [harmony]. And as the universe is made up out of all bodies to be such a body as it is, so out of all existing causes necessity [destiny] is made up to be such a cause as it is. And even those who are completely ignorant understand what I mean; for they say, It [necessity, destiny] brought this to such a person.—This then was brought and this was prescribed to him. Let us then receive these things, as well as those which Aesculapius prescribes. Many as a matter of course even among his prescriptions are disagreeable, but we accept them in the hope of health. Let the perfecting and accomplishment of the things which the common nature judges to be good, be judged by thee to be of the same kind as thy health. And so accept everything which happens, even if it seem disagreeable, because it leads to this, to the health of the universe and to the prosperity and felicity of Zeus [the universe]. For he would not have brought on any man what he has brought, if it were not useful for the whole. Neither does the nature of anything, whatever it may be, cause anything which is not suitable to that which is directed by it. For two reasons, then, it is right to be content with that which happens to thee; the one, because it was done for thee and prescribed for thee, and in a manner had reference to thee, originally from the most ancient causes spun with thy destiny; and the other, because even that which comes severally to every man is to the power which administers the universe a cause of felicity and perfection, nay even of its very continuance. For the integrity of the whole is mutilated, if thou cuttest off anything whatever from the conjunction and the continuity either of the parts or of the causes. And thou dost cut off, as far as it is in thy power, when thou art dissatisfied, and in a manner triest to put anything out of the way.

9. Be not disgusted, nor discouraged, nor dissatisfied, if thou dost not succeed in doing everything according to right principles, but when thou hast failed, return back again, and be content if the greater part of what thou dost is consistent with man's nature, and love this to which thou returnest; and do not return to philosophy as if she were a master, but act like those who have sore eyes and apply a bit of sponge and egg, or as another applies a plaster, or drenching with water. For thus thou wilt not fail to obey reason, and thou wilt repose in it. And remember that philosophy requires only the things which thy nature requires; but thou wouldst have something else which is not according to nature.—It may be objected, Why, what is more agreeable than this [which I am doing]?—But is not this the very reason why pleasure deceives us? And consider if magnanimity, freedom, simplicity, equanimity, piety, are not more agreeable. For what is more agreeable than wisdom itself, when thou thinkest of the security and the happy course of all things which depend on the faculty of understanding and knowledge?

10. Things are in such a kind of envelopment that they have seemed to philosophers, not a few nor those common philosophers, altogether unintelligible; nay even to the Stoics themselves they seem difficult to understand. And all our assent is changeable; for where is the man who never changes? Carry thy thoughts then to the objects themselves, and consider how short-lived they are and worthless, and that they may be in the possession of a filthy wretch or a robber. Then turn to the morals of

those who live with thee, and it is hardly possible to endure even the most agreeable of them, to say nothing of a man being hardly able to endure himself. In such darkness then and dirt, and in so constant a flux both of substance and of time, and of motion and of things moved, what there is worth being highly prized, or even an object of serious pursuit, I cannot imagine. But on the contrary it is a man's duty to comfort himself, and to wait for the natural dissolution, and not to be vexed at the delay, but to rest in these principles only: the one, that nothing will happen to me which is not conformable to the nature of the universe; and the other, that it is in my power never to act contrary to my god and daemon: for there is no man who will compel me to this.

11. About what am I now employing my own soul? On every occasion I must ask myself this question, and inquire, What have I now in this part of me which they call the ruling principle? and whose soul have I now,—that of a child, or of a young man, or of a feeble woman, or of a tyrant, or of a domestic animal, or of a wild beast?

12. What kind of things those are which appear good to the many, we may learn even from this. For if any man should conceive certain things as being really good, such as prudence, temperance, justice, fortitude, he would not after having first conceived these endure to listen to anything which should not be in harmony with what is really good. But if a man has first conceived as good the things which appear to the many to be good, he will listen and readily receive as very applicable that which was said by the comic writer. Thus even the many perceive the difference. For were it not so, this saying would not offend and would not be rejected [in the first case], while we receive it when it is said of wealth, and of the means which further luxury and fame, as said fitly and wittily. Go on then and ask if we should value and think those things to be good, to which after their first conception in the mind the words of the comic writer might be aptly applied,—that he who has them, through pure abundance has not a place to ease himself in.

13. I am composed of the formal and the material; and neither of them will perish into nonexistence, as neither of them came into existence out of nonexistence. Every part of me then will be reduced by change into some part of the universe, and that again will change into another part of the universe, and so on forever. And by consequence of such a change I too exist, and those who begot me, and so on forever in the other direction.

For nothing hinders us from saying so, even if the universe is administered according to definite periods [of revolution].

14. Reason and the reasoning art [philosophy] are powers which are sufficient for themselves and for their own works. They move then from a first principle which is their own, and they make their way to the end which is proposed to them; and this is the reason why such acts are named Catorthóseis or right acts, which word signifies that they proceed by the right road.

15. None of these things ought to be called a man's which do not belong to a man, as man. They are not required of a man, nor does man's nature promise them, nor are they the means of man's nature attaining its end. Neither then does the end of man lie in these things, nor yet that which aids to the accomplishment of this end, and that which aids towards this end is that which is good. Besides, if any of these things did belong to man, it would not be right for a man to despise them and to set himself against them; nor would a man be worthy of praise who showed that he did not want these things, nor would he who stinted himself in any of them be good, if indeed these things were good. But now the more of these things a man deprives himself of, or of other things like them, or even when he is deprived of any of them, the more patiently he endures the loss, just in the same degree he is a better man.

16. Such as are thy habitual thoughts, such also will be the character of thy mind; for the soul is dyed by the thoughts. Dye it then with a continuous series of such thoughts as these: for instance, that where a man can live, there he can also live well. But he must live in a palace; well then, he can also live well in a palace. And again, consider that for whatever purpose each thing has been constituted, for this it has been constituted, and towards this it is carried; and its end is in that towards which it is carried; and where the end is, there also is the advantage and the good of each thing. Now the good for the reasonable animal is society; for that we are made for society has been shown above. Is it not plain that the inferior exists for the sake of the superior? But the things which have life are superior to those which have not life, and of those which have life the superior are those which have reason.

17. To seek what is impossible is madness: and it is impossible that the bad should not do something of this kind.

18. Nothing happens to any man which he is not formed by nature to bear. The same things happen to another, and either because he does not see that they have happened, or because he would show a great spirit, he is firm and remains unharmed. It is a shame then that ignorance and conceit should be stronger than wisdom.

19. Things themselves touch not the soul, not in the least degree; nor have they admission to the soul, nor can they turn or move the soul: but the soul turns and moves itself alone, and whatever judgments it may think proper to make, such it makes for itself the things which present themselves to it.

20. In one respect man is the nearest thing to me, so far as I must do good to men and endure them. But so far as some men make themselves obstacles to my proper acts, man becomes to me one of the things which are indifferent, no less than the sun or wind or a wild beast. Now it is true that these may impede my action, but they are no impediments to my effects and disposition, which have the power of acting conditionally and changing: for the mind converts and changes every hindrance to its activity into an aid; and so that which is a hindrance is made a furtherance to an act; and that which is an obstacle on the road helps us on this road.

21. Reverence that which is best in the universe; and this is that which makes use of all things and directs all things. And in like manner also reverence that which is best in thyself; and this is of the same kind as that. For in thyself also, that which makes use of everything else is this, and thy life is directed by this.

22. That which does no harm to the state, does no harm to the citizen. In the case of every appearance of harm apply this rule: if the state is not harmed by this, neither am I harmed. But if the state is harmed, thou must not be angry with him who does harm to the state. Show him where his error is.

23. Often think of the rapidity with which things pass by and disappear, both the things which are and the things which are produced. For substance is like a river in a continual flow, and the activities of things are in constant change, and the causes work in infinite varieties; and there is hardly anything which stands still. And consider this which is near to thee, this boundless abyss of the past and of the future in which all things disappear. How then is he not a fool who is puffed up with such things or plagued about them and makes himself miserable? for they vex him only for a time, and a short time.

24. Think of the universal substance, of which thou hast a very small portion; and of universal time, of which a short and indivisible interval has been

assigned to thee; and of that which is fixed by destiny, and how small a part of it thou art.

25. Does another do me wrong? Let him look to it. He has his own disposition, his own activity. I now have what the universal nature wills me to have; and I do what my nature now wills me to do.

26. Let the part of thy soul which leads and governs be undisturbed by the movements in the flesh, whether of pleasure or of pain; and let it not unite with them, but let it circumscribe itself and limit those affects to their parts. But when these affects rise up to the mind by virtue of that other sympathy that naturally exists in a body which is all one, then thou must not strive to resist the sensation, for it is natural: but let not the ruling part of itself add to the sensation the opinion that it is either good or bad.

27. Live with the gods. And he does live with the gods who constantly shows to them that his own soul is satisfied with that which is assigned to him, and that it does all that the daemon wishes, which Zeus hath given to every man for his guardian and guide, a portion of himself. And this is every man's understanding and reason.

28. Art thou angry with him whose armpits stink? art thou angry with him whose mouth smells foul? What good will this anger do thee? He has such a mouth, he has such armpits: it is necessary that such an emanation must come from such things; but the man has reason, it will be said, and he is able, if he takes pains, to discover wherein he offends; I wish thee well of thy discovery. Well then, and thou hast reason: by thy rational faculty stir up his rational faculty; show him his error, admonish him. For if he listens, thou wilt cure him, and there is no need of anger.

29. As thou intendest to live when thou art gone out, . . . so it is in thy power to live here. But if men do not permit thee, then get away out of life, yet so as if thou wert suffering no harm. The house is smoky, and I quit it. Why dost thou think that this is any trouble? But so long as nothing of the kind drives me out, I remain, am free, and no man shall hinder me from doing what I choose; and I choose to do what is according to the nature of the rational and social animal.

30. The intelligence of the universe is social. Accordingly it has made the inferior things for the sake of the superior, and it has fitted the superior to one another. Thou seest how it has subordinated, co-ordinated, and assigned to everything its proper portion, and has brought together into concord with one another the things which are the best.

31. How hast thou behaved hitherto to the gods, thy parents, brethren, children, teachers, to those who looked after thy infancy, to thy friends, kinsfolk, to thy slaves? Consider if thou hast hitherto behaved to all in such a way that this may be said of thee,—

"Never has wronged a man in deed or word."

And call to recollection both how many things thou hast passed through, and how many things thou hast been able to endure and that the history of thy life is now complete and thy service is ended: and how many beautiful things thou hast seen; and how many pleasures and pains thou hast despised; and how many things called honorable thou hast spurned; and to how many ill-minded folks thou hast shown a kind disposition.

32. Why do unskilled and ignorant souls disturb him who has skill and knowledge? What soul then has skill and knowledge? That which knows beginning and end, and knows the reason which pervades all substance, and through all time by fixed periods [revolutions] administers the universe.

33. Soon, very soon, thou wilt be ashes, or a skeleton, and either a name or not even a name; but name is sound and echo. And the things which are much valued in life are empty and rotten and trifling, and [like] little dogs biting one another, and little children quarrelling, laughing, and then straightway weeping. But fidelity and modesty and justice and truth are fled

Up to Olympus from the wide-spread earth.

Hesiod, *Works, etc.* v. 197.

What then is there which still detains thee here, if the objects of sense are easily changed and never stand still, and the organs of perception are dull and easily receive false impressions, and the poor soul itself is an exhalation from blood? But to have good repute amid such a world as this is an empty thing. Why then dost thou not wait in tranquillity for thy end, whether it is extinction or removal to another state? And until that time comes, what is sufficient? Why, what else than to venerate the gods and bless them, and to do good to men, and to practice tolerance and self-restraint; but as to everything which is beyond the limits of the poor flesh and breath, to remember that this is neither thine nor in thy power.

34. Thou canst pass thy life in an equable flow of happiness, if thou canst go by the right way, and think and act in the right way. These two things are common both to the soul of God and to the soul of man, and to the soul of every rational being: not to be hindered by another; and to hold good to consist in the disposition to justice and the practice of it, and in this to let thy desire find its termination.
35. If this is neither my own badness, nor an effect of my own badness, and the common weal is not injured, why am I troubled about it, and what is the harm to the common weal?
36. Do not be carried along inconsiderately by the appearance of things, but give help [to all] according to thy ability and their fitness; and if they should have sustained loss in matters which are indifferent, do not imagine this to be a damage; for it is a bad habit. But as the old man, when he went away, asked back his foster-child's top, remembering that it was a top, so do thou in this case also.

    When thou art calling out on the Rostra, hast thou forgotten, man, what these things are?—Yes; but they are objects of great concern to these people—wilt thou too then be made a fool for these things? I was once a fortunate man, but I lost it, I know not how.—But fortunate means that a man has assigned to himself a good fortune: and a good fortune is good disposition of the soul, good emotions, good actions.

VI.

1. The substance of the universe is obedient and compliant; and the reason which governs it has in itself no cause for doing evil, for it has no malice, nor does it do evil to anything, nor is anything harmed by it. But all things are made and perfected according to this reason.
2. Let it make no difference to thee whether thou art cold or warm, if thou art doing thy duty; and whether thou art drowsy or satisfied with sleep; and whether ill-spoken of or praised; and whether dying or doing something else. For it is one of the acts of life, this act by which we die: it is sufficient then in this act also to do well what we have in hand (vi. 22, 28).
3. Look within. Let neither the peculiar quality of anything nor its value escape thee.

4. All existing things soon change, and they will either be reduced to vapor, if indeed all substance is one, or they will be dispersed.
5. The reason which governs knows what its own disposition is, and what it does, and on what material it works.
6. The best way of avenging thyself is not to become like [the wrong-doer].
7. Take pleasure in one thing and rest in it, in passing from one social act to another social act, thinking of God.
8. The ruling principle is that which rouses and turns itself, and while it makes itself such as it is and such as it wills to be, it also makes everything which happens appear to itself to be such as it wills.
9. In conformity to the nature of the universe every single thing is accomplished; for certainly it is not in conformity to any other nature that each thing is accomplished, either a nature which externally comprehends this, or a nature which is comprehended within this nature, or a nature external and independent of this (XI. 1; VI. 40; VIII. 50).
10. The universe is either a confusion, and a mutual involution of things, and a dispersion, or it is unity and order and providence. If then it is the former, why do I desire to tarry in a fortuitous combination of things and such a disorder? and why do I care about anything else than how I shall at last become earth? and why am I disturbed, for the dispersion of my elements will happen whatever I do? But if the other supposition is true, I venerate, and I am firm, and I trust in him who governs (IV. 27).
11. When thou hast been compelled by circumstances to be disturbed in a manner, quickly return to thyself, and do not continue out of tune longer than the compulsion lasts; for thou wilt have more mastery over the harmony by continually recurring to it.
12. If thou hadst a step-mother and a mother at the same time, thou wouldst be dutiful to thy stepmother, but still thou wouldst constantly return to thy mother. Let the court and philosophy now be to thee step-mother and mother: return to philosophy frequently and repose in her, through whom what thou meetest with in the court appears to thee tolerable, and thou appearest tolerable in the court.
13. When we have meat before us and such eatables, we receive the impression that this is the dead body of a fish, and this is the dead body of a bird or of a pig; and again, that this Falernian is only a little grape-juice, and this purple robe some sheep's wool dyed with the blood of a shell-fish:

such then are these impressions, and they reach the things themselves and penetrate them, and so we see what kind of things they are. Just in the same way ought we to act all through life, and where there are things which appear most worthy of our approbation, we ought to lay them bare and look at their worthlessness and strip them of all the words by which they are exalted. For outward show is a wonderful perverter of the reason, and when thou art most sure that thou art employed about things worth thy pains, it is then that it cheats thee most. Consider then what Crates says of Xenocrates himself.

14. Most of the things which the multitude admire are referred to objects of the most general kind, those which are held together by cohesion or natural organization, such as stones, wood, fig-trees, vines, olives. But those which are admired by men who are a little more reasonable are referred to the things which are held together by a living principle, as flocks, herds. Those which are admired by men who are still more instructed are the things which are held together by a rational soul, not however a universal soul, but rational so far as it is a soul skilled in some art, or expert in some other way, or simply rational so far as it possesses a number of slaves. But he who values a rational soul, a soul universal and fitted for political life, regards nothing else except this; and above all things he keeps his soul in a condition and in an activity comformable to reason and social life, and he co-operates to this end with those who are of the same kind as himself.

15. Some things are hurrying into existence, and others are hurrying out of it; and of that which is coming into existence part is already extinguished. Motions and changes are continually renewing the world, just as the uninterrupted course of time is always renewing the infinite duration of ages. In this flowing stream then, on which there is no abiding, what is there of the things which hurry by on which a man would set a high price? It would be just as if a man should fall in love with one of the sparrows which fly by, but it has already passed out of sight. Something of this kind is the very life of every man, like the exhalation of the blood and the respiration of the air. For such as it is to have once drawn in the air and to have given it back, which we do every moment, just the same is it with the whole respiratory power, which thou didst receive at thy birth yesterday and the day before, to give it back to the element from which thou didst first draw it.

16. Neither is transpiration, as in plants, a thing to be valued, nor respiration, as in domesticated animals and wild beasts, nor the receiving of impressions by the appearances of things, nor being moved by desires as puppets by strings, nor assembling in herds, nor being nourished by food; for this is just like the act of separating and parting with the useless part of our food. What then is worth being valued? To be received with clapping of hands? No. Neither must we value the clapping of tongues; for the praise which comes from the many is a clapping of tongues. Suppose then that thou hast given up this worthless thing called fame, what remains that is worth valuing? This, in my opinion: to move thyself and to restrain thyself in conformity to thy proper constitution, to which end both all employments and arts lead. For every art aims at this, that the thing which has been made should be adapted to the work for which it has been made; and both the vine planter who looks after the vine, and the horsebreaker, and he who trains the dog, seek this end. But the education and the teaching of youth aim at something. In this then is the value of the education and the teaching. And if this is well, thou wilt not seek anything else. Wilt thou not cease to value many other things too? Then thou wilt be neither free, nor sufficient for thy own happiness, nor without passion. For of necessity thou must be envious, jealous, and suspicious of those who can take away those things, and plot against those who have that which is valued by thee. Of necessity a man must be altogether in a state of perturbation who wants any of these things; and besides, he must often find fault with the gods. But to reverence and honor thy own mind will make thee content with thyself, and in harmony with society, and in agreement with the gods, that is, praising all that they give and have ordered.

17. Above, below, all around are the movements of the elements. But the motion of virtue is in none of these: it is something more divine, and advancing by a way hardly observed, it goes happily on its road.

18. How strangely men act! They will not praise those who are living at the same time and living with themselves; but to be themselves praised by posterity, by those whom they have never seen or ever will see, this they set much value on. But this is very much the same as if thou shouldst be grieved because those who have lived before thee did not praise thee.

19. If a thing is difficult to be accomplished by thyself, do not think that it is impossible for man: but if anything is possible for man and conformable to his nature, think that this can be attained by thyself too.

20. In the gymnastic exercises suppose that a man has torn thee with his nails, and by dashing against thy head has inflicted a wound. Well, we neither show any signs of vexation, nor are we offended, nor do we suspect him afterwards as a treacherous fellow; and yet we are on our guard against him, not however as an enemy, nor yet with suspicion, but we quietly get out of his way. Something like this let thy behavior be in all the other parts of life; let us overlook many things in those who are like antagonists in the gymnasium. For it is in our power, as I said, to get out of the way, and to have no suspicion nor hatred.

21. If any man is able to convince me and show me that I do not think or act rightly, I will gladly change; for I seek the truth, by which no man was ever injured. But he is injured who abides in his error and ignorance.

22. I do my duty: other things trouble me not; for they are either things without life, or things without reason, or things that have rambled and know not the way.

23. As to the animals which have no reason, and generally all things and objects, do thou, since thou hast reason and they have none, make use of them with a generous and liberal spirit. But towards human beings, as they have reason, behave in a social spirit. And on all occasions call on the gods, and do not perplex thyself about the length of time in which thou shalt do this; for even three hours so spent are sufficient.

24. Alexander the Macedonian and his groom by death were brought to the same state; for either they were received among the same seminal principles of the universe, or they were alike dispersed among the atoms.

25. Consider how many things in the same indivisible time take place in each of us,—things which concern the body and things which concern the soul: and so thou wilt not wonder if many more things, or rather all things which come into existence in that which is the one and all, which we call Cosmos, exist in it at the same time.

26. If any man should propose to thee the question, how the name Antoninus is written, wouldst thou with a straining of the voice utter each letter? What then if they grow angry, wilt thou be angry too? Wilt thou not go on with composure and number every letter? Just so then in this life also remember that every duty is made up of certain parts. These it is thy duty to observe, and without being disturbed or showing anger towards those who are angry with thee to go on thy way and finish that which is set before thee.

27. How cruel it is not to allow men to strive after the things which appear to them to be suitable to their nature and profitable! And yet in a manner

thou dost not allow them to do this, when thou art vexed because they do wrong. For they are certainly moved towards things because they suppose them to be suitable to their nature and profitable to them.—But it is not so.—Teach them then, and show them without being angry.

28. Death is a cessation of the impressions through the senses, and of the pulling of the strings which move the appetites, and of the discursive movements of the thoughts, and of the service to the flesh (II. 12).

29. It is a shame for the soul to be first to give way in this life, when thy body does not give way.

30. Take care that thou art not made into a Caesar, that thou art not dyed with this dye; for such things happen. Keep thyself then simple, good, pure, serious, free from affectation, a friend of justice, a worshipper of the gods, kind, affectionate, strenuous in all proper acts. Strive to continue to be such as philosophy wished to make thee. Reverence the gods, and help men. Short is life. There is only one fruit of this terrene life,—a pious disposition and social acts. Do everything as a disciple of Antoninus. Remember his constancy in every act which was conformable to reason, and his evenness in all things, and his piety, and the serenity of his countenance, and his sweetness, and his disregard of empty fame, and his efforts to understand things; and how he would never let anything pass without having first most carefully examined it and clearly understood it; and how he bore with those who blamed him unjustly without blaming them in return; how he did nothing in a hurry; and how he listened not to calumnies, and how exact an examiner of manners and actions he was; and not given to reproach people, nor timid, nor suspicious, nor a sophist; and with how little he was satisfied, such as lodging, bed, dress, food, servants; and how laborious and patient; and how he was able on account of his sparing diet to hold out to the evening; and his firmness and uniformity in his friendships; and how he tolerated freedom of speech in those who opposed his opinions; and the pleasure that he had when any man showed him anything better; and how religious he was without superstition. Imitate all this, that thou mayest have as good a conscience, when thy last hour comes, as he had.

31. Return to thy sober senses and call thyself back; and when thou hast roused thyself from sleep and hast perceived that they were only dreams which troubled thee, now in thy waking hours look at these [the things about thee] as thou didst look at those [the dreams].

32. I consist of a little body and a soul. Now to this little body all things are indifferent, for it is not able to perceive differences. But to the understanding those things only are indifferent which are not the works of its own activity. But whatever things are the works of its own activity, all these are in its power. And of these however only those which are done with reference to the present; for as to the future and the past activities of the mind, even these are for the present indifferent.

33. Neither the labor which the hand does nor that of the foot is contrary to nature, so long as the foot does the foot's work and the hand the hand's. So then neither to a man as a man is his labor contrary to nature, so long as it does the things of a man. But if the labor is not contrary to his nature, neither is it an evil to him.

34. How many pleasures have been enjoyed by robbers, patricides, tyrants.

35. Dost thou not see how the handicraftsmen accommodate themselves up to a certain point to those who are not skilled in their craft,—nevertheless they cling to the reason [the principles] of their art, and do not endure to depart from it? Is it not strange if the architect and the physician shall have more respect to the reason [the principles] of their own arts than man to his own reason, which is common to him and the gods?

36. Asia, Europe, are corners of the universe; all the sea a drop in the universe; Athos a little clod of the universe: all the present time is a point in eternity. All things are little, changeable, perishable. All things come from thence, from that universal ruling power either directly proceding or by way of sequence. And accordingly the lion's gaping jaws, and that which is poisonous, and every harmful thing, as a thorn, as mud, are after-products of the grand and beautiful. Do not then imagine that they are of another kind from that which thou dost venerate, but form a just opinion of the source of all (vii. 75).

37. He who has seen present things has seen all, both everything which has taken place from all eternity and everything which will be for time without end; for all things are of one kin and of one form.

38. Frequently consider the connection of all things in the universe and their relation to one another. For in a manner all things are implicated with one another, and all in this way are friendly to one another; for one thing comes in order after another, and this is by virtue of the active movement and mutual conspiration and the unity of the substance (ix. 1).

39. Adapt thyself to the things with which thy lot has been cast: and the men among whom thou hast received thy portion, love them, but do it truly [sincerely].

40. Every instrument, tool, vessel, if it does that for which it has been made, is well, and yet he who made it is not there. But in the things which are held together by nature there is within, and there abides in, them the power which made them; wherefore the more is it fit to reverence this power, and to think, that, if thou dost live and act according to its will, everything in thee is in conformity to intelligence. And thus also in the universe the things which belong to it are in conformity to intelligence.

41. Whatever of the things which are not within thy power thou shalt suppose to be good for thee or evil, it must of necessity be that, if such a bad thing befall thee, or the loss of such a good thing, thou wilt not blame the gods, and hate men too, those who are the cause of the misfortune or the loss, or those who are suspected of being likely to be the cause; and indeed we do much injustice because we make a difference between these things [because we do not regard these things as indifferent]. But if we judge only those things which are in our power to be good or bad, there remains no reason either for finding fault with God or standing in a hostile attitude to man.

42. We are all working together to one end, some with knowledge and design, and others without knowing what they do; as men also when they are asleep, of whom it is Heraclitus, I think, who says that they are laborers and co-operators in the things which take place in the universe. But men co-operate after different fashions: and even those cooperate abundantly, who find fault with what happens and those who try to oppose it and to hinder it; for the universe had need even of such men as these. It remains then for thee to understand among what kind of workmen thou placest thyself; for he who rules all things will certainly make a right use of thee, and he will receive thee among some part of the co-operators and of those whose labors conduce to one end. But be not thou such a part as the mean and ridiculous verse in the play, which Chrysippus speaks of.

43. Does the sun undertake to do the work of the rain, or Aesculapius the work of the Fruit-bearer [the earth]? And how is it with respect to each of the stars, are they not different and yet they work together to the same end?

44. If the gods have determined about me and about the things which must happen to me, they have determined well, for it is not easy even to imagine

a deity without forethought; and as to doing me harm, why should they have any desire towards that? for what advantage would result to them from this or to the whole, which is the special object of their providence? But if they have not determined about me individually, they have certainly determined about the whole at least, and the things which happen by way of sequence in this general arrangement I ought to accept with pleasure and to be content with them. But if they determine about nothing,—which it is wicked to believe, or if we do believe it, let us neither sacrifice nor pray nor swear by them, nor do anything else which we do as if the gods were present and lived with us,—but if however the gods determine about none of the things which concern us, I am able to determine about myself, and I can inquire about that which is useful; and that is useful to every man which is conformable to his own constitution and nature. But my nature is rational and social; and my city and country, so far as I am Antoninus, is Rome, but so far as I am a man, it is the world. The things then which are useful to these cities are alone useful to me.

45. Whatever happens to every man, this is for the interest of the universal: this might be sufficient. But further thou wilt observe this also as a general truth, if thou dost observe, that whatever is profitable to any man is profitable also to other men. But let the word profitable be taken here in the common sense as said of things of the middle kind [neither good nor bad].

46. As it happens to thee in the amphitheatre and such places, that the continual sight of the same things, and the uniformity make the spectacle wearisome, so it is in the whole of life; for all things above, below, are the same and from the same. How long then?

47. Think continually that all kinds of men and men of all kinds of pursuits and of all nations are dead, so that thy thoughts come down even to Philistion and Phoebus and Origanion. Now turn thy thoughts to the other kinds [of men]. To that place then we must remove, where there are so many great orators, and so many noble philosophers, Heraclitus, Pythagoras, Socrates; so many heroes of former days, and so many generals after them, and tyrants; besides these, Eudoxus, Hipparchus, Archimedes, and other men of acute natural talents, great minds, lovers of labor, versatile, confident, mockers even of the perishable and ephemeral life of man, as Menippus and such as are like him. As to all these consider that they have long been in the dust. What harm then is this to them; and what to those whose names are altogether unknown? One thing here is worth a great deal, to pass thy life in truth and justice, with a benevolent disposition even to liars and unjust men.

48. When thou wishest to delight thyself, think of the virtues of those who live with thee; for instance, the activity of one, and the modesty of another, and the liberality of a third, and some other good quality of a fourth. For nothing delights so much as the examples of the virtues, when they are exhibited in the morals of those who live with us and present themselves in abundance, as far as is possible. Wherefore we must keep them before us.

49. Thou art not dissatisfied, I suppose, because thou weighest only so many litrae and not three hundred. Be not dissatisfied then that thou must live only so many years and not more; for as thou art satisfied with the amount of substance which has been assigned to thee, so be content with the time.

50. Let us try to persuade them [men]. But act even against their will, when the principles of justice lead that way. If however any man by using force stands in thy way, betake thyself to contentment and tranquillity, and at the same time employ the hindrance towards the exercise of some other virtue; and remember that thy attempt was with a reservation [conditionally], that thou didst not desire to do impossibilities. What then didst thou desire?—Some such effort as this.—But thou attainest thy object, if the things to which thou wast moved are [not] accomplished.

51. He who loves fame considers another man's activity to be his own good; and he who loves pleasure, his own sensations; but he who has understanding considers his own acts to be his own good.

52. It is in our power to have no opinion about a thing, and not to be disturbed in our soul; for things themselves have no natural power to form our judgments.

53. Accustom thyself to attend carefully to what is said by another, and as much as it is possible, be in the speaker's mind.

54. That which is not good for the swarm, neither is it good for the bee.

55. If sailors abused the helmsman, or the sick the doctor, would they listen to anybody else; or how could the helmsman secure the safety of those in the ship, or the doctor the health of those whom he attends?

56. How many together with whom I came into the world are already gone out of it.

57. To the jaundiced honey tastes bitter, and to those bitten by mad dogs water causes fear; and to little children the ball is a fine thing. Why then am I angry? Dost thou think that a false opinion has less power than the bile in the jaundiced or the poison in him who is bitten by a mad dog?
58. No man will hinder thee from living according to the reason of thy own nature: nothing will happen to thee contrary to the reason of the universal nature.
59. What kind of people are those whom men wish to please, and for what objects, and by what kind of acts? How soon will time cover all things, and how many it has covered already.

VII.

1. What is badness? It is that which thou hast often seen. And on the occasion of everything which happens keep this in mind, that it is that which thou hast often seen. Everywhere up and down thou wilt find the same things, with which the old histories are filled, those of the middle ages and those of our own day; with which cities and houses are filled now. There is nothing new: all things are both familiar and short-lived.
2. How can our principles become dead, unless the impression [thoughts] which correspond to them are extinguished? But it is in thy power continuously to fan these thoughts into a flame. I can have that opinion about anything which I ought to have. If I can, why am I disturbed? The things which are external to my mind have no relation at all to my mind.—Let this be the state of thy affects, and thou standest erect. To recover thy life is in thy power. Look at things again as thou didst use to look at them; for in this consists the recovery of thy life.
3. The idle business of show, plays on the stage, flocks of sheep, herds, exercises with spears, a bone cast to little dogs, a bit of bread into fishponds, laborings of ants and burden-carrying, runnings about of frightened little mice, puppets pulled by strings—[all alike]. It is thy duty then in the midst of such things to show good humor and not a proud air; to understand however that every man is worth just so much as the things are worth about which he busies himself.
4. In discourse thou must attend to what is said, and in every movement thou must observe what is doing. And in the one thou shouldst see im-

mediately to what end it refers, but in the other watch carefully what is the thing signified.

5. Is my understanding sufficient for this or not? If it is sufficient, I use it for the work as an instrument given by the universal nature. But if it is not sufficient, then either I retire from the work and give way to him who is able to do it better, unless there be some reason why I ought not to do so; or I do it as well as I can, taking to help me the man who with the aid of my ruling principle can do what is now fit and useful for the general good. For whatsoever either by myself or with another I can do, ought to be directed to this only, to that which is useful and well suited to society.
6. How many after being celebrated by fame have been given up to oblivion; and how many who have celebrated the fame of others have long been dead.
7. Be not ashamed to be helped; for it is thy business to do thy duty like a soldier in the assault on a town. How then, if being lame thou canst not mount up on the battlements alone, but with the help of another it is possible?
8. Let not future things disturb thee, for thou wilt come to them, if it shall be necessary, having with thee the same reason which now thou usest for present things.
9. All things are implicated with one another, and the bond is holy; and there is hardly anything unconnected with any other thing. For things have been co-ordinated, and they combine to form the same universe [order]. For there is one universe made up of all things, and one god who pervades all things, and one substance, and one law, [one] common reason in all intelligent animals, and one truth; if indeed there is also one perfection for all animals which are of the same stock and participate in the same reason.
10. Everything material soon disappears in the substance of the whole; and everything formal [causal] is very soon taken back into the universal reason; and the memory of everything is very soon overwhelmed in time.
11. To the rational animal the same act is according to nature and according to reason.
12. Be thou erect, or be made erect (III. 5).
13. Just as it is with the members in those bodies which are united in one, so it is with rational beings which exist separate, for they have been constituted for one co-operation. And the perception of this will be more apparent to thee if thou often sayest to thyself that I am a member of the system of rational beings. But if thou sayest that thou art a part, thou dost

not yet love men from thy heart; beneficence does not yet delight thee for its own sake; thou still dost it barely as a thing of propriety, and not yet as doing good to thyself.

14. Let there fall externally what will on the parts which can feel the effects of this fall. For those parts which have felt will complain, if they choose. But I, unless I think that what has happened is an evil, am not injured. And it is in my power not to think so.

15. Whatever any one does or says, I must be good; just as if the gold, or the emerald, or the purple were always saying this, Whatever any one does or says, I must be emerald and keep my color.

16. The ruling faculty does not disturb itself; I mean, does not frighten itself or cause itself pain. But if any one else can frighten or pain it, let him do so. For the faculty itself will not by its own opinion turn itself into such ways. Let the body itself take care, if it can, that it suffer nothing, and let it speak, if it suffers. But the soul itself, that which is subject to fear, to pain, which has completely the power of forming an opinion about these things, will suffer nothing, for it will never deviate into such a judgment. The leading principle in itself wants nothing, unless it makes a want for itself; and therefore it is both free from perturbation and unimpeded, if it does not disturb and impede itself.

17. Eudaemonia [happiness] is a good daemon, or a good thing. What then art thou doing here, O imagination? Go away, I entreat thee by the gods, as thou didst come, for I want thee not. But thou art come according to thy old fashion. I am not angry with thee: only go away.

18. Is any man afraid of change? Why, what can take place without change? What then is more pleasing or more suitable to the universal nature? And canst thou take a bath unless the wood undergoes a change? and canst thou be nourished, unless the food undergoes a change? And can anything else that is useful be accomplished without change? Dost thou not see then that for thyself also to change is just the same, and equally necessary for the universal nature?

19. Through the universal substance as through a furious torrent all bodies are carried, being by their nature united with and co-operating with the whole, as the parts of our body with one another. How many a Chrysippus, how many a Socrates, how many an Epictetus has time already swallowed up! And let the same thought occur to thee with reference to every man and thing (v. 23; vi. 15).

20. One thing only troubles me, lest I should do something which the constitution of man does not allow, or in the way which it does not allow, or what it does not allow now.

21. Near is thy forgetfulness of all things; and near the forgetfulness of thee by all.

22. It is peculiar to man to love even those who do wrong. And this happens, if when they do wrong it occurs to thee that they are kinsmen, and that they do wrong through ignorance and unintentionally, and that soon both of you will die; and above all, that the wrong-doer has done thee no harm, for he has not made thy ruling faculty worse than it was before.

23. The universal nature out of the universal substance, as if it were wax, now moulds a horse, and when it has broken this up, it uses the material for a tree, then for a man, then for something else; and each of these things subsists for a very short time. But it is no hardship for the vessel to be broken up, just as there was none in its being fastened together (VIII. 50).

24. A scowling look is altogether unnatural; when it is often assumed,* the result is that all comeliness dies away, and at last is so completely extinguished that it cannot be again lighted up at all. Try to conclude from this very fact that it is contrary to reason. For if even the perception of doing wrong shall depart, what reason is there for living any longer?

25. Nature which governs the whole will soon change all things which thou seest, and out of their substance will make other things, and again other things from the substance of them, in order that the world may be ever new (XII. 23).

26. When a man has done thee any wrong, immediately consider with what opinion about good or evil he has done wrong. For when thou hast seen this, thou wilt pity him, and wilt neither wonder nor be angry. For either thou thyself thinkest the same thing to be good that he does or another thing of the same kind. It is thy duty then to pardon him. But if thou dost not think such things to be good or evil, thou wilt more readily be well disposed to him who is in error.

27. Think not so much of what thou hast not as of what thou hast: but of the things which thou hast select the best, and then reflect how eagerly they would have been sought, if thou hadst them not. At the same time, however, take care that thou dost not through being so pleased with them

* This is corrupt.

accustom thyself to overvalue them, so as to be disturbed if ever thou shouldst not have them.

28. Retire into thyself. The rational principle which rules has this nature, that it is content with itself when it does what is just, and so secures tranquillity.

29. Wipe out the imagination. Stop the pulling of the strings. Confine thyself to the present. Understand well what happens either to thee or to another. Divide and distribute every object into the causal [formal] and the material. Think of thy last hour. Let the wrong which is done by a man stay there where the wrong was done (viii. 29).

30. Direct thy attention to what is said. Let thy understanding enter into the things that are doing and the things which do them (vii. 4).

31. Adorn thyself with simplicity and modesty, and with indifference towards the things which lie between virtue and vice. Love mankind. Follow God. The poet says that law rules all—And it is enough to remember that law rules all.

32. About death: whether it is a dispersion, or a resolution into atoms, or annihilation, it is either extinction or change.

33. About pain: the pain which is intolerable carries us off; but that which lasts a long time is tolerable; and the mind maintains its own tranquillity by retiring into itself, and the ruling faculty is not made worse. But the parts which are harmed by pain, let them, if they can, give their opinion about it.

34. About fame: look at the minds [of those who seek fame], observe what they are, and what kind of things they avoid, and what kind of things they pursue. And consider that as the heaps of sand piled on one another hide the former sands, so in life the events which go before are soon covered by those which come after.

35. From Plato: The man who has an elevated mind and takes a view of all time and of all substance, dost thou suppose it possible for him to think that human life is anything great? It is not possible, he said.—Such a man then will think that death also is no evil.—Certainly not.

36. From Antisthenes: It is royal to do good and to be abused.

37. It is a base thing for the countenance to be obedient and to regulate and compose itself as the mind commands, and for the mind not to be regulated and composed by itself.

38. It is not right to vex ourselves at things, For they care nought about it.

39. To the immortal gods and us give joy.

40. Life must be reaped like the ripe ears of corn. One man is born; another dies.

41. If gods care not for me and for my children, There is a reason for it.

42. For the good is with me, and the just.

43. No joining others in their wailing, no violent emotion.

44. From Plato: But I would make this man a sufficient answer, which is this: Thou sayest not well, if thou thinkest that a man who is good for anything at all ought to compute the hazard of life or death, and should not rather look to this only in all that he does, whether he is doing what is just or unjust, and the works of a good or bad man.

45. For thus it is, men of Athens, in truth: wherever a man has placed himself thinking it the best place for him, or has been placed by a commander, there in my opinion he ought to stay and to abide the hazard, taking nothing into the reckoning, either death or anything else, before the baseness [of deserting his post].

46. But, my good friend, reflect whether that which is noble and good is not something different from saving and being saved; for as to a man living such or such a time, at least one who is really a man, consider if this is not a thing to be dismissed from the thoughts: and there must be no love of life: but as to these matters a man must entrust them to the Deity and believe what the women say, that no man can escape his destiny, the next inquiry being how he may best live the time that he has to live.

47. Look around at the courses of the stars, as if thou wert going along with them; and constantly consider the changes of the elements into one another, for such thoughts purge away the filth of the terrene life.

48. This is a fine saying of Plato: That he who is discoursing about men should look also at earthly things as if he viewed them from some higher place; should look at them in their assemblies, armies, agricultural labors, marriages, treaties, births, deaths, noise of the courts of justice, desert places, various nations of barbarians, feasts, lamentations, markets, a mixture of all things and an orderly combination of contraries.

49. Consider the past,—such great changes of political supremacies; thou mayest foresee also the things which will be. For they will certainly be of like form, and it is not possible that they should deviate from the order of the things which take place now; accordingly to have contemplated human life for forty years is the same as to have contemplated it for ten thousand years. For what more wilt thou see?

50. That which has grown from the earth to the earth,

> But that which has sprung from heavenly seed,
> Back to the heavenly realms returns.

This is either a dissolution of the mutual involution of the atoms, or a similar dispersion of the unsentient elements.

51. With food and drinks and cunning magic arts

> Turning the channel's course to 'scape from death.
> The breeze which heaven has sent
> We must endure, and toil without complaining.

52. Another may be more expert in casting his opponent; but he is not more social, nor more modest, nor better disciplined to meet all that happens, nor more considerate with respect to the faults of his neighbors.

53. Where any work can be done conformably to the reason which is common to gods and men, there we have nothing to fear; for where we are able to get profit by means of the activity which is successful and proceeds according to our constitution, there no harm is to be suspected.

54. Everywhere and at all times it is in thy power piously to acquiesce in thy present condition, and to behave justly to those who are about thee, and to exert thy skill upon thy present thoughts, that nothing shall steal into them without being well examined.

55. Do not look around thee to discover other men's ruling principles, but look straight to this, to what nature leads thee, both the universal nature through the things which happen to thee, and thy own nature through the acts which must be done by thee. But every being ought to do that which is according to its constitution; and all other things have been constituted for the sake of rational beings, just as among irrational things the inferior for the sake of the superior, but the rational for the sake of one another.

The prime principle then in man's constitution is the social. And the second is not to yield to the persuasions of the body,—for it is the peculiar office of the rational and intelligent motion to circumscribe itself, and never to be overpowered either by the motion of the senses or of the appetites, for both are animal; but the intelligent motion claims superiority, and does not permit itself to be overpowered by the others. And with good reason, for it is formed by nature to use all of them. The third thing in the rational constitution is freedom from error and from deception. Let then the ruling principle holding fast to these things go straight on, and it has what is its own.

56. Consider thyself to be dead, and to have completed thy life up to the present time; and live according to nature the remainder which is allowed thee.

57. Love that only which happens to thee and is spun with the thread of thy destiny. For what is more suitable?

58. In everything which happens keep before thy eyes those to whom the same things happened, and how they were vexed, and treated them as strange things, and found fault with them: and now where are they? Nowhere. Why then dost thou too choose to act in the same way; and why dost thou not leave these agitations which are foreign to nature to those who cause them and those who are moved by them; and why art thou not altogether intent upon the right way of making use of the things which happen to thee? For then thou wilt use them well, and they will be a material for thee [to work on]. Only attend to thyself, and resolve to be a good man in every act which thou dost: and remember. . . .

59. Look within. Within is the fountain of good, and it will ever bubble up, if thou wilt ever dig.

60. The body ought to be compact, and to show no irregularity either in motion or attitude. For what the mind shows in the face by maintaining in it the expression of intelligence and propriety, that ought to be required also in the whole body. But all these things should be observed without affectation.

61. The art of life is more like the wrestler's art than the dancer's, in respect of this, that it should stand ready and firm to meet onsets which are sudden and unexpected.

62. Constantly observe who those are whose approbation thou wishest to have, and what ruling principles they possess. For then thou wilt neither blame those who offend involuntarily, nor wilt thou want their approbation, if thou lookest to the sources of their opinions and appetites.

63. Every soul, the philosopher says, is involuntarily deprived of truth; consequently in the same way it is deprived of justice and temperance and

benevolence and everything of the kind. It is most necessary to bear this constantly in mind, for thus thou wilt be more gentle towards all.

64. In every pain let this thought be present, that there is no dishonor in it, nor does it make the governing intelligence worse, for it does not damage the intelligence either so far as the intelligence is rational or so far as it is social. Indeed in the case of most pains let this remark of Epicurus aid thee, that pain is neither intolerable nor everlasting, if thou bearest in mind that it has its limits, and if thou addest nothing to it in imagination: and remember this too, that we do not perceive that many things which are disagreeable to us are the same as pain, such as excessive drowsiness, and the being scorched by heat, and the having no appetite. When then thou art discontented about any of these things, say to thyself that thou art yielding to pain.

65. Take care not to feel towards the inhuman as they feel towards men.

66. How do we know if Telauges was not superior in character to Socrates? For it is not enough that Socrates died a more noble death, and disputed more skilfully with the Sophists, and passed the night in the cold with more endurance, and that when he was bid to arrest Leon of Salamis, he considered it more noble to refuse, and that he walked in a swaggering way in the streets—though as to this fact one may have great doubts if it was true. But we ought to inquire what kind of a soul it was that Socrates possessed, and if he was able to be content with being just towards men and pious towards the gods, neither idly vexed on account of men's villainy, nor yet making himself a slave to any man's ignorance, nor receiving as strange anything that fell to his share out of the universal, nor enduring it as intolerable, nor allowing his understanding to sympathize with the affects of the miserable flesh.

67. Nature has not so mingled [the intelligence] with the composition of the body, as not to have allowed thee the power of circumscribing thyself and of bringing under subjection to thyself all that is thy own; for it is very possible to be a divine man and to be recognized as such by no one. Always bear this in mind; and another thing too, that very little indeed is necessary for living a happy life. And because thou hast despaired of becoming a dialectician and skilled in the knowledge of nature, do not for this reason renounce the hope of being both free and modest, and social and obedient to God.

68. It is in thy power to live free from all compulsion in the greatest tranquillity of mind, even if all the world cry out against thee as much as

they choose, and even if wild beasts tear in pieces the members of this kneaded matter which has grown around thee. For what hinders the mind in the midst of all this from maintaining itself in tranquillity and in a just judgment of all surrounding things and in a ready use of the objects which are presented to it, so that the judgment may say to the thing which falls under its observation: This thou art in substance [reality], though in men's opinion thou mayest appear to be of a different kind; and the use shall say to that which falls under the hand: Thou art the thing that I was seeking; for to me that which presents itself is always a material for virtue both rational and political, and in a word, for the exercise of art, which belongs to man or God. For everything which happens has a relationship either to God or man, and is neither new nor difficult to handle, but a usual and apt matter to work on.

69. The perfection of moral character consists in this, in passing every day as the last, and in being neither violently excited nor torpid nor playing the hypocrite.

70. The gods who are immortal are not vexed because during so long a time they must tolerate continually men such as they are and so many of them bad; and besides this, they also take care of them in all ways. But thou, who art destined to end so soon, art thou wearied of enduring the bad, and this too when thou art one of them?

71. It is a ridiculous thing for a man not to fly from his own badness, which is indeed possible, but to fly from other men's badness, which is impossible.

72. Whatever the rational and political [social] faculty finds to be neither intelligent nor social, it properly judges to be inferior to itself.

73. When thou hast done a good act and another has received it, why dost thou still look for a third thing besides these, as fools do, either to have the reputation of having done a good act or to obtain a return?

74. No man is tired of receiving what is useful. But it is useful to act according to nature. Do not then be tired of receiving what is useful by doing it to others.

75. The nature of the All moved to make the universe. But now either everything that takes place comes by way of consequence or [continuity]; or even the chief things towards which the ruling power of the universe directs its own movement are governed by no rational principle. If this is remembered, it will make thee more tranquil in many things (vi. 44; ix. 28).

VIII.

1. This reflection also tends to the removal of the desire of empty fame, that it is no longer in thy power to have lived the whole of thy life, or at least thy life from thy youth upwards, like a philosopher; but both to many others and to thyself it is plain that thou art far from philosophy. Thou hast fallen into disorder then, so that it is no longer easy for thee to get the reputation of a philosopher; and thy plan of life also opposes it. If then thou hast truly seen where the matter lies, throw away the thought, How thou shalt seem [to others], and be content if thou shalt live the rest of thy life in such wise as thy nature wills. Observe then what it wills, and let nothing else distract thee; for thou hast had experience of many wanderings without having found happiness anywhere,—not in syllogisms, nor in wealth, nor in reputation, nor in enjoyment, nor anywhere. Where is it then? In doing what man's nature requires. How then shall a man do this? If he has principles from which come his affects and his acts. What principles? Those which relate to good and bad: the belief that there is nothing good for man which does not make him just, temperate, manly, free; and that there is nothing bad which does not do the contrary to what has been mentioned.
2. On the occasion of every act ask thyself, How is this with respect to me? Shall I repent of it? A little time and I am dead, and all is gone. What more do I seek, if what I am now doing is the work of an intelligent living being, and a social being, and one who is under the same law with God?
3. Alexander and Caius and Pompeius, what are they in comparison with Diogenes and Heraclitus and Socrates? For they were acquainted with things, and their causes [forms], and their matter, and the ruling principles of these men were the same [or conformable to their pursuits]. But as to the others, how many things had they to care for, and to how many things were they slaves!
4. [Consider] that men will do the same things nevertheless, even though thou shouldst burst.
5. This is the chief thing: Be not perturbed, for all things are according to the nature of the universal; and in a little time thou wilt be nobody and nowhere, like Hadrianus and Augustus. In the next place, having fixed thy eyes steadily on thy business look at it, and at the same time remembering that it is thy duty to be a good man, and what man's nature

demands, do that without turning aside; and speak as it seems to thee most just, only let it be with a good disposition and with modesty and without hypocrisy.

6. The nature of the universal has this work to do,—to remove to that place the things which are in this, to change them, to take them away hence, and to carry them there. All things are change, yet we need not fear anything new. All things are familiar [to us]; but the distribution of them still remains the same.

7. Every nature is contented with itself when it goes on its way well; and a rational nature goes on its way well when in its thoughts it assents to nothing false or uncertain, and when it directs its movements to social acts only, and when it confines its desires and aversions to the things which are in its power, and when it is satisfied with everything that is assigned to it by the common nature. For of this common nature every particular nature is a part, as the nature of the leaf is a part of the nature of the plant; except that in the plant the nature of the leaf is part of a nature which has not perception or reason, and is subject to be impeded; but the nature of man is part of a nature which is not subject to impediments, and is intelligent and just, since it gives to everything in equal portions and according to its worth, times, substance, cause [form], activity and incident. But examine, not to discover that any one thing compared with any other single thing is equal in all respects, but by taking all the parts together of one thing and comparing them with all the parts together of another.

8. Thou hast not leisure [or ability] to read. But thou hast leisure [or ability] to check arrogance: thou hast leisure to be superior to pleasure and pain: thou hast leisure to be superior to love of fame, and not to be vexed at stupid and ungrateful people, nay even to care for them.

9. Let no man any longer hear thee finding fault with the court life or with thy own (v. 16).

10. Repentance is a kind of self-reproof for having neglected something useful; but that which is good must be something useful, and the perfect good man should look after it. But no such man would ever repent of having refused any sensual pleasure. Pleasure then is neither good nor useful.

11. This thing, what is it in itself, in its own constitution! What is its substance and material? And what its causal nature [or form]? And what is it doing in the world? And how long does it subsist?

12. When thou risest from sleep with reluctance, remember that it is according to thy constitution and according to human nature to perform social acts, but sleeping is common also to irrational animals. But that which is according to each individual's nature is also more peculiarly its own, and more suitable to its nature, and indeed also more agreeable (v. 1).
13. Constantly and, if it be possible, on the occasion of every impression on the soul, apply to it the principles of Physic, of Ethic, and of Dialectic.
14. Whatever man thou meetest with, immediately say to thyself: What opinions has this man about good and bad? For if with respect to pleasure and pain and the causes of each, and with respect to fame and ignominy, death and life, he has such and such opinions, it will seem nothing wonderful or strange to me if he does such and such things; and I shall bear in mind that he is compelled to do so.
15. Remember that as it is a shame to be surprised if the fig-tree produces figs, so it is to be surprised if the world produces such and such things of which it is productive; and for the physician and the helmsman it is a shame to be surprised if a man has a fever, or if the wind is unfavorable.
16. Remember that to change thy opinion and to follow him who corrects thy error is as consistent with freedom as it is to persist in thy error. For it is thy own, the activity which is exerted according to thy own movement and judgment, and indeed according to thy own understanding too.
17. If a thing is in thy own power, why dost thou do it? but if it is in the power of another, whom dost thou blame,—the atoms [chance] or the gods? Both are foolish. Thou must blame nobody. For if thou canst, correct [that which is the cause]; but if thou canst not do this, correct at least the thing itself; but if thou canst not do even this, of what use is it to thee to find fault? for nothing should be done without a purpose.
18. That which has died falls not out of the universe. If it stays here, it also changes here, and is dissolved into its proper parts, which are elements of the universe and of thyself. And these too change, and they murmur not.
19. Everything exists for some end,—a horse, a vine. Why dost thou wonder? Even the sun will say, I am for some purpose, and the rest of the gods will say the same. For what purpose then art thou,—to enjoy pleasure? See if common sense allows this.
20. Nature has had regard in everything no less to the end than to the beginning and the continuance, just like the man who throws up a ball.

What good is it then for the ball to be thrown up, or harm for it to come down, or even to have fallen? and what good is it to the bubble while it holds together, or what harm when it is burst? The same may be said of a light also.

21. Turn it [the body] inside out, and see what kind of thing it is; and when it has grown old, what kind of thing it becomes, and when it is diseased.

Short lived are both the praiser and the praised, and the rememberer and the remembered: and all this in a nook of this part of the world; and not even here do all agree, no, not any one with himself: and the whole earth too is a point.

22. Attend to the matter which is before thee, whether it is an opinion or an act or a word.

Thou sufferest this justly: for thou choosest rather to become good to-morrow than to be good to-day.

23. Am I doing anything? I do it with reference to the good of mankind. Does anything happen to me? I receive it and refer it to the gods, and the source of all things, from which all that happens is derived.

24. Such as bathing appears to thee,—oil, sweat, dirt, filthy water, all things disgusting,—so is every part of life and everything.

25. Lucilla saw Verus die, and then Lucilla died. Secunda saw Maximus die, and then Secunda died. Epitynchanus saw Diotimus die, and then Epitynchanus died. Antoninus saw Faustina die, and then Antoninus died. Such is everything. Celer saw Hadrianus die, and then Celer died. And those sharp-witted men, either seers or men inflated with pride, where are they,—for instance the sharp-witted men, Charax and Demetrius the Platonist and Eudaemon, and any one else like them? All ephemeral, dead long ago. Some indeed have not been remembered even for a short time, and others have become the heroes of fables, and again others have disappeared even from fables. Remember this then, that this little compound, thyself, must either be dissolved, or thy poor breath must be extinguished, or be removed and placed elsewhere.

26. It is satisfaction to a man to do the proper works of a man. Now it is a proper work of a man to be benevolent to his own kind, to despise the movements of the senses, to form a just judgment of plausible appearances, and to take a survey of the nature of the universe and of the things which happen in it.

27. There are three relations [between thee and other things]: the one to the body which surrounds thee; the second to the divine cause from which all things come to all; and the third to those who live with thee.
28. Pain is either an evil to the body—then let the body say what it thinks of it—or to the soul; but it is in the power of the soul to maintain its own serenity and tranquillity, and not to think that pain is an evil. For every judgment and movement and desire and aversion is within, and no evil ascends so high.
29. Wipe out thy imaginations by often saying to thyself: Now it is in my power to let no badness be in this soul, nor desire, nor any perturbation at all; but looking at all things I see what is their nature, and I use each according to its value.—Remember this power which thou hast from nature.
30. Speak both in the senate and to every man, whoever he may be, appropriately, not with any affectation: use plain discourse.
31. Augustus' court, wife, daughter, descendants, ancestors, sister, Agrippa, kinsmen, intimates, friends, Areius, Maecenas, physicians, and sacrificing priests,—the whole court is dead. Then turn to the rest, not considering the death of a single man [but of a whole race], as of the Pompeii; and that which is inscribed on the tombs,—The last of his race. Then consider what trouble those before them have had that they might leave a successor; and then, that of necessity some one must be the last. Again, here consider the death of a whole race.
32. It is thy duty to order thy life well in every single act; and if every act does its duty as far as is possible, be content; and no one is able to hinder thee so that each act shall not do its duty.—But something external will stand in the way.—Nothing will stand in the way of thy acting justly and soberly and considerately.—But perhaps some other active power will be hindered.—Well, but by acquiescing in the hindrance and by being content to transfer thy efforts to that which is allowed, another opportunity of action is immediately put before thee in place of that which was hindered, and one which will adapt itself to this ordering of which we are speaking.
33. Receive [wealth or prosperity] without arrogance; and be ready to let it go.
34. If thou didst ever see a hand cut off, or a foot, or a head, lying anywhere apart from the rest of the body, such does a man make himself, as far

as he can, who is not content with what happens, and separates himself from others, or does anything unsocial. Suppose that thou hast detached thyself from the natural unity,—for thou wast made by nature a part, but now thou hast cut thyself off,—yet here there is this beautiful provision, that it is in thy power again to unite thyself. God has allowed this to no other part, after it has been separated and cut asunder, to come together again. But consider the kindness by which he has distinguished man, for he has put it in his power not to be separated at all from the universal; and when he has been separated, he has allowed him to return and to be united and to resume his place as a part.

35. As the nature of the universal has given to every rational being all the other powers that it has, so we have received from it this power also. For as the universal nature converts and fixes in its predestined place everything which stands in the way and opposes it, and makes such things a part of itself, so also the rational animal is able to make every hindrance its own material, and to use it for such purposes as it may have designed.

36. Do not disturb thyself by thinking of the whole of thy life. Let not thy thoughts at once embrace all the various troubles which thou mayest expect to befall thee: but on every occasion ask thyself, What is there in this which is intolerable and past bearing? for thou wilt be ashamed to confess. In the next place remember that neither the future nor the past pains thee, but only the present. But this is reduced to a very little, if thou only circumscribest it, and chidest thy mind if it is unable to hold out against even this.

37. Does Panthea or Pergamus now sit by the tomb of Verus? Does Chaurias or Diotimus sit by the tomb of Hadrianus? That would be ridiculous. Well, suppose they did sit there, would the dead be conscious of it? and if the dead were conscious would they be pleased? and if they were pleased, would that make them immortal? Was it not in the order of destiny that these persons too should first become old women and old men and then die? What then would those do after these were dead? All this is foul smell and blood in a bag.

38. If thou canst see sharp, look and judge wisely, says the philosopher.

39. In the constitution of the rational animal I see no virtue which is opposed to justice; but I see a virtue which is opposed to love of pleasure, and that is temperance.

40. If thou takest away thy opinion about that which appears to give thee pain, thou thyself standest in perfect security.—Who is this self?—The reason.—But I am not reason.—Be it so. Let then the reason itself not trouble itself. But if any other part of thee suffers, let it have its own opinion about itself (VII. 16).

41. Hindrance to the perceptions of sense is an evil to the animal nature. Hindrance to the movements [desires] is equally an evil to the animal nature. And something else also is equally an impediment and an evil to the constitution of plants. So then that which is a hindrance to the intelligence is an evil to the intelligent nature. Apply all these things then to thyself. Does pain or sensuous pleasure effect thee? The senses will look to that. Has any obstacle opposed thee in thy efforts towards an object? If indeed thou wast making this effort absolutely [unconditionally, or without any reservation], certainly this obstacle is an evil to thee considered as a rational animal. But if thou takest [into consideration] the usual course of things, thou hast not yet been injured nor even impeded. The things however which are proper to the understanding no other man is used to impede, for neither fire, nor iron, nor tyrant, nor abuse, touches it in any way. When it has been made a sphere, it continues a sphere (XI. 12).

42. It is not fit that I should give myself pain, for I have never intentionally given pain even to another.

43. Different things delight different people; but it is my delight to keep the ruling faculty sound without turning away either from any man or from any of the things which happen to men, but looking at and receiving all with welcome eyes and using everything according to its value.

44. See that thou secure this present time to thyself: for those who rather pursue posthumous fame do not consider that the men of after time will be exactly such as these whom they cannot bear now; and both are mortal. And what is it in any way to thee if these men of after time utter this or that sound, or have this or that opinion about thee?

45. Take me and cast me where thou wilt; for there I shall keep my divine part tranquil, that is, content, if it can feel and act conformably to its proper constitution. Is this [change of place] sufficient reason why my soul should be unhappy and worse then it was, depressed, expanded, shrinking, affrighted? and what wilt thou find which is sufficient reason for this?

46. Nothing can happen to any man which is not a human accident, nor to an ox which is not according to the nature of an ox, nor to a vine which

is not according to the nature of a vine, nor to a stone which is not proper to a stone. If then there happens to each thing both what is usual and natural, why shouldst thou complain? For the common nature brings nothing which may not be borne by thee.

47. If thou art pained by any external thing, it is not this thing that disturbs thee, but thy own judgment about it. And it is in thy power to wipe out this judgment now. But if anything in thy own disposition gives thee pain, who hinders thee from correcting thy opinion? And even if thou art pained because thou art not doing some particular thing which seems to thee to be right, why dost thou not rather act than complain?—But some insuperable obstacle is in the way?—Do not be grieved then, for the cause of its not being done depends not on thee.—But it is not worth while to live, if this cannot be done.—Take thy departure then from life contentedly, just as he dies who is in full activity, and well pleased too with the things which are obstacles.

48. Remember that the ruling faculty is invincible, when self-collected it is satisfied with itself, if it does nothing which it does not choose to do, even if it resist from mere obstinacy. What then will it be when it forms a judgment about anything aided by reason and deliberately? Therefore the mind which is free from passions is a citadel, for man has nothing more secure to which he can fly for refuge and for the future be inexpugnable. He then who has not seen this is an ignorant man; but he who has seen it and does not fly to this refuge is unhappy.

49. Say nothing more to thyself than what the first appearances report. Suppose that it has been reported to thee that a certain person speaks ill of thee. This has been reported; but that thou hast been injured, that has not been reported. I see that my child is sick. I do see; but that he is in danger, I do not see. Thus then always abide by the first appearances, and add nothing thyself from within, and then nothing happens to thee. Or rather add something like a man who knows everything that happens in the world.

50. A cucumber is bitter—Throw it away.—There are briers in the road—Turn aside from them.—This is enough. Do not add, And why were such things made in the world? For thou wilt be ridiculed by a man who is acquainted with nature, as thou wouldst be ridiculed by a carpenter and shoemaker if thou didst find fault because thou seest in their workshop shavings and cuttings from the things which they make. And yet they have places into which they can throw these shavings and cuttings, and the universal nature has no external space; but the wondrous part of her art is that though she has circumscribed herself, everything within her which appears to decay and to grow old and to be useless she changes into herself, and again makes other new things from these very same, so that she requires neither substance from without nor wants a place into which she may cast that which decays. She is content then with her own space, and her own matter, and her own art.

51. Neither in thy actions be sluggish nor in thy conversation without method, nor wandering in thy thoughts, nor let there be in thy soul inward contention nor external effusion, nor in life be so busy as to have no leisure.

Suppose that men kill thee, cut thee in pieces, curse thee. What then can these things do to prevent thy mind from remaining pure, wise, sober, just? For instance, if a man should stand by a limpid pure spring, and curse it, the spring never ceases sending up potable water; and if he should cast clay into it or filth, it will speedily disperse them and wash them out, and will not be at all polluted. How then shalt thou possess a perpetual fountain [and not a mere well]? By forming thyself hourly to freedom conjoined with contentment, simplicity, and modesty.

52. He who does not know what the world is, does not know where he is. And he who does not know for what purpose the world exists, does not know who he is, nor what the world is. But he who has failed in any one of these things could not even say for what purpose he exists himself. What then dost thou think of him who [avoids or] seeks the praise of those who applaud, of men who know not either where they are or who they are?

53. Dost thou wish to be praised by a man who curses himself thrice every hour? Wouldst thou wish to please a man who does not please himself? Does a man please himself who repents of nearly everything that he does?

54. No longer let thy breathing only act in concert with the air which surrounds thee, but let thy intelligence also now be in harmony with the intelligence which embraces all things. For the intelligent power is no less diffused in all parts and pervades all things for him who is willing to draw it to him than the aerial power for him who is able to respire it.

55. Generally, wickedness does no harm at all to the universe; and particularly the wickedness [of one man] does no harm to another. It is only harmful to him who has it in his power to be released from it as soon as he shall choose.

56. To my own free will the free will of my neighbor is just as indifferent as his poor breath and flesh. For though we are made especially for the sake of one another, still the ruling power of each of us has its own office, for otherwise my neighbor's wickedness would be my harm, which God has not willed in order that my unhappiness may not depend on another.

57. The sun appears to be poured down, and in all directions indeed it is diffused, yet it is not effused. For this diffusion is extension: Accordingly its rays are called Extensions because they are extended. But one may judge what kind of a thing a ray is, if he looks at the sun's light passing through a narrow opening into a darkened room, for it is extended in a right line, and as it were is divided when it meets with any solid body which stands in the way and intercepts the air beyond; but there the light remains fixed and does not glide or fall off. Such then ought to be the outpouring and diffusion of the understanding, and it should in no way be an effusion, but an extension, and it should make no violent or impetuous collision with the obstacles which are in its way; nor yet fall down, but be fixed, and enlighten that which receives it. For a body will deprive itself of the illumination, if it does not admit it.

58. He who fears death either fears the loss of sensation or a different kind of sensation. But if thou shalt have no sensation, neither wilt thou feel any harm; and if thou shalt acquire another kind of sensation, thou wilt be a different kind of living being and thou wilt not cease to live.

59. Men exist for the sake of one another. Teach them then or bear with them.

60. In one way an arrow moves, in another way the mind. The mind indeed, both when it exercises caution and when it is employed about inquiry, moves straight onward not the less, and to its object.

61. Enter into every man's ruling faculty; and also let every other man enter into thine.

IX.

1. He who acts unjustly acts impiously. For since the universal nature has made rational animals for the sake of one another to help one another according to their deserts, but in no way to injure one another, he who

transgresses her will is clearly guilty of impiety towards the highest divinity. And he too who lies is guilty of impiety to the same divinity; for the universal nature is the nature of things that are; and things that are have a relation to all things that come into existence. And further, this universal nature is named truth, and is the prime cause of all things that are true. He then who lies intentionally is guilty of impiety inasmuch as he acts unjustly by deceiving; and he also who lies unintentionally, inasmuch as he is at variance with the universal nature, and inasmuch as he disturbs the order by fighting against the nature of the world; for he fights against it, who is moved of himself to that which is contrary to truth, for he had received powers from nature through the neglect of which he is not able now to distinguish falsehood from truth. And indeed he who pursues pleasure as good, and avoids pain as evil, is guilty of impiety. For of necessity such a man must often find fault with the universal nature, alleging that it assigns things to the bad and the good contrary to their deserts, because frequently the bad are in the enjoyment of pleasure and possess the things which procure pleasure, but the good have pain for their share and the things which cause pain. And further, he who is afraid of pain will sometimes also be afraid of some of the things which will happen in the world, and even this is impiety. And he who pursues pleasure will not abstain from injustice, and this is plainly impiety. Now with respect to the things towards which the universal nature is equally affected,—for it would not have made both, unless it was equally affected towards both,—towards these they who wish to follow nature should be of the same mind with it, and equally affected. With respect to pain, then, and pleasure, or death and life, or honor and dishonor, which the universal nature employs equally, whoever is not equally affected is manifestly acting impiously. And I say that the universal nature employs them equally, instead of saying that they happen alike to those who are produced in continuous series and to those who come after them by virtue of a certain original movement of Providence, according to which it moved from a certain beginning to this ordering of things, having conceived certain principles of the things which were to be, and having determined powers productive of beings and of changes and of such like successions (vii. 75).

2. It would be a man's happiest lot to depart from mankind without having had any taste of lying and hypocrisy and luxury and pride. However, to breathe out one's life when a man has had enough of these things is the next best voyage, as the saying is. Hast thou determined to abide with vice, and has not experience yet induced thee to fly from this pestilence? For the destruction of the understanding is a pestilence, much more indeed than any such corruption and change of this atmosphere which surrounds us. For this corruption is a pestilence of animals so far as they are animals; but the other is a pestilence of men so far as they are men.

3. Do not despise death, but be well content with it, since this too is one of those things which nature wills. For such as it is to be young and to grow old, and to increase and to reach maturity, and to have teeth and beard and gray hairs, and to beget and to be pregnant and to bring forth, and all the other natural operations which the seasons of thy life bring, such also is dissolution. This, then, is consistent with the character of a reflecting man,—to be neither careless nor impatient nor contemptuous with respect to death, but to wait for it as one of the operations of nature. As thou now waitest for the time when the child shall come out of thy wife's womb, so be ready for the time when thy soul shall fall out of this envelope. But if thou requirest also a vulgar kind of comfort which shall reach thy heart, thou wilt be made best reconciled to death by observing the objects from which thou art going to be removed, and the morals of those with whom thy soul will no longer be mingled. For it is no way right to be offended with men, but it is thy duty to care for them and to bear with them gently; and yet to remember that thy departure will not be from men who have the same principles as thyself. For this is the only thing, if there be any, which could draw us the contrary way and attach us to life,—to be permitted to live with those who have the same principles as ourselves. But now thou seest how great is the trouble arising from the discordance of those who live together, so that thou mayest say, Come quick, O death, lest perchance I, too, should forget myself.

4. He who does wrong does wrong against himself. He who acts unjustly acts unjustly to himself, because he makes himself bad.

5. He often acts unjustly who does not do a certain thing; not only he who does a certain thing.

6. Thy present opinion founded on understanding, and thy present conduct directed to social good, and thy present disposition of contentment with everything which happens—that is enough.

7. Wipe out imagination: check desire: extinguish appetite: keep the ruling faculty in its own power.
8. Among the animals which have not reason one life is distributed; but among reasonable animals one intelligent soul is distributed: just as there is one earth of all things which are of an earthy nature, and we see by one light, and breathe one air, all of us that have the faculty of vision and all that have life.
9. All things which participate in anything which is common to them all move towards that which is of the same kind with themselves. Everything which is earthy turns towards the earth, everything which is liquid flows together, and everything which is of an aerial kind does the same, so that they require something to keep them asunder, and the application of force. Fire indeed moves upwards on account of the elemental fire, but it is so ready to be kindled together with all the fire which is here, that even every substance which is somewhat dry is easily ignited, because there is less mingled with it of that which is a hindrance to ignition. Accordingly, then, everything also which participates in the common intelligent nature moves in like manner towards that which is of the same kind with itself, or moves even more. For so much as it is superior in comparison with all other things, in the same degree also is it more ready to mingle with and to be fused with that which is akin to it. Accordingly among animals devoid of reason we find swarms of bees, and herds of cattle, and the nurture of young birds, and in a manner, loves; for even in animals there are souls, and that power which brings them together is seen to exert itself in the superior degree, and in such a way as never has been observed in plants nor in stones nor in trees. But in rational animals there are political communities and friendships, and families and meetings of people; and in wars, treaties, and armistices. But in the things which are still superior, even though they are separated from one another, unity in a manner exists, as in the stars. Thus the ascent to the higher degree is able to produce a sympathy even in things which are separated. See, then, what now takes place; for only intelligent animals have now forgotten this mutual desire and inclination, and in them alone the property of flowing together is not seen. But still, though men strive to avoid [this union], they are caught and held by it, for their nature is too strong for them; and thou wilt see what I say, if thou only observest. Sooner, then, will one find anything earthy which comes in

contact with no earthy thing, than a man altogether separated from other men.

10. Both man and God and the universe produce fruit; at the proper seasons each produces it. But and if usage has especially fixed these terms to the vine and like things, this is nothing. Reason produces fruit both for all and for itself, and there are produced from it other things of the same kind as reason itself.

11. If thou art able, correct by teaching those who do wrong; but if thou canst not, remember that indulgence is given to thee for this purpose. And the gods, too, are indulgent to such persons; and for some purposes they even help them to get health, wealth, reputation; so kind they are. And it is in thy power also; or say, who hinders thee?

12. Labor not as one who is wretched, nor yet as one who would be pitied or admired: but direct thy will to one thing only,—to put thyself in motion and to check thyself, as the social reason requires.

13. To-day I have got out of all trouble, or rather I have cast out all trouble, for it was not outside, but within and in my opinions.

14. All things are the same, familiar in experience, and ephemeral in time, and worthless in the matter. Everything now is just as it was in the time of those whom we have buried.

15. Things stand outside of us, themselves by themselves, neither knowing aught of themselves, nor expressing any judgment. What is it, then, which does judge about them? The ruling faculty.

16. Not in passivity but in activity lie the evil and the good of the rational social animal, just as his virtue and his vice lie not in passivity but in activity.

17. For the stone which has been thrown up it is no evil to come down, nor indeed any good to have been carried up (VIII. 20).

18. Penetrate inwards into men's leading principles, and thou wilt see what judges thou art afraid of, and what kind of judges they are of themselves.

19. All things are changing: and thou thyself art in continuous mutation and in a manner in continuous destruction, and the whole universe too.

20. It is thy duty to leave another man's wrongful act there where it is (VII. 29; IX. 38).

21. Termination of activity, cessation from movement and opinion, and in a sense their death, is no evil. Turn thy thoughts now to the consideration of thy life, thy life as a child, as a youth, thy manhood, thy old age, for

in these also every change was a death. Is this anything to fear? Turn thy thoughts now to thy life under thy grandfather, then to thy life under thy mother, then to thy life under thy father; and as thou findest many other differences and changes and terminations, ask thyself, Is this anything to fear? In like manner, then, neither are the termination and cessation and change of thy whole life a thing to be afraid of.

22. Hasten [to examine] thy own ruling faculty and that of the universe and that of thy neighbor: thy own that thou mayst make it just: and that of the universe, that thou mayst remember of what thou art a part; and that of thy neighbor, that thou mayst know whether he has acted ignorantly or with knowledge, and that thou mayst also consider that his ruling faculty is akin to thine.

23. As thou thyself art a component part of a social system, so let every act of thine be a component part of social life. Whatever act of thine then has no reference either immediately or remotely to a social end, this tears asunder thy life, and does not allow it to be one, and it is of the nature of a mutiny, just as when in a popular assembly a man acting by himself stands apart from the general agreement.

24. Quarrels of little children and their sports, and poor spirits carrying about dead bodies [such is everything]; and so what is exhibited in the representation of the mansions of the dead strikes our eyes more clearly.

25. Examine into the quality of the form of an object, and detach it altogether from its material part, and then contemplate it; then determine the time, the longest which a thing of this peculiar form is naturally made to endure.

26. Thou hast endured infinite troubles through not being contented with thy ruling faculty when it does the things which it is constituted by nature to do. But enough [of this].

27. When another blames thee or hates thee, or when men say about thee anything injurious, approach their poor souls, penetrate within, and see what kind of men they are. Thou wilt discover that there is no reason to take any trouble that these men may have this or that opinion about thee. However, thou must be well disposed towards them, for by nature they are friends. And the gods too aid them in all ways, by dreams, by signs, towards the attainment of those things on which they set a value.

28. The periodic movements of the universe are the same, up and down from age to age. And either the universal intelligence puts itself in motion for

every separate effect, and if this is so, be thou content with that which is the result of its activity; or it puts itself in motion once, and everything else comes by way of sequence in a manner; or indivisible elements are the origin of all things.—In a word, if there is a god, all is well; and if chance rules, do not thou also be governed by it (vi. 44; vii. 75).

Soon will the earth cover us all: then the earth, too, will change, and the things also which result from change will continue to change forever, and these again forever. For if a man reflects on the changes and transformations which follow one another like wave after wave and their rapidity, he will despise everything which is perishable (xii. 21).

29. The universal cause is like a winter torrent: it carries everything along with it. But how worthless are all these poor people who are engaged in matters political, and, as they suppose, are playing the philosopher! All drivellers. Well then, man: do what nature now requires. Set thyself in motion, if it is in thy power, and do not look about thee to see if any one will observe it; nor yet expect Plato's Republic: but be content if the smallest thing goes on well, and consider such an event to be no small matter. For who can change men's opinions? and without a change of opinions what else is there than the slavery of men who groan while they pretend to obey? Come now and tell me of Alexander and Philippus and Demetrius of Phalerum. They themselves shall judge whether they discovered what the common nature required, and trained themselves accordingly. But if they acted like tragedy heroes, no one has condemned me to imitate them. Simple and modest is the work of philosophy. Draw me not aside to insolence and pride.

30. Look down from above on the countless herds of men and their countless solemnities, and the infinitely varied voyagings in storms and calms, and the differences among those who are born, who live together, and die. And consider, too, the life lived by others in olden time, and the life of those who will live after thee, and the life now lived among barbarous nations, and how many know not even thy name, and how many will soon forget it, and how they who perhaps now are praising thee will very soon blame thee, and that neither a posthumous name is of any value, nor reputation, nor anything else.

31. Let there be freedom from perturbations with respect to the things which come from the external cause; and let there be justice in the things done by virtue of the internal cause, that is, let there be movement and action terminating in this, in social acts, for this is according to thy nature.

32. Thou canst remove out of the way many useless things among those which disturb thee, for they lie entirely in thy opinion; and thou wilt then gain for thyself ample space by comprehending the whole universe in thy mind, and by contemplating the eternity of time, and observing the rapid change of every several thing, how short is the time from birth to dissolution, and the illimitable time before birth as well as the equally boundless time after dissolution!

33. All that thou seest will quickly perish, and those who have been spectators of its dissolution will very soon perish too. And he who dies at the extremest old age will be brought into the same condition with him who died prematurely.

34. What are these men's leading principles, and about what kind of things are they busy, and for what kind of reasons do they love and honor? Imagine that thou seest their poor souls laid bare. When they think that they do harm by their blame or good by their praise, what an idea!

35. Loss is nothing else than change. But the universal nature delights in change, and in obedience to her all things are now done well, and from eternity have been done in like form, and will be such to time without end. What, then, dost thou say,—that all things have been and all things always will be bad, and that no power has ever been found in so many gods to rectify these things, but the world has been condemned to be bound in never ceasing evil (IV. 45; VII. 88)?

36. The rottenness of the matter which is the foundation of everything! water, dust, bones, filth: or again, marble rocks, the callosities of the earth; and gold and silver, the sediments; and garments, only bits of hair; and purple dye, blood; and everything else is of the same kind. And that which is of the nature of breath is also another thing of the same kind, changing from this to that.

37. Enough of this wretched life and murmuring and apish tricks. Why art thou disturbed? What is there new in this? What unsettles thee? Is it the form of the thing? Look at it. Or is it the matter? Look at it. But besides these there is nothing. Towards the gods then, now become at last more simple and better. It is the same whether we examine these things for a hundred years or three.

38. If any man has done wrong, the harm is his own. But perhaps he has not done wrong.

39. Either all things proceed from one intelligent source and come together as in one body, and the part ought not to find fault with what is done for the benefit of the whole; or there are only atoms, and nothing else than mixture and dispersion. Why, then, art thou disturbed? Say to the ruling faculty, Art thou dead, art thou corrupted, art thou playing the hypocrite, art thou become a beast, dost thou herd and feed with the rest?

40. Either the gods have no power or they have power. If, then, they have no power, why dost thou pray to them? But if they have power, why dost thou not pray for them to give thee the faculty of not fearing any of the things which thou fearest, or of not desiring any of the things which thou desirest, or not being pained at anything, rather than pray that any of these things should not happen or happen? for certainly if they can co-operate with men, they can co-operate for these purposes. But perhaps thou wilt say the gods have placed them in thy power. Well, then, is it not better to use what is in thy power like a free man than to desire in a slavish and abject way what is not in thy power? And who has told thee that the gods do not aid us even in the things which are in our power? Begin, then, to pray for such things, and thou wilt see. One man prays thus: How shall I be able to lie with that woman? Do thou pray thus: How shall I not desire to lie with her? Another prays thus: How shall I be released from this? Another prays: How shall I not desire to be released? Another thus: How shall I not lose my little son? Thou thus: How shall I not be afraid to lose him? In fine, turn thy prayers this way, and see what comes.

41. Epicurus says, In my sickness my conversation was not about my bodily sufferings, nor, says he, did I talk on such subjects to those who visited me; but I continued to discourse on the nature of things as before, keeping to this main point, how the mind, while participating in such movements as go on in the poor flesh, shall be free from perturbations and maintain its proper good. Nor did I, he says, give the physicians an opportunity of putting on solemn looks, as if they were doing something great, but my life went on well and happily. Do, then, the same that he did both in sickness, if thou art sick, and in any other circumstances; for never to desert philosophy in any events that may befall us, nor to hold trifling talk either with an ignorant man or with one unacquainted with nature, is a principle of all schools of philosophy; but to be intent only on that which thou art now doing and on the instrument by which thou dost it.

42. When thou art offended with any man's shameless conduct, immediately ask thyself, Is it possible, then, that shameless men should not be in the world? It is not possible. Do not, then, require what is impossible. For this man also is one of those shameless men who must of necessity be in the world. Let the same considerations be present to thy mind in the case of the knave, and the faithless man, and of every man who does wrong in any way. For at the same time that thou dost remind thyself that it is impossible that such kind of men should not exist, thou wilt become more kindly disposed towards every one individually. It is useful to perceive this, too, immediately when the occasion arises, what virtue nature has given to man to oppose to every wrongful act. For she has given to man, as an antidote against the stupid man, mildness, and against another kind of man some other power. And in all cases it is possible for thee to correct by teaching the man who is gone astray; for every man who errs misses his object and is gone astray. Besides, wherein hast thou been injured? For thou wilt find that no one among those against whom thou art irritated has done anything by which thy mind could be made worse; but that which is evil to thee and harmful has its foundation only in the mind. And what harm is done or what is there strange, if the man who has not been instructed does the acts of an uninstructed man? Consider whether thou shouldst not rather blame thyself, because thou didst not expect such a man to err in such a way. For thou hadst means given thee by thy reason to suppose that it was likely that he would commit this error, and yet thou hast forgotten and art amazed that he has erred. But most of all when thou blamest a man as faithless or ungrateful, turn to thyself. For the fault is manifestly thy own, whether thou didst trust that a man who had such a disposition would keep his promise, or when conferring thy kindness thou didst not confer it absolutely, nor yet in such way as to have received from thy very act all the profit. For what more dost thou want when thou hast done a man a service? art thou not content that thou hast done something comformable to thy nature, and dost thou seek to be paid for it? just as if the eye demanded a recompense for seeing, or the feet for walking. For as these members are formed for a particular purpose, and by working according to their several constitutions obtain what is their own; so also as man is formed by nature to acts of benevolence, when he has done anything benevolent or in any other way conducive to the common interest, he has acted conformably to his constitution, and he gets what is his own.

X.

1. Wilt thou, then, my soul, never be good and simple and one and naked, more manifest than the body which surrounds thee? Wilt thou never enjoy an affectionate and contented disposition? Wilt thou never be full and without a want of any kind, longing for nothing more, nor desiring anything, either animate or inanimate, for the enjoyment of pleasures? nor yet desiring time wherein thou shalt have longer enjoyment, or place, or pleasant climate, or society of men with whom thou mayest live in harmony? but wilt thou be satisfied with thy present condition, and pleased with all that is about thee, and wilt thou convince thyself that thou hast everything, and that it comes from the gods, that everything is well for thee, and will be well whatever shall please them, and whatever they shall give for the conservation of the perfect living being, the good and just and beautiful, which generates and holds together all things, and contains and embraces all things which are dissolved for the production of other like things? Wilt thou never be such that thou shalt so dwell in community with gods and men as neither to find fault with them at all, nor to be condemned by them?
2. Observe what thy nature requires, so far as thou art governed by nature only: then do it and accept it, if thy nature, so far as thou art a living being, shall not be made worse by it. And next thou must observe what thy nature requires so far as thou art a living being. And all this thou mayest allow thyself, if thy nature, so far as thou art a rational animal, shall not be made worse by it. But the rational animal is consequently also a political [social] animal. Use these rules, then, and trouble thyself about nothing else.
3. Everything which happens either happens in such wise as thou art formed by nature to bear it, or as thou art not formed by nature to bear it. If, then, it happens to thee in such way as thou art formed by nature to bear it, do not complain, but bear it as thou art formed by nature to bear it. But if it happens in such wise as thou art not formed by nature to bear it, do not complain, for it will perish after it has consumed thee. Remember, however,

that thou art formed by nature to bear everything, with respect to which it depends on thy own opinion to make it endurable and tolerable, by thinking that it is either thy interest or thy duty to do this.

4. If a man is mistaken, instruct him kindly and show him his error. But if thou art not able, blame thyself, or blame not even thyself.
5. Whatever may happen to thee, it was prepared for thee from all eternity; and the implication of causes was from eternity spinning the thread of thy being, and of that which is incident to it (III. 11; IV. 26).
6. Whether the universe is [a concourse of] atoms, or nature [is a system], let this first be established, that I am a part of the whole which is governed by nature; next, I am in a manner intimately related to the parts which are of the same kind with myself. For remembering this, inasmuch as I am a part, I shall be discontented with none of the things which are assigned to me out of the whole; for nothing is injurious to the part if it is for the advantage of the whole. For the whole contains nothing which is not for its advantage; and all natures indeed have this common principle, but the nature of the universe has this principle besides, that it cannot be compelled even by any external cause to generate anything harmful to itself. By remembering, then, that I am a part of such a whole, I shall be content with everything that happens. And inasmuch as I am in a manner intimately related to the parts which are of the same kind with myself, I shall do nothing unsocial, but I shall rather direct myself to the things which are of the same kind with myself, and I shall turn all my efforts to the common interest, and divert them from the contrary. Now, if these things are done so, life must flow on happily, just as thou mayest observe that the life of a citizen is happy, who continues a course of action which is advantageous to his fellow citizens, and is content with whatever the state may assign to him.
7. The parts of the whole, everything, I mean, which is naturally comprehended in the universe, must of necessity perish; but let this be understood in this sense, that they must undergo change. But if this is naturally both an evil and a necessity for the parts, the whole would not continue to exist in a good condition, the parts being subject to change and constituted so as to perish in various ways. For whether did Nature herself design to do evil to the things which are parts of herself, and to make them subject to evil and of necessity fall into evil, or have such results happened without her knowing it? Both these suppositions, indeed, are incredible.

But if a man should even drop the term Nature [as an efficient power], and should speak of these things as natural, even then it would be ridiculous to affirm at the same time that the parts of the whole are in their nature subject to change, and at the same time to be surprised or vexed as if something were happening contrary to nature, particularly as the dissolution of things is into those things of which each thing is composed. For there is either a dispersion of the elements out of which everything has been compounded, or a change from the solid to the earthy and from the airy to the aerial, so that these parts are taken back into the universal reason, whether this at certain periods is consumed by fire or renewed by eternal changes. And do not imagine that the solid and the airy part belongs to thee from the time of generation. For all this received its accretion only yesterday and the day before, as one may say, from the food and the air which is inspired. This, then, which has received [the accretion], changes, not that which thy mother brought forth. But suppose that this [which thy mother brought forth] implicates thee very much with that other part, which has the peculiar quality [of change], this is nothing in fact in the way of objection to what is said.

8. When thou hast assumed these names, good, modest, true, rational, a man of equanimity, and magnanimous, take care that thou dost not change these names; and if thou shouldst lose them, quickly return to them. And remember that the term Rational was intended to signify a discriminating attention to every several thing, and freedom from negligence; and that Equanimity is the voluntary acceptance of the things which are assigned to thee by the common nature; and that Magnanimity is the elevation of the intelligent part above the pleasurable or painful sensations of the flesh, and above that poor thing called fame, and death, and all such things. If, then, thou maintainest thyself in the possession of these names, without desiring to be called by these names by others, thou wilt be another person and wilt enter on another life. For to continue to be such as thou hast hitherto been, and to be torn in pieces and defiled in such a life, is the character of a very stupid man and one over-fond of his life, and like those half-devoured fighters with wild beasts who, though covered with wounds and gore, still entreat to be kept to the following day, though they will be exposed in the same state to the same claws and bites. Therefore fix thyself in the possession of these few names: and if thou art able to abide in them, abide as if thou wast removed to certain islands of the Happy. But if thou shalt perceive that thou fallest out of them and dost not maintain thy hold, go courageously into some nook where thou shalt maintain them, or even depart at once from life, not in passion, but with simplicity and freedom and modesty, after doing this one [laudable] thing at least in thy life, to have gone out of it thus. In order, however, to the remembrance of these names, it will greatly help thee if thou rememberest the gods, and that they wish not to be flattered, but wish all reasonable beings to be made like themselves; and if thou rememberest that what does the work of a fig-tree is a fig-tree, and that what does the work of a dog is a dog, and that what does the work of a bee is a bee, and that what does the work of a man is a man.

9. Mimi, war, astonishment, torpor, slavery, will daily wipe out those holy principles of thine. How many things without studying nature dost thou imagine, and how many dost thou neglect? But it is thy duty so to look on and so to do everything, that at the same time the power of dealing with circumstances is perfected, and the contemplative faculty is exercised, and the confidence which comes from the knowledge of each several thing is maintained without showing it, but yet not concealed. For when wilt thou enjoy simplicity, when gravity, and when the knowledge of every several thing, both what it is in substance, and what place it has in the universe, and how long it is formed to exist, and of what things it is compounded, and to whom it can belong, and who are able both to give it and take it away?

10. A spider is proud when it has caught a fly, and another when he has caught a poor hare, and another when he has taken a little fish in a net, and another when he has taken wild boars, and another when he has taken bears, and another when he has taken Sarmatians. Are not these robbers, if thou examinest their opinions?

11. Acquire the contemplative way of seeing how all things change into one another, and constantly attend to it, and exercise thyself about this part [of philosophy]. For nothing is so much adapted to produce magnanimity. Such a man has put off the body, and as he sees that he must, no one knows how soon, go away from among men and leave everything here, he gives himself up entirely to just doing in all his actions, and in everything else that happens he resigns himself to the universal nature. But as to what any man shall say or think about him or do against him, he never

even thinks of it, being himself contented with these two things,—with acting justly in what he now does, and being satisfied with what is now assigned to him; and he lays aside all distracting and busy pursuits, and desires nothing else than to accomplish the straight course through the law, and by accomplishing the straight course to follow God.

12. What need is there of suspicious fear, since it is in thy power to inquire what ought to be done? And if thou seest clear, go by this way content, without turning back: but if thou dost not see clear, stop and take the best advisers. But if any other things oppose thee, go on according to thy powers with due consideration, keeping to that which appears to be just. For it is best to reach this object, and if thou dost fail, let thy failure be in attempting this. He who follows reason in all things is both tranquil and active at the same time, and also cheerful and collected.

13. Inquire of thyself as soon as thou wakest from sleep whether it will make any difference to thee if another does what is just and right. It will make no difference (vi. 32; viii. 55).

Thou hast not forgotten, I suppose, that those who assume arrogant airs in bestowing their praise or blame on others are such as they are at bed and at board, and thou hast not forgotten what they do, and what they avoid, and what they pursue, and how they steal and how they rob, not with hands and feet, but with their most valuable part, by means of which there is produced, when a man chooses, fidelity, modesty, truth, law, a good daemon [happiness] (vii. 17)?

14. To her who gives and takes back all, to nature, the man who is instructed and modest says, Give what thou wilt; take back what thou wilt. And he says this not proudly, but obediently, and well pleased with her.

15. Short is the little which remains to thee of life. Live as on a mountain. For it makes no difference whether a man lives there or here, if he lives everywhere in the world as in a state [political community]. Let men see, let them know a real man who lives according to nature. If they cannot endure him, let them kill him. For that is better than to live thus [as men do].

16. No longer talk at all about the kind of man that a good man ought to be, but be such.

17. Constantly contemplate the whole of time and the whole of substance, and consider that all individual things as to substance are a grain of a fig, and as to time the turning of a gimlet.

18. Look at everything that exists, and observe that it is already in dissolution and in change, and as it were putrefaction or dispersion, or that everything is so constituted by nature as to die.
19. Consider what men are when they are eating, sleeping, generating, easing themselves, and so forth. Then what kind of men they are when they are imperious and arrogant, or angry and scolding from their elevated place. But a short time ago to how many they were slaves and for what things; and after a little time consider in what a condition they will be.
20. That is for the good of each thing, which the universal nature brings to each. And it is for its good at the time when nature brings it.
21. "The earth loves the shower"; and "the solemn ether loves"; and the universe loves to make whatever is about to be. I say then to the universe, that I love as thou lovest. And is not this too said, that "this or that loves [is wont] to be produced"?
22. Either thou livest here and hast already accustomed thyself to it, or thou art going away, and this was thy own will; or thou art dying and hast discharged thy duty. But besides these things there is nothing. Be of good cheer, then.
23. Let this always be plain to thee, that this piece of land is like any other; and that all things here are the same with things on the top of a mountain, or on the sea-shore, or wherever thou choosest to be. For thou wilt find just what Plato says, Dwelling within the walls of a city as in a shepherd's fold on a mountain. [The three last words are omitted in the translation.]
24. What is my ruling faculty now to me? and of what nature am I now making it? and for what purpose am I now using it? is it void of understanding? is it loosed and rent asunder from social life? is it melted into and mixed with the poor flesh so as to move together with it?
25. He who flies from his master is a runaway; but the law is master, and he who breaks the law is a runaway. And he also who is grieved or angry or afraid, is dissatisfied because something has been or is or shall be of the things which are appointed by him who rules all things, and he is Law and assigns to every man what is fit. He then who fears or is grieved or is angry is a run-away.
26. A man deposits seed in a womb and goes away, and then another cause takes it, and labors on it and makes a child. What a thing from such a material! Again, the child passes food down through the throat, and then

another cause takes it and makes perception and motion, and in fine, life and strength and other things; how many and how strange! Observe then the things which are produced in such a hidden way, and see the power just as we see the power which carries things downwards and upwards, not with the eyes, but still no less plainly (vii. 75).

27. Constantly consider how all things such as they now are, in time past also were; and consider that they will be the same again. And place before thy eyes entire dramas and stages of the same form, whatever thou hast learned from thy experience or from older history; for example, the whole court of Hadrianus, and the whole court of Antoninus, and the whole court of Philippus, Alexander, Croesus; for all those were such dramas as we see now, only with different actors.

28. Imagine every man who is grieved at anything or discontented to be like a pig which is sacrificed and kicks and screams.

Like this pig also is he who on his bed in silence laments the bonds in which we are held. And consider that only to the rational animal is it given to follow voluntarily what happens; but simply to follow is a necessity imposed on all.

29. Severally on the occasion of everything that thou doest, pause and ask thyself if death is a dreadful thing because it deprives thee of this.

30. When thou art offended at any man's fault, forthwith turn to thyself and reflect in what like manner thou dost err thyself; for example, in thinking that money is a good thing, or pleasure, or a bit of reputation, and the like. For by attending to this thou wilt quickly forget thy anger, if this consideration also is added, that the man is compelled: for what else could he do? or, if thou art able, take away from him the compulsion.

31. When thou hast seen Satyron the Socratic, think of either Eutyches or Hymen, and when thou hast seen Euphrates, think of Eutychion or Silvanus, and when thou hast seen Alciphron think of Tropaeophorus, and when thou hast seen Xenophon, think of Crito or Severus, and when thou hast looked on thyself, think of any other Caesar, and in the case of every one do in like manner. Then let this thought be in thy mind, Where then are those men? Nowhere, or nobody knows where. For thus continuously thou wilt look at human things as smoke and nothing at all; especially if thou reflectest at the same time that what has once changed will never exist again in the infinite duration of time. But thou, in what a brief space of time is thy existence? And why art thou not content to pass through this short time in an orderly way? What matter and opportunity [for thy activity] art thou avoiding? For what else are all these things, except exercises for the reason, when it has viewed carefully and by examination into their nature the things which happen in life? Persevere then until thou shalt have made these things thy own, as the stomach which is strengthened makes all things its own, as the blazing fire makes flame and brightness out of everything that is thrown into it.

32. Let it not be in any man's power to say truly of thee that thou art not simple or that thou art not good; but let him be a liar whoever shall think anything of this kind about thee; and this is altogether in thy power. For who is he that shall hinder thee from being good and simple? Do thou only determine to live no longer unless thou shalt be such. For neither does reason allow [thee to live], if thou art not such.

33. What is that which as to this material [our life] can be done or said in the way most conformable to reason? For whatever this may be, it is in thy power to do it or to say it, and do not make excuses that thou art hindered. Thou wilt not cease to lament till thy mind is in such a condition that, what luxury is to those who enjoy pleasure, such shall be to thee, in the matter which is subjected and presented to thee, the doing of the things which are conformable to man's constitution; for a man ought to consider as an enjoyment everything which it is in his power to do according to his own nature. And it is in his power everywhere. Now, it is not given to a cylinder to move everywhere by its own motion, nor yet to water nor to fire, nor to anything else which is governed by nature or an irrational soul, for the things which check them and stand in the way are many. But intelligence and reason are able to go through everything that opposes them, and in such manner as they are formed by nature and as they choose. Place before thy eyes this facility with which the reason will be carried through all things, as fire upwards, as a stone downwards, as a cylinder down an inclined surface, and seek for nothing further. For all other obstacles either affect the body only, which is a dead thing; or, except through opinion and the yielding of the reason itself, they do not crush nor do any harm of any kind; for if they did, he who felt it would immediately become bad. Now, in the case of all things which have a certain constitution, whatever harm may happen to any of them, that which is so affected becomes consequently worse; but in the like case, a man becomes both better, if one may say so, and more worthy of praise by making a right use of these accidents. And finally remember that nothing harms him who is really a citizen, which does not harm the state; nor yet does anything harm the state, which does not harm law [order]; and of these things which are called misfortunes not one harms law. What then does not harm law does not harm either state or citizen.

34. To him who is penetrated by true principles even the briefest precept is sufficient, and any common precept, to remind him that he should be free from grief and fear. For example,—

> "Leaves, some the wind scatters on the ground—
> So is the race of men."

Leaves, also, are thy children; and leaves, too, are they who cry out as if they were worthy of credit and bestow their praise, or on the contrary curse, or secretly blame and sneer; and leaves, in like manner, are those who shall receive and transmit a man's fame to after-times. For all such things as these "are produced in the season of spring," as the poet says; then the wind casts them down; then the forest produces other leaves in their places. But a brief existence is common to all things, and yet thou avoidest and pursuest all things as if they would be eternal. A little time, and thou shalt close thy eyes; and him who has attended thee to thy grave another will soon lament.

35. The healthy eye ought to see all visible things and not to say, I wish for green things; for this is the condition of a diseased eye. And the healthy hearing and smelling ought to be ready to perceive all that can be heard and smelled. And the healthy stomach ought to be with respect to all food just as the mill with respect to all things which it is formed to grind. And accordingly the healthy understanding ought to be prepared for everything which happens; but that which says, Let my dear children live, and let all men praise whatever I may do, is an eye which seeks for green things, or teeth which seek for soft things.

36. There is no man so fortunate that there shall not be by him when he is dying some who are pleased with what is going to happen. Suppose that he was a good and wise man, will there not be at last some one to say to himself, Let us at last breathe freely, being relieved from this schoolmaster? It is true that he was harsh to none of us, but I perceived that he tacitly condemns us.—This is what is said of a good man. But in our own case how many other things are there for which there are many who wish to get rid of us. Thou wilt consider this, then, when thou art dying, and thou wilt depart more contentedly by reflecting thus: I am going away from such a life, in which even my associates in behalf of whom I have striven so much, prayed, and cared, themselves wish me to depart, hoping perchance to get some little advantage by it. Why then should a man cling to a longer stay here? Do not however for this reason go away less kindly disposed to them, but preserving thy own character, and friendly and benevolent and mild, and on the other hand not as if thou wast torn away; but as when a man dies a quiet death, the poor soul is easily separated from the body, such also ought thy departure from men to be, for nature united thee to them and associated thee. But does she now dissolve the union? Well, I am separated as from kinsmen, not however dragged resisting, but without compulsion; for this, too, is one of the things according to nature.

37. Accustom thyself as much as possible on the occasion of anything being done by any person to inquire with thyself, For what object is this man doing this? But begin with thyself, and examine thyself first.

38. Remember that this which pulls the strings is the thing which is hidden within: this is the power of persuasion, this is life, this, if one may so say, is man. In contemplating thyself never include the vessel which surrounds thee and these instruments which are attached about it. For they are like to an axe, differing only in this, that they grow to the body. For indeed there is no more use in these parts without the cause which moves and checks them than in the weaver's shuttle, and the writer's pen, and the driver's whip.

XI.

1. These are the properties of the rational soul: it sees itself, analyzes itself, and makes itself such as it chooses; the fruit which it bears itself enjoys,—for the fruits of plants and that in animals which corresponds to fruits others enjoy,—it obtains its own end, wherever the limit of life may be fixed. Not as in a dance and in a play and in such like things, where the whole action is incomplete if anything cuts it short; but in every part, and wherever it may be stopped, it makes what has been set before it full and complete, so that it can say, I have what is my own. And further it

traverses the whole universe, and the surrounding vacuum, and surveys its form, and it extends itself into the infinity of time, and embraces and comprehends the periodical renovation of all things, and it comprehends that those who come after us will see nothing new, nor have those before us seen anything more, but in a manner he who is forty years old, if he has any understanding at all, has seen by virtue of the uniformity that prevails all things which have been and all that will be. This too is a property of the rational soul, love of one's neighbor, and truth and modesty, and to value nothing more than itself, which is also the property of Law. Thus then right reason differs not at all from the reason of justice.

2. Thou wilt set little value on pleasing song and dancing and the pancratium, if thou wilt distribute the melody of the voice into its several sounds, and ask thyself as to each, if thou art mastered by this; for thou wilt be prevented by shame from confessing it: and in the matter of dancing, if at each movement and attitude thou wilt do the same; and the like also in the matter of the pancratium. In all things, then, except virtue and the acts of virtue, remember to apply thyself to their several parts, and by this division to come to value them little: and apply this rule also to thy whole life.
3. What a soul that is which is ready, if at any moment it must be separated from the body, and ready either to be extinguished or dispersed or continue to exist; but so that this readiness comes from a man's own judgment, not from mere obstinacy, as with the Christians, but considerately and with dignity and in a way to persuade another, without tragic show.
4. Have I done something for the general interest? Well then I have had my reward. Let this always be present to thy mind, and never stop [doing such good].
5. What is thy art? To be good. And how is this accomplished well except by general principles, some about the nature of the universe, and others about the proper constitution of man?
6. At first tragedies were brought on the stage as means of reminding men of the things which happen to them, and that it is according to nature for things to happen so, and that, if you are delighted with what is shown on the stage, you should not be troubled with that which takes place on the larger stage. For you see that these things must be accomplished thus, and that even they bear them who cry out, "O Cithaeron." And, indeed, some things are said well by the dramatic writers, of which kind is the following especially:—

"Me and my children if the gods neglect,
This has its reason too."

And again,—

"We must not chafe and fret at that which happens."

And,—

"Life's harvest reap like the wheat's fruitful ear."

And other things of the same kind.

After tragedy the old comedy was introduced, which had a magisterial freedom of speech, and by its very plainness of speaking was useful in reminding men to beware of insolence; and for this purpose too Diogenes used to take from these writers.

But as to the middle comedy, which came next, observe what it was, and again, for what object the new comedy was introduced, which gradually sank down into a mere mimic artifice. That some good things are said even by these writers, everybody knows: but the whole plan of such poetry and dramaturgy, to what end does it look?

7. How plain does it appear that there is not another condition of life so well suited for philosophizing as this in which thou now happenest to be.

8. A branch cut off from the adjacent branch must of necessity be cut off from the whole tree also. So too a man when he is separated from another man has fallen off from the whole social community. Now as to a branch, another cuts it off; but a man by his own act separates himself from his neighbor when he hates him and turns away from him, and he does not know that he has at the same time cut himself off from the whole social system. Yet he has this privilege certainly from Zeus, who framed society, for it is in our power to grow again to that which is near to us, and again to become a part which helps to make up the whole. However, if it often happens, this kind of separation, it makes it difficult for that which detaches itself to be brought to unity and to be restored to its former condition. Finally, the branch, which from the first grew together with the tree, and has continued to have one life with it, is not like that which after being cut off is then ingrafted, for this is something like what the gardeners mean when they say that it grows with the rest of the tree, but that it has not the same mind with it.

9. As those who try to stand in thy way when thou art proceeding according to right reason will not be able to turn thee aside from thy proper action, so neither let them drive thee from thy benevolent feelings towards them, but be on thy guard equally in both matters, not only in the matter of steady judgment and action, but also in the matter of gentleness to those who try to hinder or otherwise trouble thee. For this also is a weakness, to be vexed at them, as well as to be diverted from thy course of action and to give way through fear; for both are equally deserters from their post,—the man who does it through fear, and the man who is alienated from him who is by nature a kinsman and a friend.

10. There is no nature which is inferior to art, for the arts imitate the natures of things. But if this is so, that nature which is the most perfect and the most comprehensive of all natures, cannot fall short of the skill of art. Now all arts do the inferior things for the sake of the superior; therefore the universal nature does so too. And, indeed, hence is the origin of justice, and in justice the other virtues have their foundation: for justice will not be observed, if we either care for middle things [things indifferent], or are easily deceived and careless and changeable (v. 16, 30; vii. 55).

11. If the things do not come to thee, the pursuits and avoidances of which disturb thee, still in a manner thou goest to them. Let then thy judgment about them be at rest, and they will remain quiet, and thou wilt not be seen either pursuing or avoiding.

12. The spherical form of the soul maintains its figure when it is neither extended towards any object, nor contracted inwards, nor dispersed nor sinks down, but is illuminated by light, by which it sees the truth,—the truth of all things and the truth that is in itself (viii. 41, 45; xii. 3).

13. Suppose any man shall despise me. Let him look to that himself. But I will look to this, that I be not discovered doing or saying anything deserving of contempt. Shall any man hate me? Let him look to it. But I will be mild and benevolent towards every man, and ready to show even him his mistake, not reproachfully, nor yet as making a display of my endurance, but nobly and honestly, like the great Phocion, unless indeed he only assumed it. For the interior [parts] ought to be such, and a man ought to be seen by the gods neither dissatisfied with anything nor complaining.

For what evil is it to thee, if thou art now doing what is agreeable to thy own nature, and art satisfied with that which at this moment is suitable to the nature of the universe, since thou art a human being placed at thy post in order that what is for the common advantage may be done in some way?

14. Men despise one another and flatter one another; and men wish to raise themselves above one another, and crouch before one another.

15. How unsound and insincere is he who says, I have determined to deal with thee in a fair way!—What art thou doing, man? There is no occasion to give this notice. It will soon show itself by acts. The voice ought to be plainly written on the forehead. Such as a man's character is, he immediately shows it in his eyes, just as he who is beloved forthwith reads everything in the eyes of lovers. The man who is honest and good ought to be exactly like a man who smells strong, so that the bystander as soon as he comes near him must smell whether he choose or not. But the affectation of simplicity is like a crooked stick. Nothing is more disgraceful than a wolfish friendship [false friendship]. Avoid this most of all. The good and simple and benevolent show all these things in the eyes, and there is no mistaking.

16. As to living in the best way, this power is in the soul, if it be indifferent to things which are indifferent. And it will be indifferent, if it looks on each of these things separately and all together, and if it remembers that not one of them produces in us an opinion about itself, nor comes to us; but these things remain immovable, and it is we ourselves who produce the judgments about them, and, as we may say, write them in ourselves, it being in our power not to write them, and it being in our power, if perchance these judgments have imperceptibly got admission to our minds, to wipe them out; and if we remember also that such attention will only be for a short time, and then life will be at an end. Besides, what trouble is there at all in doing this? For if these things are according to nature, rejoice in them and they will be easy to thee: but if contrary to nature, seek what is conformable to thy own nature, and strive towards this, even if it bring no reputation; for every man is allowed to seek his own good.

17. Consider whence each thing is come, and of what it consists, and into what it changes, and what kind of a thing it will be when it has changed, and that it will sustain no harm.

18. [If any have offended against thee, consider first]: What is my relation to men, and that we are made for one another; and in another respect I

was made to be set over them, as a ram over the flock or a bull over the herd. But examine the matter from first principles, from this: If all things are not mere atoms, it is nature which orders all things: if this is so, the inferior things exist for the sake of the superior, and these for the sake of one another (II. 1; IX. 39; V. 16; III. 4).

Second, consider what kind of men they are at table, in bed, and so forth: and particularly, under what compulsions in respect of opinions they are; and as to their acts, consider with what pride they do what they do (VIII. 14; IX. 34).

Third, that if men do rightly what they do, we ought not to be displeased: but if they do not right, it is plain that they do so involuntarily and in ignorance. For as every soul is unwillingly deprived of the truth, so also is it unwillingly deprived of the power of behaving to each man according to his deserts. Accordingly men are pained when they are called unjust, ungrateful, and greedy, and in a word wrong-doers to their neighbors (VII. 62, 63; II. 1; VII. 26; VIII. 29).

Fourth, consider that thou also dost many things wrong, and that thou art a man like others; and even if thou dost abstain from certain faults, still thou hast the disposition to commit them, though either through cowardice, or concern about reputation, or some such mean motive, thou dost abstain from such faults (I. 17).

Fifth, consider that thou dost not even understand whether men are doing wrong or not, for many things are done with a certain reference to circumstances. And in short, a man must learn a great deal to enable him to pass a correct judgment on another man's acts (IX. 38; IV. 51).

Sixth, consider when thou art much vexed or grieved, that man's life is only a moment, and after a short time we are all laid out dead (VII. 58; IV. 48).

Seventh, that it is not men's acts which disturb us, for those acts have their foundation in men's ruling principles, but it is our own opinions which disturb us. Take away these opinions then, and resolve to dismiss thy judgment about an act as if it were something grievous, and thy anger is gone. How then shall I take away these opinions? By reflecting that no wrongful act of another brings shame on thee: for unless that which is shameful is alone bad, thou also must of necessity do many things wrong, and become a robber and everything else (V. 25; VII. 16).

Eighth, consider how much more pain is brought on us by the anger and vexation caused by such acts than by the acts themselves, at which we are angry and vexed (IV. 39, 49; VII. 24).

Ninth, consider that a good disposition is invincible if it be genuine, and not an affected smile and acting a part. For what will the most violent man do to thee, if thou continuest to be of a kind disposition towards him, and if, as opportunity offers, thou gently admonishest him and calmly correctest his errors at the very time when he is trying to do thee harm, saying, Not so, my child: we are constituted by nature for something else: I shall certainly not be injured, but thou art injuring thyself, my child.—And show him with gentle tact and by general principles that this is so, and that even bees do not do as he does, nor any animals which are formed by nature to be gregarious. And thou must do this neither with any double meaning nor in the way of reproach, but affectionately and without any rancor in thy soul; and not as if thou wert lecturing him, nor yet that any bystander may admire, but either when he is alone, and if others are present. . . . *

Remember these nine rules, as if thou hadst received them as a gift from the Muses, and begin at last to be a man while thou livest. But thou must equally avoid flattering men and being vexed at them, for both are unsocial and lead to harm. And let this truth be present to thee in the excitement of anger, that to be moved by passion is not manly, but that mildness and gentleness, as they are more agreeable to human nature, so also are they more manly; and he who possesses these qualities possesses strength, nerves, and courage, and not the man who is subject to fits of passion and discontent. For in the same degree in which a man's mind is nearer to freedom from all passion, in the same degree also is it nearer to strength: and as the sense of pain is a characteristic of weakness, so also is anger. For he who yields to pain and he who yields to anger, both are wounded and both submit.

But if thou wilt, receive also a tenth present from the leader of the [Muses, Apollo], and it is this,—that to expect bad men not to do wrong is madness, for he who expects this desires an impossibility. But to allow men to behave so to others, and to expect them not to do thee any wrong, is irrational and tyrannical.

19. There are four principal aberrations of the superior faculty against

* It appears that there is a defect in the text here.

which thou shouldst be constantly on thy guard, and when thou hast detected them, thou shouldst wipe them out and say on each occasion thus: This thought is not necessary: this tends to destroy social union: this which thou art going to say comes not from the real thoughts; for thou shouldst consider it among the most absurd of things for a man not to speak from his real thoughts. But the fourth is when thou shalt reproach thyself for anything, for this is an evidence of the diviner part within thee being overpowered and yielding to the less honorable and to the perishable part, the body, and to its gross pleasures (IV. 24; II. 16).

20. Thy aerial part and all the fiery parts which are mingled in thee, though by nature they have an upward tendency, still in obedience to the disposition of the universe they are overpowered here in the compound mass [the body]. And also the whole of the earthy part in thee and the watery, though their tendency is downward, still are raised up and occupy a position which is not their natural one. In this manner then the elemental parts obey the universal; for when they have been fixed in any place, perforce they remain there until again the universal shall sound the signal for dissolution. Is it not then strange that thy intelligent part only should be disobedient and discontented with its own place? And yet no force is imposed on it, but only those things which are comformable to its nature: still it does not submit, but is carried in the opposite direction. For the movement towards injustice and intemperance and to anger and grief and fear is nothing else than the act of one who deviates from nature. And also when the ruling faculty is discontented with anything that happens, then too it deserts its post: for it is constituted for piety and reverence towards the gods no less than for justice. For these qualities also are comprehended under the generic term of contentment with the constitution of things, and indeed they are prior to acts of justice.

21. He who has not one and always the same object in life, cannot be one and the same all through his life. But what I have said is not enough, unless this also is added, what this object ought to be. For as there is not the same opinion about all the things which in some way or other are considered by the majority to be good, but only about some certain things, that is, things which concern the common interest, so also ought we to propose to ourselves an object which shall be of a common kind [social] and political. For he who directs all his own efforts to this object, will make all his acts alike, and thus will always be the same.

22. Think of the country mouse and of the town mouse, and of the alarm and trepidation of the town mouse.*
23. Socrates used to call the opinions of the many by the name of Lamiae,—bugbears to frighten children.
24. The Lacedaemonians at their public spectacles used to set seats in the shade for strangers, but themselves sat down anywhere.
25. Socrates excused himself to Perdiccas for not going to him, saying, It is because I would not perish by the worst of all ends; that is, I would not receive a favor and then be unable to return it.
26. In the writings of the [Ephesians] there was this precept, constantly to think of some one of the men of former times who practised virtue.
27. The Pythagoreans bid us in the morning look to the heavens that we may be reminded of those bodies which continually do the same things and in the same manner perform their work, and also be reminded of their purity and nudity. For there is no veil over a star.
28. Consider what a man Socrates was when he dressed himself in a skin, after Xanthippe had taken his cloak and gone out, and what Socrates said to his friends who were ashamed of him and drew back from him when they saw him dressed thus.
29. Neither in writing nor in reading wilt thou be able to lay down rules for others before thou shalt have first learned to obey rules thyself. Much more is this so in life.
30. A slave thou art: free speech is not for thee.

> 31. And my heart laughed within.
>
> *Odyssey,* ix. 413

> 32. And virtue they will curse, speaking harsh words.
>
> *Hesiod, Works and Days,* 184

33. To look for the fig in winter is a madman's act: such is he who looks for his child when it is no longer allowed (Epictetus, III. 24, 87).
34. When a man kisses his child, said Epictetus, he should whisper to himself, "To-morrow perchance thou wilt die."—But those are words of bad omen.—"No word is a word of bad omen," said Epictetus, "which ex-

* The story is told by Horace in his Satires and by others since, but not better.

presses any work of nature; or if it is so, it is also a word of bad omen to speak of the ears of corn being reaped" (Epictetus, III. 24, 88).

35. The unripe grape, the ripe bunch, the dried grape all are changes, not into nothing, but into something which exists not yet (Epictetus, III. 24).

36. No man can rob us of our free will (Epictetus III. 22, 105).

37. Epictetus also said, a man must discover an art [or rules] with respect to giving his assent; and in respect to his movements he must be careful that they be made with regard to circumstances, that they be consistent with social interests, that they have regard to the value of the object; and as to sensual desire, he should altogether keep away from it; and as to avoidance [aversion], he should not show it with respect to any of the things which are not in our power.

38. The dispute then, he said, is not about any common matter, but about being mad or not.

39. Socrates used to say, What do you want, souls of rational men or irrational?—souls of rational men.—Of what rational men, sound or unsound?—Sound.—Why then do you not seek for them?—Because we have them.—Why then do you fight and quarrel?

XII.

1. All those things at which thou wishest to arrive by a circuitous road thou canst have now, if thou dost not refuse them to thyself. And this means, if thou wilt take no notice of all the past, and trust the future to providence, and direct the present only conformably to piety and justice. Conformably to piety, that thou mayest be content with the lot which is assigned to thee, for nature designed it for thee and thee for it. Conformably to justice, that thou mayest always speak the truth freely and without disguise, and do the things which are agreeable to law and according to the worth of each. And let neither another man's wickedness hinder thee, nor opinion nor voice, nor yet the sensations of the poor flesh which has grown about thee; for the passive part will look to this. If, then, whatever the time may be when thou shalt be near to thy departure, neglecting everything else thou shalt respect only thy ruling faculty and the divinity within thee, and if thou shalt be afraid not because thou must some time cease to live, but if thou shalt fear never to have begun to live according to nature,—then thou wilt be a man worthy of the universe which hast produced thee, and thou wilt cease to be a stranger in thy native land, and to wonder at things which happen daily as if they were something unexpected, and not to be dependent on this or that.

2. God sees the minds [ruling principles] of all men bared of the material vesture and rind and impurities. For with his intellectual part alone he touches the intelligence only which has flowed and been derived from himself into these bodies. And if thou also usest thyself to do this, thou wilt rid thyself of thy much trouble. For he who regards not the poor flesh which envelops him, surely will not trouble himself by looking after raiment and dwelling and fame and such like externals and show.

3. The things are three of which thou art composed: a little body, a little breath [life], intelligence. Of these the first two are thine, so far as it is thy duty to take care of them; but the third alone is properly thine. Therefore if thou shalt separate from thyself, that is, from thy understanding, whatever others do or say, and whatever thou hast done or said thyself, and whatever future things trouble thee because they may happen, and whatever in the body which envelops thee or in the breath [life], which is by nature associated with the body, is attached to thee independent of thy will, and whatever the external circumfluent vortex whirls round, so that the intellectual power exempt from the things of fate can live pure and free by itself, doing what is just and accepting what happens and saying the truth: if thou wilt separate, I say, from this ruling faculty the things which are attached to it by the impressions of sense, and the things of time to come and of time that is past, and wilt make thyself like Empedocles' sphere,

"All round and in its joyous rest reposing";

and if thou shalt strive to live only what is really thy life, that is, the present,—then thou wilt be able to pass that portion of life which remains for thee up to the time of thy death free from perturbations, nobly, and obedient to thy own daemon [to the god that is within thee] (II. 13, 17; III. 5, 6; XI. 12).

4. I have often wondered how it is that every man loves himself more than all the rest of men, but yet sets less value on his own opinion of himself

than on the opinion of others. If then a god or a wise teacher should present himself to a man and bid him to think of nothing and to design nothing which he would not express as soon as he conceived it, he could not endure it even for a single day. So much more respect have we to what our neighbors shall think of us than to what we shall think of ourselves.

5. How can it be that the gods, after having arranged all things well and benevolently for mankind, have overlooked this alone, that some men, and very good men, and men who, as we may say, have had most communion with the divinity, and through pious acts and religious observances have been most intimate with the divinity, when they have once died should never exist again, but should be completely extinguished?

But if this is so, be assured that if it ought to have been otherwise, the gods would have done it. For if it were just, it would also be possible; and if it were according to nature, nature would have had it so. But because it is not so, if in fact it is not so, be thou convinced that it ought not to have been so: for thou seest even of thyself that in this inquiry thou art disputing with the Deity; and we should not thus dispute with the gods, unless they were most excellent and most just; but if this is so, they would not have allowed anything in the ordering of the universe to be neglected unjustly and irrationally.

6. Practise thyself even in the things which thou despairest of accomplishing. For even the left hand, which is ineffectual for all other things for want of practice, holds the bridle more vigorously than the right hand; for it has been practised in this.

7. Consider in what condition both in body and soul a man should be when he is overtaken by death; and consider the shortness of life, the boundless abyss of time past and future, the feebleness of all matter.

8. Contemplate the formative principles [forms] of things bare of their coverings; the purposes of actions; consider what pain is, what pleasure is, and death, and fame; who is to himself the cause of his uneasiness; how no man is hindered by another; that everything is opinion.

9. In the application of thy principles thou must be like the pancratiast, not like the gladiator; for the gladiator lets fall the sword which he uses and is killed; but the other always has his hand, and needs to do nothing else than use it.

10. See what things are in themselves, dividing them into matter, form, and purpose.

11. What a power man has to do nothing except what God will approve, and to accept all that God may give him.

12. With respect to that which happens conformably to nature, we ought to blame neither gods, for they do nothing wrong either voluntarily or involuntarily, nor men, for they do nothing wrong except involuntarily. Consequently we should blame nobody (II. 11, 12, 13; VII. 62; VIII. 17, 18).

13. How ridiculous and what a stranger he is who is surprised at anything which happens in life.

14. Either there is a fatal necessity and invincible order, or a kind providence, or a confusion without a purpose and without a director (IV. 27). If then there is an invincible necessity, why dost thou resist? But if there is a providence which allows itself to be propitiated, make thyself worthy of the help of the divinity. But if there is a confusion without a governor, be content that in such a tempest thou hast in thyself a certain ruling intelligence. And even if the tempest carry thee away, let it carry away the poor flesh, the poor breath, everything else; for the intelligence at least it will not carry away.

15. Does the light of the lamp shine without losing its splendor until it is extinguished; and shall the truth which is in thee and justice and temperance be extinguished [before thy death]?

16. When a man has presented the appearance of having done wrong [say], How then do I know if this is a wrongful act? And even if he has done wrong, how do I know that he has not condemned himself? And so this is like tearing his own face. Consider that he who would not have the bad man do wrong, is like the man who would not have the fig-tree bear juice in the figs, and infants cry, and the horse neigh, and whatever else must of necessity be. For what must a man do who has such a character? If then thou art irritable, cure this man's disposition.

17. If it is not right, do not do it: if it is not true, do not say it. [For let thy efforts be—]

18. In everything always observe what the thing is which produces for thee an appearance, and resolve it by dividing it into the formal, the material, the purpose, and the time within which it must end.

19. Perceive at last that thou hast in thee something better and more divine than the things which cause the various effects, and as it were pull thee by the strings. What is there now in my mind,—is it fear, or suspicion, or desire, or anything of the kind (V. 11)?

20. First, do nothing inconsiderately, nor without a purpose. Second, make thy acts refer to nothing else than to a social end.

21. Consider that before long thou wilt be nobody and nowhere, nor will any of the things exist which thou now seest, nor any of those who are now living. For all things are formed by nature to change and be turned and to perish, in order that other things in continuous succession may exist (IX. 28).

22. Consider that everything is opinion, and opinion is in thy power. Take away then, when thou choosest, thy opinion, and like a mariner who has doubled the promontory, thou wilt find calm, everything stable, and a waveless bay.

23. Any one activity, whatever it may be, when it has ceased at its proper time, suffers no evil because it has ceased; nor he who has done this act, does he suffer any evil for this reason, that the act has ceased. In like manner then the whole which consists of all the acts, which is our life, if it cease at its proper time, suffers no evil for this reason, that it has ceased; nor he who has terminated this series at the proper time, has he been ill dealt with. But the proper time and the limit nature fixes, sometimes as in old age the peculiar nature of man, but always the universal nature, by the change of whose parts the whole universe continues ever young and perfect. And everything which is useful to the universal is always good and in season. Therefore the termination of life for every man is no evil, because neither is it shameful, since it is both independent of the will and not opposed to the general interest, but it is good, since it is seasonable, and profitable to and congruent with the universal. For thus too he is moved by the Deity who is moved in the same manner with the Deity, and moved towards the same things in his mind.

24. These three principles thou must have in readiness: In the things which thou dost do nothing either inconsiderately or otherwise than as Justice herself would act; but with respect to what may happen to thee from without, consider that it happens either by chance or according to providence, and thou must neither blame chance nor accuse providence. Second, consider what every being is from the seed to the time of its receiving a soul, and from the reception of a soul to the giving back of the same, and of what things every being is compounded, and into what things it is resolved. Third, if thou shouldst suddenly be raised up above the earth, and shouldst look down on human things, and observe the variety of them how great it is, and at the same time also shouldst see at a glance how great is the number of beings who dwell all around in the air and the ether, consider that as often as thou shouldst be raised up, thou wouldst see the same things, sameness of form and shortness of duration. Are these things to be proud of?

25. Cast away opinion: thou art saved. Who then hinders thee from casting it away?

26. When thou art troubled about anything, thou hast forgotten this, that all things happen according to the universal nature; and forgotten this, that a man's wrongful act is nothing to thee; and further thou hast forgotten this, that everything which happens, always happened so and will happen so, and now happens so everywhere; forgotten this too, how close is the kinship between a man and the whole human race, for it is a community, not of a little blood or seed, but of intelligence. And thou hast forgotten this too, that every man's intelligence is a god and is an efflux of the Deity; and forgotten this, that nothing is a man's own, but that his child and his body and his very soul came from the Deity; forgotten this, that everything is opinion; and lastly thou hast forgotten that every man lives the present time only, and loses only this.

27. Constantly bring to thy recollection those who have complained greatly about anything, those who have been most conspicuous by the greatest fame or misfortunes or enmities or fortunes of any kind: then think where are they all now? Smoke and ash and a tale, or not even a tale. And let there be present to thy mind also everything of this sort, how Fabius Catullinus lived in the country, and Lucius Lupus in his gardens, and Stertinius at Baiae, and Tiberius at Capreae, and Velius Rufus [or Rufus at Velia]; and in fine think of the eager pursuit of anything conjoined with pride; and how worthless everything is after which men violently strain; and how much more philosophical it is for a man in the opportunities presented to him to show himself just, temperate, obedient to the gods, and to do this with all simplicity: for the pride which is proud of its want of pride is the most intolerable of all.

28. To those who ask, Where hast thou seen the gods, or how dost thou comprehend that they exist and so worshippest them, I answer, in the first place, they may be seen even with the eyes;* in the second place, neither

* "Seen even with the eyes." It is supposed that this may be explained by the Stoic doctrine, that the universe is a god or living being (IV. 40), and that the celestial bodies are gods (VIII. 19). But

have I seen even my own soul, and yet I honor it. Thus then with respect to the gods, from what I constantly experience of their power, from this I comprehend that they exist, and I venerate them.

29. The safety of life is this, to examine everything all through, what it is itself, that is its material, what the formal part; with all thy soul to do justice and to say the truth, What remains, except to enjoy life by joining one good thing to another so as not to leave even the smallest intervals between?

30. There is one light of the sun, though it is interrupted by walls, mountains, and other things infinite. There is one common substance, though it is distributed among countless bodies which have their several qualities. There is one soul, though it is distributed among infinite natures and individual circumscriptions [or individuals]. There is one intelligent soul, though it seems to be divided. Now in the things which have been mentioned, all the other parts, such as those which are air and matter, are without sensation and have no fellowship: and yet even these parts the intelligent principle holds together and the gravitation towards the same. But intellect in a peculiar manner tends to that which is of the same kin, and combines with it, and the feeling for communion is not interrupted.

31. What dost thou wish,—to continue to exist? Well, dost thou wish to have sensation, movement, growth, and then again to cease to grow, to use thy speech, to think? What is there of all these things which seems to thee worth desiring? But if it is easy to set little value on all these things, turn to that which remains, which is to follow reason and God. But it is inconsistent with honoring reason and God to be troubled because by death a man will be deprived of the other things.

32. How small a part of the boundless and unfathomable time is assigned to every man, for it is very soon swallowed up in the eternal! And how small a part of the whole substance; and how small a part of the universal soul; and on what a small clod of the whole earth thou creepest! Reflecting on all this, consider nothing to be great, except to act as thy nature leads thee, and to endure that which the common nature brings.

---

the emperor may mean that we know that the gods exist, as he afterwards states it, because we see what they do; as we know that man has intellectual powers, because we see what he does, and in no other way do we know it.

33. How does the ruling faculty make use of itself? for all lies in this. But everything else, whether it is in the power of thy will or not, is only lifeless ashes and smoke.

34. This reflection is most adapted to move us to contempt of death, that even those who think pleasure to be a good and pain an evil still have despised it.

35. The man to whom that only is good which comes in due season, and to whom it is the same thing whether he has done more or fewer acts conformable to right reason, and to whom it makes no difference whether he contemplates the world for a longer or a shorter time,—for this man neither is death a terrible thing (III. 7; VI. 23; X. 20; XII. 23).

36. Man, thou hast been a citizen in this great state [the world]; what difference does it make to thee whether for five years [or three]? for that which is conformable to the laws is just for all. Where is the hardship then, if no tyrant nor yet an unjust judge sends thee away from the state, but nature, who brought thee into it? the same as if a praetor who has employed an actor dismisses him from the stage.—"But I have not finished the five acts, but only three of them."—Thou sayest well, but in life the three acts are the whole drama; for what shall be a complete drama is determined by him who was once the cause of its composition, and now of its dissolution: but thou art the cause of neither. Depart then satisfied, for he also who releases thee is satisfied.

The Philosophy of Marcus Aurelius Antoninus

It has been said that the Stoic philosophy first showed its real value when it passed from Greece to Rome. The doctrines of Zeno and his successors were well suited to the gravity and practical good sense of the Romans; and even in the Republican period we have an example of a man, M. Cato Uticensis, who lived the life of a Stoic and died consistently with the opinions which he professed. He was a man, says Cicero, who embraced the Stoic philosophy from conviction; not for the purpose of vain discussion, as most did, but in order to make his life conformable to the Stoic precepts. In the wretched times from the death of Augustus to the murder of Domitian, there was nothing but the Stoic philosophy which could console and support the followers of the old religion under imperial tyranny and amidst universal corruption. There were even then noble minds that could dare and endure, sustained by a good conscience and an elevated idea of the purposes of man's existence. Such were Paetus Thrasea, Helvidius Priscus, Cornutus, C. Musonius Rufus, and the poets Persius and Juvenal, whose energetic language and manly thoughts may be as instructive to us now as they might have been to their contemporaries. Persius died under Nero's bloody reign; but Juvenal had the good fortune to survive the tyrant Domitian and to see the better times of Nerva, Trajan, and Hadrian. His best precepts are derived from the Stoic school, and they are enforced in his finest verses by the unrivalled vigor of the Latin language.

The best two expounders of the later Stoical philosophy were a Greek slave and a Roman emperor. Epictetus, a Phrygian Greek, was brought to Rome, we know not how, but he was there the slave and afterwards the freedman of his unworthy master, Epaphroditus. Like other great teachers he wrote nothing, and we are indebted to his grateful pupil Arrian for what we have of Epictetus' discourses. Arrian wrote eight books of the discourses of Epictetus, of which only four remain and some fragments. We have also from Arrian's hand the small Enchiridion or

Manual of the chief precepts of Epictetus. There is a valuable commentary on the Enchiridion by Simplicius, who lived in the time of the emperor Justinian.

Antoninus in his first book (I. 7), in which he gratefully commemorates his obligations to his teachers, says that he was made acquainted by Junius Rusticus with the discourses of Epictetus, whom he mentions also in other passages (IV. 41; XI. 34, 36). Indeed, the doctrines of Epictetus and Antoninus are the same, and Epictetus is the best authority for the explanation of the philosophical language of Antoninus and the exposition of his opinions. But the method of the two philosophers is entirely different. Epictetus addressed himself to his hearers in a continuous discourse and in a familiar and simple manner. Antoninus wrote down his reflections for his own use only, in short, unconnected paragraphs, which are often obscure.*

* The Stoics made three divisions of philosophy,—Physic, Ethic, and Logic (VIII. 13). This division, we are told by Diogenes, was made by Zeno of Citium, the founder of the Stoic sect, and by Chrysippus; but these philosophers placed the three divisions in the following order,—Logic, Physic, Ethic. It appears, however, that this division was made before Zeno's time, and acknowledged by Plato, as Cicero remarks. Logic is not synonymous with our term Logic in the narrower sense of that word.

Cleanthes, a Stoic, subdivided the three divisions, and made six,—Dialectic and Rhetoric, comprised in Logic; Ethic and Politic; Physic and Theology. This division was merely for practical use, for all Philosophy is one. Even among the earliest Stoics Logic, or Dialectic, does not occupy the same place as in Plato: it is considered only as an instrument which is to be used for the other divisions of Philosophy. An exposition of the earlier Stoic doctrines and of their modifications would require a volume. My object is to explain only the opinions of Antoninus, so far as they can be collected from his book.

According to the subdivision of Cleanthes, Physic and Theology go together, or the study of the nature of Things, and the study of the nature of the Deity, so far as man can understand the Deity, and of his government of the universe. This division or subdivision is not formally adopted by Antoninus, for, as already observed, there is no method in his book; but it is virtually contained in it.

Cleanthes also connects Ethic and Politic, or the study of the principles of morals and the study of the constitution of civil society; and undoubtedly he did well in subdividing Ethic into two parts, Ethic in the narrower sense and Politic; for though the two are intimately connected, they are also very distinct, and many questions can only be properly discussed by carefully observing the distinction. Antoninus does not treat of Politic. His subject is Ethic, and Ethic in its practical application to his own conduct in life as a man and as a governor. His Ethic is founded on his doctrines about man's nature, the Universal Nature, and the relation of every man to everything else. It is therefore intimately and inseparably connected with Physic, or the nature of Things, and with Theology, or the Nature of the Deity. He advises us to examine well all the impressions on our minds and to form a right judgment of them, to make just conclusions, and to inquire into the meaning of words, and so far to apply Dialectic; but he has no attempt at any exposition of Dialectic, and his philosophy is in substance purely moral and practical. He says, "Constantly and, if it be possible, on the occasion of every impression on the soul, apply

The want of arrangement in the original and of connection among the numerous paragraphs, the corruption of the text, the obscurity of the language and the style, and sometimes perhaps the confusion in the writer's own ideas,—besides all this, there is occasionally an apparent contradiction in the emperor's thoughts, as if his principles were sometimes unsettled, as if doubt sometimes clouded his mind. A man who leads a life of tranquillity and reflection, who is not disturbed at home and meddles not with the affairs of the world, may keep his mind at ease and his thoughts in one even course. But such a man has not been tried. All his Ethical philosophy and his passive virtue might turn out to be idle words, if he were once exposed to the rude realities of human existence. Fine thoughts and moral dissertations from men who have not worked and suffered may be read, but they will be forgotten. No religion, no Ethical philosophy is worth anything, if the teacher has not lived the "life of an apostle," and been ready to die "the death of a martyr." "Not in passivity (the passive affects) but in activity lie the evil and the good of the rational social animal, just as his virtue and his vice lie not in passivity, but in activity" (IX. 16). The emperor Antoninus was a practical moralist. From his youth he followed a laborious discipline, and though his high station placed him above all want or the fear of it, he lived as frugally and temperately as the poorest philosopher. Epictetus wanted little, and it seems that he always had the little that he wanted and he was content with it, as he had been with his servile station. But Antoninus after his accession to the empire sat on an uneasy seat. He had the administration of an empire which extended from the Euphrates to the Atlantic, from the cold mountains of Scotland to the hot sands of Africa; and we may imagine, though we cannot know it by experience, what must be the trials, the troubles, the anxiety, and the sorrows of him who has the world's business on his hands, with the wish to do the best that he can, and the certain knowledge that he can do very little of the good which he wishes.

In the midst of war, pestilence, conspiracy, general corruption, and with the

---

to it the principles of Physic, of Ethic, and of Dialectic": which is only another way of telling us to examine the impression in every possible way. In another passage (III. 11) he says, "To the aids which have been mentioned, let this one still be added: make for thyself a definition or description of the object which is presented to thee, so as to see distinctly what kind of a thing it is in its substance, in its nudity, in its complete entirety, and tell thyself its proper name, and the names of the things of which it has been compounded, and into which it will be resolved." Such an examination implies a use of Dialectic, which Antoninus accordingly employed as a means towards establishing his Physical, Theological, and Ethical principles.

weight of so unwieldy an empire upon him, we may easily comprehend that Antoninus often had need of all his fortitude to support him. The best and the bravest men have moments of doubt and of weakness; but if they are the best and the bravest, they rise again from their depression by recurring to first principles, as Antoninus does. The emperor says that life is smoke, a vapor, and St. James in his Epistle is of the same mind; that the world is full of envious, jealous, malignant people, and a man might be well content to get out of it. He has doubts perhaps sometimes even about that to which he holds most firmly. There are only a few passages of this kind, but they are evidence of the struggles which even the noblest of the sons of men had to maintain against the hard realities of his daily life. A poor remark it is which I have seen somewhere, and made in a disparaging way, that the emperor's reflections show that he had need of consolation and comfort in life, and even to prepare him to meet his death. True that he did need comfort and support, and we see how he found it. He constantly recurs to his fundamental principle that the universe is wisely ordered, that every man is a part of it and must conform to that order which he cannot change, that whatever the Deity has done is good, that all mankind are a man's brethren, that he must love and cherish them and try to make them better, even those who would do him harm. This is his conclusion (II. 17): "What then is that which is able to conduct a man? One thing and only one, Philosophy. But this consists in keeping the divinity within a man free from violence and unharmed, superior to pains and pleasures, doing nothing without a purpose nor yet falsely and with hypocrisy, not feeling the need of another man's doing or not doing anything; and besides, accepting all that happens and all that is allotted, as coming from thence, wherever it is, from whence he himself came; and finally waiting for death with a cheerful mind as being nothing else than a dissolution of the elements of which every living being is compounded. But if there is no harm to the elements themselves in each continually changing into another, why should a man have any apprehension about the change and dissolution of all the elements [himself]? for it is according to nature; and nothing is evil that is according to nature."

The Physic of Antoninus is the knowledge of the Nature of the Universe, of its government, and of the relation of man's nature to both. He names the universe (VI. 1), "the universal substance," and he adds that "reason" governs the universe. He also (VI. 9) uses the terms "universal nature" or "nature of the universe." He (VI. 25) calls the universe "the one and all, which we name Cosmos or Order." If he ever seems to use these general terms as significant of the All, of all that man can in any way conceive to exist, he still on other occasions plainly distinguishes between Matter, Material things, and Cause, Origin, Reason. This is conformable to Zeno's doctrine that there are two original principles of all things, that which acts and that which is acted upon. That which is acted on is the formless matter: that which acts is the reason, God, who is eternal and operates through all matter, and produces all things. So Antoninus (v. 32) speaks of the reason which pervades all substance, and through all time by fixed periods (revolutions) administers the universe. God is eternal, and Matter is eternal. It is God who gives form to matter, but he is not said to have created matter. According to this view, which is as old as Anaxagoras, God and matter exist independently, but God governs matter. This doctrine is simply the expression of the fact of the existence both of matter and of God. The Stoics did not perplex themselves with the insoluble question of the origin and nature of matter. Antoninus also assumes a beginning of things, as we now know them; but his language is sometimes very obscure.

Matter consists of elemental parts of which all material objects are made. But nothing is permanent in form. The nature of the universe, according to Antoninus' expression (IV. 36), "loves nothing so much as to change the things which are, and to make new things like them. For everything that exists is in a manner the seed of that which will be. But thou art thinking only of seeds which are cast into the earth or into a womb: but this is a very vulgar notion." All things then are in a constant flux and change: some things are dissolved into the elements, others come in their places; and so the "whole universe continues ever young and perfect."

When we look at the motions of the planets, the action of what we call gravitation, the elemental combination of unorganized bodies and their resolution, the production of plants and of living bodies, their generation, growth, and their dissolution, which we call their death, we observe a regular sequence of phenomena, which within the limits of experience present and past, so far as we know the past, is fixed and invariable. But if this is not so, if the order and sequence of phenomena, as known to us, are subject to change in the course of an infinite progression,—and such change is conceivable,—we have not discovered, nor shall we ever discover, the whole of the order and sequence of phenomena, in which sequence there may be involved according to its very nature, that is, according to its fixed order, some variation of what we now call the Order or Nature of Things. It is also conceivable that such changes have taken place,—changes in the order of things, as we are compelled by the imperfection of language to call them, but which are no changes; and further it is certain that our knowledge of the true sequence of all actual phenomena, as for instance the phenomena of generation, growth, and dissolution, is and ever must be imperfect.

We do not fare much better when we speak of Causes and Effects than when we speak of Nature. For the practical purposes of life we may use the terms cause and effect conveniently, and we may fix a distinct meaning to them, distinct enough at least to prevent all misunderstanding. But the case is different when we speak of causes and effects as of Things. All that we know is phenomena, as the Greeks called them, or appearances which follow one another in a regular order, as we conceive it, so that if some one phenomenon should fail in the series, we conceive that there must either be an interruption of the series, or that something else will appear after the phenomenon which has failed to appear, and will occupy the vacant place; and so the series in its progression may be modified or totally changed. Cause and effect then mean nothing in the sequence of natural phenomena beyond what I have said; and the real cause, or the transcendent cause, as some would call it, of each successive phenomenon is in that which is the cause of all things which are, which have been, and which will be forever. Thus the word Creation may have a real sense if we consider it as the first, if we can conceive a first, in the present order of natural phenomena; but in the vulgar sense a creation of all things at a certain time, followed by a quiescence of the first cause, and an abandonment of all sequences of Phenomena to the laws of Nature, or to the other words that people may use, is absolutely absurd.

Man being conscious that he is a spiritual power or an intellectual power, or that he has such a power, in whatever way he conceives that he has it,—for I wish simply to state a fact,—from this power which he has in himself, he is led, as Antoninus says, to believe that there is a greater power, which, as the old Stoics tell us, pervades the whole universe as the intellect pervades man.

God exists then, but what do we know of his nature? Antoninus says that the soul of man is an efflux from the divinity. We have bodies like animals, but we have reason, intelligence, as the gods. Animals have life and what we call instincts or natural principles of action: but the rational animal man alone has a rational, intelligent soul. Antoninus insists on this continually: God is in man, and so we must constantly attend to the divinity within us, for it is only in this way that we can have any knowledge of the nature of God. The human soul is in a sense a portion of the divinity, and the soul alone has any communication with the Deity; for as he says (XII. 2): "With his intellectual part alone God touches the intelligence only which has flowed and been derived from himself into these bodies." In fact he says that which is hidden within a man is life, that is the man himself. All the rest is vesture, covering, organs, instrument, which the living man, the real man, uses for the purpose of his present existence. The air is universally diffused for him who is able to respire; and so for him who is willing to partake of it the intelligent power, which holds within it all things, is diffused as wide and free as the air (viii. 54). It is by living a divine life that man approaches to a knowledge of the divinity. It is by following the divinity within, as Antoninus calls it, that man comes nearest to the Deity, the supreme good; for man can never attain to perfect agreement with his internal guide. "Live with the gods. And he does live with the gods who constantly shows to them that his own soul is satisfied with that which is assigned to him, and that it does all the daemon wishes, which Zeus hath given to every man for his guardian and guide, and a portion of himself. And this daemon is every man's understanding and reason" (v. 27).

There is in man, that is in the reason, the intelligence, a superior faculty which if it is exercised rules all the rest. A man must reverence only his ruling faculty and the divinity within him. As we must reverence that which is supreme in the universe, so we must reverence that which is supreme in ourselves; and this is that which is of like kind with that which is supreme in the universe (v. 21). Antoninus speaks of a man's condemnation of himself when the diviner part within him has been overpowered and yields to the less honorable and to the perishable part, the body, and its gross pleasures.

Antoninus did not view God and the material universe as the same, any more than he viewed the body and soul of man as one. Antoninus has no speculations on the absolute nature of the Deity. It was not his fashion to waste his time on what man cannot understand. He was satisfied that God exists, that he governs all things, that man can only have an imperfect knowledge of his nature, and he must attain this imperfect knowledge by reverencing the divinity which is within him, and keeping it pure.

From all that has been said, it follows that the universe is administered by the Providence of God and that all things are wisely ordered. There are passages in which Antoninus expresses doubts, or states different possible theories of the constitution and government of the universe; but he always recurs to his fundamental principle; that if we admit the existence of a deity, we must also admit that he orders all things wisely and well (iv. 27; vi. 1; ix. 28; xii. 5).

But if all things are wisely ordered, how is the world so full of what we call evil, physical and moral? If instead of saying that there is evil in the world, we use the expression which I have used, "what we call evil," we have partly anticipated the emperor's answer. We see and feel and know imperfectly very few things in the few years that we live, and all the knowledge and all the experience of all the human race is positive ignorance of the whole, which is infinite. Now, as our reason teaches us that everything is in some way related to and connected with every other thing, all notion of evil as being in the universe of things is a contradiction; for if the whole comes from and is governed by an intelligent being, it is impossible to conceive anything in it which tends to the evil or destruction of the whole (VIII. 55; X. 6).

Everything is in constant mutation, and yet the whole subsists. We might imagine the solar system resolved into its elemental parts, and yet the whole would still subsist "ever young and perfect."

All things, all forms, are dissolved and new forms appear. All living things undergo the change which we call death. If we call death an evil, then all change is an evil. Living beings also suffer pain, and man suffers most of all, for he suffers both in and by his body and by his intelligent part. Men suffer also from one another, and perhaps the largest part of human suffering comes to man from those whom he calls his brothers. Antoninus says, (VIII. 55) "Generally, wickedness does no harm at all to the universe; and particularly, the wickedness [of one man] does no harm to another. It is only harmful to him who has it in his power to be released from it as soon as he shall choose." The first part of this is perfectly consistent with the doctrine that the whole can sustain no evil or harm. The second part must be explained by the Stoic principle that there is no evil in anything which is not in our power. What wrong we suffer from another is his evil, not ours. But this is an admission that there is evil in a sort, for he who does wrong does evil, and if others can endure the wrong, still there is evil in the wrong-doer. Antoninus (XI. 18) gives many excellent precepts with respect to wrongs and injuries, and his precepts are practical. He teaches us to bear what we cannot avoid, and his lessons may be just as useful to him who denies the being and the government of God as to him who believes in both. There is no direct answer in Antoninus to the objections which may be made to the existence and providence of God because of the moral disorder and suffering which are in the world, except this answer which he makes in reply to the supposition that even the best men may be extinguished by death. He says if it is so, we may be sure that if it ought to have been otherwise, the gods would have ordered it otherwise (XII. 5). His conviction of the wisdom which we may observe in the government of the world is too strong to be disturbed by any apparent irregularities in the order of things. That these disorders exist is a fact, and those who would conclude from them against the being and government of God conclude too hastily. We all admit that there is an order in the material world, a constitution, a system, a relation of parts to one another and a fitness of the whole for something. So in the constitution of plants and of animals there is an order, a fitness for some end. Sometimes the order, as we conceive it, is interrupted and the end, as we conceive it, is not attained. The seed, the plant, or the animal sometimes perishes before it has passed through all its changes and done all its uses. It is according to Nature, that is a fixed order, for some to perish early and for others to do all their uses and leave successors to take their place. So man has a corporeal and intellectual and moral constitution fit for certain uses, and on the whole man performs these uses, dies, and leaves other men in his place. So society exists, and a social state is manifestly the natural state of man,—the state for which his nature fits him, and society amidst innumerable irregularities and disorders still subsists; and perhaps we may say that the history of the past and our present knowledge give us a reasonable hope that its disorders will diminish, and that order, its governing principle may be more firmly established. As order then, a fixed order, we may say, subject to deviations real or apparent, must be admitted to exist in the whole nature of things, that which we call disorder or evil, as it seems to us, does not in any way alter the fact of the general constitution of things having a nature or fixed order. Nobody will conclude from the existence of disorder that order is not the rule, for the existence of order both physical and moral is proved by daily experience and all past experience. We cannot conceive how the order of the universe is maintained: we cannot even conceive how our own life from day to day is continued, nor how we perform the simplest movements of the body, nor how we grow and think and act, though we know many of the conditions which are necessary for all these functions. Knowing nothing then of the unseen power which acts in ourselves except by what is done, we know nothing of the power which acts through what we call all time and all space; but seeing that there is a nature or fixed order in all things known to us, it is conformable to the nature of our minds to believe that this universal Nature has a cause which operates continually, and that we are totally unable to speculate on the reason of any of those disorders or evils which we perceive. This I believe is the answer which may be collected from all that Antoninus has said.

The origin of evil is an old question. Achilles tells Priam that Zeus has two casks, one filled with good things, and the other with bad, and that he gives to men out of each according to his pleasure; and so we must be content, for we cannot alter the will of Zeus. One of the Greek commentators asks how must we reconcile this doctrine with what we find in the first book of the Odyssey, where the king of the gods says, "Men say that evil comes to them from us, but they bring it on themselves through their own folly." The answer is plain enough even to the Greek commentator. The poets make both Achilles and Zeus speak appropriately to their several characters. Indeed, Zeus says plainly that men do attribute their sufferings to the gods, but they do it falsely, for they are the cause of their own sorrows.

Epictetus in his Enchiridion makes short work of the question of evil. He says, "As a mark is not set up for the purpose of missing it, so neither does the nature of evil exist in the universe." This will appear obscure enough to those who are not acquainted with Epictetus, but he always knows what he is talking about. We do not set up a mark in order to miss it, though we may miss it. God, whose existence Epictetus assumes, has not ordered all things so that his purpose shall fail. Whatever there may be of what we call evil, the nature of evil, as he expresses it, does not exist; that is, evil is not a part of the constitution or nature of things. If there were a principle of evil in the constitution of things, evil would no longer be evil, as Simplicius argues, but evil would be good.

One passage more will conclude this matter. It contains all that the emperor could say: "To go from among men, if there are gods, is not a thing to be afraid of, for the gods will not involve thee in evil; but if indeed they do not exist, or if they have no concern about human affairs, what is it to me to live in a universe devoid of gods or devoid of providence? But in truth they do exist, and they do care for human things, and they have put all the means in man's power to enable him not to fall into real evils. And as to the rest, if there was anything evil, they would have provided for this also, that it should be altogether in a man's power not to fall into it. But that which does not make a man worse, how can it make a man's life worse? But neither through ignorance, nor having the knowledge but not the power to guard against or correct these things, is it possible that the nature of the universe has overlooked them; nor is it possible that it has made so great a mistake, either through want of power or want of skill, that good and evil should happen indiscriminately to the good and the bad. But death certainly and life, honor and dishonor, pain and pleasure, all these things equally happen to good and bad men, being things which make us neither better nor worse. Therefore they are neither good nor evil."

The Ethical part of Antoninus' Philosophy follows from his general principles. The end of all his philosophy is to live conformably to Nature, both a man's own nature and the nature of the universe. Bishop Butler has explained what the Greek philosophers meant when they spoke of living according to Nature, and he says that when it is explained, as he has explained it and as they understood it, it is, "a manner of speaking not loose and undeterminate, but clear and distinct, strictly just and true." To live according to Nature is to live according to a man's whole nature, not according to a part of it, and to reverence the divinity within him as the governor of all his actions. "To the rational animal the same act is according to nature and according to reason." That which is done contrary to reason is also an act contrary to nature, to the whole nature, though it is certainly conformable to some part of man's nature, or it could not be done. Man is made for action, not for idleness or pleasure. As plants and animals do the uses of their nature, so man must do his (v. 1).

Man must also live conformably to the universal nature, conformably to the nature of all things of which he is one; and as a citizen of a political community he must direct his life and actions with reference to those among whom, and for whom, among other purposes, he lives. A man must not retire into solitude and cut himself off from his fellow-men. He must be ever active to do his part in the great whole. All men are his kin, not only in blood, but still more by participating in the same intelligence and by being a portion of the same divinity. A man cannot really be injured by his brethren, for no act of theirs can make him bad, and he must not be angry with them nor hate them: "For we are made for co-operation, like feet, like hands, like eyelids, like the rows of the upper and lower teeth. To act against one another then is contrary to nature; and it is acting against one another to be vexed and to turn away" (II. 1).

Further he says: "Take pleasure in one thing, and rest in it in passing from one social act to another social act, thinking of God" (VI. 7). Again: "Love mankind. Follow God" (VII. 31). It is the characteristic of the rational soul for a man to love his neighbor (XI. 1). Antoninus teaches in various passages the forgiveness of injuries, and we know that he also practiced what he taught. Bishop Butler remarks that "this divine precept to forgive injuries and to love our enemies, though to be met with in Gentile moralists, yet is in a peculiar sense a precept of Christianity, as our Saviour has insisted more upon it than on any other single virtue." The practise of this precept is the most difficult of all virtues. Antoninus often enforces it and gives us aid towards following it. When we are injured, we feel anger and resentment, and the feeling is natural, just, and useful for the conservation of society. It is useful that wrong-doers should feel the natural consequences of their actions, among which is the disapprobation of society and the resentment of him who is wronged. But revenge, in the proper sense of that word, must not be practiced. "The best way of avenging thyself," says the emperor, "is not to become like the wrongdoer." It is plain by this that he does not mean that we should in any case practise revenge; but he says to those who talk of revenging wrongs, "Be not like him who has done the wrong. When a man has done thee any wrong, immediately consider with what opinion about good or evil he has done wrong. For when thou hast seen this, thou wilt pity him, and wilt neither wonder nor be angry" (VII. 26). Antoninus would not deny that wrong naturally produces the feeling of anger and resentment, for this is implied in the recommendation to reflect on the nature of the man's mind who has done the wrong, and then you will have pity instead of resentment; and so it comes to the same as St. Paul's advice to be angry and sin not; which, as Butler well explains it, is not a recommendation to be angry, which nobody needs, for anger is a natural passion, but it is a warning against allowing anger to lead us into sin. In short the emperor's doctrine about wrongful acts is this: wrong-doers do not know what good and bad are: they offend out of ignorance, and in the sense of the Stoics this is true. Though this kind of ignorance will never be admitted as a legal excuse, and ought not to be admitted as a full excuse in any way by society, there may be grievous injuries, such as it is in a man's power to forgive without harm to society; and if he forgives because he sees that his enemies know not what they do, he is acting in the spirit of the sublime prayer, "Father, forgive them, for they know not what they do."

The emperor's moral philosophy was not a feeble, narrow system, which teaches a man to look directly to his own happiness, though a man's happiness or tranquillity is indirectly promoted by living as he ought to do. A man must live conformably to the universal nature, which means, as the emperor explains it in many passages, that a man's actions must be conformable to his true relations to all other human beings, both as a citizen of a political community and as a member of the whole human family. This implies, and he often expresses it in the most forcible language, that a man's words and action, so far as they affect others, must be measured by a fixed rule, which is their consistency with the conservation and the interests of the particular society of which he is a member, and of the whole human race. To live conformably to such a rule, a man must use his rational faculties in order to discern clearly the consequences and full effect of all his actions and of the actions of others: he must not live a life of contemplation and reflection only, though he must often retire within himself to calm and purify his soul by thought, but he must mingle in the work of man and be a fellow-laborer for the general good.

A man should have an object or purpose in life, that he may direct all his energies to it; of course a good object (II. 7). He who has not one object or purpose of life, cannot be one and the same all through his life (XI. 21). Bacon has a remark to the same effect, on the best means of "reducing of the mind unto virtue and good estate; which is, the electing and propounding unto a man's self good and virtuous ends of his life, such as may be in a reasonable sort within his compass to attain." He is a happy man who has been wise enough to do this when he was young and has had the opportunities; but the emperor seeing well that a man cannot always be so wise in his youth, encourages himself to do it when he can, and not to let life slip away before he has begun. He who can propose to himself good and virtuous ends of life, and be true to them, cannot fail to live conformably to his own interest and the universal interest, for in the nature of things they are one. If a thing is not good for the hive, it is not good for the bee (VI. 54).

One passage may end this matter. "If the gods have determined about me and about the things which must happen to me, they have determined well, for it is not easy even to imagine a deity without forethought; and as to doing me harm, why should they have any desire towards that? For what advantage would result to them from this or to the whole, which is the special object of their providence? But if they have not determined about me individually, they have certainly determined about the whole at least; and the things which happen by way of sequence in this general arrangement I ought to accept with pleasure and to be content with them. But if they determine about nothing—which it is wicked to believe, or if we do believe it, let us neither sacrifice nor pray nor swear by them, nor do anything else which we do as if the gods were present and lived with us; but if however the gods determine about none of the things which concern us, I am able to determine about myself, and I can inquire about that which is useful; and that is useful to every man which is conformable to his own constitution and nature. But my nature is rational and social; and my city and country, so far as I am Antoninus, is Rome; but so far as I am a man, it is the world."

It would be tedious, and it is not necessary to state the emperor's opinions on all the ways in which a man may profitably use his understanding towards perfecting himself in practical virtue. The passages to this purpose are in all parts of his book, but as they are in no order or connection, a man must use the book a long time before he will find out all that is in it. A few words may be added here. If we analyze all other things, we find how insufficient they are for human life, and how truly worthless many of them are. Virtue alone is indivisible, one, and perfectly satisfying. The notion of Virtue cannot be considered vague or unsettled, because a man may find it difficult to explain the notion fully to himself, or to expound it to others in such a way as to prevent cavilling. Virtue is a whole, and no more consists of parts than man's intelligence does; and yet we speak of various intellectual faculties as a convenient way of expressing the various powers which man's intellect shows by his works. In the same way we may speak of various virtues or parts of virtue, in a practical sense, for the purpose of showing what particular virtues we ought to practise in order to the exercise of the whole of virtue, that is, as much as man's nature is capable of.

The prime principle in man's constitution is social. The next in order is not to yield to the persuasions of the body, when they are not conformable to the rational principle, which must govern. The third is freedom from error and from deception. "Let then the ruling principle holding fast to these things go straight on and it has what is its own" (VII. 53). The emperor selects justice as the virtue which is the basis of all the rest (X. 11), and this had been said long before his time.

It is true that all people have some notion of what is meant by justice as a disposition of the mind, and some notion about acting in conformity to this disposition; but experience shows that men's notions about justice are as confused as their actions are inconsistent with the true notion of justice. The emperor's notion of justice is clear enough, but not practical enough for all mankind. "Let there be freedom from perturbations with respect to the things which come from the external cause; and let there be justice in the things done by virtue of the internal cause, that is, let there be movement and action terminating in this, in social acts, for this is according to thy nature" (IX. 31). In another place (IX. 1) he says that "he who acts unjustly acts impiously," which follows of course from all that he says in various places. He insists on the practice of truth as a virtue and as a means to virtue, which no doubt it is: for lying even in indifferent things weakens the understanding; and lying maliciously is as great a moral offence as a man can be guilty of, viewed both as showing an habitual disposition, and viewed with respect to consequences. He couples the notion of justice with action. A man must not pride himself on having some fine notion of justice in his head, but he must exhibit his justice in act.

The Stoics, and Antoninus among them, call some things beautiful and some ugly, and as they are beautiful so they are good, and as they are ugly so they are evil, or bad (II. 1). All these things, good and evil, are in our power, absolutely some of the stricter Stoics would say; in a manner only, as those who would not depart altogether from common sense would say; practically they are to a great degree in the power of some persons and in some circumstances, but in a small degree only in other persons and in other circumstances. The Stoics maintain man's free will as to the things which are in his power; for as to the things which are out of his power, free will terminating in action is of course excluded by the very terms of the expression. I hardly know if we can discover exactly Antoninus' notion of the free will of man, nor is the question worth the inquiry. What he does mean and does say is intelligible. All the things which are not in our power are indifferent: they are neither good nor bad, morally. Such are life, health, wealth, power, disease, poverty, and death. Life and death are all men's portion. Health, wealth, power, disease, and poverty happen to men, indifferently to the good and to the bad; to those who live according to nature and to those who do not. "Life," says the emperor, "is a warfare and a stranger's sojourn, and after fame is oblivion" (II. 17). After speaking of those men who have disturbed the world and then died, and of the death of philosophers such as Heraclitus, and Democritus, who was destroyed by lice, and of Socrates whom other lice (his enemies) destroyed, he says: "What means all this? Thou hast embarked, thou hast made the voyage, thou art come to shore; get out. If indeed to another life, there is no want of gods, not even there. But if to a state without sensation, thou wilt cease to be held by pains and pleasures, and to be a slave to the vessel which is as much inferior as that which serves it is superior: for the one is intelligence and Deity; the other is earth and corruption" (III. 3). It is not death that a man should fear, but he should fear never beginning to live according to nature (XII. 1). Every man should live in such a way as to discharge his duty, and to trouble himself about nothing else. He should live such a life that he shall always be ready for death, and shall depart content when the summons comes. For what is death? "A cessation of the impressions through the senses, and of the pulling of the strings which move the appetites, and of the discursive movements of the thoughts, and of the service to the flesh" (VI. 28). Death is such as generation is, a mystery of nature (IV. 5). In another passage (IX. 3), the exact meaning of which is perhaps doubtful, he speaks of the child which leaves the womb, and so he says the soul at death leaves its envelope.

Antoninus' opinion of a future life is nowhere clearly expressed. His doctrine of the nature of the soul of necessity implies that it does not perish absolutely, for a portion of the divinity cannot perish. The opinion is at least as old as the time of Epicharmus and Euripides; what comes from earth goes back to earth, and what comes from heaven, the divinity, returns to him who gave it. But I find nothing clear in Antoninus as to the notion of the man existing after death so as to be conscious of his sameness with that soul which occupied his vessel of clay. He seems to be perplexed on this matter, and finally to have rested in this, that God or the gods will do whatever is best, and consistent with the university of things.

Nor, I think, does he speak conclusively on another Stoic doctrine, which some Stoics practiced,—the anticipating the regular course of nature by a man's own act. The reader will find some passages in which this is touched on, and he may make of them what he can. But there are passages in which the emperor encourages himself to wait for the end patiently and with tranquillity; and certainly it is consistent with all his best teaching that a man should bear all that falls to his lot and do useful acts as long as he lives. He should not therefore abridge the time of his usefulness by his own act.

Happiness was not the direct object of a Stoic's life. There is no rule of life contained in the precept that a man should pursue his own happiness. Many men think that they are seeking happiness when they are only seeking the gratification of some particular passion, the strongest that they have. The end of a man is, as already explained, to live conformably to nature, and he will thus obtain happiness, tranquillity of mind, and contentment (III. 12; VIII. 2). As a means of living conformably to nature he must study the four chief virtues, each of which has its proper sphere: wisdom, or the knowledge of good and evil; justice, or the giving to every man his due; fortitude, or the enduring of labor and pain; and temperance, which is moderation in all things. By thus living conformably to nature the Stoic obtained all that he wished or expected. His reward was in his virtuous life, and he was satisfied with that.

Epictetus and Antoninus both by precept and example labored to improve themselves and others; and if we discover imperfections in their teaching, we must still honor these great men who attempted to show that there is in man's nature and in the constitution of things sufficient reason for living a virtuous life. It is difficult enough to live as we ought to live, difficult even for any man to live in such a way as to satisfy himself, if he exercises only in a moderate degree the power of reflecting upon and reviewing his own conduct; and if all men cannot be brought to the same opinions in morals and religion, it is at least worth while to give them good reasons for as much as they can be persuaded to accept.

EPICTETUS

The Golden Sayings

Translated by Hastings Crossley

Contents

Section 1

1

Are these the only works of Providence within us? What words suffice to praise or set them forth? Had we but understanding, should we ever cease hymning and blessing the Divine Power, both openly and in secret, and telling of His gracious gifts? Whether digging or ploughing or eating, should we not sing the hymn to God:—Great is God, for that He hath given us such instruments to till the ground withal: Great is God, for that He hath given us hands and the power of swallowing and digesting; of unconsciously growing and breathing while we sleep! Thus should we ever have sung; yea and this, the grandest and divinest hymn of all:—Great is God, for that He hath given us a mind to apprehend these things, and duly to use them! What then! seeing that most of you are blinded, should there not be some one to fill this place, and sing the hymn to God on behalf of all men? What else can I that am old and lame do but sing to God? Were I a nightingale, I should do after the manner of a nightingale. Were I a swan, I should do after the manner of a swan. But now, since I am a reasonable being, I must sing to God: that is my work: I do it, nor will I desert this my post, as long as it is granted me to hold it; and upon you too I call to join in this self–same hymn.

2

How then do men act? As though one returning to his country who had sojourned for the night in a fair inn, should be so captivated thereby as to take up his abode there. "Friend, thou hast forgotten thine intention! This was not thy destination, but only lay on the way thither." "Nay, but it is a proper place." "And how many more of the sort there may be; only to pass through upon thy way! Thy purpose was to return to thy country; to relieve thy kinsmen's fears for thee; thyself to discharge the duties of a citizen; to marry a wife, to beget offspring, and to fill the appointed round of office. Thou didst not come to choose out what places are most pleasant; but rather to return to that wherein thou wast born and where wert appointed to be a citizen."

3

Try to enjoy the great festival of life with other men.

4

But I have one whom I must please, to whom I must be subject, whom I must obey:—God, and those who come next to Him. He hath entrusted me with myself: He hath made my will subject to myself alone and given me rules for the right use thereof.

5

Rufus used to say, If you have leisure to praise me, what I say is naught. In truth he spoke in such wise, that each of us who sat there, though that some one had accused him to Rufus:—so surely did he lay his finger on the very deeds we did: so surely display the faults of each before his very eyes.

6

But what saith God?—"Had it been possible, Epictetus, I would have made both that body of thine and thy possessions free and unimpeded, but as it is, be not deceived:—it is not thine own; it is but finely tempered clay. Since then this I could not do, I have given thee a portion of Myself, in the power of desiring and declining and of pursuing and avoiding, and is a word the power of dealing with the things of sense. And if thou neglect not this, but place all that thou hast therein, thou shalt never be let or hindered; thou shalt never lament; thou shalt not blame or flatter any. What then? Seemth this to thee a little thing?"—God forbid!—"Be content then therewith!" And so I pray the Gods.

7

What saith Antisthenes? Hast thou never heard?—It is a kingly thing, O Cyrus, to do well and to be evil spoken of.

8

"Aye, but to debase myself thus were unworthy of me." "That," said Epictetus, "is for you to consider, not for me. You know yourself what you are worth in your own eyes; and at what price you will sell yourself. For men sell themselves at various prices. This was why, when Florus was deliberating whether he should appear at Nero's shows, taking part in the performance himself, Agrippinus replied, 'But why do not you appear?' he answered, 'Because I do not even consider the question.' For the man who has once stooped to consider such questions, and to reckon up the value of external things, is not far from forgetting what manner of man he is. Why, what is it that you ask me? Is death preferable, or life? I reply, Life. Pain or pleasure? I reply, Pleasure." "Well, but if I do not act, I shall lose my head." "Then go and act! But for my part I will not act." "Why?" "Because you think yourself but one among the many threads which make up the texture of the doublet. You should aim at being like men in general—just as your thread has no ambition either to be anything distinguished compared with the other threads. But I desire to be the purple—that small and shining part which makes the rest seem fair and beautiful. Why then do you bid me become even as the multitude? Then were I no longer the purple."

9

If a man could be thoroughly penetrated, as he ought, with this thought, that we are all in an especial manner sprung from God, and that God is the Father of men as well as of Gods, full surely he would never conceive aught ignoble or base of himself. Whereas if Caesar were to adopt you, your haughty looks would be intolerable;

will you not be elated at knowing that you are the son of God? Now however it is not so with us: but seeing that in our birth these two things are commingled—the body which we share with the animals, and the Reason and Thought which we share with the Gods, many decline towards this unhappy kinship with the dead, few rise to the blessed kinship with the Divine. Since then every one must deal with each thing according to the view which he forms about it, those few who hold that they are born for fidelity, modesty, and unerring sureness in dealing with the things of sense, never conceive aught base or ignoble of themselves: but the multitude the contrary. Why, what am I?—A wretched human creature; with this miserable flesh of mine. Miserable indeed! but you have something better than that paltry flesh of yours. Why then cling to the one, and neglect the other?

10

Thou art but a poor soul laden with a lifeless body.

11

The other day I had an iron lamp placed beside my household gods. I heard a noise at the door and on hastening down found my lamp carried off. I reflected that the culprit was in no very strange case. "Tomorrow, my friend," I said, "you will find an earthenware lamp; for a man can only lose what he has."

12

The reason why I lost my lamp was that the thief was superior to me in vigilance. He paid however this price for the lamp, that in exchange for it he consented to become a thief: in exchange for it, to become faithless.

13

But God hath introduced Man to be a spectator of Himself and of His works; and not a spectator only, but also an interpreter of them. Wherefore it is a shame for man to begin and to leave off where the brutes do. Rather he should begin there, and leave off where Nature leaves off in us: and that is at contemplation, and understanding, and a manner of life that is in harmony with herself. See then that ye die not without being spectators of these things.

14

You journey to Olympia to see the work of Phidias; and each of you holds it a misfortune not to have beheld these things before you die. Whereas when there is no need even to take a journey, but you are on the spot, with the works before you, have you no care to contemplate and study these? Will you not then perceive either who you are or unto what end you were born: or for what purpose the power of contemplation has been bestowed on you? "Well, but in life there are some things disagreeable and hard to bear." And are there none at Olympia? Are you not scorched by the heat? Are you not cramped for room? Have you not to bathe with discomfort? Are you not drenched when it rains? Have you not to endure the clamor and shouting and such annoyances as these? Well, I suppose you set all this over against the splendour of the spectacle and bear it patiently. What then? have you not received greatness of heart, received courage, received fortitude? What care I, if I am great of heart, for aught that can come to pass? What shall cast me down or disturb me? What shall seem painful? Shall I not use the power to the end for which I received it, instead of moaning and wailing over what comes to pass?

15

If what philosophers say of the kinship of God and Man be true, what remains for men to do but as Socrates did:—never, when asked one's country, to answer, "I am an Athenian or a Corinthian," but "I am a citizen of the world."

16

He that hath grasped the administration of the World, who hath learned that this Community, which consists of God and men, is the foremost and mightiest and most comprehensive of all:—that from God have descended the germs of life, not to my father only and father's father, but to all things that are born and grow upon the earth, and in an especial manner to those endowed with Reason (for those only are by their nature fitted to hold communion with God, being by means of Reason conjoined with Him)—why should not such an one call himself a citizen of the world? Why not a son of God? Why should he fear aught that comes to pass among men? Shall kinship with Caesar, or any other of the great at Rome, be enough to hedge men around with safety and consideration, without a thought of apprehension: while to have God for our Maker, and Father, and Kinsman, shall not this set us free from sorrows and fears?

17

I do not think that an old fellow like me need have been sitting here to try and prevent your entertaining abject notions of yourselves, and talking of yourselves in an abject and ignoble way: but to prevent there being by chance among you any such young men as, after recognising their kindred to the Gods, and their bondage in these chains of the body and its manifold necessities, should desire to cast them off as burdens too grievous to be borne, and depart their true kindred. This is the struggle in which your Master and Teacher, were he worthy of the name, should be engaged. You would come to me and say: "Epictetus, we can no longer endure being chained to this wretched body, giving food and drink and rest and purification: aye, and for its sake forced to be subservient to this man and that. Are these not things indifferent and nothing to us? Is it not true that death is no evil? Are we not in a manner kinsmen of the Gods, and have we not come from them? Let us depart thither, whence we came: let us be freed from these chains that confine and press us down. Here are thieves and robbers and tribunals: and they that are called tyrants, who deem that they have after a fashion power over us, because of the miserable body and what appertains to it. Let us show them that they have power over none."

18

And to this I reply:—"Friends, wait for God. When He gives the signal, and releases you from this service, then depart to Him. But for the present, endure to dwell in the place wherein He hath assigned you your post. Short indeed is the time of your habitation therein, and easy to those that are minded. What tyrant, what robber, what tribunals have any terrors for those who thus esteem the body and all that belong to it as of no account? Stay; depart not rashly hence!"

19

Something like that is what should pass between a teacher and ingenuous youths. As it is, what does pass? The teacher is a lifeless body, and you are lifeless bodies yourselves. When you have had enough to eat today, you sit down and weep about tomorrow's food. Slave! if you have it, well and good; if not, you will depart: the door is open—why lament? What further room is there for tears? What further occasion for flattery? Why should one envy another? Why should you stand in awe of them that have much or are placed in power, especially if they be also strong and passionate? Why, what should they do to us? What they can do, we will not regard: what does concern us, that they cannot do. Who then shall rule one that is thus minded?

20

Seeing this then, and noting well the faculties which you have, you should say,—"Send now, O God, any trial that Thou wilt; lo, I have means and powers given me by Thee to acquit myself with honour through whatever comes to pass!"—No; but there you sit, trembling for fear certain things should come to pass, and moaning and groaning and lamenting over what does come to pass. And then you upbraid the Gods. Such meanness of spirit can have but one result—impiety. Yet God has not only given us these faculties by means of which we may bear everything that comes to pass without being crushed or depressed thereby; but like a good King and Father, He has given us this without let or hindrance, placed wholly at our own disposition, without reserving to Himself any power of impediment or restraint. Though possessing all these things free and all you own, you do not use them! you do not perceive what it is you have received nor whence it comes, but sit moaning and groaning; some of you blind to the Giver, making no acknowledgment to your Benefactor; others basely giving themselves to complaints and accusations against God. Yet what faculties and powers you possess for attaining courage and greatness of heart, I can easily show you; what you have for upbraiding and accusation, it is for you to show me!

21

How did Socrates bear himself in this regard? How else than as became one who was fully assured that he was the kinsman of Gods?

22

If God had made that part of His own nature which He severed from Himself and gave to us, liable to be hindered or constrained either by Himself or any other, He would not have been God, nor would He have been taking care of us as He ought. . . . If you choose, you are free; if you choose, you need blame no man—accuse no man. All things will be at once according to your mind and according to the Mind of God.

23

Petrifaction is of two sorts. There is petrifaction of the understanding; and also of the sense of shame. This happens when a man obstinately refuses to acknowledge plain truths, and persists in maintaining what is self-contradictory. Most of us dread mortification of the body, and would spare no pains to escape anything of that kind. But of mortification of the soul we are utterly heedless. With regard, indeed, to the soul, if a man is in such a state as to be incapable of following or understanding anything, I grant you we do think him in a bad way. But mortification of the sense of shame and modesty we go so far as to dub strength of mind!

24

If we were as intent upon our business as the old fellows at Rome are upon what interests them, we too might perhaps accomplish something. I know a man older than I am, now Superintendent of the Corn-market at Rome, and I remember when he passed through this place on his way back from exile, what an account he gave me of his former life, declaring that for the future, once home again, his only care should be to pass his remaining years in quiet and tranquility. "For how few years have I left!" he cried. "That," I said, "you will not do; but the moment the scent of Rome is in your nostrils, you will forget it all; and if you can but gain admission to Court, you will be glad enough to elbow your way in, and thank God for it." "Epictetus," he replied, "if ever you find me setting as much as one foot within the Court, think what you will of me." Well, as it was, what did he do? Ere ever he entered the city, he was met by a despatch from the Emperor. He took it, and forgot the whole of his resolutions. From that moment, he has been piling one thing upon another. I should like to be beside him to remind him of what he said when passing this way, and to add, How much better a prophet I am than you! What then? do I say man is not made for an active life? Far from it! . . . But there is a great difference between other men's occupations and ours. . . . A glance at theirs will make it clear to you. All day long they do nothing but calculate, contrive, consult how to wring their profit out of food-stuffs, farm-plots and the like. . . . Whereas, I entreat you to learn what the administration of the World is, and what place a Being endowed with reason holds therein: to consider what you are yourself, and wherein your Good and Evil consists.

25

A man asked me to write to Rome on his behalf who, as most people thought, had met with misfortune; for having been before wealthy and distinguished, he had afterwards lost all and was living here. So I wrote about him in a humble style. He however on reading the letter returned it to me, with the words: "I asked for your help, not for your pity. No evil has happened unto me."

26

True instruction is this:—to learn to wish that each thing should come to pass as it does. And how does it come to pass? As the Disposer has disposed it. Now He has disposed that there should be summer and winter, and plenty and dearth, and vice and virtue, and all such opposites, for the harmony of the whole.

27

Have this thought ever present with thee, when thou losest any outward thing, what thou gainest in its stead; and if this be the more precious, say not, I have suffered loss.

28

Concerning the Gods, there are who deny the very existence of the Godhead; others say that it exists, but neither bestirs nor concerns itself nor has forethought for anything. A third party attribute to it existence and forethought, but only for great and heavenly matters, not for anything that is on earth. A fourth party admit things on earth as well as in heaven, but only in general, and not with respect to each individual. A fifth, of whom were Ulysses and Socrates are those that cry:—I move not without Thy knowledge!

29

Considering all these things, the good and true man submits his judgment to Him that administers the Universe, even as good citizens to the law of the State. And he that is being instructed should come thus minded:—How may I in all things follow the Gods; and, How may I rest satisfied with the Divine Administration; and, How may I become free? For he is free for whom all things come to pass according to his will, and whom none can hinder. What then, is freedom madness? God forbid. For madness and freedom exist not together. "But I wish all that I desire to come to pass and in the manner that I desire."—You are mad, you are beside yourself. Know you not that Freedom is a glorious thing and of great worth? But that what I desired at random I should wish at random to come to pass, so far from being noble, may well be exceeding base.

30

You must know that it is no easy thing for a principle to become a man's own, unless each day he maintain it and hear it maintained, as well as work it out in life.

31

You are impatient and hard to please. If alone, you call it solitude: if in the company of men, you dub them conspirators and thieves, and find fault with your very parents, children, brothers, and neighbours. Whereas when by yourself you should have called it Tranquillity and Freedom: and herein deemed yourself like unto the Gods. And when in the company of many, you should not have called it a wearisome crowd and tumult, but an assembly and a tribunal; and thus accepted all with contentment.

32

What then is the chastisement of those who accept it not? To be as they are. Is any discontented with being alone? let him be in solitude. Is any discontented with his parents? let him be a bad son, and lament. Is any discontented with his children? let him be a bad father.—"Throw him into prison!"—What prison?—Where he is already: for he is there against his will; and wherever a man is against his will, that to him is a prison. Thus Socrates was not in prison, since he was there with his own consent.

33

Knowest thou what a speck thou art in comparison with the Universe?—That is, with respect to the body; since with respect to Reason, thou art not inferior to the Gods, nor less than they. For the greatness of Reason is not measured by length or height, but by the resolves of the mind. Place then thy happiness in that wherein thou art equal to the Gods.

34

Asked how a man might eat acceptably to the Gods, Epictetus replied:—If when he eats, he can be just, cheerful, equable, temperate, and orderly, can he not thus eat acceptably to the Gods? But when you call for warm water, and your slave does not answer, or when he answers brings it lukewarm, or is not even found to be in the house at all, then not to be vexed nor burst with anger, is not that acceptable to the Gods? "But how can one endure such people?" Slave, will you not endure your own brother, that has God to his forefather, even as a son sprung from the same stock, and of the same high descent as yourself? And if you are stationed in a high position, are you therefor forthwith set up for a tyrant? Remember who you are, and whom you rule, that they are by nature your kinsmen, your brothers, the offspring of God. "But I paid a price for them, not they for me." Do you see whither you are looking—down to the earth, to the pit, to those despicable laws of the dead? But to the laws of the Gods you do not look.

35

When we are invited to a banquet, we take what is set before us; and were one to call upon his host to set fish upon the table or sweet things, he would be deemed absurd. Yet in a word, we ask the Gods for what they do not give; and that, although they have given us so many things!

36

Asked how a man might convince himself that every single act of his was under the eye of God, Epictetus answered:—"Do you not hold that things on earth and things in heaven are continuous and in unison with each other?" "I do," was the reply. "Else how should the trees so regularly, as though by God's command, at His bidding flower; at His bidding send forth shoots, bear fruit and ripen it; at His bidding let it fall and shed their leaves, and folded up upon themselves lie in quietness and rest? How else, as the Moon waxes and wanes, as the Sun approaches and recedes, can it be that such vicissitude and alternation is seen in earthly things? "If then all things that grow, nay, our own bodies, are thus bound up with the whole, is not this still truer of our souls? And if our souls are bound up and in contact with God, as being very parts and fragments plucked from Himself, shall He not feel every movement of theirs as though it were His own, and belonging to His own nature?"

37

"But," you say, "I cannot comprehend all this at once." "Why, who told you that your powers were equal to God's?" Yet God hath placed by the side of each a man's own Guardian Spirit, who is charged to watch over him—a Guardian who sleeps not nor is deceived. For to what better or more watchful Guardian could He have committed watch of us? So when you have shut the doors and made a darkness within, remember never to say that you are alone; for you are not alone, but God is within, and your Guardian Spirit, and what light do they need to behold what you do? To this God you also should have sworn allegiance, even as soldiers unto Caesar. They, when their service is hired, swear to hold the life of Caesar dearer than all else: and will you not swear your oath, that are deemed worthy of so many and great gifts? And will you not keep your oath when you have sworn it? And what oath will you swear? Never to disobey, never to arraign or murmur at aught that comes to you from His hand: never unwillingly to do or suffer aught that necessity lays upon you. "Is this oath like theirs?" They swear to hold no other dearer than Caesar: you, to hold our true selves dearer than all else beside.

38

"How shall my brother cease to be wroth with me?" Bring him to me, and I will tell him. But to thee I have nothing to say about his anger.

39

When one took counsel of Epictetus, saying, "What I seek is this, how even though my brother be not reconciled to me, I may still remain as Nature would have me to be," he replied: "All great things are slow of growth; nay, this is true even of a grape or of a fig. If then you say to me now, I desire a fig, I shall answer, It needs time: wait till it first flower, then cast its blossom, then ripen. Whereas then the fruit of the fig-tree reaches not maturity suddenly nor yet in a single hour, do you nevertheless desire so quickly, and easily to reap the fruit of the mind of man?—Nay, expect it not, even though I bade you!"

40

Epaphroditus had a shoemaker whom he sold as being good-for-nothing. This fellow, by some accident, was afterwards purchased by one of Caesar's men, and became a shoemaker to Caesar. You should have seen what respect Epaphroditus paid him then. "How does the good Felicion? Kindly let me know!" And if any of us inquired, "What is Epaphroditus doing?" the answer was, "He is consulting about so and so with Felicion."—Had he not sold him as good-for-nothing? Who had in a trice converted him into a wiseacre? This is what comes of holding of importance anything but the things that depend on the Will.

41

What you shun enduring yourself, attempt not to impose on others. You shun slavery—beware of enslaving others! If you can endure to do that, one would think you had been once upon a time a slave yourself. For Vice has nothing in common with virtue, nor Freedom with slavery.

42

Has a man been raised to tribuneship? Every one that he meets congratulates him. One kisses him on the eyes, another on the neck, while the slaves kiss his hands. He goes home to find torches burning; he ascends to the Capitol to sacrifice.—Who ever sacrificed for having had right desires; for having conceived such inclinations as Nature would have him? In truth we thank the Gods for that wherein we place our happiness.

43

A man was talking to me to-day about the priesthood of Augustus. I said to him, "Let the thing go, my good Sir; you will spend a good deal to no purpose." "Well, but my name will be inserted in all documents and contracts." "Will you be standing there to tell those that read them, That is my name written there? And even if you could now be there in every case, what will you do when you are dead?" "At all events my name will remain." "Inscribe it on a stone and it will remain just as well. And think, beyond Nicopolis what memory of you will there be?"

"But I shall have a golden wreath to wear."

"If you must have a wreath, get a wreath of roses and put it on; you will look more elegant!"

44

Above all, remember that the door stands open. Be not more fearful than children; but as they, when they weary of the game, cry, "I will play no more," even so, when thou art in the like case, cry, "I will play no more" and depart. But if thou stayest, make no lamentation.

45

Is there smoke in the room? If it be slight, I remain; if grievous, I quit it. For you must remember this and hold it fast, that the door stands open.

"You shall not dwell at Nicopolis!"

Well and good.

"Nor at Athens."

Then I will not dwell at Athens either.

"Nor at Rome."

Nor at Rome either.

"You shall dwell in Gyara!"

Well: but to dwell in Gyara seems to me like a grievous smoke; I depart to a place where none can forbid me to dwell: that habitation is open unto all! As for the last garment of all, that is the poor body; beyond that, none can do aught unto me. This why Demetrius said to Nero: "You threaten me with death; it is Nature who threatens you!"

46

The beginning of philosophy is to know the condition of one's own mind. If a man recognises that this is in a weakly state, he will not then want to apply it to questions of the greatest moment. As it is, men who are not fit to swallow even a morsel, buy whole treatises and try to devour them. Accordingly they either vomit them up again, or suffer from indigestion, whence come gripings, fluxions, and fevers. Whereas they should have stopped to consider their capacity.

47

In theory it is easy to convince an ignorant person: in actual life, men not only object to offer themselves to be convinced, but hate the man who has convinced them. Whereas Socrates used to say that we should never lead a life not subjected to examination.

48

This is the reason why Socrates, when reminded that he should prepare for his trial, answered: "Thinkest thou not that I have been preparing for it all my life?"

"In what way?"

"I have maintained that which in me lay."

"How so?"

"I have never, secretly or openly, done a wrong unto any."

49

In what character dost thou now come forward?

As a witness summoned by God. "Come thou," saith God, "and testify for me, for thou art worthy of being brought forward as a witness by Me. Is aught that is outside thy will either good or bad? Do I hurt any man? Have I placed the good of each in the power of any other than himself? What witness dost thou bear to God?"

"I am in evil state, Master, I am undone! None careth for me, none giveth me aught: all men blame, all speak evil of me."

Is this the witness thou wilt bear, and do dishonour to the calling wherewith He hath called thee, because He hath done thee so great honour, and deemed thee worthy of being summoned to bear witness in so great a cause?

50

Wouldst thou have men speak good of thee? speak good of them. And when thou hast learned to speak good of them, try to do good unto them, and thus thou wilt reap in return their speaking good of thee.

51

When thou goest in to any of the great, remember that Another from above sees what is passing, and that thou shouldst please Him rather than man. He therefore asks thee:—

"In the Schools, what didst thou call exile, imprisionment, bonds, death and shame?"

"I called them things indifferent."

'What then dost thou call them now? Are they at all changed?"

"No."

"Is it then thou that art changed?"

"No."

"Say then, what are things indifferent?"

"Things that are not in our power."

"Say then, what follows?"

"That things which are not in our power are nothing to me."

"Say also what things you hold to be good."

"A will such as it ought to be, and a right use of the things of sense."

"And what is the end?"

"To follow Thee!"

52

"That Socrates should ever have been so treated by the Athenians!"

Slave! why say "Socrates"? Speak of the thing as it is: That ever then the poor body of Socrates should have been dragged away and haled by main force to prision! That ever hemlock should have been given to the body of Socrates; that that should have breathed its life away!—Do you marvel at this? Do you hold this unjust? Is it for this that you accuse God? Had Socrates no compensation for this? Where then for him was the ideal Good? Whom shall we hearken to, you or him? And what says he?

"Anytus and Melitus may put me to death: to injure me is beyond their power."

And again:—

"If such be the will of God, so let it be."

53

Nay, young man, for heaven's sake; but once thou hast heard these words, go home and say to thyself:—"It is not Epictetus that has told me these things: how indeed should he? No, it is some gracious God through him. Else it would never have entered his head to tell me them—he that is not used to speak to any one thus. Well, then, let us not lie under the wrath of God, but be obedient unto Him."—Nay, indeed; but if a raven by its croaking bears thee any sign, it is not the raven but God that sends the sign through the raven; and if He signifies anything to thee through human voice, will He not cause the man to say these words to thee, that thou mayest know the power of the Divine—how He sends a sign to some in one way and to others in another, and on the greatest and highest matters of all signifies His will through the noblest messenger?

What else does the poet mean:—

I spake unto him erst Myself, and sent
Hermes the shining One, to check and warn him,
The husband not to slay, nor woo the wife!

54

In the same way my friend Heraclitus, who had a trifling suit about a petty farm at Rhodes, first showed the judges that his cause was just, and then at the finish cried, "I will not entreat you: nor do I care what sentence you pass. It is you who are on your trial, not I!"—And so he ended the case.

55

As for us, we behave like a herd of deer. When they flee from the huntsman's feathers in affright, which way do they turn? What haven of safety do they make for? Why, they rush upon the nets! And thus they perish by confounding what they should fear with that wherein no danger lies. . . . Not death or pain is to be feared, but the fear of death or pain. Well said the poet therefore:—

Death has no terror; only a Death of shame!

56

How is it then that certain external things are said to be natural, and other contrary to Nature?

Why, just as it might be said if we stood alone and apart from others. A foot, for instance, I will allow it is natural should be clean. But if you take it as a foot, and as a thing which does not stand by itself, it will beseem it (if need be) to walk in the mud, to tread on thorns, and sometimes even to be cut off, for the benefit of the whole body; else it is no longer a foot. In some such way we should conceive of ourselves also. What art thou?—A man.—Looked at as standing by thyself and separate, it is natural for thee in health and wealth long to live. But looked at as a Man, and only as a part of a Whole, it is for that Whole's sake that thou shouldest at one time fall sick, at another brave the perils of the sea, again, know the meaning of want and perhaps die an early death. Why then repine? Knowest thou not that as the foot is no more a foot if detached from the body, so thou in like case art no longer a Man? For what is a Man? A part of a City:—first of the City of Gods and Men; next, of that which ranks nearest it, a minature of the universal City. . . . In such a body, in such a world enveloping us, among lives like these, such things must happen to one or another. Thy part, then, being here, is to speak of these things as is meet, and to order them as befits the matter.

57

That was a good reply which Diogenes made to a man who asked him for letters of recommendation.—"That you are a man, he will know when he sees you;—whether a good or bad one, he will know if he has any skill in discerning the good or bad. But if he has none, he will never know, though I write him a thousand times."—It is as though a piece of silver money desired to be recommended to some one to be tested. If the man be a good judge of silver, he will know: the coin will tell its own tale.

58

Even as the traveller asks his way of him that he meets, inclined in no wise to bear to the right rather than to the left (for he desires only the way leading whither he would go), so should we come unto God as to a guide; even as we use our eyes without admonishing them to show us some things rather than others, but content to receive the images of such things as they present to us. But as it is we stand anxiously watching the victim, and with the voice of supplication call upon the augur:—"Master, have mercy on me: vouchsafe unto me a way of escape!" Slave, would you then have aught else then what is best? is there anything better than what is God's good pleasure? Why, as far as in you lies, would you corrupt your Judge, and lead your Counsellor astray?

59

God is beneficent. But the Good also is beneficent. It should seem then that where the real nature of God is, there too is to be found the real nature of the Good. What then is the real nature of God?—Intelligence, Knowledge, Right Reason. Here then without more ado seek the real nature of the Good. For surely thou dost not seek it in a plant or in an animal that reasoneth not.

60

Seek then the real nature of the Good in that without whose presence thou wilt not admit the Good to exist in aught else.—What then? Are not these other things also works of God?—They are; but not preferred to honour, nor are they portions of God. But thou art a thing preferred to honour: thou art thyself a fragment torn from God:—thou hast a portion of Him within thyself. How is it then that thou dost not know thy high descent—dost not know whence thou comest? When thou eatest, wilt thou not remember who thou art that eatest and whom thou feedest? In intercourse, in exercise, in discussion knowest thou not that it is a God whom thou feedest, a God whom thou exercisest, a God whom thou bearest about with thee, O miserable! and thou perceivest it not. Thinkest thou that I speak of a God of silver or gold, that is without thee? Nay, thou bearest Him within thee! all unconcious of polluting Him with thoughts impure and unclean deeds. Were an image of God present, thou wouldest not dare to act as thou dost, yet, when God Himself is present within thee, beholding and hearing all, thou dost not blush to think such thoughts and do such deeds, O thou that art insensible of thine own nature and liest under the wrath of God!

61

Why then are we afraid when we send a young man from the Schools into active life, lest he should indulge his appetites intemperately, lest he should debase himself by ragged clothing, or be puffed up by fine raiment? Knows he not the God within him; knows he not with whom he is starting on his way? Have we patience to hear him say to us, Would I had thee with me!—Hast thou not God where thou art, and having Him dost thou still seek for any other! Would He tell thee aught else than these things? Why, wert thou a statue of Phidias, an Athena or a Zeus, thou wouldst bethink thee both of thyself and thine artificer; and hadst thou any sense, thou wouldst strive to do no dishonour to thyself or him that fashioned thee, nor appear to beholders in unbefitting guise. But now, because God is thy Maker, is that why thou carest not of what sort thou shalt show thyself to be? Yet how different the artists and their workmanship! What human artist's work, for example, has in it the faculties that are displayed in fashioning it? Is it aught but marble, bronze, gold, or ivory? Nay, when the Athena of Phidias has put forth her hand and received therein a Victory, in that attitude she stands for evermore. But God's works move and breathe; they use and judge the things of sense. The workmanship of such an Artist, wilt thou dishonor Him? Ay, when he not only fashioned thee, but placed thee, like a ward, in the care and guardianship of thyself alone, wilt thou not only forget this, but also do dishonour to what is committed to thy care! If God had entrusted thee with an orphan, wouldst thou have thus neglected him? He hath delivered thee to thine own care, saying, I had none more faithful than myself: keep this man for me such as Nature hath made him—modest, faithful, high-minded, a stranger to fear, to passion, to perturbation. . . .

Such will I show myself to you all.—"What, exempt from sickness also: from age, from death?"—Nay, but accepting sickness, accepting death as becomes a God!

62

No labour, according to Diogenes, is good but that which aims at producing courage and strength of soul rather than of body.

63

A guide, on finding a man who has lost his way, brings him back to the right path—he does not mock and jeer at him and then take himself off. You also must show the unlearned man the truth, and you will see that he will follow. But so long as you do not show it him, you should not mock, but rather feel your own incapacity.

64

It was the first and most striking characteristic of Socrates never to become heated in discourse, never to utter an injurious or insulting word—on the contrary, he persistently bore insult from others and thus put an end to the fray. If you care to know the extent of his power in this direction, read Xenophon's

Banquet, and you will see how many quarrels he put an end to. This is why the Poets are right in so highly commending this faculty:—

Quickly and wisely withal even bitter feuds would he settle.

Nevertheless the practice is not very safe at present, especially in Rome. One who adopts it, I need not say, ought not to carry it out in an obscure corner, but boldly accost, if occasion serve, some personage of rank or wealth.

"Can you tell me, sir, to whose care you entrust your horses?"

"I can."

"Is it to the first corner, who knows nothing about them?"

"Certainly not."

"Well, what of the man who takes care of your gold, your silver or your raiment?"

"He must be experienced also."

"And your body—have you ever considered about entrusting it to any one's care?"

"Of course I have."

"And no doubt to a person of experience as a trainer, a physician?"

"Surely."

"And these things the best you possess, or have you anything more precious?"

"What can you mean?"

"I mean that which employs these; which weights all things; which takes counsel and resolve."

"Oh, you mean the soul."

"You take me rightly; I do mean the soul. By Heaven, I hold that far more precious than all else I possess. Can you show me then what care you bestow on a soul? For it can scarcely be thought that a man of your wisdom and consideration in the city would suffer your most precious possession to go to ruin through carelessness and neglect."

"Certainly not."

"Well, do you take care of it yourself? Did any one teach you the right method, or did you discover it yourself?"

Now here comes in the danger: first, that the great man may answer, "Why, what is that to you, my good fellow? are you my master?" And then, if you persist in troubling him, may raise his hand to strike you. It is a practice of which I was myself a warm admirer until such experiences as these befell me.

65

When a youth was giving himself airs in the Theatre and saying, "I am wise, for I have conversed with many wise men." Epictetus replied, "I too have conversed with many rich men, yet I am not rich!"

66

We see that a carpenter becomes a carpenter by learning certain things: that a pilot, by learning certain things, becomes a pilot. Possibly also in the present case the mere desire to be wise and good is not enough. It is necessary to learn certain things. This is then the object of our search. The Philosophers would have us first learn that there is a God, and that His Providence directs the Universe; further, that to hide from Him not only one's acts but even one's thoughts and intentions is impossible; secondly, what the nature of God is. Whatever that nature is discovered to be, the man who would please and obey Him must strive with all his might to be made like unto him. If the Divine is faithful, he also must be faithful; if free, he also must be free; if beneficent, he also must be beneficent; if magnanimous, he also must be magnanimous. Thus as an imitator of God must he follow Him in every deed and word.

67

If I show you, that you lack just what is most important and necessary to happiness, that hitherto your attention has been bestowed on everything rather than that which claims it most; and, to crown all, that you know neither what God nor Man is—neither what Good or Evil is: why, that you are ignorant of everything else, perhaps you may bear to be told; but to hear that you know nothing of yourself, how could you submit to that? How could you stand your ground and suffer that to be proved? Clearly not at all. You instantly turn away in wrath. Yet what harm have I done to you? Unless indeed the mirror harms the ill–favoured man by showing him to himself just as he is; unless the physician can be thought to insult his patient, when he tells him:—"Friend, do you suppose there is nothing wrong with you? why, you have a fever. Eat nothing to-day, and drink only water." Yet no one says, "What an insufferable insult!" Whereas if you say to a man, "Your desires are inflamed, your instincts of rejection are weak and low, your aims are inconsistent, your impulses are not in harmony with Nature, your opinions are rash and false," he forthwith goes away and complains that you have insulted him.

68

Our way of life resembles a fair. The flocks and herds are passing along to be sold, and the greater part of the crowd to buy and sell. But there are some few who come only to look at the fair, to inquire how and why it is being held, upon what authority and with what object. So too, in this great Fair of life, some, like the cattle, trouble themselves about nothing but the fodder. Know all of you, who are busied about land, slaves and public posts, that these are nothing but fodder! Some few there are attending the Fair, who love to contemplate what the world is, what He that administers it. Can there be no Administrator? is it possible, that while neither city nor household could endure even a moment without one to administer and see to its welfare, this Fabric, so fair, so vast, should be administered in order so harmonious, without a purpose and by blind chance? There is therefore an Administrator. What is His nature and how does He administer? And who are we that are His children and what work were we born to perform? Have we any close connection or relation with Him or not?

Such are the impressions of the few of whom I speak. And further, they apply themselves solely to considering and examining the great assembly before they depart. Well, they are derided by the multitude. So are the lookers-on by the traders: aye, and if the beasts had any sense, they would deride those who thought much of anything but fodder!

69

I think I know now what I never knew before—the meaning of the common saying, A fool you can neither bend nor break. Pray heaven I may never have a wise fool for my friend! There is nothing more intractable.—"My resolve is fixed!"—Why so madman say too; but the more firmly they believe in their delusions, the more they stand in need of treatment.

70

—"O! when shall I see Athens and its Acropolis again?"—Miserable man! art thou not contented with the daily sights that meet thine eyes? canst thou behold aught greater or nobler than the Sun, Moon, and Stars; than the outspread Earth and Sea? If indeed thous apprehendest Him who administers the universe, if thou bearest Him about within thee, canst thou still hanker after mere fragments of stone and fine rock? When thou art about to bid farewell to the Sun and Moon itself, wilt thou sit down and cry like a child? Why, what didst thou hear, what didst thou learn? why didst thou write thyself down a philosopher, when thou mightest have written what was the fact, namely, "I have made one or two Compendiums, I have read some works of Chrysippus, and I have not even touched the hem of Philosophy's robe"!

71

Friend, lay hold with a desperate grasp, ere it is too late, on Freedom, on Tranquility, on Greatness of soul! Lift up thy head, as one escaped from slavery; dare to look up to God, and say:—"Deal with me henceforth as Thou wilt; Thou and I are of one mind. I am Thine: I refuse nothing that seeeth good to Thee; lead on whither Thou wilt; clothe me in what garb Thou pleasest; wilt Thou have me a ruler or a subject—at home or in exile—poor or rich? All these things will I justify unto men for Thee. I will show the true nature of each. . . ."

Who would Hercules have been had he loitered at home? no Hercules, but Eurystheus. And in his wanderings through the world how many friends and comrades did he find? but nothing dearer to him than God. Wherefore he was believed to be God's son, as indeed he was. So then in obedience to Him, he went about delivering the earth from injustice and lawlessness.

But thou art not Hercules, thou sayest, and canst not deliver others from their iniquity—not even Theseus, to deliver the soil of Attica from its monsters? Purge away thine own, cast forth thence—from thine own mind, not robbers and monsters, but Fear, Desire, Envy, Malignity, Avarice, Effeminacy, Intemperance. And these may not be cast out, except by looking to God alone, by fixing thy affections on Him only, and by consecrating thyself to His commands. If thou choosest aught else, with sighs and groans thou wilt be forced to follow a Might greater than thine own, ever seeking Tranquillity without, and never able to attain unto her. For thou seekest her where she is not to be found; and where she is, there thou seekest her not!

72

If a man would pursue Philosophy, his first task is to throw away conceit. For it is impossible for a man to begin to learn what he has a conceit that he already knows.

73

Give me but one young man, that has come to the School with this intention, who stands forth a champion of this cause, and says, "All else I renounce, content if I am but able to pass my life free from hindrance and trouble; to raise my head aloft and face all things as a free man; to look up to heaven as a friend of God, fearing nothing that may come to pass!" Point out such a one to me, that I may say, "Enter, young man, into possession of that which is thine own. For thy lot is to adorn Philosophy. Thine are these possessions; thine these books, these discourses!"

And when our champion has duly exercised himself in this part of the subject, I hope he will come back to me and say:—"What I desire is to be free from passion and from perturbation; as one who grudges no pains in the pursuit of piety and philosophy, what I desire is to know my duty to the Gods, my duty to my parents, to my brothers, to my country, to strangers."

"Enter then on the second part of the subject; it is thine also."

"But I have already mastered the second part; only I wished to stand firm and unshaken—as firm when asleep as when awake, as firm when elated with wine as in despondency and dejection."

"Friend, you are verily a God! you cherish great designs."

74

"The question at stake," said Epictetus, "is no common one; it is this:—Are we in our senses, or are we not?"

75

If you have given way to anger, be sure that over and above the evil involved therein, you have strengthened the habit, and added fuel to the fire. If overcome by a temptation of the flesh, do not reckon it a single defeat, but that you have also strengthened your dissolute habits. Habits and faculties are necessarily affected by the corresponding acts. Those that were not there before, spring up: the rest gain in strength and extent. This is the account which Philosophers give of the origin of diseases of the mind:—Suppose you have once lusted after money: if reason sufficient to produce a sense of evil be applied, then the lust is checked, and the mind at once regains its original authority; whereas if you have recourse to no remedy, you can no longer look for this return—on the contrary, the next time it is excited by the corresponding object, the flame of desire leaps up more quickly than before. By frequent repetition, the mind in the long run becomes callous; and thus this mental disease produces confirmed Avarice.

One who has had fever, even when it has left him, is not in the same condition of health as before, unless indeed his cure is complete. Something of the same sort is true also of diseases of the mind. Behind, there remains a legacy of traces and blisters: and unless these are effectually erased, subsequent blows on the same spot will produce no longer mere blisters, but sores. If you do not wish to be prone to anger, do not feed the habit; give it nothing which may tend its increase. At first, keep quiet and count the days when you were not angry: "I used to be angry every day, then every other day: next every two, next every three days!" and if you succeed in passing thirty days, sacrifice to the Gods in thanksgiving.

76

How then may this be attained?—Resolve, now if never before, to approve thyself to thyself; resolve to show thyself fair in God's sight; long to be pure with thine own pure self and God!

77

That is the true athlete, that trains himself to resist such outward impressions as these.

"Stay, wretched man! suffer not thyself to be carried away!" Great is the combat, divine the task! you are fighting for Kingship, for Liberty, for Happiness, for Tranquillity. Remember God: call upon Him to aid thee, like a comrade that stands beside thee in the fight.

78

Who then is a Stoic—in the sense that we call a statue of Phidias which is modelled after that master's art? Show me a man in this sense modelled after the doctrines that are ever upon his lips. Show me a man that is sick—and happy; an exile—and happy; in evil report—and happy! Show me him, I ask again. So help me Heaven, I long to see one Stoic! Nay, if you cannot show me one fully modelled, let me at least see one in whom the process is at work—one whose bent is in that direction. Do me that favour! Grudge it not to an old man, to behold a sight he has never yet beheld. Think you I wish to see the Zeus or Athena of Phidias, bedecked with gold and ivory?—Nay, show me, one of you, a human soul, desiring to be of one mind with God, no more to lay blame on God or man, to suffer nothing to disappoint, nothing to cross him, to yield neither to anger, envy, nor jealousy—in a word, why disguise the matter? one that from a man would fan become a God; one that while still imprisoned in this dead body makes fellowship with God his aim. Show me him!—Ah, you cannot! Then why mock yourselves and delude others? why stalk about tricked out in other men's attire, thieves and robbers that you are of names and things to which you can show no title!

79

If you have assumed a character beyond your strength, you have both played a poor figure in that, and neglected one that is within your powers.

80

Fellow, you have come to blows at home with a slave: you have turned the household upside down, and thrown the neighbourhood into confusion; and do you come to me then with airs of assumed modesty—do you sit down like a sage and criticise my explanation of the readings, and whatever idle babble you say has come into my head? Have you come full of envy, and dejected because nothing is sent you from home; and while the discussion is going on, do you sit brooding on nothing but how your father or your brother are disposed towards you:—"What are they saying about me there? at this moment they imagine I am making progress and saying, He will return perfectly omniscient! I wish I could become omniscient before I return; but that would be very troublesome. No one sends me anything—the baths at Nicopolis are dirty; things are wretched at home and wretched here." And then they say, "Nobody is any the better for the School."—Who comes to the School with a sincere wish to learn: to submit his principles to correction and himself to treatment? Who, to gain a sense of his wants? Why then be surprised if you carry home from the School exactly what you bring into it?

81

"Epictetus, I have often come desiring to hear you speak, and you have never given me any answer; now if possible, I entreat you, say something to me."

"Is there, do you think," replied Epictetus, "an art of speaking as of other things, if it is to be done skilfully and with profit to the hearer?"

"Yes."

"And are all profited by what they hear, or only some among them? So that it seems there is an art of hearing as well as of speaking. . . . To make a statue needs skill: to view a statue aright needs skill also."

"Admitted."

"And I think all will allow that one who proposes to hear philosophers speak needs a considerable training in hearing. Is that not so? Then tell me on what subject you are able to hear me."

"Why, on good and evil."

"The good and evil of what? a horse, an ox?"

"No; of a man."

"Do we know then what Man is? what his nature is? what is the idea we have of him? And are our ears practised in any degree on the subject? Nay, do you understand what Nature is? can you follow me in any degree when I say that I shall have to use demonstration? Do you understand what Demonstration is? what True or False is? . . . must I drive you to Philosophy? . . . Show me what good I am to do by discoursing with you. Rouse my desire to do so. The sight of a pasture it loves stirs in a sheep the desire to feed: show it a stone or a bit of bread and it remains unmoved. Thus we also have certain natural desires, aye, and one that moves us to speak when we find a listener that is worth his salt: one that himself stirs the spirit. But if he sits by like a stone or a tuft of grass, how can he rouse a man's desire?"

"Then you will say nothing to me?"

"I can only tell you this: that one who knows not who he is and to what end he was born; what kind of world this is and with whom he is associated therein; one who cannot distinguish Good and Evil, Beauty and Foulness, . . . Truth and Falsehood, will never follow Reason in shaping his desires and impulses and repulsions, nor yet in assent, denial, or suspension of judgement; but will in one word go about deaf and blind, thinking himself to be somewhat, when he is in truth of no account. Is there anything new in all this? Is not this ignorance the cause of all the mistakes and mischances of men since the human race began? . . ."

"This is all I have to say to you, and even this against the grain. Why? Because you have not stirred my spirit. For what can I see in you to stir me, as a spirited horse will stir a judge of horses? Your body? That you maltreat. Your dress? That is luxurious. Your behavior, your look?—Nothing whatever. When you want to hear a philosopher, do not say, You say nothing to me; only show yourself worthy or fit to hear, and then you will see how you will move the speaker."

82

And now, when you see brothers apparently good friends and living in accord, do not immediately pronounce anything upon their friendship, though they should affirm it with an oath, though they should declare, "For us to live apart in a thing impossible!" For the heart of a bad man is faithless, unprincipled, inconstant: now overpowered by one impression, now by another. Ask not the usual questions, Were they born of the same parents, reared together, and under the same tutor?; but ask this only, in what they place their real interest—whether in outward things or in the Will. If in outward things, call them not friends, any more than faithful, constant, brave or free: call them not even human beings, if you have any sense. . . . But should you hear that these men hold the Good to lie only in the Will, only in rightly dealing with the things of sense, take no more trouble to inquire whether they are father and son or brothers, or comrades of long standing; but, sure of this one thing, pronounce as boldly that they are friends as that they are faithful and just: for where else can Friendship be found than where Modesty is, where there is an interchange of things fair and honest, and of such only?

83

No man can rob us of our Will—no man can lord it over that!

Section 2

84

When disease and death overtake me, I would fain be found engaged in the task of liberating mine own Will from the assaults of passion, from hindrance, from resentment, from slavery.

Thus would I fain to be found employed, so that I may say to God, "Have I in aught transgressed Thy commands? Have I in aught perverted the faculties, the senses, the natural principles that Thou didst give me? Have I ever blamed Thee or found fault with Thine administration? When it was Thy good pleasure, I fell sick—and so did other men: by my will consented. Because it was Thy pleasure, I became poor: but my heart rejoiced. No power in the State was mine, because Thou wouldst not: such power I never desired! Hast Thou ever seen me of more doleful countenance on that account? Have I not ever drawn nigh unto Thee with cheerful look, waiting upon Thy commands, attentive to Thy signals? Wilt Thou that I now depart from the great Assembly of men? I go: I give Thee all thanks, that Thou hast deemed me worthy to take part with Thee in this Assembly: to behold Thy works, to comprehend this Thine administration."

Such I would were the subject of my thoughts, my pen, my study, when death overtakes me.

85

Seemeth it nothing to you, never to accuse, never to blame either God or Man? to wear ever the same countenance in going forth as in coming in? This was the secret of Socrates: yet he never said that he knew or taught anything. . . . Who amongst you makes this his aim? Were it indeed so, you would gladly endure sickness, hunger, aye, death itself.

86

How are we constituted by Nature? To be free, to be noble, to be modest (for what other living thing is capable of blushing, or of feeling the impression of shame?) and to subordinate pleasure to the ends for which Nature designed us, as a handmaid and a minister, in order to call forth our activity; in order to keep us constant to the path prescribed by Nature.

87

The husbandman deals with land; physicians and trainers with the body; the wise man with his own Mind.

88

Which of us does not admire what Lycurgus the Spartan did? A young citizen had put out his eye, and been handed over to him by the people to be punished at his own discretion. Lycurgus abstained from all vengeance, but on the contrary instructed and made a good man of him. Producing him in public in the theatre, he said to the astonished Spartans:—"I received this young man at your hands full of violence and wanton insolence; I restore him to you in his right mind and fit to serve his country."

89

A money-changer may not reject Caesar's coin, nor may the seller of herbs, but must when once the coin is shown, deliver what is sold for it, whether he will or no. So is it also with the Soul. Once the Good appears, it attracts towards itself; evil repels. But a clear and certain impression of the Good the Soul will never reject, any more than men do Caesar's coin. On this hangs every impulse alike of Man and God.

90

Asked what Common Sense was, Epictetus replied:—

As that may be called a Common Ear which distinguishes only sounds, while that which distinguishes musical notes is not common but produced by training; so there are certain things which men not entirely perverted see by the natural principles common to all. Such a constitution of the Mind is called Common Sense.

91

Canst thou judge men? . . . then make us imitators of thyself, as Socrates did. Do this, do not do that, else will I cast thee into prison; this is not governing men like reasonable creatures. Say rather, As God hath ordained, so do; else thou wilt suffer chastisement and loss. Askest thou what loss? None other than this: To have left undone what thou shouldst have done: to have lost the faithfulness, the reverence, the modesty that is in thee! Greater loss than this seek not to find!

92

"His son is dead."

What has happened?

"His son is dead."

Nothing more?

"Nothing."

"His ship is lost."

"He has been haled to prison."

What has happened?

"He has been haled to prison."

But that any of these things are misfortunes to him, is an addition which every one makes of his own. But (you say) God is unjust is this.—Why? For having given thee endurance and greatness of soul? For having made such things to be no evils? For placing happiness within thy reach, even when enduring them? For open unto thee a door, when things make not for thy good?—Depart, my friend and find fault no more!

93

You are sailing to Rome (you tell me) to obtain the post of Governor of Cnossus. You are not content to stay at home with the honours you had before; you want something on a larger scale, and more conspicuous. But when did you ever undertake a voyage for the purpose of reviewing your own principles and getting rid of any of them that proved unsound? Whom did you ever visit for that object? What time did you ever set yourself for that? What age? Run over the times of your life—by yourself, if you are ashamed before me. Did you examine your principles when a boy? Did you not do everything just as you do now? Or when you were a stripling, attending the school of oratory and practising the art yourself, what did you ever imagine you lacked? And when you were a young man, entered upon public life, and were pleading causes and making a name, who any longer seemed equal to you? And at what moment would you have endured another examining your principles and proving that they were unsound? What then am I to say to you? "Help me in this matter!" you cry. Ah, for that I have no rule! And neither did you, if that was your object, come to me as a philosopher, but as you might have gone to a herb-seller or a cobbler.—"What do philosophers have rules for, then?"—Why, that whatever may betide, our ruling faculty may be as Nature would have it, and so remain. Think you this a small matter? Not so! but the greatest thing there is. Well, does it need but a short time? Can it be grasped by a passer-by?—grasp it, if you can!

Then you will say, "Yes, I met Epictetus!"

Aye, just as you might a statue or a monument. You saw me! and that is all. But a man who meets a man is one who learns the other's mind, and lets him see his in turn. Learn my mind—show me yours; and then go and say that you met me. Let us try each other; if I have any wrong principle, rid me of it; if you have, out with it. That is what meeting a philosopher means. Not so, you think;

this is only a flying visit; while we are hiring the ship, we can see Epictetus too! Let us see what he has to say. Then on leaving you cry, "Out on Epictetus for a worthless fellow, provincial and barbarous of speech!" What else indeed did you come to judge of?

94

Whether you will or no, you are poorer than I!

"What then do I lack?"

What you have not: Constancy of mind, such as Nature would have it be: Tranquillity. Patron or no patron, what care I? but you do care. I am richer than you: I am not racked with anxiety as to what Caesar may think of me; I flatter none on that account. This is what I have, instead of vessels of gold and silver! your vessels may be of gold, but your reason, your principles, your accepted views, your inclinations, your desires are of earthenware.

95

To you, all you have seems small: to me, all I have seems great. Your desire is insatiable, mine is satisfied. See children thrusting their hands into a narrow-necked jar, and striving to pull out the nuts and figs it contains: if they fill the hand, they cannot pull it out again, and then they fall to tears.—"Let go a few of them, and then you can draw out the rest!"—You, too, let your desire go! covet not many things, and you will obtain.

96

Pittacus wronged by one whom he had it in his power to punish, let him go free, saying, Forgiveness is better than revenge. The one shows native gentleness, the other savagery.

97

"My brother ought not to have treated me thus."

True: but he must see to that. However he may treat me, I must deal rightly by him. This is what lies with me, what none can hinder.

98

Nevertheless a man should also be prepared to be sufficient unto himself—to dwell with himself alone, even as God dwells with Himself alone, shares His repose with none, and considers the nature of His own administration, intent upon such thoughts as are meet unto Himself. So should we also be able to converse with ourselves, to need none else beside, to sigh for no distraction, to bend our thoughts upon the Divine Administration, and how we stand related to all else; to observe how human accidents touched us of old, and how they touch us now; what things they are that still have power to hurt us, and how they may be cured or removed; to perfect what needs perfecting as Reason would direct.

99

If a man has frequent intercourse with others, either in the way of conversation, entertainment, or simple familiarity, he must either become like them, or change them to his own fashion. A live coal placed next a dead one will either kindle that or be quenched by it. Such being the risk, it is well to be cautious in admitting intimacies of this sort, remembering that one cannot rub shoulders with a soot-stained man without sharing the soot oneself. What will you do, supposing the talk turns on gladiators, or horses, or prize-fighters, or (what is worse) on persons, condemning this and that, approving the other? Or suppose a man sneers and jeers or shows a malignant temper? Has any among us the skill of the lute-player, who knows at the first touch which strings are out of tune and sets the instrument right: has any of you such power as Socrates had, in all his intercourse with men, of winning them over to his own convictions? Nay, but you must needs be swayed hither and thither by the uninstructed. How comes it then that they prove so much stronger than you? Because they speak from the fulness of the heart—their low, corrupt views are their real convictions: whereas your fine sentiments are but from the lips, outwards; that is why they are so nerveless and dead. It turns one's stomach to listen to your exhortations, and hear of your miserable Virtue, that you prate of up and down. Thus it is that the Vulgar prove too strong for you. Everywhere strength, everywhere victory waits your conviction!

100

In general, any methods of discipline applied to the body which tend to modify its desires or repulsions, are good—for ascetic ends. But if done for display, they betray at once a man who keeps an eye on outward show; who has an ulterior purpose, and is looking for spectators to shout, "Oh what a great man!" This is why Apollonius so well said: "If you are bent upon a little private discipline, wait till you are choking with heat some day—then take a mouthful of cold water, and spit it out again, and tell no man!"

101

Study how to give as one that is sick: that thou mayest hereafter give as one that is whole. Fast; drink water only; abstain altogether from desire, that thou mayest hereafter conform thy desire to Reason.

102

Thou wouldst do good unto men? then show them by thine own example what kind of men philosophy can make, and cease from foolish trifling. Eating, do good to them that eat with thee; drinking, to them that drink with thee; yield unto all, give way, and bear with them. Thus shalt thou do them good: but vent not upon them thine own evil humour!

103

Even as bad actors cannot sing alone, but only in chorus: so some cannot walk alone.

Man, if thou art aught, strive to walk alone and hold converse with thyself, instead of skulking in the chorus! at length think; look around thee; bestir thyself, that thou mayest know who thou art!

104

You would fain be victor at the Olympic games, you say. Yes, but weigh the conditions, weigh the consequences; then and then only, lay to your hand—if it be for your profit. You must live by rule, submit to diet, abstain from dainty meats, exercise your body perforce at stated hours, in heat or in cold; drink no cold water, nor, it may be, wine. In a word, you must surrender yourself wholly to your trainer, as though to a physician.

Then in the hour of contest, you will have to delve the ground, it may chance dislocate an arm, sprain an ankle, gulp down abundance of yellow sand, be scourge with the whip—and with all this sometimes lose the victory. Count the cost—and then, if your desire still holds, try the wrestler's life. Else let me tell you that you will be behaving like a pack of children playing now at wrestlers, now at gladiators; presently falling to trumpeting and anon to stageplaying, when the fancy takes them for what they have seen. And you are even the same: wrestler, gladiator, philosopher, orator all by turns and none of them with your whole soul. Like an ape, you mimic what you see, to one thing constant never; the thing that is familiar charms no more. This is because you never undertook aught with due consideration, nor after strictly testing and viewing it from every side; no, your choice was thoughtless; the glow of your desire had waxed cold. . . .

Friend, bethink you first what it is you would do, and then what your own nature is able to bear. Would you be a wrestler, consider your shoulders, your thighs, your loins—not all men are formed to the same end. Think you to be a philosopher while acting as you do? think you go on thus eating, thus drinking, giving way in like manner to wrath and to displeasure? Nay, you must watch, you must labour; overcome certain desires; quit your familiar friends, submit to be despised by your slave, to be held in derision by them that meet you, to take the lower place in all things, in office, in positions of authority, in courts of law.

Weigh these things fully, and then, if you will, lay to your hand; if as the price of these things you would gain Freedom, Tranquillity, and passionless Serenity.

105

He that hath no musical instruction is a child in Music; he that hath no letters is a child in Learning; he that is untaught is a child in Life.

106

Can any profit be derived from these men? Aye, from all.

"What, even from a reviler?"

"Why, tell me what profit a wrestler gains from him who exercises him beforehand? The very greatest: he trains me in the practice of endurance, of controlling my temper, of gentle ways. You deny it. What, the man who lays hold of my neck, and disciplines loins and shoulders, does me good, . . . while he that trains me to keep my temper does me none? This is what it means, not knowing how to gain advantage from men! Is my neighbour bad? Bad to himself, but good to me: he brings my good temper, my gentleness into play. Is my father bad? Bad to himself, but good to me. This is the rod of Hermes; touch what you will with it, they say, and it becomes gold. Nay, but bring what you will and I will transmute it into Good. Bring sickness, bring death, bring poverty and reproach, bring trial for life—all these things through the rod of Hermes shall be turned to profit.

107

Till then these sound opinions have taken firm root in you, and you have gained a measure of strength for your security, I counsel you to be cautious in associating with the uninstructed. Else whatever impressions you receive upon the tablets of your mind in the School will day by day melt and disappear, like wax in the sun. Withdraw then somewhere far from the sun, while you have these waxen sentiments.

108

We must approach this matter in a different way; it is great and mystical: it is no common thing; nor given to every man. Wisdom alone, it may be, will not suffice for the care of youth: a man needs also a certain measure of readiness—an aptitude for the office; aye, and certain bodily qualities; and above all, to be counselled of God Himself to undertake this post; even as He counselled Socrates to fill the post of one who confutes error, assigning to Diogenes the royal office of high reproof, and to Zeno that of positive instruction. Whereas you would fain set up for a physician provided with nothing but drugs! Where and how they should be applied you neither know nor care.

109

If what charms you is nothing but abstract principles, sit down and turn them over quietly in your mind: but never dub yourself a Philosopher, nor suffer others to call you so. Say rather: He is in error; for my desires, my impulses are unaltered. I give in my adhesion to what I did before; nor has my mode of dealing with the things of sense undergone any change.

110

When a friend inclined to Cynic views asked Epictetus, what sort of person a true Cynic should be, requesting a general sketch of the system, he answered:—"We will consider that at leisure. At present I content myself with saying this much: If a man put his hand to so weighty a matter without God, the wrath of God abides upon him. That which he covets will but bring upon him public shame. Not even on finding himself in a well-ordered house does a man step forward and say to himself, I must be master here! Else the lord of that house takes notice of it, and, seeing him insolently giving orders, drags him forth and chastises him. So it is also in this great City, the World. Here also is there a Lord of the House, who orders all things:—

"Thou are the Sun! in thine orbit thou hast power to make the year and the seasons; to bid the fruits of the earth to grow and increase, the winds arise and fall; thou canst in due measure cherish with thy warmth the frames of men; go make thy circuit, and thus minister unto all from the greatest to the least! . . .

"Thou canst lead a host against Troy; be Agamemnon!" "Thou canst meet Hector in single combat; be Achilles!"

"But had Thersites stepped forward and claimed the chief command, he had been met with a refusal, or obtained it only to his own shame and confusion of face, before a cloud of witnesses."

111

Others may fence themselves with walls and houses, when they do such deeds as these, and wrap themselves in darkness—aye, they have many a device to hide themselves. Another may shut his door and station one before his chamber to say, if any comes, He has gone forth! he is not at leisure! But the true Cynic will have none of these things; instead of them, he must wrap himself in Modesty: else he will but bring himself to shame, naked and under the open sky. That is his house; that is his door; that is the slave that guards his chamber; that is his darkness!

112

Death? let it come when it will, whether it smite but a part of the whole: Fly, you tell me—fly! But whither shall I fly? Can any man cast me beyond the limits of the World? It may not be! And whithersoever I go, there shall I still find Sun, Moon, and Stars; there I shall find dreams, and omens, and converse with the Gods!

113

Furthermore the true Cynic must know that he is sent as a Messenger from God to men, to show unto them that as touching good and evil they are in error; looking for these where they are not to be found, nor ever bethinking themselves where they are. And like Diogenes when brought before Philip after the battle of Chaeronea, the Cynic must remember that he is a Spy. For a Spy he really is—to bring back word what things are on Man's side, and what against him. And when he had diligently observed all, he must come back with a true report, not terrified into announcing them to be foes that are no foes, nor otherwise perturbed or confounded by the things of sense.

114

How can it be that one who hath nothing, neither raiment, nor house, nor home, nor bodily tendance, nor servant, nor city, should yet live tranquil and contented? Behold God hath sent you a man to show you in act and deed that it may be so. Behold me! I have neither house nor possessions nor servants: the ground is my couch; I have no wife, no children, no shelter—nothing but earth and sky, and one poor cloak. And what lack I yet? am I not untouched by sorrow, by fear? am I not free? . . . when have I laid anything to the charge of God or Man? when have I accused any? hath any of you seen me with a sorrowful countenance? And in what wise treat I those of whom you stand in fear and awe? Is it not as slaves? Who when he seeth me doth not think that he beholdeth his Master and his King?

115

Give thyself more diligently to reflection: know thyself: take counsel with the Godhead: without God put thine hand unto nothing!

116

"But to marry and to rear offspring," said the young man, "will the Cynic hold himself bound to undertake this as a chief duty?"

Grant me a republic of wise men, answered Epictetus, and perhaps none will lightly take the Cynic life upon him. For on whose account should he embrace that method of life? Suppose however that he does, there will then be nothing to hinder his marrying and rearing offspring. For his wife will be even such another as himself, and likewise her father; and in like manner will his children be brought up.

But in the present condition of things, which resembles an Army in battle array, ought not the Cynic to be free from all distraction and given wholly to the service of God, so that he can go in and out among men, neither fettered by the duties nor entangled by the relations of common life? For if he transgress them, he will forfeit the character of a good man and true; whereas if he observe them, there is an end to him as the Messenger, the Spy, the Herald of the Gods!

117

Ask me if you choose if a Cynic shall engage in the administration of the State. O fool, seek you a nobler administration than that in which he is engaged? Ask you if a man shall come forward in the Athenian assembly and talk about revenue and supplies, when his business is to converse with all men, Athenians, Corinthians, and Romans alike, not about supplies, not about revenue, nor yet peace and war, but about Happiness and Misery, Prosperity and Adversity, Slavery and Freedom?

Ask you whether a man shall engage in the administration of the State who has engaged in such an Administration as this? Ask me too if he shall govern; and again I will answer, Fool, what greater government shall he hold than he holds already?

118

Such a man needs also to have a certain habit of body. If he appears consumptive, thin and pale, his testimony has no longer the same authority. He must not only prove to the unlearned by showing them what his Soul is that it is possible to be a good man apart from all that they admire; but he must also show them, by his body, that a plain and simple manner of life under the open sky does no harm to the body either. "See, I am proof of this! and my body also." As Diogenes used to do, who went about fresh of look and by the very appearance of his body drew men's eyes. But if a Cynic is an object of pity, he seems a mere beggar; all turn away, all are offended at him. Nor should he be slovenly of look, so as not to scare men from him in this way either; on the contrary, his very roughness should be clean and attractive.

119

Kings and tyrants have armed guards wherewith to chastise certain persons, though they themselves be evil. But to the Cynic conscience gives this power—not arms and guards. When he knows that he has watched and laboured on behalf of mankind: that sleep hath found him pure, and left him purer still: that his thoughts have been the thought of a Friend of the Gods—of a servant, yet one that hath a part in the government of the Supreme God: that the words are ever on his lips:—

Lead me, O God, and thou, O Destiny!
as well as these:—
If this be God's will, so let it be!

why should he not speak boldly unto his own brethren, unto his children—in a word, unto all that are akin to him!

120

Does a Philosopher apply to people to come and hear him? does he not rather, of his own nature, attract those that will be benefited by him—like the sun that warms, the food that sustains them? What Physician applies to men to come and be healed? (Though indeed I hear that the Physicians at Rome do nowadays apply for patients—in my time they were applied to.) I apply to you to come and hear that you are in evil case; that what deserves your attention most is the last thing to gain it; that you know not good from evil, and are in short a hapless wretch; a fine way to apply! though unless the words of the Philosopher affect you thus, speaker and speech are alike dead.

121

A Philosopher's school is a Surgery: pain, not pleasure, you should have felt therein. For on entering none of you is whole. One has a shoulder out of joint, another an abscess: a third suffers from an issue, a fourth from pains in the head. And am I then to sit down and treat you to pretty sentiments and empty flourishes, so that you may applaud me and depart, with neither shoulder, nor head, nor issue, nor abscess a whit the better for your visit? Is it then for this that young men are to quit their homes, and leave parents, friends, kinsmen and substance to mouth out Bravo to your empty phrases!

122

If any be unhappy, let him remember that he is unhappy by reason of himself alone. For God hath made all men to enjoy felicity and constancy of good.

123

Shall we never wean ourselves—shall we never heed the teachings of Philosophy (unless perchance they have been sounding in our ears like an enchanter's drone):—

This World is one great City, and one if the substance whereof it is fashioned: a certain period indeed there needs must be, while these give place to those; some must perish for others to succeed; some move and some abide: yet all is full of friends—first God, then Men, whom Nature hath bound by ties of kindred each to each.

124

Nor did the hero weep and lament at leaving his children orphans. For he knew that no man is an orphan, but it is the Father that careth for all continually and for evermore. Not by mere report had he heard that the Supreme God is the Father of men: seeing that he called Him Father believing Him so to be, and in all that he did had ever his eyes fixed upon Him. Wherefore in whatsoever place he was, there is was given him to live happily.

125

Know you not that the thing is a warfare? one man's duty is to mount guard, another must go out to reconnoitre, a third to battle; all cannot be in one place, nor would it even be expedient. But you, instead of executing you Commander's orders, complain if aught harsher than usual is enjoined; not understanding to what condition you are bringing the army, so far as in you lies. If all were to follow your example, none would dig a trench, none would cast a rampart around the camp, none would keep watch, or expose himself to danger; but all turn out useless for the service of war. . . . Thus it is here also. Every life is a warfare, and that long and various. You must fulfil a soldier's duty, and obey each order at your commander's nod: aye, if it be possible, divine what he would have done; for between that Command and this, there is no comparison, either in might or in excellence.

126

Have you again forgotten? Know you not that a good man does nothing for appearance' sake, but for the sake of having done right? . . .

"Is there no reward then?"

Reward! do you seek any greater reward for a good man than doing what is right and just? Yet at the Great Games you look for nothing else; there the victor's crown you deem enough. Seems it to you so small a thing and worthless, to be a good man, and happy therein?

127

It befits thee not to be unhappy by reason of any, but rather to be happy by reason of all men, and especially by reason of God, who formed us to this end.

128

What, did Diogenes love no man, he that was so gentle, so true a friend to men as cheerfully to endure such bodily hardships for the common weal of all mankind? But how loved he them? As behooved a minister of the Supreme God, alike caring for men and subject unto God.

129

I am by Nature made for my own good; not for my own evil.

130

Remind thyself that he whom thou lovest is mortal—that what thou lovest is not thine own; it is given thee for the present, not irrevocably nor for ever, but even as a fig or a bunch of grapes at the appointed season of the year. . . .

"But these are words of evil omen." . . .

What, callest thou aught of evil omen save that which signifies some evil thing? Cowardice is a word of evil omen, if thou wilt, and meanness of spirit, and lamentation and mourning, and shamelessness. . . .

But do not, I pray thee, call of evil omen a word that is significant of any natural thing:—as well call of evil omen the reaping of the corn; for that means the destruction of the ears, though not of the World!—as well say that the fall of the leaf is of evil omen; that the dried fig should take the place of the green; that raisins should be made from grapes. All these are changes from a former state into another; not destruction, but an ordered economy, a fixed administration. Such is leaving home, a change of small account; such is Death, a greater change, from what now is, not to what is not, but to what is not now.

"Shall I then no longer be?"

Not so; thou wilt be; but something different, of which the World now hath need. For thou too wert born not when thou chosest, but when the World had need of thee.

131

Wherefore a good man and true, bearing in mind who he is and whence he came and from whom he sprang, cares only how he may fill his post with due discipline and obedience to God.

Wilt thou that I continue to live? Then will I live, as one that is free and noble, as Thou wouldst have me. For Thou hast made me free from hindrance in what appertaineth unto me. But hast Thou no further need of me? I thank Thee! Up to this hour have I stayed for Thy sake and none other's; and now in obedience to Thee I depart.

"How dost thou depart?"

Again I say, as Thou wouldst have me; as one that is free, as Thy servant, as one whose ear is open unto what Thou dost enjoin, what Thou dost forbid.

132

Whatsoever place or post Thou assignest me, sooner will I die a thousand deaths, as Socrates said, then depart it. And where wilt Thou have be me? At Rome or Athens? At Thebes or on a desert island? Only remember me there! Shouldst Thou send me where man cannot live as Nature would have him, I will depart, not in disobedience to Thee, but as though Thou wert sounding the signal for my retreat: I am not deserting Thee—far be that from me! I only perceive that thou needest me no longer.

133

If you are in Gyaros, do not let your mind dwell upon life at Rome, and all the pleasures it offered to you when living there, and all that would attend your return. Rather be intent on this—how he that lives in Gyaros may live in Gyaros like a man of spirit. And if you are at Rome, do not let your mind dwell upon the life at Athens, but study only how to live at Rome.

Finally, in the room of all other pleasures put this—the pleasure which springs from concious obedience to God.

134

To a good man there is no evil, either in life or death. And if God supply not food, has He not, as a wise Commander, sounded the signal for retreat and nothing more? I obey, I follow—speaking good of my Commander, and praising His acts. For at His good pleasure I came; and I depart when it pleases Him; and while I was yet alive that was my work, to sing praises unto God!

135

Reflect that the chief source of all evils to Man, and of baseness and cowardice, is not death, but the fear of death.

Against this fear then, I pray you, harden yourself; to this let all your reasonings, your exercises, your reading tend. Then shall you know that thus alone are men set free.

136

He is free who lives as he wishes to live; to whom none can do violence, none hinder or compel; whose impulses are unimpeded, whose desires are attain their purpose, who falls not into what he would avoid. Who then would live in error?—None. Who would live deceived and prone to fall, unjust, intemperate, in abject whining at his lot?—None. Then doth no wicked man live as he would, and therefore neither is he free.

137

Thus do the more cautious of travellers act. The road is said to be beset by robbers. The traveller will not venture alone, but awaits the companionship on the road of an ambassador, a quaestor or a proconsul. To him he attaches himself and thus passes by in safety. So doth the wise man in the world. Many are the companies of robbers and tyrants, many the storms, the straits, the losses of all a man holds dearest. Whither shall he fall for refuge—how shall he pass by unassailed? What companion on the road shall he await for protection? Such and such a wealthy man, of consular rank? And how shall I be profited, if he is stripped and falls to lamentation and weeping? And how if my fellow-traveller himself turns upon me and robs me? What am I to do? I will become a friend of Caesar's! in his train none will do me wrong! In the first place—O the indignities I must endure to win distinction! O the multitude of hands there will be to rob me! And if I succeed, Caesar too is but a mortal. While should it come to pass that I offend him, whither shall I flee from his presence? To the wilderness? And may not fever await me there? What then is to be done? Cannot a fellow-traveller be found that is honest and loyal, strong and secure against surprise? Thus doth the wise man reason, considering that if he would pass through in safety, he must attach himself unto God.

138

"How understandest thou attach himself to God?"

That what God wills, he should will also; that what God wills not, neither should he will.

"How then may this come to pass?"

By considering the movements of God, and His administration.

139

And dost thou that hast received all from another's hands, repine and blame the Giver, if He takes anything from thee? Why, who art thou, and to what end comest thou here? was it not He that made the Light manifest unto thee, that gave thee fellow-workers, and senses, and the power to reason? And how brought He thee into the world? Was it not as one born to die; as one bound to live out his earthly life in some small tabernacle of flesh; to behold His administration, and for a little while share with Him in the mighty march of this great Festival Procession? Now therefore that thou hast beheld, while it was permitted thee, the Solemn Feast and Assembly, wilt thou not cheerfully depart, when He summons thee forth, with adoration and thanksgiving for what thou hast seen and heard?—"Nay, but I would fain have stayed longer at the Festival."—Ah, so would the mystics fain have the rites prolonged; so perchance would the crowd at the Great Games fain behold more wrestlers still. But the Solemn Assembly is over! Come forth, depart with thanksgiving and modesty—give place to others that must come into being even as thyself.

140

Why art thou thus insatiable? why thus unreasonable? why encumber the world?—"Aye, but I fain would have my wife and children with me too."—What, are they then thine, and not His that gave them—His that made thee? Give up then that which is not thine own: yield it to One who is better than thou. "Nay, but why did He bring one into the world on these conditions?"—If it suits thee not, depart! He hath no need of a spectator who finds fault with his lot! Them that will take part in the Feast he needeth—that will lift their voices with the rest, that men may applaud the more, and exalt the Great Assembly in hymns and songs of praise. But the wretched and the fearful He will not be displeased to see absent from it: for when they were present, they did not behave as at a Feast, nor fulfil their proper office; but moaned as though in pain, and found fault with their fate, their fortune and their companions; insensible to what had fallen to their lot, insensible to the powers they had received for a very different purpose—the powers of Magnanimity, Nobility of Heart, of Fortitude, or Freedom!

141

Art thou then free? a man may say. So help me heaven, I long and pray for freedom! But I cannot look my masters boldly in the face; I still value the poor body; I still set much store on its preservation whole and sound.

But I can point thee out a free man, that thou mayest be no more in search of an example. Diogenes was free. How so? Not because he was of free parentage (for that, indeed, was not the case), but because he was himself free. He had cast away every handle whereby slavery might lay hold of him to enslave him, nor was it possible for any to approach and take hold of him to enslave him. All things sat loose upon him—all things were to him attached by but slender ties. Hadst thou seized upon his possessions, he would rather have let them go than have followed thee for them—aye, had it been even a limb, or mayhap his whole body; and in like manner, relatives, friends, and country. For he knew whence they came—from whose hands and on what terms he had received them. His true forefathers, the Gods, his true Country, he never would have abandoned; nor would he have yielded to any man in obedience and submission to the one nor in cheerfully dying for the other. For he was ever mindful that everything that comes to pass has its source and origin there; being indeed brought about for the weal of that his true Country, and directed by Him in whose governance it is.

142

Ponder on this—on these convictions, on these words: fix thine eyes on these examples, if thou wouldst be free, if thou hast thine heart set upon the matter according to its worth. And what marvel if thou purchase so great a thing at so great and high a price? For the sake of this that men deem liberty, some hang themselves, others cast themselves down from the rock; aye, time has been when whole cities came utterly to an end: while for the sake of Freedom that is true, and sure, and unassailable, dost thou grudge to God what He gave, when He claims it? Wilt thou not study, as Plato saith, to endure, not death alone, but torture, exile, stripes—in a word, to render up all that is not thine own? Else thou wilt be a slave amid slaves, wert thou ten thousand times a consul; aye, not a whit the less, though thou climb the Palace steps. And thou shalt know how true the saying of Cleanthes, that though the words of philosophers may run counter to the opinions of the world, yet have they reason on their side.

143

Asked how a man should best grieve his enemy, Epictetus replied, "By setting himself to live the noblest life himself."

144

I am free, I am a friend of God, ready to render Him willing obedience. Of all else I may set store by nothing—neither by mine own body, nor possessions, nor office, nor good report, nor, in a word, aught else beside. For it is not His Will, that I should so set store by these things. Had it been His pleasure, He would have placed my Good therein. But now He hath not done so: therefore I cannot transgress one jot of His commands. In everything hold fast to that which is thy Good—but to all else (as far as is given thee) within the measure of Reason only, contented with this alone. Else thou wilt meet with failure, ill success, let and hindrance. These are the Laws ordained of God—these are His Edicts; these a man should expound and interpret; to these submit himself, not to the laws of Masurius and Cassius.

145

Remember that not the love of power and wealth sets us under the heel of others, but even the love of tranquillity, of leisure, of change of scene—of learning in general, it matters not what the outward thing may be—to set store by it is to place thyself in subjection to another. Where is the difference then between desiring to be a Senator, and desiring not to be one: between thirsting for office and thirsting to be quit of it? Where is the difference between crying, Woe is me, I know not what to do, bound hand and foot as I am to my books so that I cannot stir! and crying, Woe is me, I have not time to read! As though a book were not as much an outward thing and independent of the will, as office and power and the receptions of the great.

Or what reason hast thou (tell me) for desiring to read? For if thou aim at nothing beyond the mere delight of it, or gaining some scrap of knowledge, thou art but a poor, spiritless knave. But if thou desirest to study to its proper end, what else is this than a life that flows on tranquil and serene? And if thy reading secures thee not serenity, what profits it?—"Nay, but it doth secure it," quoth he, "and that is why I repine at being deprived of it."—And what serenity is this that lies at the mercy of every passer-by? I say not at the mercy of the Emperor or Emperor's favorite, but such as trembles at a raven's croak and piper's din, a fever's touch or a thousand things of like sort! Whereas the life serene has no more certain mark than this, that it ever moves with constant unimpeded flow.

146

If thou hast put malice and evil speaking from thee, altogether, or in some degree: if thou hast put away from thee rashness, foulness of tongue, intemperance, sluggishness: if thou art not moved by what once moved thee, or in like manner as thou once wert moved—then thou mayest celebrate a daily festival, to-day because thou hast done well in this manner, to-morrow in that. How much greater cause is here for offering sacrifice, than if a man should become Consul or Prefect?

147

These things hast thou from thyself and from the Gods: only remember who it is that giveth them—to whom and for what purpose they were given. Feeding thy soul on thoughts like these, dost thou debate in what place happiness awaits thee? in what place thou shalt do God's pleasure? Are not the Gods nigh unto all places alike; see they not alike what everywhere comes to pass?

148

To each man God hath granted this inward freedom. These are the principles that in a house create love, in a city concord, among nations peace, teaching a man gratitude towards God and cheerful confidence, wherever he may be, in dealing with outward things that he knows are neither his nor worth striving after.

149

If you seek Truth, you will not seek to gain a victory by every possible means; and when you have found Truth, you need not fear being defeated.

150

What foolish talk is this? how can I any longer lay claim to right principles, if I am not content with being what I am, but am all aflutter about what I am supposed to be?

151

God hath made all things in the world, nay, the world itself, free from hindrance and perfect, and its parts for the use of the whole. Not other creature is capable of comprehending His administration thereof; but the reasonable being Man possesses faculties for the consideration of all these things—not only that he is himself a part, but what part he is, and how it is meet that the parts should give place to the whole. Nor is this all. Being naturally constituted noble, magnanimous, and free, he sees that the things which surround him are of two kinds. Some are free from hindrance and in the power of the will. Other are subject to hindrance, and depend on the will of other men. If then he place his own good, his own best interest, only in that which is free from hindrance and in his power, he will be free, tranquil, happy, unharmed, noble-hearted, and pious; giving thanks to all things unto God, finding fault with nothing that comes to pass, laying no charge against anything. Whereas if he place his good in outward things, depending not on the will, he must perforce be subject to hindrance and restraint, the slave of those that have power over the things he desires and fears; he must perforce be impious, as deeming himself injured at the hands of God; he must be unjust, as ever prone to claim more than his due; he must perforce be of a mean and abject spirit.

152

Whom then shall I fear? the lords of the Bedchamber, lest they should shut me out? If they find me desirous of entering in, let them shut me out, if they will.

"Then why comest thou to the door?"

Because I think it meet and right, so long as the Play lasts, to take part therein.

"In what sense art thou then shut out?"

Because, unless I am admitted, it is not my will to enter: on the contrary, my will is simply that which comes to pass. For I esteem what God wills better than what I will. To Him will I cleave as His minister and attendant; having the same movements, the same desires, in a word the same Will as He. There is no such thing as being shut out for me, but only for them that would force their way in.

153

But what says Socrates?—"One man finds pleasure in improving his land, another his horses. My pleasure lies in seeing that I myself grow better day by day."

154

The dress is suited to the craft; the craftsman takes his name from the craft, not from the dress. For this reason Euphrates was right in saying, "I long endeavoured to conceal my following the philosophic life; and this profited me much. In the first place, I knew that what I did aright, I did not for the sake of lookers-on, but for my own. I ate aright—unto myself; I kept the even tenor of my walk, my glance composed and serene—all unto myself and unto God. Then as I fought alone, I was alone in peril. If I did anything amiss or shameful, the cause of Philosophy was not in me endangered; nor did I wrong the multitude by transgressing as a professed philosopher. Wherefore those that knew not my purpose marvelled how it came about, that whilst all my life and conversation was passed with philosophers without exception, I was yet none myself. And what harm that the philosopher should be known by his acts, instead of mere outward signs and symbols?"

155

First study to conceal what thou art; seek wisdom a little while unto thyself. Thus grows the fruit; first, the seed must be buried in the earth for a little space; there it must be hid and slowly grow, that it may reach maturity. But if it produce the ear before the jointed stalk, it is imperfect—a thing from the garden of Adonis. Such a sorry growth art thou; thou hast blossomed too soon: the winter cold will wither thee away!

156

First of all, condemn the life thou art now leading: but when thou hast condemned it, do not despair of thyself—be not like them of mean spirit, who once they have yielded, abandon themselves entirely and as it were allow the torrent to sweep them away. No; learn what the wrestling masters do. Has the boy fallen? "Rise," they say, "wrestle again, till thy strength come to thee." Even thus should it be with thee. For know that there is nothing more tractable than the human soul. It needs but to will, and the thing is done; the soul is set upon the right path: as on the contrary it needs but to nod over the task, and all is lost. For ruin and recovery alike are from within.

157

It is the critical moment that shows the man. So when the crisis is upon you, remember that God, like a trainer of wrestlers, has matched you with a rough and stalwart antagonist.—"To what end?" you ask. That you may prove the victor at the Great Games. Yet without toil and sweat this may not be!

158

If thou wouldst make progress, be content to seem foolish and void of understanding with respect to outward things. Care not to be thought to know anything. If any should make account of thee, distrust thyself.

159

Remember that in life thou shouldst order thy conduct as at a banquet. Has any dish that is being served reached thee? Stretch forth thy hand and help thyself modestly. Doth it pass thee by? Seek not to detain it. Has it not yet come? Send not forth thy desire to meet it, but wait until it reaches thee. Deal thus with children, thus with wife; thus with office, thus with wealth—and one day thou wilt be meet to share the Banquets of the Gods. But if thou dost not so much as touch that which is placed before thee, but despisest it, then shalt thou not only share the Banquets of the Gods, but their Empire also.

160

Remember that thou art an actor in a play, and of such sort as the Author chooses, whether long or short. If it be his good pleasure to assign thee the part of a beggar, a ruler, or a simple citizen, thine it is to play it fitly. For thy business is to act the part assigned thee, well: to choose it, is another's.

161

Keep death and exile daily before thine eyes, with all else that men deem terrible, but more especially Death. Then wilt thou never think a mean thought, nor covet anything beyond measure.

162

As a mark is not set up in order to be missed, so neither is such a thing as natural evil produced in the World.

163

Piety toward the Gods, to be sure, consists chiefly in thinking rightly concerning them—that they are, and that they govern the Universe with goodness and justice; and that thou thyself art appointed to obey them, and to submit under all circumstances that arise; acquiescing cheerfully in whatever may happen, sure it is brought to pass and accomplished by the most Perfect Understanding. Thus thou wilt never find fault with the Gods, nor charge them with neglecting thee.

164

Lose no time in setting before you a certain stamp of character and behaviour both when by yourself and in company with others. Let silence be your general rule; or say only what is necessary and in few words. We shall, however, when occasion demands, enter into discourse sparingly, avoiding common topics as gladiators, horse-races, athletes; and the perpetual talk about food and drink. Above all avoid speaking of persons, either in way of praise or blame, or comparison.

If you can, win over the conversation of your company to what it should be by your own. But if you find yourself cut off without escape among strangers and aliens, be silent.

165

Laughter should not be much, nor frequent, nor unrestrained.

166

Refuse altogether to take an oath if you can, if not, as far as may be.

167

Banquets of the unlearned and of them that are without, avoid. But if you have occasion to take part in them, let not your attention be relaxed for a moment, lest you slip after all into evil ways. For you may rest assured that be a man ever so pure himself, he cannot escape defilement if his associates are impure.

168

Take what relates to the body as far as the bare use warrants—as meat, drink, raiment, house and servants. But all that makes for show and luxury reject.

169

If you are told that such an one speaks ill of you, make no defence against what was said, but answer, He surely knew not my other faults, else he would not have mentioned these only!

170

When you visit any of those in power, bethink yourself that you will not find him in: that you may not be admitted: that the door may be shut in your face: that he may not concern himself about you. If with all this, it is your duty to go, bear what happens, and never say to yourself, It was not worth the trouble! For that would smack of the foolish and unlearned who suffer outward things to touch them.

171

In company avoid frequent and undue talk about your own actions and dangers. However pleasant it may be to you to enlarge upon the risks you have run, others may not find such pleasure in listening to your adventures. Avoid provoking laughter also: it is a habit from which one easily slides into the ways of the foolish, and apt to diminish the respect which your neighbors feel for you. To border on coarse talk is also dangerous. On such occasions, if a convenient opportunity offer, rebuke the speaker. If not, at least by relapsing into silence, colouring, and looking annoyed, show that you are displeased with the subject.

172

When you have decided that a thing ought to be done, and are doing it, never shun being seen doing it, even though the multitude should be likely to judge the matter amiss. For if you are not acting rightly, shun the act itself; if rightly, however, why fear misplaced censure?

173

It stamps a man of mean capacity to spend much time on the things of the body, as to be long over bodily exercises, long over eating, long over drinking, long over other bodily functions. Rather should these things take the second place, while all your care is directed to the understanding.

174

Everything has two handles, one by which it may be borne, the other by which it may not. If your brother sin against you lay not hold of it by the handle of injustice, for by that it may not be borne: but rather by this, that he is your brother, the comrade of your youth; and thus you will lay hold on it so that it may be borne.

175

Never call yourself a Philosopher nor talk much among the unlearned about Principles, but do that which follows from them. Thus at a banquet, do not discuss how people ought to eat; but eat as you ought. Remember that Socrates thus entirely avoided ostentation. Men would come to him desiring to be recommended to philosophers, and he would conduct them thither himself—so well did he bear being overlooked. Accordingly if any talk concerning principles should arise among the unlearned, be you for the most part silent. For you run great risk of spewing up what you have ill digested. And when a man tells you that you know nothing and you are not nettled at it, then you may be sure that you have begun the work.

176

When you have brought yourself to supply the needs of the body at small cost, do not pique yourself on that, nor if you drink only water, keep saying on each occasion, I drink water! And if you ever want to practise endurance and toil, do so unto yourself and not unto others—do not embrace statues!

177

When a man prides himself on being able to understand and interpret the writings of Chrysippus, say to yourself:—

If Chrysippus had not written obscurely, this fellow would have had nothing to be proud of. But what is it that I desire? To understand Nature, and to follow her! Accordingly I ask who is the Interpreter. On hearing that it is Chrysippus, I go to him. But it seems I do not understand what he wrote. So I seek one to interpret that. So far there is nothing to pride myself on. But when I have found my interpreter, what remains is to put in practice his instructions. This itself is the only thing to be proud of. But if I admire the interpretation and that alone, what else have I turned out but a mere commentator instead of a lover of wisdom?—except indeed that I happen to be interpreting Chrysippus instead of Homer. So when any one says to me, Prithee, read me Chrysippus, I am more inclined to blush, when I cannot show my deeds to be in harmony and accordance with his sayings.

178

At feasts, remember that you are entertaining two guests, body and soul. What you give to the body, you presently lose; what you give to the soul, you keep for ever.

179

At meals, see to it that those who serve be not more in number than those who are served. It is absurd for a crowd of persons to be dancing attendance on half a dozen chairs.

180

It is best to share with your attendants what is going forward, both in the labour of preparation and in the enjoyment of the feast itself. If such a thing be difficult at the time, recollect that you who are not weary are being served by those that are; you who are eating and drinking by those who do neither; you who are talking by those who are silent; you who are at ease by those who are under constraint. Thus no sudden wrath will betray you into unreasonable conduct, nor will you behave harshly by irritating another.

181

When Xanthippe was chiding Socrates for making scanty preparation for entertaining his friends, he answered:—"If they are friends of our, they will not care for that; if they are not, we shall care nothing for them!"

182

Asked, Who is the rich man? Epictetus replied, "He who is content."

183

Favorinus tells us how Epictetus would also say that there were two faults far graver and fouler than any others—inability to bear, and inability to forbear, when we neither patiently bear the blows that must be borne, nor abstain from the things and the pleasures we ought to abstain from. "So," he went on, "if a man will only have these two words at heart, and heed them carefully by ruling and watching over himself, he will for the most part fall into no sin, and his life will be tranquil and serene." He meant the words—"Bear and Forbear."

184

On all occasions these thoughts should be at hand:—

Lead me, O God, and Thou, O Destiny Be what it may the goal appointed me, Bravely I'll follow; nay, and if I would not, I'd prove a coward, yet must follow still!

Again:

Who to Necessity doth bow aright, Is learn'd in wisdom and the things of God.

Once more:—

Crito, if this be God's will, so let it be. As for me, Anytus and Meletus can indeed put me to death, but injure me, never!

185

We shall then be like Socrates, when we can indite hymns of praise to the Gods in prison.

186

It is hard to combine and unite these two qualities, the carefulness of one who is affected by circumstances, and the intrepidity of one who heeds them not. But it is not impossible: else were happiness also impossible. We should act as we do in seafaring.

"What can I do?"—Choose the master, the crew, the day, the opportunity. Then comes a sudden storm. What matters it to me? my part has been fully done. The matter is in the hands of another—the Master of the ship. The ship is foundering. What then have I to do? I do the only thing that remains to me—to be drowned without fear, without a cry, without upbraiding God, but knowing that what has been born must likewise perish. For I am not Eternity, but a human being—a part of the whole, as an hour is part of the day. I must come like the hour, and like the hour must pass!

187

And now we are sending you to Rome to spy out the land; but none send a coward as such a spy, that, if he hear but a noise and see a shadow moving anywhere, loses his wits and comes flying to say, The enemy are upon us!

So if you go now, and come and tell us: "Everything at Rome is terrible: Death is terrible, Exile is terrible, Slander is terrible, Want is terrible; fly, comrades! the enemy are upon us!" we shall reply, Get you gone, and prophesy to yourself! we have but erred in sending such a spy as you. Diogenes, who was sent as a spy long before you, brought us back another report than this. He says that Death is no evil; for it need not even bring shame with it. He says that Fame is but the empty noise of madmen. And what report did this spy bring us of Pain, what of Pleasure, what of Want? That to be clothed in sackcloth is better than any purple robe; that sleeping on the bare ground is the softest couch; and in proof of each assertion he points to his own courage, constancy, and freedom; to his own healthy and muscular frame. "There is no enemy near," he cries, "all is perfect peace!"

188

If a man has this peace—not the peace proclaimed by Caesar (how indeed should he have it to proclaim?), nay, but the peace proclaimed by God through reason, will not that suffice him when alone, when he beholds and reflects:—Now can no evil happen unto me; for me there is no robber, for me no earthquake; all things are full of peace, full of tranquillity; neither highway nor city nor gathering of men, neither neighbor nor comrade can do me hurt. Another supplies my food, whose care it is; another my raiment; another hath given me perceptions of sense and primary conceptions. And when He supplies my necessities no more, it is that He is sounding the retreat, that He hath opened the door, and is saying to thee, Come!—Wither? To nought that thou needest fear, but to the friendly kindred elements whence thou didst spring. Whatsoever of fire is in thee, unto fire shall return; whatsoever of earth, unto earth; of spirit, unto spirit; of water, unto water. There is no Hades, no fabled rivers of Sighs, of Lamentation, or of Fire: but all things are full of Beings spiritual and divine. With thoughts like these, beholding the Sun, Moon, and Stars, enjoying earth and sea, a man is neither helpless nor alone!

189

What wouldst thou be found doing when overtaken by Death? If I might choose, I would be found doing some deed of true humanity, of wide import, beneficent and noble. But if I may not be found engaged in aught so lofty, let me hope at least for this—what none may hinder, what is surely in my power—that I may be found raising up in myself that which had fallen; learning to deal more wisely with the things of sense; working out my own tranquillity, and thus rendering that which is its due to every relation of life. . . .

If death surprise me thus employed, it is enough if I can stretch forth my hands to God and say, "The faculties which I received at Thy hands for apprehending this thine Administration, I have not neglected. As far as in me lay, I have done Thee no dishonour. Behold how I have used the senses, the primary conceptions which Thous gavest me. Have I ever laid anything to Thy charge? Have I ever murmured at aught that came to pass, or wished it otherwise? Have I in anything transgressed the relations of life? For that Thou didst beget me, I thank Thee for that Thou hast given: for the time during which I have used the things that were Thine, it suffices me. Take them back and place them wherever Thou wilt! They were all Thine, and Thou gavest them me."—If a man depart thus minded, is it not enough? What life is fairer and more noble, what end happier than his?

Section 3

Fragments

1

A life entangled with Fortune is like a torrent. It is turbulent and muddy; hard to pass and masterful of mood: noisy and of brief continuance.

2

The soul that companies with Virtue is like an ever-flowing source. It is a pure, clear, and wholesome draught; sweet, rich, and generous of its store; that injures not, neither destroys.

3

It is a shame that one who sweetens his drink with the gifts of the bee, should embitter God's gift Reason with vice.

4

Crows pick out the eyes of the dead, when the dead have no longer need of them; but flatterers mar the soul of the living, and her eyes they blind.

5

Keep neither a blunt knife nor an ill-disciplined looseness of tongue.

6

Nature hath given men one tongue but two ears, that we may hear from others twice as much as we speak.

7

Do not give sentence in another tribunal till you have been yourself judged in the tribunal of Justice.

8

If is shameful for a Judge to be judged by others.

9

Give me by all means the shorter and nobler life, instead of one that is longer but of less account!

10

Freedom is the name of virtue: Slavery, of vice. . . . None is a slave whose acts are free.

11

Of pleasures, those which occur most rarely give the most delight.

12

Exceed due measure, and the most delightful things become the least delightful.

13

The anger of an ape—the threat of a flatterer:—these deserve equal regard.

14

Chastise thy passions that they avenge not themselves upon thee.

15

No man is free who is not master of himself.

16

A ship should not ride on a single anchor, nor life on a single hope.

17

Fortify thyself with contentment: that is an impregnable stronghold.

18

No man who is a lover of money, of pleasure, of glory, is likewise a lover of Men; but only he that is a lover of whatsoever things are fair and good.

19

Think of God more often than thou breathest.

20

Choose the life that is noblest, for custom can make it sweet to thee.

21

Let thy speech of God be renewed day by day, aye, rather than thy meat and drink.

22

Even as the Sun doth not wait for prayers and incantations to rise, but shines forth and is welcomed by all: so thou also wait not for clapping of hands and shouts and praise to do thy duty; nay, do good of thine own accord, and thou wilt be loved like the Sun.

23

Let no man think that he is loved by any who loveth none.

24

If thou rememberest that God standeth by to behold and visit all that thou doest; whether in the body or in the soul, thou surely wilt not err in any prayer or deed; and thou shalt have God to dwell with thee.

Appendix

The Hymn of Cleanthes

Chiefest glory of deathless Gods, Almighty for ever,
Sovereign of Nature that rulest by law, what Name shall we give Thee?—
Blessed be Thou! for on Thee should call all things that are mortal.
For that we are Thine offspring; nay, all that in myriad motion
Lives for its day on the earth bears one impress—Thy likeness—upon it.
Wherefore my song is of Thee, and I hymn thy power for ever.

Lo, the vast orb of the Worlds, round the Earth evermore as it rolleth,
Feels Thee its Ruler and Guide, and owns Thy lordship rejoicing.
Aye, for Thy conquering hands have a servant of living fire—
Sharp is the bolt!—where it falls, Nature shrinks at the shock
and doth shudder.
Thus Thou directest the Word universal that pulses through all things,
Mingling its life with Lights that are great and Lights that are lesser,
E'en as beseemeth its birth, High King through ages unending.

Nought is done that is done without Thee in the earth or the waters
Or in the heights of heaven, save the deed of the fool and the sinner.
Thou canst make rough things smooth; at Thy voice, lo, jarring disorder
Moveth to music, and Love is born where hatred abounded.
Thus hast Thou fitted alike things good and things evil together,
That over all might reign one Reason, supreme and eternal;
Though thereunto the hearts of the wicked be hardened and heedless—

Woe unto them!—for while ever their hands are grasping at good things,
Blind are their eyes, yea, stopped are their ears to God's Law universal,
Calling through wise disobedience to live the life that is noble.
This they mark not, but heedless of right, turn each to his own way,
Here, a heart fired with ambition, in strife and straining unhallowed;
There, thrusting honour aside, fast set upon getting and gaining;
Others again given over to lusts and dissolute softness,
Working never God's Law, but that which warreth upon it.

Nay, but, O Giver of all things good, whose home is the dark cloud,
Thou that wieldesy Heaven's bolt, save men from their ignorance grievous;
Scatter its night from their souls, and grant them to come to that Wisdom
Wherewithal, sistered with Justice, Thou rulest and governest all things;
That we, honoured by Thee, may requite Thee with worship and honour,
Evermore praising thy works, as is meet for men that shall perish;
Seeing that none, be he mortal or God, hath privilege nobler
Than without stint, without stay, to extol Thy Law universal.

LUCIUS ANNAEUS SENECA

Collected Letters

Translated by Richard Mott Gummere

Contents

Introduction

Among the personalities of the early Roman Empire there are few who offer to the readers of today* such dramatic interest as does Lucius Annaeus Seneca, the author of the Epistles which are translated in this volume. Born in a province, educated at Rome, prominent at the bar, a distinguished exile, a trusted minister of State, and a doomed victim of a capricious emperor, Seneca is so linked with the age in which he lived that in reading his works we read those of a true representative of the most thrilling period of Roman history.

Seneca was born in the year 4 BC, a time of great opportunity, at Corduba (now Cordoba), in Spain, son of the talented rhetorician Annaeus Seneca. We gather that the family moved to Rome during the boyhood of Lucius, that he was educated for the bar, and that he was soon attracted by the Stoic philosophy, the stern nurse of heroes during the first century of the Empire. That his social connexions were distinguished we infer from the prominence and refinement of his brother Gallio—the Gallio of the New Testament—from the fact that he himself was noticed and almost condemned to death by the Emperor Caligula soon after he began to speak in public, and especially because his aunt, whom he visited in Egypt, was the wife of the governor of that country.

Up to the year 41 he prospered. He makes mention of his children, of his mother who, like the mother of Goethe, seems to have imbued him with idealism and a certain amount of mysticism, and of many valued friends. But during that year, as a result of court intrigue, he was banished to the island of Corsica. The charge against him was a too great intimacy with Iulia Livilla, unfortunate sister of the late emperor, and the arch-foe of Messalina, whose husband, Claudius, had recalled the princess from exile. We may discount any

* Originally published in 1916.

crime on Seneca's part because even the gossip-laden Suetonius says: "The charge was vague and the accused was given no opportunity to defend himself."

The eight years of exile were productive of much literary work. The tragedies, which have had such influence on later drama, are the fruit of this period, besides certain essays on philosophic subjects, and a rather cringing letter to Polybius, a rich freedman at the court of Claudius. In 49, however, Fortune, whom Seneca as a Stoic so often ridicules, came to his rescue. Agrippina had him recalled and appointed tutor to her young son, later to become the Emperor Nero. Holding the usual offices of state, and growing in prominence, Seneca administered the affairs of the prince, in partnership with Burrus, the praetorian. Together they maintained the balance of power between throne and Senate until the death of Burrus in the year 62. After that time, a philosopher without the support of military power was unable to cope with the vices and whims of the monster on the throne.

The last two years of Seneca's life were spent in travelling about southern Italy, composing essays on natural history and relieving his burdened soul by correspondence with his friend Lucilius. In the year 65 came his suicide, anticipating an act of violence on the Emperor's part; in this deed of heroism he was nobly supported by his young wife Paulina. The best account of these dark days is given in Tacitus.

These letters are all addressed to Lucilius. From internal evidence we gather that the native country of this Lucilius was Campania, and his native city Pompeii or Naples. He was a Roman knight, having gained that position, as Seneca tells us, by sheer industry. Prominent in the civil service, he had filled many important positions and was, at the time when the *Letters* were written, procurator in Sicily. He seems to have had Epicurean tendencies, like so many men from this part of Italy; the author argues and tries to win him over to Stoicism, in the kindliest manner. Lucilius wrote books, was interested in philosophy and geography, knew intimately many persons in high places, and is thought by some to be the author of the extant poem *Aetna*.

When their friendship began we cannot say. The *Naturales Quaestiones* and the *Letters* are the work of Seneca's closing years. Both are addressed to Lucilius. The essay *De Providentia*, which was also dedicated to him, is of doubtful date, and may be fixed at any time between the beginning of the exile in Corsica and the period when the *Letters* were written.

In spite of the many problems which confront us, it may be safely said that the years 63–65 constitute the period of the *Letters*. We find possible allusions to the Campanian earthquake of 63, a reference to the conflagration at Lyons, which took place either in 64 or in 65, and various hints that the philosopher was travelling about Italy in order to forget politics. The form of this work, as Bacon says, is a collection of essays rather than of letters. The recipient is often mentioned by name; but his identity is secondary to the main purpose. . . . The ingenious juxtaposition of effective words, the balance in style and thought, and the continual striving after point, indicate that the language of the diatribe had affected the informality of the epistle.

The structure of each letter is interesting. A concrete fact, such as the mention of an illness, a voyage by sea or land, an incident like the adventure in the Naples tunnel, a picnic party, or an assemblage of friends who discuss questions from Plato, or Aristotle, or Epicurus—these are the elements which serve to justify the reflections which follow. After such an introduction, the writer takes up his theme; he deals with abstract subjects such as the contempt of death, the stout-heartedness of the sage, or the quality of the Supreme Good. We shall not mention the sources of all these topics in footnotes, but shall aim only to explain that which is obscure in meaning or unusual in its import. Plato's Theory of Ideas, Aristotle's Categories, Theophrastus on Friendship, Epicurus on Pleasure, and all the countless doctrinal shades of difference which we find in the Stoic leaders, are at least sketched in outline.

But we must give full credit to the philosopher's own originality. In these letters, it is impossible to ignore the advance from a somewhat stiff and Ciceronian point of view into the attractive and debatable land of what one may fairly call modern ideas. The style of the Epistles is bold, and so is the thought. . . .

The Epistles contain also, of course, the usual literary types which every Roman epistolographer would feel bound to introduce. There is the *consolatio*; there is the theme of friendship; there are second-hand lectures on philosophy taken from Plato and Aristotle and Theophrastus. . . . and several characteristically Roman laudations of certain old men (including the author himself) who wrestle with physical infirmities. But the Stoic doctrine is interpreted better, from the Roman point of view, by no other Latin writer. The facts of Seneca's life prove the sincerity of his utterances, and blunt the edge of many of the sneers which we find in Dio Cassius, regarding the fabulous sums which he had out at interest and the costly tables purchased for the palace of a millionaire.

Finally, in no pagan author, save perhaps Vergil, is the beauty of holiness so sincerely presented from a Roman standpoint. Although his connexion with the early Church has been disproved, Seneca shows the modern, the Christian, spirit.

—*Richard M. Gummere*
Haverford College
May 1916

Letters

1. ON SAVING TIME

Greetings from Seneca to his friend Lucilius.

Continue to act thus, my dear Lucilius—set yourself free for your own sake; gather and save your time, which till lately has been forced from you, or filched away, or has merely slipped from your hands. Make yourself believe the truth of my words—that certain moments are torn from us, that some are gently removed, and that others glide beyond our reach. The most disgraceful kind of loss, however, is that due to carelessness. Furthermore, if you will pay close heed to the problem, you will find that the largest portion of our life passes while we are doing ill, a goodly share while we are doing nothing, and the whole while we are doing that which is not to the purpose. What man can you show me who places any value on his time, who reckons the worth of each day, who understands that he is dying daily? For we are mistaken when we look forward to death; the major portion of death has already passed. Whatever years be behind us are in death's hands.

Therefore, Lucilius, do as you write me that you are doing: hold every hour in your grasp. Lay hold of today's task, and you will not need to depend so much upon tomorrow's. While we are postponing, life speeds by. Nothing, Lucilius, is ours, except time. We were entrusted by nature with the ownership of this single thing, so fleeting and slippery that anyone who will can oust us from possession. What fools these mortals be! They allow the cheapest and most useless things, which can easily be replaced, to be charged in the reckoning, after they have acquired them; but they never regard themselves as in debt when they have received some of that precious commodity—time! And yet time is the one loan which even a grateful recipient cannot repay.

You may desire to know how I, who preach to you so freely, am practising.

I confess frankly: my expense account balances, as you would expect from one who is free-handed but careful. I cannot boast that I waste nothing, but I can at least tell you what I am wasting, and the cause and manner of the loss; I can give you the reasons why I am a poor man. My situation, however, is the same as that of many who are reduced to slender means through no fault of their own: every one forgives them, but no one comes to their rescue.

What is the state of things, then? It is this: I do not regard a man as poor, if the little which remains is enough for him. I advise you, however, to keep what is really yours; and you cannot begin too early. For, as our ancestors believed, it is too late to spare when you reach the dregs of the cask. Of that which remains at the bottom, the amount is slight, and the quality is vile. Farewell.

2. ON DISCURSIVENESS IN READING

Judging by what you write me, and by what I hear, I am forming a good opinion regarding your future. You do not run hither and thither and distract yourself by changing your abode; for such restlessness is the sign of a disordered spirit. The primary indication, to my thinking, of a well-ordered mind is a man's ability to remain in one place and linger in his own company. Be careful, however, lest this reading of many authors and books of every sort may tend to make you discursive and unsteady. You must linger among a limited number of master thinkers, and digest their works, if you would derive ideas which shall win firm hold in your mind. Everywhere means nowhere. When a person spends all his time in foreign travel, he ends by having many acquaintances, but no friends. And the same thing must hold true of men who seek intimate acquaintance with no single author, but visit them all in a hasty and hurried manner. Food does no good and is not assimilated into the body if it leaves the stomach as soon as it is eaten; nothing hinders a cure so much as frequent change of medicine; no wound will heal when one salve is tried after another; a plant which is often moved can never grow strong. There is nothing so efficacious that it can be helpful while it is being shifted about. And in reading of many books is distraction.

Accordingly, since you cannot read all the books which you may possess, it is enough to possess only as many books as you can read. "But," you reply, "I wish to dip first into one book and then into another." I tell you that it is the sign of an overnice appetite to toy with many dishes; for when they are manifold and varied, they cloy but do not nourish. So you should always read standard authors; and when you crave a change, fall back upon those whom you read before. Each day acquire something that will fortify you against poverty, against death, indeed against other misfortunes as well; and after you have run over many thoughts, select one to be thoroughly digested that day. This is my own custom; from the many things which I have read, I claim some one part for myself.

The thought for today is one which I discovered in Epicurus; for I am wont to cross over even into the enemy's camp—not as a deserter, but as a scout. He says: "Contented poverty is an honourable estate." Indeed, if it be contented, it is not poverty at all. It is not the man who has too little, but the man who craves more, that is poor. What does it matter how much a man has laid up in his safe, or in his warehouse, how large are his flocks and how fat his dividends, if he covets his neighbour's property, and reckons, not his past gains, but his hopes of gains to come? Do you ask what is the proper limit to wealth? It is, first, to have what is necessary, and, second, to have what is enough. Farewell.

3. ON TRUE AND FALSE FRIENDSHIP

You have sent a letter to me through the hand of a "friend" of yours, as you call him. And in your very next sentence you warn me not to discuss with him all the matters that concern you, saying that even you yourself are not accustomed to do this; in other words, you have in the same letter affirmed and denied that he is your friend. Now if you used this word of ours in the popular sense, and called him "friend" in the same way in which we speak of all candidates for election as "honourable gentlemen," and as we greet all men whom we meet casually, if their names slip us for the moment, with the salutation "my dear sir,"—so be it. But if you consider any man a friend whom you do not trust as you trust yourself, you are mightily mistaken and you do not sufficiently understand what true friendship means. Indeed, I would have you discuss everything with a friend; but first of all discuss the man himself. When friendship is settled, you must trust; before friendship is formed, you must pass judgment. Those persons indeed put last first and confound their duties, who, violating the rules of Theophrastus, judge a man after they have made him their friend, instead of making him their friend after they have judged him. Ponder for a long time whether you shall admit a given person to your friendship; but when you have decided to admit him, welcome him with all your heart and soul. Speak as boldly with him as with yourself. As to yourself, although you should live in such a way that you trust your own self with nothing which you could not entrust even to your enemy, yet, since certain matters occur which convention keeps secret, you should share with a friend at least all your worries and reflections. Regard him as loyal, and you will make him loyal. Some, for example, fearing to be deceived, have taught men to deceive; by their suspicions they have given their friend the right to do wrong. Why need I keep back any words in the presence of my friend? Why should I not regard myself as alone when in his company?

There is a class of men who communicate, to anyone whom they meet, matters which should be revealed to friends alone, and unload upon the chance listener whatever irks them. Others, again, fear to confide in their closest intimates; and if it were possible, they would not trust even themselves, burying their secrets deep in their hearts. But we should do neither. It is equally faulty to trust everyone and to trust no one. Yet the former fault is, I should say, the more ingenuous, the latter the more safe. In like manner you should rebuke these two kinds of men,—both those who always lack repose, and those who are always in repose. For love of bustle is not industry,—it is only the restlessness of a hunted mind. And true repose does not consist in condemning all motion as merely vexation; that kind of repose is slackness and inertia. Therefore, you should note the following saying, taken from my reading in Pomponius: "Some men shrink into dark corners, to such a degree that they see darkly by day." No, men should combine these tendencies, and he who reposes should act and he who acts should take repose. Discuss the problem with Nature; she will tell you that she has created both day and night. Farewell.

7. ON CROWDS

Do you ask me what you should regard as especially to be avoided? I say, crowds; for as yet you cannot trust yourself to them with safety. I shall admit my own weakness, at any rate; for I never bring back home the same character that I took abroad with me. Something of that which I have forced to be calm within me is disturbed; some of the foes that I have routed return again. Just as the sick man, who has been weak for a long time, is in such a condition that he cannot be taken out of the house without suffering a relapse, so we ourselves are affected when our souls are recovering from a lingering disease. To consort with the crowd is harmful; there is no person who does not make some vice attractive to us, or stamp it upon us, or taint us unconsciously therewith. Certainly, the greater the mob with which we mingle, the greater the danger.

But nothing is so damaging to good character as the habit of lounging at the games; for then it is that vice steals subtly upon one through the avenue of pleasure. What do you think I mean? I mean that I come home more greedy, more ambitious, more voluptuous, and even more cruel and inhuman, because I have been among human beings. By chance I attended a mid-day exhibition, expecting some fun, wit, and relaxation—an exhibition at which men's eyes have respite from the slaughter of their fellow-men. But it was quite the reverse. The previous combats were the essence of compassion: but now all the trifling is put aside and it is pure murder.* The men have no defensive armour. They are exposed to blows at all points, and no one ever strikes in vain. Many persons prefer this programme to the usual pairs and to the bouts "by request." Of course they do; there is no helmet or shield to deflect the weapon. What is the need of defensive armour, or of skill? All these mean delaying death. In the morning they throw men to the lions and the bears; at noon, they throw them to the spectators. The spectators demand that the slayer shall face the man who is to slay him in his turn; and they always reserve the latest conqueror for another butchering. The outcome of every fight is death, and the means are fire and sword. This sort of thing goes on while the arena is empty. You may retort: "But he was a highway robber; he killed a man!" And what of it? Granted that, as a murderer, he deserved this punishment, what crime have you committed, poor fellow, that you should deserve to sit and see this show? In the morning they cried "Kill him! Lash him! Burn him! Why does he meet the sword in so cowardly a way? Why does he strike so feebly? Why doesn't he die game? Whip him to meet his wounds! Let them receive blow for blow, with chests bare and exposed to the stroke!" And when the games stop for the intermission, they announce: "A little throatcutting in the meantime, so that there may still be something going on!"

Come now; do you† not understand even this truth, that a bad example reacts on the agent? Thank the immortal gods that you are teaching cruelty

---

* During the luncheon interval, condemned criminals were often driven into the arena and compelled to fight, for the amusement of those spectators who remained throughout the day.

† The remark is addressed to the brutalized spectators.

to a person who cannot learn to be cruel. The young character, which cannot hold fast to righteousness, must be rescued from the mob; it is too easy to side with the majority. Even Socrates, Cato, and Laelius might have been shaken in their moral strength by a crowd that was unlike them; so true it is that none of us, no matter how much he cultivates his abilities, can withstand the shock of faults that approach, as it were, with so great a retinue. Much harm is done by a single case of indulgence or greed; the familiar friend, if he be luxurious, weakens and softens us imperceptibly; the neighbour, if he be rich, rouses our covetousness; the companion, if he be slanderous, rubs off some of his rust upon us, even though we be spotless and sincere. What then do you think the effect will be on character, when the world at large assaults it! You must either imitate or loathe the world.

But both courses are to be avoided; you should not copy the bad simply because they are many, nor should you hate the many because they are unlike you. Withdraw into yourself, as far as you can. Associate with those who will make a better man of you. Welcome those whom you yourself can improve. The process is mutual; for men learn while they teach. There is no reason why pride in advertising your abilities should lure you into publicity, so that you should desire to recite or harangue before the general public. Of course I should be willing for you to do so if you had a stock-in-trade that suited such a mob; as it is, there is not a man of them who can understand you. One or two individuals will perhaps come in your way, but even these will have to be moulded and trained by you so that they will understand you. You may say: "For what purpose did I learn all these things?" But you need not fear that you have wasted your efforts; it was for yourself that you learned them.

In order, however, that I may not today have learned exclusively for myself, I shall share with you three excellent sayings, of the same general purport, which have come to my attention. This letter will give you one of them as payment of my debt; the other two you may accept as a contribution in advance. Democritus says: "One man means as much to me as a multitude, and a multitude only as much as one man." The following also was nobly spoken by someone or other, for it is doubtful who the author was; they asked him what was the object of all this study applied to an art that would reach but very few. He replied: "I am content with few, content with one, content with none at all." The third saying—and a noteworthy one, too—is by Epicurus, written to one of the partners of his studies: "I write this not for the many, but for you; each of us is enough of an audience for the other." Lay these words to heart,

Lucilius, that you may scorn the pleasure which comes from the applause of the majority. Many men praise you; but have you any reason for being pleased with yourself, if you are a person whom the many can understand? Your good qualities should face inwards. Farewell.

9. ON PHILOSOPHY AND FRIENDSHIP

You desire to know whether Epicurus is right when, in one of his letters, he rebukes those who hold that the wise man is self-sufficient and for that reason does not stand in need of friendships. This is the objection raised by Epicurus against Stilbo and those who believe* that the Supreme Good is a soul which is insensible to feeling.

We are bound to meet with a double meaning if we try to express the Greek term "lack of feeling" summarily, in a single word, rendering it by the Latin word *impatientia*. For it may be understood in the meaning the opposite to that which we wish it to have. What we mean to express is, a soul which rejects any sensation of evil; but people will interpret the idea as that of a soul which can endure no evil. Consider, therefore, whether it is not better to say "a soul that cannot be harmed," or "a soul entirely beyond the realm of suffering." There is this difference between ourselves and the other school:† our ideal wise man feels his troubles, but overcomes them; their wise man does not even feel them. But we and they alike hold this idea—that the wise man is self-sufficient. Nevertheless, he desires friends, neighbours, and associates, no matter how much he is sufficient unto himself. And mark how self-sufficient he is; for on occasion he can be content with a part of himself. If he lose a hand through disease or war, or if some accident puts out one or both of his eyes, he will be satisfied with what is left, taking as much pleasure in his impaired and maimed body as he took when it was sound. But while he does not pine for these parts if they are missing, he prefers not to lose them. In this sense the wise man is self-sufficient, that he can do without friends, not that he desires to do without them. When I say "can," I mean this: he endures the loss of a friend with equanimity.

But he need never lack friends, for it lies in his own control how soon he shall make good a loss. Just as Phidias, if he lose a statue, can straightway carve

---

* *i.e.*, the Cynics.

† *i.e.*, the Cynics.

another, even so our master in the art of making friendships can fill the place of a friend he has lost. If you ask how one can make oneself a friend quickly, I will tell you, provided we are agreed that I may pay my debt at once and square the account, so far as this letter is concerned. Hecato says: "I can show you a philtre, compounded without drugs, herbs, or any witch's incantation: 'If you would be loved, love.'" Now there is great pleasure, not only in maintaining old and established friendships, but also in beginning and acquiring new ones. There is the same difference between winning a new friend and having already won him, as there is between the farmer who sows and the farmer who reaps. The philosopher Attalus used to say: "It is more pleasant to make than to keep a friend, as it is more pleasant to the artist to paint than to have finished painting." When one is busy and absorbed in one's work, the very absorption affords great delight; but when one has withdrawn one's hand from the completed masterpiece, the pleasure is not so keen. Henceforth it is the fruits of his art that he enjoys; it was the art itself that he enjoyed while he was painting. In the case of our children, their young manhood yields the more abundant fruits, but their infancy was sweeter.

Let us now return to the question. The wise man, I say, self-sufficient though he be, nevertheless desires friends if only for the purpose of practising friendship, in order that his noble qualities may not lie dormant. Not, however, for the purpose mentioned by Epicurus in the letter quoted above: "That there may be someone to sit by him when he is ill, to help him when he is in prison or in want;" but that he may have someone by whose sick-bed he himself may sit, someone a prisoner in hostile hands whom he himself may set free. He who regards himself only, and enters upon friendships for this reason, reckons wrongly. The end will be like the beginning: he has made friends with one who might assist him out of bondage; at the first rattle of the chain such a friend will desert him. These are the so-called "fair-weather" friendships; one who is chosen for the sake of utility will be satisfactory only so long as he is useful. Hence prosperous men are blockaded by troops of friends; but those who have failed stand amid vast loneliness their friends fleeing from the very crisis which is to test their worth. Hence, also, we notice those many shameful cases of persons who, through fear, desert or betray. The beginning and the end cannot but harmonize. He who begins to be your friend because it pays will also cease because it pays. A man will be attracted by some reward offered in exchange for his friendship, if he be attracted by aught in friendship other than friendship itself.

For what purpose, then, do I make a man my friend? In order to have someone for whom I may die, whom I may follow into exile, against whose death I may stake my own life, and pay the pledge, too. The friendship which you portray is a bargain and not a friendship; it regards convenience only, and looks to the results. Beyond question the feeling of a lover has in it something akin to friendship; one might call it friendship run mad. But, though this is true, does anyone love for the sake of gain, or promotion, or renown? Pure* love, careless of all other things, kindles the soul with desire for the beautiful object, not without the hope of a return of the affection. What then? Can a cause which is more honourable produce a passion that is base? You may retort: "We are now discussing the question whether friendship is to be cultivated for its own sake." On the contrary, nothing more urgently requires demonstration; for if friendship is to be sought for its own sake, he may seek it who is self-sufficient. "How, then," you ask, "does he seek it?" Precisely as he seeks an object of great beauty, not attracted to it by desire for gain, nor yet frightened by the instability of Fortune. One who seeks friendship for favourable occasions, strips it of all its nobility.

"The wise man is self-sufficient." This phrase, my dear Lucilius, is incorrectly explained by many; for they withdraw the wise man from the world, and force him to dwell within his own skin. But we must mark with care what this sentence signifies and how far it applies; the wise man is sufficient unto himself for a happy existence, but not for mere existence. For he needs many helps towards mere existence; but for a happy existence he needs only a sound and upright soul, one that despises Fortune.

I should like also to state to you one of the distinctions of Chrysippus, who declares that the wise man is in want of nothing, and yet needs many things. "On the other hand," he says, "nothing is needed by the fool, for he does not understand how to use anything, but he is in want of everything." The wise man needs hands, eyes, and many things that are necessary for his daily use; but he is in want of nothing. For want implies a necessity, and nothing is necessary to the wise man. Therefore, although he is self-sufficient, yet he has need of friends. He craves as many friends as possible, not, however, that he may live happily; for he will live happily even without friends. The Supreme Good calls for no practical aids from outside; it is developed at home, and arises entirely within itself. If the good seeks any portion of itself from without, it begins to be subject to the play of Fortune.

* "Pure love," *i.e.*, love in its essence, unalloyed with other emotions.

People may say: "But what sort of existence will the wise man have, if he be left friendless when thrown into prison, or when stranded in some foreign nation, or when delayed on a long voyage, or when out upon a lonely shore?" His life will be like that of Jupiter, who, amid the dissolution of the world, when the gods are confounded together and Nature rests for a space from her work, can retire into himself and give himself over to his own thoughts. In some such way as this the sage will act; he will retreat into himself, and live with himself. As long as he is allowed to order his affairs according to his judgment, he is self-sufficient—and marries a wife; he is self-sufficient—and brings up children; he is self-sufficient—and yet could not live if he had to live without the society of man. Natural promptings, and not his own selfish needs, draw him into Friendships. For just as other things have for us an inherent attractiveness, so has friendship. As we hate solitude and crave society, as nature draws men to each other, so in this matter also there is an attraction which makes us desirous of friendship. Nevertheless, though the sage may love his friends dearly, often comparing them with himself, and putting them ahead of himself, yet all the good will be limited to his own being, and he will speak the words which were spoken by the very Stilbo whom Epicurus criticizes in his letter. For Stilbo, after his country was captured and his children and his wife lost, as he emerged from the general desolation alone and yet happy, spoke as follows to Demetrius, called Sacker of Cities because of the destruction he brought upon them, in answer to the question whether he had lost anything: "I have all my goods with me!" There is a brave and stout-hearted man for you! The enemy conquered, but Stilbo conquered his conqueror. "I have lost nothing!" Aye, he forced Demetrius to wonder whether he himself had conquered after all. "My goods are all with me!" In other words, he deemed nothing that might be taken from him to be a good.

We marvel at certain animals because they can pass through fire and suffer no bodily harm; but how much more marvellous is a man who has marched forth unhurt and unscathed through fire and sword and devastation! Do you understand now how much easier it is to conquer a whole tribe than to conquer one *man*? This saying of Stilbo makes common ground with Stoicism; the Stoic also can carry his goods unimpaired through cities that have been burned to ashes; for he is self-sufficient. Such are the bounds which he sets to his own happiness.

But you must not think that our school alone can utter noble words; Epicurus himself, the reviler of Stilbo, spoke similar language; put it down to my credit, though I have already wiped out my debt for the present day. He says: "Whoever does not regard what he has as most ample wealth, is unhappy, though he be master of the whole world." Or, if the following seems to you a more suitable phrase—for we must try to render the meaning and not the mere words: "A man may rule the world and still be unhappy, if he does not feel that he is supremely happy." In order, however, that you may know that these sentiments are universal, suggested, of course, by Nature, you will find in one of the comic poets this verse:

Unblest is he who thinks himself unblest.

Or what does your condition matter, if it is bad in your own eyes? You may say: "What then? If yonder man, rich by base means, and yonder man, lord of many but slave of more, shall call themselves happy, will their own opinion make them happy?" It matters not what one says, but what one feels; also, not how one feels on one particular day, but how one feels at all times. There is no reason, however, why you should fear that this great privilege will fall into unworthy hands; only the wise man is pleased with his own. Folly is ever troubled with weariness of itself. Farewell.

11. ON THE BLUSH OF MODESTY

Your friend and I have had a conversation. He is a man of ability; his very first words showed what spirit and understanding he possesses, and what progress he has already made. He gave me a foretaste, and he will not fail to answer thereto. For he spoke not from forethought, but was suddenly caught off his guard. When he tried to collect himself, he could scarcely banish that hue of modesty, which is a good sign in a young man; the blush that spread over his face seemed so to rise from the depths. And I feel sure that his habit of blushing will stay with him after he has strengthened his character, stripped off all his faults, and become wise. For by no wisdom can natural weaknesses of the body be removed. That which is implanted and inborn can be toned down by training, but not overcome. The steadiest speaker, when before the public, often breaks into a perspiration, as if he had wearied or over-heated himself; some tremble in the knees when they rise to speak; I know of some whose teeth chatter, whose tongues falter, whose lips quiver. Training and experience can never shake off this habit; nature exerts her own power and through such a weakness makes her presence known even to the strongest. I know that the blush, too, is a habit of this sort, spreading suddenly over the faces of the most dignified men. It is, indeed, more prevalent in youth, because of the warmer blood and the sensitive countenance; nevertheless, both seasoned men and aged men are affected by it. Some are most dangerous when they redden, as if they were letting all their sense of shame escape. Sulla, when the blood mantled his cheeks, was in his fiercest mood. Pompey had the most sensitive cast of countenance; he always blushed in the presence of a gathering, and especially at a public assembly. Fabianus also, I remember, reddened when he appeared as a witness before the Senate; and his embarrassment became him to a remarkable degree. Such a habit is not due to mental weakness, but to the novelty of a situation; an inexperienced person is not necessarily confused, but is usually affected, because he slips into this habit by natural tendency of the body. Just as certain men are full-blooded, so others are of a quick and mobile blood, that rushes to the face at once.

As I remarked, Wisdom can never remove this habit; for if she could rub out all our faults, she would be mistress of the universe. Whatever is assigned to us by the terms of our birth and the blend in our constitutions will stick with us, no matter how hard or how long the soul may have tried to master itself. And we cannot forbid these feelings any more than we can summon them. Actors in the theatre, who imitate the emotions, who portray fear and nervousness, who depict sorrow, imitate bashfulness by hanging their heads, lowering their voices, and keeping their eyes fixed and rooted upon the ground. They cannot, however, muster a blush; for the blush cannot be prevented or acquired. Wisdom will not assure us of a remedy, or give us help against it; it comes or goes unbidden, and is a law unto itself.

But my letter calls for its closing sentence. Hear and take to heart this useful and wholesome motto: "Cherish some man of high character, and keep him ever before your eyes, living as if he were watching you, and ordering all your actions as if he beheld them." Such, my dear Lucilius, is the counsel of Epicurus; he has quite properly given us a guardian and an attendant. We can get rid of most sins, if we have a witness who stands near us when we are likely to go wrong. The soul should have someone whom it can respect,—one by whose authority it may make even its inner shrine more hallowed. Happy is the man who can make others better, not merely when he is in their company, but even when he is in their thoughts! And happy also is he who can so revere a man as to calm and regulate himself by calling him to mind! One who can so revere another, will soon be himself worthy of reverence. Choose therefore a Cato; or, if Cato seems too severe a model, choose some Laelius, a gentler spirit. Choose a master whose life, conversation, and soul-expressing face have satisfied you; picture him always to yourself as your protector or your pattern. For we must indeed have someone according to whom we may regulate our characters; you can never straighten that which is crooked unless you use a ruler. Farewell.

12. ON OLD AGE

Wherever I turn, I see evidences of my advancing years. I visited lately my country-place, and protested against the money which was spent on the tumble-down building. My bailiff maintained that the flaws were not due to his own carelessness; "he was doing everything possible, but the house was old." And this was the house which grew under my own hands! What has the future in store for me, if stones of my own age are already crumbling? I was angry, and I embraced the first opportunity to vent my spleen in the bailiff's presence. "It is clear," I cried, "that these plane-trees are neglected; they have no leaves. Their branches are so gnarled and shrivelled; the boles are so rough and unkempt! This would not happen, if someone loosened the earth at their feet, and watered them." The bailiff swore by my protecting deity that "he was doing everything possible, and never relaxed his efforts, but those trees were old." Between you and me, I had planted those trees myself; I had seen them in their first leaf. Then I turned to the door and asked: "Who is that broken-down dotard? You have done well to place him at the entrance; for he is outward bound.* Where did you get him? What pleasure did it give you to take up for burial some other man's dead?"† But the slave said: "Don't you know me, sir? I am Felicio; you used to bring me little images.‡ My father was Philositus the steward, and I am your pet slave." "The man is clean crazy," I remarked. "Has my pet slave become a little boy again? But it is quite possible; his teeth are just dropping out."§

---

* A jesting allusion to the Roman funeral: the corpse's feet pointed to the door.

† His former owner should have kept him and buried him.

‡ Small figures, generally of terra-cotta, were frequently given to children as presents at the Saturnalia.

§ *i.e.*, the old slave resembles a child in that he is losing his teeth (but for the second time).

I owe it to my country-place that my old age became apparent whithersoever I turned. Let us cherish and love old age; for it is full of pleasure if one knows how to use it. Fruits are most welcome when almost over; youth is most charming at its close; the last drink delights the toper, the glass which souses him and puts the finishing touch on his drunkenness. Each pleasure reserves to the end the greatest delights which it contains. Life is most delightful when it is on the downward slope, but has not yet reached the abrupt decline. And I myself believe that the period which stands, so to speak, on the edge of the roof, possesses pleasures of its own. Or else the very fact of our not wanting pleasures has taken the place of the pleasures themselves. How comforting it is to have tired out one's appetites, and to have done with them! "But," you say, "it is a nuisance to be looking death in the face!" Death, however, should be looked in the face by young and old alike. We are not summoned according to our rating on the censor's list. Moreover, no one is so old that it would be improper for him to hope for another day of existence. And one day, mind you, is a stage on life's journey.

Our span of life is divided into parts; it consists of large circles enclosing smaller. One circle embraces and bounds the rest; it reaches from birth to the last day of existence. The next circle limits the period of our young manhood. The third confines all of childhood in its circumference. Again, there is, in a class by itself, the year; it contains within itself all the divisions of time by the multiplication of which we get the total of life. The month is bounded by a narrower ring. The smallest circle of all is the day; but even a day has its beginning and its ending, its sunrise and its sunset. Hence Heraclitus, whose obscure style gave him his surname, remarked: "One day is equal to every day." Different persons have interpreted the saying in different ways. Some hold that days are equal in number of hours, and this is true; for if by "day" we mean twenty-four hours' time, all days must be equal, inasmuch as the night acquires what the day loses. But others maintain that one day is equal to all days through resemblance, because the very longest space of time possesses no element which cannot be found in a single day—namely, light and darkness—and even to eternity day makes these alternations more numerous, not different when it is shorter and different again when it is longer. Hence, every day ought to be regulated as if it closed the series, as if it rounded out and completed our existence.

Pacuvius, who by long occupancy made Syria his own, used to hold a regular burial sacrifice in his own honour, with wine and the usual funeral feasting, and then would have himself carried from the dining-room to his chamber, while eunuchs applauded and sang in Greek to a musical accompaniment: "He has lived his life, he has lived his life!" Thus Pacuvius had himself carried out to burial every day. Let us, however, do from a good motive what he used to do from a debased motive; let us go to our sleep with joy and gladness; let us say:

I have lived; the course which Fortune set for me
Is finished.

And if God is pleased to add another day, we should welcome it with glad hearts. That man is happiest, and is secure in his own possession of himself, who can await the morrow without apprehension. When a man has said: "I have lived!" every morning he arises he receives a bonus.

But now I ought to close my letter. "What?" you say; "shall it come to me without any little offering?" Be not afraid; it brings something,—nay, more than something, a great deal. For what is more noble than the following saying of which I make this letter the bearer: "It is wrong to live under constraint; but no man is constrained to live under constraint." Of course not. On all sides lie many short and simple paths to freedom; and let us thank God that no man can be kept in life. We may spurn the very constraints that hold us. "Epicurus," you reply, "uttered these words; what are you doing with another's property?" Any truth, I maintain, is my own property. And I shall continue to heap quotations from Epicurus upon you, so that all persons who swear by the words of another, and put a value upon the speaker and not upon the thing spoken, may understand that the best ideas are common property. Farewell.

13. ON GROUNDLESS FEARS

I know that you have plenty of spirit; for even before you began to equip yourself with maxims which were wholesome and potent to overcome obstacles, you were taking pride in your contest with Fortune; and this is all the more true, now that you have grappled with Fortune and tested your powers. For our powers can never inspire in us implicit faith in ourselves except when many difficulties have confronted us on this side and on that, and have occasionally even come to close quarters with us. It is only in this way that the true spirit can be tested—the spirit that will never consent to come under the jurisdiction of things external to ourselves. This is the touchstone of such a spirit; no prize-fighter can go with high spirits into the strife if he has never been beaten black and blue; the only contestant who can confidently enter the lists is the man who has seen his own blood, who has felt his teeth rattle beneath his opponent's fist, who has been tripped and felt the full force of his adversary's charge, who has been downed in body but not in spirit, one who, as often as he falls, rises again with greater defiance than ever. So then, to keep up my figure, Fortune has often in the past got the upper hand of you, and yet you have not surrendered, but have leaped up and stood your ground still more eagerly. For manliness gains much strength by being challenged; nevertheless, if you approve, allow me to offer some additional safeguards by which you may fortify yourself.

There are more things, Lucilius, likely to frighten us than there are to crush us; we suffer more often in imagination than in reality. I am not speaking with you in the Stoic strain but in my milder style. For it is our Stoic fashion to speak of all those things, which provoke cries and groans, as unimportant and beneath notice; but you and I must drop such great-sounding words, although, heaven knows, they are true enough. What I advise you to do is, not to be unhappy before the crisis comes; since it may be that the dangers before which you paled as if they were threatening you, will never come upon you; they certainly have not yet come. Accordingly, some things torment us more than they ought; some torment us before they ought; and some torment us when they ought not to torment us at all. We are in the habit of exaggerating, or imagining, or anticipating, sorrow.

The first of these three faults* may be postponed for the present, because the subject is under discussion and the case is still in court, so to speak. That which I should call trifling, you will maintain to be most serious; for of course I know that some men laugh while being flogged, and that others wince at a box on the ear. We shall consider later whether these evils derive their power from their own strength, or from our own weakness.

Do me the favour, when men surround you and try to talk you into believing that you are unhappy, to consider not what you hear but what you yourself feel, and to take counsel with your feelings and question yourself independently, because you know your own affairs better than anyone else does. Ask: "Is there any reason why these persons should condole with me?

* Seneca dismisses the topic of "exaggerated ills," because judgments will differ regarding present troubles; the Stoics, for example, would not admit that torture was an evil at all.

Why should they be worried or even fear some infection from me, as if troubles could be transmitted? Is there any evil involved, or is it a matter merely of ill report, rather than an evil?" Put the question voluntarily to yourself: "Am I tormented without sufficient reason, am I morose, and do I convert what is not an evil into what is an evil?" You may retort with the question: "How am I to know whether my sufferings are real or imaginary?" Here is the rule for such matters: we are tormented either by things present, or by things to come, or by both. As to things present, the decision is easy. Suppose that your person enjoys freedom and health, and that you do not suffer from any external injury. As to what may happen to it in the future, we shall see later on. Today there is nothing wrong with it. "But," you say, "something will happen to it." First of all, consider whether your proofs of future trouble are sure. For it is more often the case that we are troubled by our apprehensions, and that we are mocked by that mocker, rumour, which is wont to settle wars, but much more often settles individuals. Yes, my dear Lucilius; we agree too quickly with what people say. We do not put to the test those things which cause our fear; we do not examine into them; we blench and retreat just like soldiers who are forced to abandon their camp because of a dust-cloud raised by stampeding cattle, or are thrown into a panic by the spreading of some unauthenticated rumour. And somehow or other it is the idle report that disturbs us most. For truth has its own definite boundaries, but that which arises from uncertainty is delivered over to guesswork and the irresponsible license of a frightened mind. That is why no fear is so ruinous and so uncontrollable as panic fear. For other fears are groundless, but this fear is witless.

Let us, then, look carefully into the matter. It is likely that some troubles will befall us; but it is not a present fact. How often has the unexpected happened! How often has the expected never come to pass! And even though it is ordained to be, what does it avail to run out to meet your suffering? You will suffer soon enough, when it arrives; so look forward meanwhile to better things. What shall you gain by doing this? Time. There will be many happenings meanwhile which will serve to postpone, or end, or pass on to another person, the trials which are near or even in your very presence. A fire has opened the way to flight. Men have been let down softly by a catastrophe. Sometimes the sword has been checked even at the victim's throat. Men have survived their own executioners. Even bad Fortune is fickle. Perhaps it will come, perhaps not; in the meantime it is not. So look forward to better things.

The mind at times fashions for itself false shapes of evil when there are no signs that point to any evil; it twists into the worst construction some word of doubtful meaning; or it fancies some personal grudge to be more serious than it really is, considering not how angry the enemy is, but to what lengths he may go if he is angry. But life is not worth living, and there is no limit to our sorrows, if we indulge our fears to the greatest possible extent; in this matter, let prudence help you, and contemn with a resolute spirit even when it is in plain sight. If you cannot do this, counter one weakness with another, and temper your fear with hope. There is nothing so certain among these objects of fear that it is not more certain still that things we dread sink into nothing and that things we hope for mock us.

Accordingly, weigh carefully your hopes as well as your fears, and whenever all the elements are in doubt, decide in your own favour; believe what you prefer. And if fear wins a majority of the votes, incline in the other direction anyhow, and cease to harass your soul, reflecting continually that most mortals, even when no troubles are actually at hand or are certainly to be expected in the future, become excited and disquieted. No one calls a halt on himself, when he begins to be urged ahead; nor does he regulate his alarm according to the truth. No one says, "The author of the story is a fool, and he who has believed it is a fool, as well as he who fabricated it." We let ourselves drift with every breeze; we are frightened at uncertainties, just as if they were certain. We observe no moderation. The slightest thing turns the scales and throws us forthwith into a panic.

But I am ashamed either to admonish you sternly or to try to beguile you with such mild remedies. Let another say: "Perhaps the worst will not happen." You yourself must say, "Well, what if it does happen? Let us see who wins! Perhaps it happens for my best interests; it may be that such a death will shed credit upon my life." Socrates was ennobled by the hemlock draught. Wrench from Cato's hand his sword, the vindicator of liberty, and you deprive him of the greatest share of his glory. I am exhorting you far too long, since you need reminding rather than exhortation. The path on which I am leading you is not different from that on which your nature leads you; you were born to such conduct as I describe. Hence there is all the more reason why you should increase and beautify the good that is in you.

But now, to close my letter, I have only to stamp the usual seal upon it, in other words, to commit thereto some noble message to be delivered to you: "The fool, with all his other faults, has this also, he is always getting ready to live." Reflect, my esteemed Lucilius, what this saying means, and you will see how revolting is the fickleness of men who lay down every day new foundations of life, and begin to build up fresh hopes even at the brink of the grave. Look within your own mind for individual instances; you will think of old men who are preparing themselves at that very hour for a political career, or for travel, or for business. And what is baser than getting ready to live when you are already old? I should not name the author of this motto, except that it is somewhat unknown to fame and is not one of those popular sayings of Epicurus which I have allowed myself to praise and to appropriate. Farewell.

16. ON PHILOSOPHY, THE GUIDE OF LIFE

It is clear to you, I am sure, Lucilius, that no man can live a happy life, or even a supportable life, without the study of wisdom; you know also that a happy life is reached when our wisdom is brought to completion, but that life is at least endurable even when our wisdom is only begun. This idea, however, clear though it is, must be strengthened and implanted more deeply by daily reflection; it is more important for you to keep the resolutions you have already made than to go on and make noble ones. You must persevere, must develop new strength by continuous study, until that which is only a good inclination becomes a good settled purpose. Hence you no longer need to come to me with much talk and protestations; I know that you have made great progress. I understand the feelings which prompt your words; they are not feigned or specious words. Nevertheless I shall tell you what I think—that at present I have hopes for you, but not yet perfect trust. And I wish that you would adopt the same attitude towards yourself; there is no reason why you should put confidence in yourself too quickly and readily. Examine yourself; scrutinize and observe yourself in divers ways; but mark, before all else, whether it is in philosophy or merely in life itself that you have made progress. Philosophy is no trick to catch the public; it is not devised for show. It is a matter, not of words, but of facts. It is not pursued in order that the day may yield some amusement before it is spent, or that our leisure may be relieved of a tedium that irks us. It moulds and constructs the soul; it orders our life, guides our conduct, shows us what we should do and what we should leave undone; it sits at the helm and directs our course as we waver amid uncertainties. Without it, no one can live fearlessly or in peace of mind. Countless things that happen every hour call for advice; and such advice is to be sought in philosophy.

Perhaps someone will say: "How can philosophy help me, if Fate exists? Of what avail is philosophy, if God rules the universe? Of what avail is it, if Chance governs everything? For not only is it impossible to change things that are determined, but it is also impossible to plan beforehand against what is undetermined; either God has forestalled my plans, and decided what I am to do, or else Fortune gives no free play to my plans." Whether the truth, Lucilius, lies in one or in all of these views, we must be philosophers; whether Fate binds us down by an inexorable law, or whether God as arbiter of the universe has arranged everything, or whether Chance drives and tosses human affairs without method, philosophy ought to be our defence. She will encourage us to obey God cheerfully, but Fortune defiantly; she will teach us to follow God and endure Chance. But it is not my purpose now to be led into a discussion as to what is within our own control—if foreknowledge is supreme, or if a chain of fated events drags us along in its clutches, or if the sudden and the unexpected play the tyrant over us; I return now to my warning and my exhortation, that you should not allow the impulse of your spirit to weaken and grow cold. Hold fast to it and establish it firmly, in order that what is now impulse may become a habit of the mind.

If I know you well, you have already been trying to find out, from the very beginning of my letter, what little contribution it brings to you. Sift the letter, and you will find it. You need not wonder at any genius of mine; for as yet I am lavish only with other men's property. But why did I say "other men"? Whatever is well said by anyone is mine. This also is a saying of Epicurus: "If you live according to nature, you will never be poor; if you live according to opinion, you will never be rich." Nature's wants are slight; the demands of opinion are boundless. Suppose that the property of many millionaires is heaped up in your possession. Assume that Fortune carries you far beyond the limits of a private income, decks you with gold, clothes you in purple, and brings you to such a degree of luxury and wealth that you can bury the earth under your marble floors; that you may not only possess, but tread upon, riches. Add statues, paintings, and whatever any art has devised for the luxury; you will only learn from such things to crave still greater.

Natural desires are limited; but those which spring from false opinion can have no stopping-point. The false has no limits. When you are travelling on a road, there must be an end; but when astray, your wanderings are limitless. Recall your steps, therefore, from idle things, and when you would know whether that which you seek is based upon a natural or upon a misleading desire, consider whether it can stop at any definite point. If you find, after having travelled far, that there is a more distant goal always in view, you may be sure that this condition is contrary to nature. Farewell.

17. ON PHILOSOPHY AND RICHES

Cast away everything of that sort, if you are wise; nay, rather that you may be wise; strive toward a sound mind at top speed and with your whole strength. If any bond holds you back, untie it, or sever it. "But," you say, "my estate delays me; I wish to make such disposition of it that it may suffice for me when I have nothing to do, lest either poverty be a burden to me, or I myself a burden to others." You do not seem, when you say this, to know the strength and power of that good which you are considering. You do indeed grasp the all important thing, the great benefit which philosophy confers, but you do not yet discern accurately its various functions, nor do you yet know how great is the help we receive from philosophy in everything, everywhere—how, (to use Cicero's language) it not only succours us in the greatest matters but also descends to the smallest. Take my advice; call wisdom into consultation; she will advise you not to sit for ever at your ledger. Doubtless, your object, what you wish to attain by such postponement of your studies, is that poverty may not have to be feared by you. But what if it is something to be desired? Riches have shut off many a man from the attainment of wisdom; poverty is unburdened and free from care. When the trumpet sounds, the poor man knows that he is not being attacked; when there is a cry of "Fire," he only seeks a way of escape, and does not ask what he can save; if the poor man must go to sea, the harbour does not resound, nor do the wharves bustle with the retinue of one individual. No throng of slaves surrounds the poor man—slaves for whose mouths the master must covet the fertile crops of regions beyond the sea. It is easy to fill a few stomachs, when they are well trained and crave nothing else but to be filled. Hunger costs but little; squeamishness costs much. Poverty is contented with fulfilling pressing needs.

Why, then, should you reject Philosophy as a comrade? Even the rich man copies her ways when he is in his senses. If you wish to have leisure for your mind, either be a poor man, or resemble a poor man. Study cannot be helpful unless you take pains to live simply; and living simply is voluntary poverty. Away, then, with all excuses like: "I have not yet enough; when I have gained the desired amount, then I shall devote myself wholly to philosophy." And yet this ideal, which you are putting off and placing second to other interests, should be secured first of all; you should begin with it. You retort: "I wish to acquire something to live on." Yes, but learn while you are acquiring it; for if anything forbids you to live nobly, nothing forbids you to die nobly. There is no reason why poverty should call us away from philosophy—no, nor even actual want. For when hastening after wisdom, we must endure even hunger. Men have endured hunger when their towns were besieged, and what other reward for their endurance did they obtain than that they did not fall under the conqueror's power? How much greater is the promise of the prize of everlasting liberty, and the assurance that we need fear neither God nor man! Even though we starve, we must reach that goal. Armies have endured all manner of want, have lived on roots, and have resisted hunger by means of food too revolting to mention. All this they have suffered to gain a kingdom, and—what is more marvellous—to gain a kingdom that will be another's. Will any man hesitate to endure poverty, in order that he may free his mind from madness?

Therefore one should not seek to lay up riches first; one may attain to philosophy, however, even without money for the journey. It is indeed so. After you have come to possess all other things, shall you then wish to possess wisdom also? Is philosophy to be the last requisite in life—a sort of supplement? Nay, your plan should be this: be a philosopher now, whether you have anything or not—for if you have anything, how do you know that you have not too much already?—but if you have nothing, seek understanding first, before anything else. "But," you say, "I shall lack the necessities of life." In the first place, you cannot lack them; because nature demands but little, and the wise man suits his needs to nature. But if the utmost pinch of need arrives, he will quickly take leave of life and cease being a trouble to himself. If, however, his means of existence are meagre and scanty, he will make the best of them, without being anxious or worried about anything more than the bare necessities; he will do justice to his belly and his shoulders; with free and happy spirit he will laugh at the bustling of rich men, and the flurried ways of those who are hastening after wealth, and say: "Why of your own accord postpone your real life to the distant future? Shall you wait for some interest to fall due, or for some income on your merchandise, or for a place in the will of some wealthy old man, when you can be rich here and now. Wisdom offers wealth in ready money, and pays it over to those in whose eyes she has made wealth superfluous." These remarks refer to other men; you are nearer the rich class.

Change the age in which you live, and you have too much. But in every age, what is enough remains the same.

I might close my letter at this point, if I had not got you into bad habits. One cannot greet Parthian royalty without bringing a gift; and in your case I cannot say farewell without paying a price. But what of it? I shall borrow from Epicurus: "The acquisition of riches has been for many men, not an end, but a change, of troubles." I do not wonder. For the fault is not in the wealth, but in the mind itself. That which had made poverty a burden to us, has made riches also a burden. Just as it matters little whether you lay a sick man on a wooden or on a golden bed, for whithersoever he be moved he will carry his malady with him; so one need not care whether the diseased mind is bestowed upon riches or upon poverty. His malady goes with the man. Farewell.

18. ON FESTIVALS AND FASTING

It is the month of December, and yet the city is at this very moment in a sweat. License is given to the general merrymaking. Everything resounds with mighty preparations—as if the Saturnalia differed at all from the usual business day! So true it is that the difference is nil, that I regard as correct the remark of the man who said: "Once December was a month; now it is a year."*

If I had you with me, I should be glad to consult you and find out what you think should be done—whether we ought to make no change in our daily routine, or whether, in order not to be out of sympathy with the ways of the public, we should dine in gayer fashion and doff the toga. As it is now, we Romans have changed our dress for the sake of pleasure and holiday-making, though in former times that was only customary when the State was disturbed and had fallen on evil days. I am sure that, if I know you aright, playing the part of an umpire you would have wished that we should be neither like the liberty-capped† throng in all ways, nor in all ways unlike them; unless, perhaps, this is just the season when we ought to lay down the law to the soul, and bid it be alone in refraining from pleasures just when the whole mob has let itself go in pleasures; for this is the surest proof which a man can get of his own constancy, if he neither seeks the things which are seductive and allure him to luxury, nor

---

* *i.e.*, the whole year is a Saturnalia.

† The *pilleus* was worn by newly freed slaves and by the Roman populace on festal occasions.

is led into them. It shows much more courage to remain dry and sober when the mob is drunk and vomiting; but it shows greater self-control to refuse to withdraw oneself and to do what the crowd does, but in a different way—thus neither making oneself conspicuous nor becoming one of the crowd. For one may keep holiday without extravagance.

I am so firmly determined, however, to test the constancy of your mind that, drawing from the teachings of great men, I shall give you also a lesson: Set aside a certain number of days, during which you shall be content with the scantiest and cheapest fare, with coarse and rough dress, saying to yourself the while: "Is this the condition that I feared?" It is precisely in times of immunity from care that the soul should toughen itself beforehand for occasions of greater stress, and it is while Fortune is kind that it should fortify itself against her violence. In days of peace the soldier performs manoeuvres, throws up earthworks with no enemy in sight, and wearies himself by gratuitous toil, in order that he may be equal to unavoidable toil. If you would not have a man flinch when the crisis comes, train him before it comes. Such is the course which those men have followed who, in their imitation of poverty, have every month come almost to want, that they might never recoil from what they had so often rehearsed.

You need not suppose that I mean meals like Timon's, or "paupers' huts," or any other device which luxurious millionaires use to beguile the tedium of their lives. Let the pallet be a real one, and the coarse cloak; let the bread be hard and grimy. Endure all this for three or four days at a time, sometimes for more, so that it may be a test of yourself instead of a mere hobby. Then, I assure you, my dear Lucilius, you will leap for joy when filled with a pennyworth of food, and you will understand that a man's peace of mind does not depend upon Fortune; for, even when angry she grants enough for our needs.

There is no reason, however, why you should think that you are doing anything great; for you will merely be doing what many thousands of slaves and many thousands of poor men are doing every day. But you may credit yourself with this item—that you will not be doing it under compulsion, and that it will be as easy for you to endure it permanently as to make the experiment from time to time. Let us practise our strokes on the "dummy";* let us become intimate with poverty, so that Fortune may not catch us off our guard. We shall be rich with all the more comfort, if we once learn how far poverty is from being a burden.

* The post which gladiators used when preparing themselves for combats in the arena.

Even Epicurus, the teacher of pleasure, used to observe stated intervals, during which he satisfied his hunger in niggardly fashion; he wished to see whether he thereby fell short of full and complete happiness, and, if so, by what amount he fell short, and whether this amount was worth purchasing at the price of great effort. At any rate, he makes such a statement in the well known letter written to Polyaenus in the archonship of Charinus. Indeed, he boasts that he himself lived on less than a penny, but that Metrodorus, whose progress was not yet so great, needed a whole penny. Do you think that there can be fullness on such fare? Yes, and there is pleasure also—not that shifty and fleeting Pleasure which needs a fillip now and then, but a pleasure that is steadfast and sure. For though water, barley-meal, and crusts of barley-bread, are not a cheerful diet, yet it is the highest kind of Pleasure to be able to derive pleasure from this sort of food, and to have reduced one's needs to that modicum which no unfairness of Fortune can snatch away. Even prison fare is more generous; and those who have been set apart for capital punishment are not so meanly fed by the man who is to execute them. Therefore, what a noble soul must one have, to descend of one's own free will to a diet which even those who have been sentenced to death have not to fear! This is indeed forestalling the spear thrusts of Fortune.

So begin, my dear Lucilius, to follow the custom of these men, and set apart certain days on which you shall withdraw from your business and make yourself at home with the scantiest fare. Establish business relations with poverty.

Dare, O my friend, to scorn the sight of wealth,
And mould thyself to kinship with thy God.

For he alone is in kinship with God who has scorned wealth. Of course I do not forbid you to possess it, but I would have you reach the point at which you possess it dauntlessly; this can be accomplished only by persuading yourself that you can live happily without it as well as with it, and by regarding riches always as likely to elude you.

But now I must begin to fold up my letter. "Settle your debts first," you cry. Here is a draft on Epicurus; he will pay down the sum: "Ungoverned anger begets madness." You cannot help knowing the truth of these words, since you have had not only slaves, but also enemies. But indeed this emotion blazes out against all sorts of persons; it springs from love as much as from hate, and shows itself not less in serious matters than in jest and sport. And it makes no difference how important the provocation may be, but into what kind of soul it penetrates. Similarly with fire; it does not matter how great is the flame, but what it falls upon. For solid timbers have repelled a very great fire; conversely, dry and easily inflammable stuff nourishes the slightest spark into a conflagration. So it is with anger, my dear Lucilius; the outcome of a mighty anger is madness, and hence anger should be avoided, not merely that we may escape excess, but that we may have a healthy mind. Farewell.

23. ON THE TRUE JOY WHICH COMES FROM PHILOSOPHY

Do you suppose that I shall write you how kindly the winter season has dealt with us—a short season and a mild one—or what a nasty spring we are having—cold weather out of season—and all the other trivialities which people write when they are at a loss for topics of conversation? No; I shall communicate something which may help both you and myself. And what shall this "something" be, if not an exhortation to soundness of mind? Do you ask what is the foundation of a sound mind? It is, not to find joy in useless things. I said that it was the foundation; it is really the pinnacle. We have reached the heights if we know what it is that we find joy in and if we have not placed our happiness in the control of externals. The man who is goaded ahead by hope of anything, though it be within reach, though it be easy of access, and though his ambitions have never played him false, is troubled and unsure of himself. Above all, my dear Lucilius, make this your business: learn how to feel joy.

Do you think that I am now robbing you of many pleasures when I try to do away with the gifts of chance, when I counsel the avoidance of hope, the sweetest thing that gladdens our hearts? Quite the contrary; I do not wish you ever to be deprived of gladness. I would have it born in your house; and it is born there, if only it be inside of you. Other objects of cheer do not fill a man's bosom; they merely smooth his brow and are inconstant—unless perhaps you believe that he who laughs has joy. The very soul must be happy and confident, lifted above every circumstance.

Real joy, believe me, is a stern matter. Can one, do you think, despise death with a care-free countenance, or with a "blithe and gay" expression, as our young dandies are accustomed to say? Or can one thus open his door to poverty, or hold the curb on his pleasures, or contemplate the endurance of pain?

He who ponders these things* in his heart is indeed full of joy; but it is not a cheerful joy. It is just this joy, however, of which I would have you become the owner; for it will never fail you when once you have found its source. The yield of poor mines is on the surface; those are really rich whose veins lurk deep, and they will make more bountiful returns to him who delves unceasingly. So too those baubles which delight the common crowd afford but a thin pleasure, laid on as a coating, and even joy that is only plated lacks a real basis. But the joy of which I speak, that to which I am endeavouring to lead you, is something solid, disclosing itself the more fully as you penetrate into it. Therefore I pray you, my dearest Lucilius, do the one thing that can render you really happy: cast aside and trample under foot all the things that glitter outwardly and are held out to you by another or as obtainable from another; look toward the true good, and rejoice only in that which comes from your own store. And what do I mean by "from your own store"? I mean from your very self, that which is the best part of you. The frail body, also, even though we can accomplish nothing without it, is to be regarded as necessary rather than as important; it involves us in vain pleasures, short-lived, and soon to be regretted, which, unless they are reined in by extreme self-control, will be transformed into the opposite. This is what I mean: pleasure, unless it has been kept within bounds, tends to rush headlong into the abyss of sorrow.

But it is hard to keep within bounds in that which you believe to be good. The real good may be coveted with safety. Do you ask me what this real good is, and whence it derives? I will tell you: it comes from a good conscience, from honourable purposes, from right actions, from contempt of the gifts of chance, from an even and calm way of living which treads but one path. For men who leap from one purpose to another, or do not even leap but are carried over by a sort of hazard—how can such wavering and unstable persons possess any good that is fixed and lasting? There are only a few who control themselves and their affairs by a guiding purpose; the rest do not proceed; they are merely swept along, like objects afloat in a river. And of these objects, some are held back by sluggish waters and are transported gently; others are torn along by a more violent current; some, which are nearest the bank, are left there as the current slackens; and others are carried out to sea by the onrush of the stream. Therefore, we should decide what we wish, and abide by the decision.

Now is the time for me to pay my debt. I can give you a saying of your

---

* Death, poverty, temptation, and suffering.

friend Epicurus and thus clear this letter of its obligation. "It is bothersome always to be beginning life." Or another, which will perhaps express the meaning better: "They live ill who are always beginning to live." You are right in asking why; the saying certainly stands in need of a commentary. It is because the life of such persons is always incomplete. But a man cannot stand prepared for the approach of death if he has just begun to live. We must make it our aim already to have lived long enough. No one deems that he has done so, if he is just on the point of planning his life. You need not think that there are few of this kind; practically everyone is of such a stamp. Some men, indeed, only begin to live when it is time for them to leave off living. And if this seems surprising to you, I shall add that which will surprise you still more: Some men have left off living before they have begun. Farewell.

24. ON DESPISING DEATH

You write me that you are anxious about the result of a lawsuit, with which an angry opponent is threatening you; and you expect me to advise you to picture to yourself a happier issue, and to rest in the allurements of hope. Why, indeed, is it necessary to summon trouble—which must be endured soon enough when it has once arrived, or to anticipate trouble and ruin the present through fear of the future? It is indeed foolish to be unhappy now because you may be unhappy at some future time. But I shall conduct you to peace of mind by another route: if you would put off all worry, assume that what you fear may happen will certainly happen in any event; whatever the trouble may be, measure it in your own mind, and estimate the amount of your fear. You will thus understand that what you fear is either insignificant or short-lived. And you need not spend a long time in gathering illustrations which will strengthen you; every epoch has produced them. Let your thoughts travel into any era of Roman or foreign history, and there will throng before you notable examples of high achievement or of high endeavour.

If you lose this case, can anything more severe happen to you than being sent into exile or led to prison? Is there a worse fate that any man may fear than being burned or being killed? Name such penalties one by one, and mention the men who have scorned them; one does not need to hunt for them—it is simply a matter of selection. Sentence of conviction was borne by Rutilius as if the injustice of the decision were the only thing which annoyed him. Exile was endured by Metellus with courage, by Rutilius even with gladness; for the former consented to come back only because his country called him; the latter refused to return when Sulla summoned him—and nobody in those days said "No" to Sulla! Socrates in prison discoursed, and declined to flee when certain persons gave him the opportunity; he remained there, in order to free mankind from the fear of two most grievous things, death and imprisonment. Mucius put his hand into the fire. It is painful to be burned; but how much more painful to inflict such suffering upon oneself! Here was a man of no learning, not primed to face death and pain by any words of wisdom, and equipped only with the courage of a soldier, who punished himself for his fruitless daring; he stood and watched his own right hand falling away piecemeal on the enemy's brazier, nor did he withdraw the dissolving limb, with its uncovered bones, until his foe removed the fire. He might have accomplished something more successful in that camp, but never anything more brave. See how much keener a brave man is to lay hold of danger than a cruel man is to inflict it: Porsenna was more ready to pardon Mucius for wishing to slay him than Mucius to pardon himself for failing to slay Porsenna!

"Oh," say you, "those stories have been droned to death in all the schools; pretty soon, when you reach the topic 'On Despising Death,' you will be telling me about Cato." But why should I not tell you about Cato, how he read Plato's* book on that last glorious night, with a sword laid at his pillow? He had provided these two requisites for his last moments—the first, that he might have the will to die, and the second, that he might have the means. So he put his affairs in order—as well as one could put in order that which was ruined and near its end—and thought that he ought to see to it that no one should have the power to slay or the good Fortune to save† Cato. Drawing the sword—which he had kept unstained from all bloodshed against the final day, he cried: "Fortune, you have accomplished nothing by resisting all my endeavours. I have fought, till now, for my country's freedom, and not for my own; I did not strive so doggedly to be free, but only to live among the free. Now, since the affairs of mankind are beyond hope, let Cato be withdrawn to safety." So saying, he inflicted a mortal wound upon his body. After the physicians had bound it up, Cato had less blood and less strength, but no less courage; angered now not only at Caesar but also at himself, he rallied his unarmed hands against his

---

* The *Phaedo*, on the immortality of the soul

† *i.e.*, to save and bring back to Rome as a prisoner.

wound, and expelled, rather than dismissed, that noble soul which had been so defiant of all worldly power.

I am not now heaping up these illustrations for the purpose of exercising my wit, but for the purpose of encouraging you to face that which is thought to be most terrible. And I shall encourage you all the more easily by showing that not only resolute men have despised that moment when the soul breathes its last, but that certain persons, who were craven in other respects, have equalled in this regard the courage of the bravest. Take, for example, Scipio, the father-in-law of Gnaeus Pompeius: he was driven back upon the African coast by a head-wind and saw his ship in the power of the enemy. He therefore pierced his body with a sword; and when they asked where the commander was, he replied: "All is well with the commander." These words brought him up to the level of his ancestors and suffered not the glory which fate gave to the Scipios in Africa* to lose its continuity. It was a great deed to conquer Carthage, but a greater deed to conquer death. "All is well with the commander!" Ought a general to die otherwise, especially one of Cato's generals? I shall not refer you to history, or collect examples of those men who throughout the ages have despised death; for they are very many. Consider these times of ours, whose enervation and over-refinement call forth our complaints; they nevertheless will include men of every rank, of every lot in life, and of every age, who have cut short their misfortunes by death.

Believe me, Lucilius; death is so little to be feared that through its good offices nothing is to be feared. Therefore, when your enemy threatens, listen unconcernedly. Although your conscience makes you confident, yet, since many things have weight which are outside your case, both hope for that which is utterly just, and prepare yourself against that which is utterly unjust. Remember, however, before all else, to strip things of all that disturbs and confuses, and to see what each is at bottom; you will then comprehend that they contain nothing fearful except the actual fear. That you see happening to boys happens also to ourselves, who are only slightly bigger boys: when those whom they love, with whom they daily associate, with whom they play, appear with masks on, the boys are frightened out of then wits. We should strip the mask, not only from men, but from things, and restore to each object its own aspect.

---

* Scipio Africanus defeated Hannibal at Zama in 202 B.C. Scipio Aemilianus, also surnamed Africanus, was by adoption the grandson of Hannibal's conqueror. He captured Carthage in the Third Punic War, 146 B.C. The Scipio mentioned by Seneca died in 46 B.C.

"Why dost thou hold up before my eyes swords, fires, and a throng of executioners raging about thee? Take away all that vain show, behind which thou lurkest and scarest fools! Ah! thou art naught but Death, whom only yesterday a manservant of mine and a maidservant did despise! Why dost thou again unfold and spread before me, with all that great display, the whip and the rack? Why are those engines of torture made ready, one for each several member of the body, and all the other innumerable machines for tearing a man apart piecemeal? Away with all such stuff, which makes us numb with terror! And thou, silence the groans, the cries, and the bitter shrieks ground out of the victim as he is torn on the rack! Forsooth thou are naught but Pain, scorned by yonder gout-ridden wretch, endured by yonder dyspeptic in the midst of his dainties, borne bravely by the girl in travail. Slight thou art, if I can bear thee; short thou art if I cannot bear thee!"

Ponder these words which you have often heard and often uttered. Moreover, prove by the result whether that which you have heard and uttered is true. For there is a very disgraceful charge often brought against our school—that we deal with the words, and not with the deeds, of philosophy.

What, have you only at this moment learned that death is hanging over your head, at this moment exile, at this moment grief? You were born to these perils. Let us think of everything that can happen as something which will happen. I know that you have really done what I advise you to do; I now warn you not to drown your soul in these petty anxieties of yours; if you do, the soul will be dulled and will have too little vigour left when the time comes for it to arise. Remove the mind from this case of yours to the case of men in general. Say to yourself that our petty bodies are mortal and frail; pain can reach them from other sources than from wrong or the might of the stronger. Our pleasures themselves become torments; banquets bring indigestion, carousals paralysis of the muscles and palsy, sensual habits affect the feet, the hands, and every joint of the body.

I may become a poor man; I shall then be one among many. I may be exiled; I shall then regard myself as born in the place to which I shall be sent. They may put me in chains. What then? Am I free from bonds now? Behold this clogging burden of a body, to which nature has fettered me! "I shall die," you say; you mean to say, "I shall cease to run the risk of sickness; I shall cease to run the risk of imprisonment; I shall cease to run the risk of death." I am not so foolish as to go through at this juncture the arguments which Epicurus harps upon, and say that the terrors of the world below are idle—that Ixion does not whirl round on his wheel, that Sisyphus does not shoulder his stone uphill, that a man's entrails cannot be restored and devoured every day; no one is so childish as to fear Cerberus, or the shadows, or the spectral garb of those who are held together by naught but their unfleshed bones. Death either annihilates us or strips us bare. If we are then released, there remains the better part, after the burden has been withdrawn; if we are annihilated, nothing remains; good and bad are alike removed.

Allow me at this point to quote a verse of yours, first suggesting that, when you wrote it, you meant it for yourself no less than for others. It is ignoble to say one thing and mean another; and how much more ignoble to write one thing and mean another! I remember one day you were handling the well-known commonplace—that we do not suddenly fall on death, but advance towards it by slight degrees; we die every day. For every day a little of our life is taken from us; even when we are growing, our life is on the wane. We lose our childhood, then our boyhood, and then our youth. Counting even yesterday, all past time is lost time; the very day which we are now spending is shared between ourselves and death. It is not the last drop that empties the water-clock, but all that which previously has flowed out; similarly, the final hour when we cease to exist does not of itself bring death; it merely of itself completes the death-process. We reach death at that moment, but we have been a long time on the way. In describing this situation, you said in your customary style (for you are always impressive, but never more pungent than when you are putting the truth in appropriate words):

Not single is the death which comes; the death
Which takes us off is but the last of all.

I prefer that you should read your own words rather than my letter; for then it will be clear to you that this death, of which we are afraid, is the last but not the only death. I see what you are looking for; you are asking what I have packed into my letter, what inspiriting saying from some master-mind, what useful precept. So I shall send you something dealing with this very subject which has been under discussion. Epicurus upbraids those who crave, as much as those who shrink from, death: "It is absurd," he says, "to run towards death because you are tired of life, when it is your manner of life that has made you run towards death." And in another passage: "What is so absurd as to seek death, when it is through fear of death that you have robbed your life of peace?"

And you may add a third statement, of the same stamp: "Men are so thoughtless, nay, so mad, that some, through fear of death, force themselves to die."

Whichever of these ideas you ponder, you will strengthen your mind for the endurance alike of death and of life. For we need to be warned and strengthened in both directions—not to love or to hate life overmuch; even when reason advises us to make an end of it, the impulse is not to be adopted without reflection or at headlong speed. The grave and wise man should not beat a hasty retreat from life; he should make a becoming exit. And above all, he should avoid the weakness which has taken possession of so many—the lust for death. For just as there is an unreflecting tendency of the mind towards other things, so, my dear Lucilius, there is an unreflecting tendency towards death; this often seizes upon the noblest and most spirited men, as well as upon the craven and the abject. The former despise life; the latter find it irksome.

Others also are moved by a satiety of doing and seeing the same things, and not so much by a hatred of life as because they are cloyed with it. We slip into this condition, while philosophy itself pushes us on, and we say; "How long must I endure the same things? Shall I continue to wake and sleep, be hungry and be cloyed, shiver and perspire? There is an end to nothing; all things are connected in a sort of circle; they flee and they are pursued. Night is close at the heels of day, day at the heels of night; summer ends in autumn, winter rushes after autumn, and winter softens into spring; all nature in this way passes, only to return. I do nothing new; I see nothing new; sooner or later one sickens of this, also." There are many who think that living is not painful, but superfluous. Farewell.

27. ON THE GOOD WHICH ABIDES

"What," say you, "are you giving me advice? Indeed, have you already advised yourself, already corrected your own faults? Is this the reason why you have leisure to reform other men?" No, I am not so shameless as to undertake to cure my fellow-men when I am ill myself. I am, however, discussing with you troubles which concern us both, and sharing the remedy with you, just as if we were lying ill in the same hospital. Listen to me, therefore, as you would if I were talking to myself. I am admitting you to my inmost thoughts, and am having it out with myself, merely making use of you as my pretext. I keep crying out to myself: "Count your years, and you will be ashamed to desire and pursue the same things you desired in your boyhood days. Of this one thing make sure against your dying day—let your faults die before you die. Away with those disordered pleasures, which must be dearly paid for; it is not only those which are to come that harm me, but also those which have come and gone. Just as crimes, even if they have not been detected when they were committed, do not allow anxiety to end with them; so with guilty pleasures, regret remains even after the pleasures are over. They are not substantial, they are not trustworthy; even if they do not harm us, they are fleeting. Cast about rather for some good which will abide. But there can be no such good except as the soul discovers it for itself within itself. Virtue alone affords everlasting and peace-giving joy; even if some obstacle arise, it is but like an intervening cloud, which floats beneath the sun but never prevails against it."

When will it be your lot to attain this joy? Thus far, you have indeed not been sluggish, but you must quicken your pace. Much toil remains; to confront it, you must yourself lavish all your waking hours, and all your efforts, if you wish the result to be accomplished. This matter cannot be delegated to someone else. The other kind of literary activity* admits of outside assistance. Within our own time there was a certain rich man named Calvisius Sabinus; he had the bank-account and the brains of a freedman. I never saw a man whose good Fortune was a greater offence against propriety. His memory was so faulty that he would sometimes forget the name of Ulysses, or Achilles, or Priam—names which we know as well as we know those of our own attendants. No major-domo in his dotage, who cannot give men their right names, but is compelled to invent names for them—no such man, I say, calls off the names† of his master's tribesmen so atrociously as Sabinus used to call off the Trojan and Achaean heroes. But none the less did he desire to appear learned. So he devised this short cut to learning: he paid fabulous prices for slaves—one to know Homer by heart and another to know Hesiod; he also delegated a special slave to each of the nine lyric poets. You need not wonder that he paid high prices for these slaves; if he did not find them ready to hand he had them made to order. After collecting this retinue, he began to make life miserable for his guests; he would keep these fellows at the foot of his couch, and ask them from time to time for verses which he might repeat, and then frequently break

* *i.e.*, ordinary studies, or literature, as contrasted with philosophy.

† At the *salutatio*, or morning call. The position of *nomenclator*, "caller of names," was originally devoted more strictly to political purposes. Here it is primarily social.

down in the middle of a word. Satellius Quadratus, a feeder, and consequently a fawner, upon addle-pated millionaires, and also (for this quality goes with the other two) a flouter of them, suggested to Sabinus that he should have philologists to gather up the bits.* Sabinus remarked that each slave cost him one hundred thousand sesterces; Satellius replied: "You might have bought as many book-cases for a smaller sum." But Sabinus held to the opinion that what any member of his household knew, he himself knew also. This same Satellius began to advise Sabinus to take wrestling lessons—sickly, pale, and thin as he was, Sabinus answered: "How can I? I can scarcely stay alive now." "Don't say that, I implore you," replied the other, "consider how many perfectly healthy slaves you have!" No man is able to borrow or buy a sound mind; in fact, as it seems to me, even though sound minds were for sale, they would not find buyers. Depraved minds, however, are bought and sold every day.

But let me pay off my debt and say farewell: "Real wealth is poverty adjusted to the law of Nature." Epicurus has this saying in various ways and contexts; but it can never be repeated too often, since it can never be learned too well. For some persons the remedy should be merely prescribed; in the case of others, it should be forced down their throats. Farewell.

28. ON TRAVEL AS A CURE FOR DISCONTENT

Do you suppose that you alone have had this experience? Are you surprised, as if it were a novelty, that after such long travel and so many changes of scene you have not been able to shake off the gloom and heaviness of your mind? You need a change of soul rather than a change of climate. Though you may cross vast spaces of sea, and though, as our Vergil remarks,

> *Lands and cities are left astern,*

your faults will follow you whithersoever you travel. Socrates made the same remark to one who complained; he said: "Why do you wonder that globe-trotting does not help you, seeing that you always take yourself with you? The reason which set you wandering is ever at your heels." What pleasure is there in

* *i.e.*, all the ideas that dropped out of the head of Sabinus. The slave who picked up the crumbs was called *analecta*.

seeing new lands? Or in surveying cities and spots of interest? All your bustle is useless. Do you ask why such flight does not help you? It is because you flee along with yourself. You must lay aside the burdens of the mind; until you do this, no place will satisfy you. Reflect that your present behaviour is like that of the prophetess whom Vergil describes: she is excited and goaded into fury, and contains within herself much inspiration that is not her own:

The priestess raves, if haply she may shake
The great god from her heart.

You wander hither and yon, to rid yourself of the burden that rests upon you, though it becomes more troublesome by reason of your very restlessness, just as in a ship the cargo when stationary makes no trouble, but when it shifts to this side or that, it causes the vessel to heel more quickly in the direction where it has settled. Anything you do tells against you, and you hurt yourself by your very unrest; for you are shaking up a sick man.

That trouble once removed, all change of scene will become pleasant; though you may be driven to the uttermost ends of the earth, in whatever corner of a savage land you may find yourself, that place, however forbidding, will be to you a hospitable abode. The person you are matters more than the place to which you go; for that reason we should not make the mind a bondsman to any one place. Live in this belief: "I am not born for any one corner of the universe; this whole world is my country." If you saw this fact clearly, you would not be surprised at getting no benefit from the fresh scenes to which you roam each time through weariness of the old scenes. For the first would have pleased you in each case, had you believed it wholly yours. As it is, however, you are not journeying; you are drifting and being driven, only exchanging one place for another, although that which you seek—to live well—is found everywhere. Can there be any spot so full of confusion as the Forum? Yet you can live quietly even there, if necessary. Of course, if one were allowed to make one's own arrangements, I should flee far from the very sight and neighbourhood of the Forum. For just as pestilential places assail even the strongest constitution, so there are some places which are also unwholesome for a healthy mind which is not yet quite sound, though recovering from its ailment. I disagree with those who strike out into the midst of the billows and, welcoming a stormy existence, wrestle daily in hardihood of soul with life's problems. The wise man will endure all that, but will not choose it; he will prefer to be at peace rather than at war. It helps little to have cast out your own faults if you must quarrel with those of others. Says one: "There were thirty tyrants surrounding Socrates, and yet they could not break his spirit"; but what does it matter how many masters a man has? "Slavery" has no plural; and he who has scorned it is free—no matter amid how large a mob of over-lords he stands.

It is time to stop, but not before I have paid duty. "The knowledge of sin is the beginning of salvation." This saying of Epicurus seems to me to be a noble one. For he who does not know that he has sinned does not desire correction; you must discover yourself in the wrong before you can reform yourself. Some boast of their faults. Do you think that the man has any thought of mending his ways who counts over his vices as if they were virtues? Therefore, as far as possible, prove yourself guilty, hunt up charges against yourself; play the part, first of accuser, then of judge, last of intercessor. At times be harsh with yourself. Farewell.

33. ON THE FUTILITY OF LEARNING MAXIMS

You wish me to close these letters also, as I closed my former letters, with certain utterances taken from the chiefs of our school. But they did not interest themselves in choice extracts; the whole texture of their work is full of strength. There is unevenness, you know, when some objects rise conspicuous above others. A single tree is not remarkable if the whole forest rises to the same height. Poetry is crammed with utterances of this sort, and so is history. For this reason I would not have you think that these utterances belong to Epicurus. They are common property and are emphatically our own. They are, however, more noteworthy in Epicurus, because they appear at infrequent intervals and when you do not expect them, and because it is surprising that brave words should be spoken at any time by a man who made a practise of being effeminate. For that is what most persons maintain. In my own opinion, however, Epicurus is really a brave man, even though he did wear long sleeves. Fortitude, energy, and readiness for battle are to be found among the Persians, just as much as among men who have girded themselves up high.

Therefore, you need not call upon me for extracts and quotations; such thoughts as one may extract here and there in the works of other philosophers run through the whole body of our writings. Hence we have no "show-window goods," nor do we deceive the purchaser in such a way that, if he enters our shop, he will find nothing except that which is displayed in the window. We allow the purchasers themselves to get their samples from anywhere they please. Suppose we should desire to sort out each separate motto from the general stock; to whom shall we credit them? To Zeno, Cleanthes, Chrysippus, Panaetius, or Posidonius? We Stoics are not subjects of a despot: each of us lays claim to his own freedom. With them, on the other hand, whatever Hermarchus says or Metrodorus, is ascribed to one source. In that brotherhood, everything that any man utters is spoken under the leadership and commanding authority of one alone. We cannot, I maintain, no matter how we try, pick out anything from so great a multitude of things equally good.

Only the poor man counts his flock.

Wherever you direct your gaze, you will meet with something that might stand out from the rest, if the context in which you read it were not equally notable.

For this reason, give over hoping that you can skim, by means of epitomes, the wisdom of distinguished men. Look into their wisdom as a whole; study it as a whole. They are working out a plan and weaving together, line upon line, a masterpiece, from which nothing can be taken away without injury to the whole. Examine the separate parts, if you like, provided you examine them as parts of the man himself. She is not a beautiful woman whose ankle or arm is praised, but she whose general appearance makes you forget to admire her single attributes.

If you insist, however, I shall not be niggardly with you, but lavish; for there is a huge multitude of these passages; they are scattered about in profusion—they do not need to be gathered together, but merely to be picked up. They do not drip forth occasionally; they flow continuously. They are unbroken and are closely connected. Doubtless they would be of much benefit to those who are still novices and worshipping outside the shrine; for single maxims sink in more easily when they are marked off and bounded like a line of verse. That is why we give to children a proverb, or that which the Greeks call *Chria*, to be learned by heart; that sort of thing can be comprehended by the young mind, which cannot as yet hold more. For a man, however, whose progress is definite, to chase after choice extracts and to prop his weakness by the best known and the briefest sayings and to depend upon his memory, is disgraceful; it is time for him to lean on himself. He should make such maxims and not memorize them.

For it is disgraceful even for an old man, or one who has sighted old age, to have a note-book knowledge. "This is what Zeno said." But what have you yourself said? "This is the opinion of Cleanthes." But what is your own opinion? How long shall you march under another man's orders? Take command, and utter some word which posterity will remember. Put forth something from your own stock. For this reason I hold that there is nothing of eminence in all such men as these, who never create anything themselves, but always lurk in the shadow of others, playing the rôle of interpreters, never daring to put once into practise what they have been so long in learning. They have exercised their memories on other men's material. But it is one thing to remember, another to know. Remembering is merely safeguarding something entrusted to the memory; knowing, however, means making everything your own; it means not depending upon the copy and not all the time glancing back at the master. "Thus said Zeno, thus said Cleanthes, indeed!" Let there be a difference between yourself and your book! How long shall you be a learner? From now on be a teacher as well! "But why," one asks, "should I have to continue hearing lectures on what I can read?" "The living voice," one replies, "is a great help." Perhaps, but not the voice which merely makes itself the mouthpiece of another's words, and only performs the duty of a reporter.

Consider this fact also. Those who have never attained their mental independence begin, in the first place, by following the leader in cases where everyone has deserted the leader; then, in the second place, they follow him in matters where the truth is still being investigated. However, the truth will never be discovered if we rest contented with discoveries already made. Besides, he who follows another not only discovers nothing but is not even investigating. What then? Shall I not follow in the footsteps of my predecessors? I shall indeed use the old road, but if I find one that makes a shorter cut and is smoother to travel, I shall open the new road. Men who have made these discoveries before us are not our masters, but our guides. Truth lies open for all; it has not yet been monopolized. And there is plenty of it left even for posterity to discover. Farewell.

36. ON THE VALUE OF RETIREMENT

Encourage your friend to despise stout-heartedly those who upbraid him because he has sought the shade of retirement and has abdicated his career of

honours, and, though he might have attained more, has preferred tranquillity to them all. Let him prove daily to these detractors how wisely he has looked out for his own interests. Those whom men envy will continue to march past him; some will be pushed out of the ranks, and others will fall. Prosperity is a turbulent thing; it torments itself. It stirs the brain in more ways than one, goading men on to various aims—some to power, and others to high living. Some it puffs up; others it slackens and wholly enervates.

"But," the retort comes, "so-and-so carries his prosperity well." Yes; just as he carries his liquor. So you need not let this class of men persuade you that one who is besieged by the crowd is happy; they run to him as crowds rush for a pool of water, rendering it muddy while they drain it. But you say: "Men call our friend a trifler and a sluggard." There are men, you know, whose speech is awry, who use the contrary terms. They called him happy; what of it? Was he happy? Even the fact that to certain persons he seems a man of a very rough and gloomy cast of mind, does not trouble me. Aristo used to say that he preferred a youth of stern disposition to one who was a jolly fellow and agreeable to the crowd. "For," he added, "wine which, when new, seemed harsh and sour, becomes good wine; but that which tasted well at the vintage cannot stand age." So let them call him stern and a foe to his own advancement, it is just this sternness that will go well when it is aged, provided only that he continues to cherish virtue and to absorb thoroughly the studies which make for culture—not those with which it is sufficient for a man to sprinkle himself, but those in which the mind should be steeped. Now is the time to learn. "What? Is there any time when a man should not learn?" By no means; but just as it is creditable for every age to study, so it is not creditable for every age to be instructed. An old man learning his A B C is a disgraceful and absurd object; the young man must store up, the old man must use. You will therefore be doing a thing most helpful to yourself if you make this friend of yours as good a man as possible; those kindnesses, they tell us, are to be both sought for and bestowed, which benefit the giver no less than the receiver; and they are unquestionably the best kind.

Finally, he has no longer any freedom in the matter; he has pledged his word. And it is less disgraceful to compound with a creditor than to compound with a promising future. To pay his debt of money, the business man must have a prosperous voyage, the farmer must have fruitful fields and kindly weather; but the debt which your friend owes can be completely paid by mere goodwill. Fortune has no jurisdiction over character. Let him so regulate his character

that in perfect peace he may bring to perfection that spirit within him which feels neither loss nor gain, but remains in the same attitude, no matter how things fall out. A spirit like this, if it is heaped with worldly goods, rises superior to its wealth; if, on the other hand, chance has stripped him of a part of his wealth, or even all, it is not impaired.

If your friend had been born in Parthia, he would have begun, when a child, to bend the bow; if in Germany, he would forthwith have been brandishing his slender spear; if he had been born in the days of our forefathers, he would have learned to ride a horse and smite his enemy hand to hand. These are the occupations which the system of each race recommends to the individual—yes, prescribes for him. To what, then, shall this friend of yours devote his attention? I say, let him learn that which is helpful against all weapons, against every kind of foe—contempt of death; because no one doubts that death has in it something that inspires terror, so that it shocks even our souls, which nature has so moulded that they love their own existence; for otherwise there would be no need to prepare ourselves, and to whet our courage, to face that towards which we should move with a sort of voluntary instinct, precisely as all men tend to preserve their existence. No man learns a thing in order that, if necessity arises, he may lie down with composure upon a bed of roses; but he steels his courage to this end, that he may not surrender his plighted faith to torture, and that, if need be, he may some day stay out his watch in the trenches, even though wounded, without even leaning on his spear; because sleep is likely to creep over men who support themselves by any prop whatsoever.

In death there is nothing harmful; for there must exist something to which it is harmful. And yet, if you are possessed by so great a craving for a longer life, reflect that none of the objects which vanish from our gaze and are reabsorbed into the world of things, from which they have come forth and are soon to come forth again, is annihilated; they merely end their course and do not perish. And death, which we fear and shrink from, merely interrupts life, but does not steal it away; the time will return when we shall be restored to the light of day; and many men would object to this, were they not brought back in forgetfulness of the past.

But I mean to show you later, with more care, that everything which seems to perish merely changes. Since you are destined to return, you ought to depart with a tranquil mind. Mark how the round of the universe repeats its course; you will see that no star in our firmament is extinguished, but that they all set and rise in alternation. Summer has gone, but another year will bring it again;

winter lies low, but will be restored by its own proper months; night has overwhelmed the sun, but day will soon rout the night again. The wandering stars retrace their former courses; a part of the sky is rising unceasingly, and a part is sinking. One word more, and then I shall stop; infants, and boys, and those who have gone mad, have no fear of death, and it is most shameful if reason cannot afford us that peace of mind to which they have been brought by their folly. Farewell.

38. ON QUIET CONVERSATION

You are right when you urge that we increase our mutual traffic in letters. But the greatest benefit is to be derived from conversation, because it creeps by degrees into the soul. Lectures prepared beforehand and spouted in the presence of a throng have in them more noise but less intimacy. Philosophy is good advice; and no one can give advice at the top of his lungs. Of course we must sometimes also make use of these harangues, if I may so call them, when a doubting member needs to be spurred on; but when the aim is to make a man learn and not merely to make him wish to learn, we must have recourse to the low-toned words of conversation. They enter more easily, and stick in the memory; for we do not need many words, but, rather, effective words.

Words should be scattered like seed; no matter how small the seed may be, if it has once found favourable ground, it unfolds its strength and from an insignificant thing spreads to its greatest growth. Reason grows in the same way; it is not large to the outward view, but increases as it does its work. Few words are spoken; but if the mind has truly caught them, they come into their strength and spring up. Yes, precepts and seeds have the same quality; they produce much, and yet they are slight things. Only, as I said, let a favourable mind receive and assimilate them. Then of itself the mind also will produce bounteously in its turn, giving back more than it has received. Farewell.

40. ON THE PROPER STYLE FOR A PHILOSOPHER'S DISCOURSE

I thank you for writing to me so often; for you are revealing your real self to me in the only way you can. I never receive a letter from you without being in your company forthwith. If the pictures of our absent friends are pleasing to us, though they only refresh the memory and lighten our longing by a solace that is unreal and unsubstantial, how much more pleasant is a letter, which brings us real traces, real evidences, of an absent friend! For that which is sweetest when we meet face to face is afforded by the impress of a friend's hand upon his letter—recognition.

You write me that you heard a lecture by the philosopher Serapio, when he landed at your present place of residence. "He is wont," you say, "to wrench up his words with a mighty rush, and he does not let them flow forth one by one, but makes them crowd and dash upon each other. For the words come in such quantity that a single voice is inadequate to utter them." I do not approve of this in a philosopher; his speech, like his life, should be composed; and nothing that rushes headlong and is hurried is well ordered. That is why, in Homer, the rapid style, which sweeps down without a break like a snow-squall, is assigned to the younger speaker; from the old man eloquence flows gently, sweeter than honey.

Therefore, mark my words; that forceful manner of speech, rapid and copious, is more suited to a mountebank than to a man who is discussing and teaching an important and serious subject. But I object just as strongly that he should drip out his words as that he should go at top speed; he should neither keep the ear on the stretch, nor deafen it. For that poverty-stricken and thin-spun style also makes the audience less attentive because they are weary of its stammering slowness; nevertheless, the word which has been long awaited sinks in more easily than the word which flits past us on the wing. Finally, people speak of "handing down" precepts to their pupils; but one is not "handing down" that which eludes the grasp. Besides, speech that deals with the truth should be unadorned and plain. This popular style has nothing to do with the truth; its aim is to impress the common herd, to ravish heedless ears by its speed; it does not offer itself for discussion, but snatches itself away from discussion. But how can that speech govern others which cannot itself be governed? May I not also remark that all speech which is employed for the purpose of healing our minds ought to sink into us? Remedies do not avail unless they remain in the system.

Besides, this sort of speech contains a great deal of sheer emptiness; it has more sound than power. My terrors should be quieted, my irritations soothed, my illusions shaken off, my indulgences checked, my greed rebuked. And which of these cures can be brought about in a hurry? What physician can heal his patient on a flying visit? May I add that such a jargon of confused and ill-chosen words cannot afford pleasure, either? No; but just as you are well satisfied, in the majority of cases, to have seen through tricks which you did not think could possibly be done, so in the case of these word-gymnasts to have heard them once is amply sufficient. For what can a man desire to learn or to imitate in them? What is he to think of their souls, when their speech is sent into the charge in utter disorder, and cannot be kept in hand? Just as, when you run downhill, you cannot stop at the point where you had decided to stop, but your steps are carried along by the momentum of your body and are borne beyond the place where you wished to halt; so this speed of speech has no control over itself, nor is it seemly for philosophy; since philosophy should carefully place her words, not fling them out, and should proceed step by step.

"What then?" you say; "should not philosophy sometimes take a loftier tone?" Of course she should; but dignity of character should be preserved, and this is stripped away by such violent and excessive force. Let philosophy possess great forces, but kept well under control; let her stream flow unceasingly, but never become a torrent. And I should hardly allow even to an orator a rapidity of speech like this, which cannot be called back, which goes lawlessly ahead; for how could it be followed by jurors, who are often inexperienced and untrained? Even when the orator is carried away by his desire to show off his powers, or by uncontrollable emotion, even then he should not quicken his pace and heap up words to an extent greater than the ear can endure.

You will be acting rightly, therefore, if you do not regard those men who seek how much they may say, rather than how they shall say it, and if for yourself you choose, provided a choice must be made, to speak as Publius Vinicius the stammerer does. When Asellius was asked how Vinicius spoke, he replied: "Gradually!" (It was a remark of Geminus Varius, by the way: "I don't see how you can call that man 'eloquent'; why, he can't get out three words together.") Why, then, should you not choose to speak as Vinicius does? Though of course some wag may cross your path, like the person who said, when Vinicius was dragging out his words one by one, as if he were dictating and not speaking: "Say, haven't you anything to say?" And yet that was the better choice, for the rapidity of Quintus Haterius, the most famous orator of his age, is, in my opinion, to be avoided by a man of sense. Haterius never hesitated, never paused; he made only one start, and only one stop.

However, I suppose that certain styles of speech are more or less suitable to nations also; in a Greek you can put up with the unrestrained style, but we

Romans, even when writing, have become accustomed to separate our words.* And our compatriot Cicero, with whom Roman oratory sprang into prominence, was also a slow pacer. The Roman language is more inclined to take stock of itself, to weigh, and to offer something worth weighing. Fabianus, a man noteworthy because of his life, his knowledge, and, less important than either of these, his eloquence also, used to discuss a subject with dispatch rather than with haste; hence you might call it ease rather than speed. I approve this quality in the wise man; but I do not demand it; only let his speech proceed unhampered, though I prefer that it should be deliberately uttered rather than spouted.

However, I have this further reason for frightening you away from the latter malady, namely, that you could only be successful in practising this style by losing your sense of modesty; you would have to rub all shame from your countenance, and refuse to hear yourself speak. For that heedless flow will carry with it many expressions which you would wish to criticize. And, I repeat, you could not attain it and at the same time preserve your sense of shame. Moreover, you would need to practise every day, and transfer your attention from subject matter to words. But words, even if they came to you readily and flowed without any exertion on your part, yet would have to be kept under control. For just as a less ostentatious gait becomes a philosopher, so does a restrained style of speech, far removed from boldness. Therefore, the ultimate kernel of my remarks is this: I bid you be slow of speech. Farewell.

41. ON THE GOD WITHIN US

You are doing an excellent thing, one which will be wholesome for you, if, as you write me, you are persisting in your effort to attain sound understanding; it is foolish to pray for this when you can acquire it from yourself. We do not need to uplift our hands towards heaven, or to beg the keeper of a temple to let us approach his idol's ear, as if in this way our prayers were more likely to be heard. God is near you, he is with you, he is within you. This is what I mean, Lucilius: a holy spirit indwells within us, one who marks our good and bad deeds, and is our guardian. As we treat this spirit, so are we treated by it.

---

* The Greek texts were still written without separation of the words, in contrast with the Roman.

Indeed, no man can be good without the help of God. Can one rise superior to Fortune unless God helps him to rise? He it is that gives noble and upright counsel. In each good man

A god doth dwell, but what god know we not.

If ever you have come upon a grove that is full of ancient trees which have grown to an unusual height, shutting out a view of the sky by a veil of pleached and intertwining branches, then the loftiness of the forest, the seclusion of the spot, and your marvel at the thick unbroken shade in the midst of the open spaces, will prove to you the presence of deity. Or if a cave, made by the deep crumbling of the rocks, holds up a mountain on its arch, a place not built with hands but hollowed out into such spaciousness by natural causes, your soul will be deeply moved by a certain intimation of the existence of God. We worship the sources of mighty rivers; we erect altars at places where great streams burst suddenly from hidden sources; we adore springs of hot water as divine, and consecrate certain pools because of their dark waters or their immeasurable depth. If you see a man who is unterrified in the midst of dangers, untouched by desires, happy in adversity, peaceful amid the storm, who looks down upon men from a higher plane, and views the gods on a footing of equality, will not a feeling of reverence for him steal over you, will you not say: "This quality is too great and too lofty to be regarded as resembling this petty body in which it dwells? A divine power has descended upon that man." When a soul rises superior to other souls, when it is under control, when it passes through every experience as if it were of small account, when it smiles at our fears and at our prayers, it is stirred by a force from heaven. A thing like this cannot stand upright unless it be propped by the divine. Therefore, a greater part of it abides in that place from whence it came down to earth. Just as the rays of the sun do indeed touch the earth, but still abide at the source from which they are sent; even so the great and hallowed soul, which has come down in order that we may have a nearer knowledge of divinity, does indeed associate with us, but still cleaves to its origin; on that source it depends, thither it turns its gaze and strives to go, and it concerns itself with our doings only as a being superior to ourselves.

What, then, is such a soul? One which is resplendent with no external good, but only with its own. For what is more foolish than to praise in a man the qualities which come from without? And what is more insane than to marvel at characteristics which may at the next instant be passed on to someone else? A golden bit does not make a better horse. The lion with gilded mane, in process of being trained and forced by weariness to endure the decoration, is sent into the arena in quite a different way from the wild lion whose spirit is unbroken; the latter, indeed, bold in his attack, as nature wished him to be, impressive because of his wild appearance—and it is his glory that none can look upon him without fear—is favoured* in preference to the other lion, that languid and gilded brute.

No man ought to glory except in that which is his own. We praise a vine if it makes the shoots teem with increase, if by its weight it bends to the ground the very poles which hold its fruit; would any man prefer to this vine one from which golden grapes and golden leaves hang down? In a vine the virtue peculiarly its own is fertility; in man also we should praise that which is his own. Suppose that he has a retinue of comely slaves and a beautiful house, that his farm is large and large his income; none of these things is in the man himself; they are all on the outside. Praise the quality in him which cannot be given or snatched away, that which is the peculiar property of the man. Do you ask what this is? It is soul, and reason brought to perfection in the soul. For man is a reasoning animal. Therefore, man's highest good is attained, if he has fulfilled the good for which nature designed him at birth. And what is it which this reason demands of him? The easiest thing in the world—to live in accordance with his own nature. But this is turned into a hard task by the general madness of mankind; we push one another into vice. And how can a man be recalled to salvation, when he has none to restrain him, and all mankind to urge him on? Farewell.

42. ON VALUES

Has that friend of yours already made you believe that he is a good man? And yet it is impossible in so short a time for one either to become good or be known as such. Do you know what kind of man I now mean when I speak of "a good man"? I mean one of the second grade, like your friend. For one of the first class perhaps springs into existence, like the phoenix, only once in five hundred

* The spectators of the fight, which is to take place between two lions, applaud the wild lion and bet on him.

years. And it is not surprising, either, that greatness develops only at long intervals; Fortune often brings into being commonplace powers, which are born to please the mob; but she holds up for our approval that which is extraordinary by the very fact that she makes it rare.

This man, however, of whom you spoke, is still far from the state which he professes to have reached. And if he knew what it meant to be "a good man," he would not yet believe himself such; perhaps he would even despair of his ability to become good. "But," you say, "he thinks ill of evil men." Well, so do evil men themselves; and there is no worse penalty for vice than the fact that it is dissatisfied with itself and all its fellows. "But he hates those who make an ungoverned use of great power suddenly acquired." I retort that he will do the same thing as soon as he acquires the same powers. In the case of many men, their vices, being powerless, escape notice; although, as soon as the persons in question have become satisfied with their own strength, the vices will be no less daring than those which prosperity has already disclosed. These men simply lack the means whereby they may unfold their wickedness. Similarly, one can handle even a poisonous snake while it is stiff with cold; the poison is not lacking; it is merely numbed into inaction. In the case of many men, their cruelty, ambition, and indulgence only lack the favour of Fortune to make them dare crimes that would match the worst. That their wishes are the same you will in a moment discover, in this way: give them the power equal to their wishes.

Do you remember how, when you declared that a certain person was under your influence, I pronounced him fickle and a bird of passage, and said that you held him not by the foot but merely by a wing? Was I mistaken? You grasped him only by a feather; he left it in your hands and escaped. You know what an exhibition he afterwards made of himself before you, how many of the things he attempted were to recoil upon his own head. He did not see that in endangering others he was tottering to his own downfall. He did not reflect how burdensome were the objects which he was bent upon attaining, even if they were not superfluous.

Therefore, with regard to the objects which we pursue, and for which we strive with great effort, we should note this truth; either there is nothing desirable in them, or the undesirable is preponderant. Some objects are superfluous; others are not worth the price we pay for them. But we do not see this clearly, and we regard things as free gifts when they really cost us very dear. Our stupidity may be clearly proved by the fact that we hold that "buying" refers only to the objects for which we pay cash, and we regard as free gifts the things for which we spend our very selves. These we should refuse to buy, if we were compelled to give in payment for them our houses or some attractive and profitable estate; but we are eager to attain them at the cost of anxiety, of danger, and of lost honour, personal freedom, and time; so true it is that each man regards nothing as cheaper than himself.

Let us therefore act, in all our plans and conduct, just as we are accustomed to act whenever we approach a huckster who has certain wares for sale; let us see how much we must pay for that which we crave. Very often the things that cost nothing cost us the most heavily; I can show you many objects the quest and acquisition of which have wrested freedom from our hands. We should belong to ourselves, if only these things did not belong to us.

I would therefore have you reflect thus, not only when it is a question of gain, but also when it is a question of loss. "This object is bound to perish." Yes, it was a mere extra; you will live without it just as easily as you have lived before. If you have possessed it for a long time, you lose it after you have had your fill of it; if you have not possessed it long, then you lose it before you have become wedded to it. "You will have less money." Yes, and less trouble. "Less influence." Yes, and less envy. Look about you and note the things that drive us mad, which we lose with a flood of tears; you will perceive that it is not the loss that troubles us with reference to these things, but a notion of loss. No one feels that they have been lost, but his mind tells him that it has been so. He that owns himself has lost nothing. But how few men are blessed with ownership of self! Farewell.

48. ON QUIBBLING AS UNWORTHY OF THE PHILOSOPHER

In answer to the letter which you wrote me while travelling—a letter as long as the journey itself—I shall reply later. I ought to go into retirement, and consider what sort of advice I should give you. For you yourself, who consult me, also reflected for a long time whether to do so; how much more, then, should I myself reflect, since more deliberation is necessary in settling than in propounding a problem! And this is particularly true when one thing is advantageous to you and another to me. Am I speaking again in the guise of an Epicurean? But the fact is, the same thing is advantageous to me which is advantageous to you; for I am not your friend unless whatever is at issue concerning you is my concern also. Friendship produces between us a partnership in all our interests. There is no such thing as good or bad Fortune for the individual; we live in common. And no one can live happily who has regard to himself alone and transforms everything into a question of his own utility; you must live for your neighbour, if you would live for yourself. This fellowship, maintained with scrupulous care, which makes us mingle as men with our fellow-men and holds that the human race have certain rights in common, is also of great help in cherishing the more intimate fellowship which is based on friendship, concerning which I began to speak above. For he that has much in common with a fellow-man will have all things in common with a friend.

And on this point, my excellent Lucilius, I should like to have those subtle dialecticians of yours advise me how I ought to help a friend, or how a fellow-man, rather than tell me in how many ways the word "friend" is used, and how many meanings the word "man" possesses. Lo, Wisdom and Folly are taking opposite sides. Which shall I join? Which party would you have me follow? On that side, "man" is the equivalent of "friend"; on the other side, "friend" is not the equivalent of "man." The one wants a friend for his own advantage; the other wants to make himself an advantage to his friend. What *you* have to offer me is nothing but distortion of words and splitting of syllables. It is clear that unless I can devise some very tricky premises and by false deductions tack on to them a fallacy which springs from the truth, I shall not be able to distinguish between what is desirable and what is to be avoided! I am ashamed! Old men as we are, dealing with a problem so serious, we make play of it!

"'Mouse' is a syllable.* Now a mouse eats its cheese; therefore, a syllable eats cheese." Suppose now that I cannot solve this problem; see what peril hangs over my head as a result of such ignorance! What a scrape I shall be in! Without doubt I must beware, or some day I shall be catching syllables in a mousetrap, or, if I grow careless, a book may devour my cheese! Unless, perhaps, the following syllogism is shrewder still: "'Mouse' is a syllable. Now a syllable does not eat cheese. Therefore a mouse does not eat cheese." What childish nonsense! Do we knit our brows over this sort of problem? Do we let our beards grow long for this reason? Is this the matter which we teach with sour and pale faces?

---

* In this paragraph Seneca exposes the folly of trying to prove a truth by means of logical tricks, and offers a caricature of those which were current among the philosophers whom he derides.

Would you really know what philosophy offers to humanity? Philosophy offers counsel. Death calls away one man, and poverty chafes another; a third is worried either by his neighbour's wealth or by his own. So-and-so is afraid of bad luck; another desires to get away from his own good fortune. Some are ill-treated by men, others by the gods. Why, then, do you frame for me such games as these? It is no occasion for jest; you are retained as counsel for unhappy mankind. You have promised to help those in peril by sea, those in captivity, the sick and the needy, and those whose heads are under the poised axe. Whither are you straying? What are you doing?

This friend, in whose company you are jesting, is in fear. Help him, and take the noose from about his neck. Men are stretching out imploring hands to you on all sides; lives ruined and in danger of ruin are begging for some assistance; men's hopes, men's resources, depend upon you. They ask that you deliver them from all their restlessness, that you reveal to them, scattered and wandering as they are, the clear light of truth. Tell them what nature has made necessary, and what superfluous; tell them how simple are the laws that she has laid down, how pleasant and unimpeded life is for those who follow these laws, but how bitter and perplexed it is for those who have put their trust in opinion rather than in nature.

I should deem your games of logic to be of some avail in relieving men's burdens, if you could first show me what part of these burdens they will relieve. What among these games of yours banishes lust? Or controls it? Would that I could say that they were merely of no profit! They are positively harmful. I can make it perfectly clear to you whenever you wish, that a noble spirit when involved in such subtleties is impaired and weakened. I am ashamed to say what weapons they supply to men who are destined to go to war with Fortune, and how poorly they equip them! Is this the path to the greatest good? Is philosophy to proceed by such claptrap and by quibbles which would be a disgrace and a reproach even for expounders of the law? For what else is it that you men are doing, when you deliberately ensnare the person to whom you are putting questions, than making it appear that the man has lost his case on a technical error? But just as the judge can reinstate those who have lost a suit in this way, so philosophy has reinstated these victims of quibbling to their former condition. Why do you men abandon your mighty promises, and, after having assured me in high-sounding language that you will permit the glitter of gold to dazzle my eyesight no more than the gleam of the sword, and that I shall, with mighty steadfastness, spurn both that which all men crave and that which all men fear, why do you descend to the ABC's of scholastic pedants? What is your answer?

Is this the path to heaven?

For that is exactly what philosophy promises to me, that I shall be made equal to God. For this I have been summoned, for this purpose have I come. Philosophy, keep your promise!

Therefore, my dear Lucilius, withdraw yourself as far as possible from these exceptions and objections of so-called philosophers. Frankness, and simplicity beseem true goodness. Even if there were many years left to you, you would have had to spend them frugally in order to have enough for the necessary things; but as it is, when your time is so scant, what madness it is to learn superfluous things! Farewell.

52. ON CHOOSING OUR TEACHERS

What is this force, Lucilius, that drags us in one direction when we are aiming in another, urging us on to the exact place from which we long to withdraw? What is it that wrestles with our spirit, and does not allow us to desire anything once for all? We veer from plan to plan. None of our wishes is free, none is unqualified, none is lasting. "But it is the fool," you say, "who is inconsistent; nothing suits him for long." But how or when can we tear ourselves away from this folly? No man by himself has sufficient strength to rise above it; he needs a helping hand, and some one to extricate him.

Epicurus remarks that certain men have worked their way to the truth without anyone's assistance, carving out their own passage. And he gives special praise to these, for their impulse has come from within, and they have forged to the front by themselves. Again, he says, there are others who need outside help, who will not proceed unless someone leads the way, but who will follow faithfully. Of these, he says, Metrodorus was one; this type of man is also excellent, but belongs to the second grade. We ourselves are not of that first class, either; we shall be well treated if we are admitted into the second. Nor need you despise a man who can gain salvation only with the assistance of another; the will to be saved means a great deal, too.

You will find still another class of man—and a class not to be despised—

who can be forced and driven into righteousness, who do not need a guide as much as they require someone to encourage and, as it were, to force them along. This is the third variety. If you ask me for a man of this pattern also, Epicurus tells us that Hermarchus was such. And of the two last-named classes, he is more ready to congratulate the one, but he feels more respect for the other; for although both reached the same goal, it is a greater credit to have brought about the same result with the more difficult material upon which to work.

Suppose that two buildings have been erected, unlike as to their foundations, but equal in height and in grandeur. One is built on faultless ground, and the process of erection goes right ahead. In the other case, the foundations have exhausted the building materials, for they have been sunk into soft and shifting ground and much labour has been wasted in reaching the solid rock. As one looks at both of them, one sees clearly what progress the former has made but the larger and more difficult part of the latter is hidden. So with men's dispositions; some are pliable and easy to manage, but others have to be laboriously wrought out by hand, so to speak, and are wholly employed in the making of their own foundations. I should accordingly deem more fortunate the man who has never had any trouble with himself; but the other, I feel, has deserved better of himself, who has won a victory over the meanness of his own nature, and has not gently led himself, but has wrestled his way, to wisdom.

You may be sure that this refractory nature, which demands much toil, has been implanted in us. There are obstacles in our path; so let us fight, and call to our assistance some helpers. "Whom," you say, "shall I call upon? Shall it be this man or that?" There is another choice also open to you; you may go to the ancients; for they have the time to help you. We can get assistance not only from the living, but from those of the past. Let us choose, however, from among the living, not men who pour forth their words with the greatest glibness, turning out commonplaces and holding, as it were, their own little private exhibitions—not these, I say, but men who teach us by their lives, men who tell us what we ought to do and then prove it by practise, who show us what we should avoid, and then are never caught doing that which they have ordered us to avoid.

Choose as a guide one whom you will admire more when you see him act than when you hear him speak. Of course I would not prevent you from listening also to those philosophers who are wont to hold public meetings and discussions, provided they appear before the people for the express purpose of improving themselves and others, and do not practise their profession for the sake of self-seeking. For what is baser than philosophy courting applause? Does the sick man praise the surgeon while he is operating? In silence and with reverent awe submit to the cure. Even though you cry applause, I shall listen to your cries as if you were groaning when your sores were touched. Do you wish to bear witness that you are attentive, that you are stirred by the grandeur of the subject? You may do this at the proper time; I shall of course allow you to pass judgment and cast a vote as to the better course. Pythagoras made his pupils keep silence for five years; do you think that they had the right on that account to break out immediately into applause?

How mad is he who leaves the lecture-room in a happy frame of mind simply because of applause from the ignorant! Why do you take pleasure in being praised by men whom you yourself cannot praise? Fabianus used to give popular talks, but his audience listened with self-control. Occasionally a loud shout of praise would burst forth, but it was prompted by the greatness of his subject, and not by the sound of oratory that slipped forth pleasantly and softly. There should be a difference between the applause of the theatre and the applause of the school; and there is a certain decency even in bestowing praise. If you mark them carefully, all acts are always significant, and you can gauge character by even the most trifling signs. The lecherous man is revealed by his gait, by a movement of the hand, sometimes by a single answer, by his touching his head with a finger, by the shifting of his eye. The scamp is shown up by his laugh; the madman by his face and general appearance. These qualities become known by certain marks; but you can tell the character of every man when you see how he gives and receives praise. The philosopher's audience, from this corner and that, stretch forth admiring hands, and sometimes the adoring crowd almost hang over the lecturer's head. But, if you really understand, that is not praise; it is merely applause. These outcries should be left for the arts which aim to please the crowd; let philosophy be worshipped in silence. Young men, indeed, must sometimes have free play to follow their impulses, but it should only be at times when they act from impulse, and when they cannot force themselves to be silent. Such praise as that gives a certain kind of encouragement to the hearers themselves, and acts as a spur to the youthful mind. But let them be roused to the matter, and not to the style; otherwise, eloquence does them harm, making them enamoured of itself, and not of the subject.

I shall postpone this topic for the present; it demands a long and special investigation, to show how the public should be addressed, what indulgences should be allowed to a speaker on a public occasion, and what should be allowed to the crowd itself in the presence of the speaker. There can be no doubt that philosophy has suffered a loss, now that she has exposed her charms for sale. But she can still be viewed in her sanctuary, if her exhibitor is a priest and not a pedlar. Farewell.

53. ON THE FAULTS OF THE SPIRIT

You can persuade me into almost anything now, for I was recently persuaded to travel by water. We cast off when the sea was lazily smooth; the sky, to be sure, was heavy with nasty clouds, such as usually break into rain or squalls. Still, I thought that the few miles between Puteoli and your dear Parthenope* might be run off in quick time, despite the uncertain and lowering sky. So, in order to get away more quickly, I made straight out to sea for Nesis,† with the purpose of cutting across all the inlets. But when we were so far out that it made little difference to me whether I returned or kept on, the calm weather, which had enticed me, came to naught. The storm had not yet begun, but the ground-swell was on, and the waves kept steadily coming faster. I began to ask the pilot to put me ashore somewhere; he replied that the coast was rough and a bad place to land, and that in a storm he feared a lee shore more than anything else. But I was suffering too grievously to think of the danger, since a sluggish seasickness which brought no relief was racking me, the sort that upsets the liver without clearing it. Therefore I laid down the law to my pilot, forcing him to make for the shore, willy-nilly. When we drew near, I did not wait for things to be done in accordance with Vergil's orders, until

Prow faced seawards

or

Anchor plunged from bow;

---

* The poetical name for Naples; perhaps it was once a town nearby which gave a sort of romantic second title to the larger city.

† An islet near the mouth of the bay wherein Baiae was situated. Puteoli was on the opposite side of the bay from Baiae.

I remembered my profession as a veteran devotee of cold water, and, clad as I was in my cloak, let myself down into the sea, just as a cold-water bather should. What do you think my feelings were, scrambling over the rocks, searching out the path, or making one for myself? I understood that sailors have good reason to fear the land. It is hard to believe what I endured when I could not endure myself; you may be sure that the reason why Ulysses was shipwrecked on every possible occasion was not so much because the sea-god was angry with him from his birth; he was simply subject to seasickness. And in the future I also, if I must go anywhere by sea, shall only reach my destination in the twentieth year.*

When I finally calmed my stomach (for you know that one does not escape seasickness by escaping from the sea) and refreshed my body with a rubdown, I began to reflect how completely we forget or ignore our failings, even those that affect the body, which are continually reminding us of their existence—not to mention those which are more serious in proportion as they are more hidden. A slight ague deceives us; but when it has increased and a genuine fever has begun to burn, it forces even a hardy man, who can endure much suffering, to admit that he is ill. There is pain in the foot, and a tingling sensation in the joints; but we still hide the complaint and announce that we have sprained a joint, or else are tired from over-exercise. Then the ailment, uncertain at first, must be given a name; and when it begins to swell the ankles also, and has made both our feet "right" feet, we are bound to confess that we have the gout. The opposite holds true of diseases of the soul; the worse one is, the less one perceives it. You need not be surprised, my beloved Lucilius. For he whose sleep is light pursues visions during slumber, and sometimes, though asleep, is conscious that he is asleep; but sound slumber annihilates our very dreams and sinks the spirit down so deep that it has no perception of self. Why will no man confess his faults? Because he is still in their grasp; only he who is awake can recount his dream, and similarly a confession of sin is a proof of sound mind.

Let us, therefore, rouse ourselves, that we may be able to correct our mistakes. Philosophy, however, is the only power that can stir us, the only power that can shake off our deep slumber. Devote yourself wholly to philosophy. You are worthy of her; she is worthy of you; greet one another with a loving embrace. Say farewell to all other interests with courage and frankness. Do not study philosophy merely during your spare time.

---

* Ulysses took ten years on his journey, because of seasickness; Seneca will need twice as many.

If you were ill, you would stop caring for your personal concerns and forget your business duties; you would not think highly enough of any client to take active charge of his case during a slight abatement of your sufferings. You would try your hardest to be rid of the illness as soon as possible. What, then? Shall you not do the same thing now? Throw aside all hindrances and give up your time to getting a sound mind; for no man can attain it if he is engrossed in other matters. Philosophy wields her own authority; she appoints her own time and does not allow it to be appointed for her. She is not a thing to be followed at odd times, but a subject for daily practise; she is mistress, and she commands our attendance. Alexander, when a certain state promised him a part of its territory and half its entire property, replied: "I invaded Asia with the intention, not of accepting what you might give, but of allowing you to keep what I might leave." Philosophy likewise keeps saying to all occupations: "I do not intend to accept the time which you have left over, but I shall allow you to keep what I myself shall leave."

Turn to her, therefore, with all your soul, sit at her feet, cherish her; a great distance will then begin to separate you from other men. You will be far ahead of all mortals, and even the gods will not be far ahead of you. Do you ask what will be the difference between yourself and the gods? They will live longer. But, by my faith, it is the sign of a great artist to have confined a full likeness to the limits of a miniature. The wise man's life spreads out to him over as large a surface as does all eternity to a god. There is one point in which the sage has an advantage over the god; for a god is freed from terrors by the bounty of nature, the wise man by his own bounty. What a wonderful privilege, to have the weaknesses of a man and the serenity of a god! The power of philosophy to blunt the blows of chance is beyond belief. No missile can settle in her body; she is well-protected and impenetrable. She spoils the force of some missiles and wards them off with the loose folds of her gown, as if they had no power to harm; others she dashes aside, and hurls them back with such force that they recoil upon the sender. Farewell.

56. ON QUIET AND STUDY

Beshrew me if I think anything more requisite than silence for a man who secludes himself in order to study! Imagine what a variety of noises reverberates about my ears! I have lodgings right over a bathing establishment. So picture to yourself the assortment of sounds, which are strong enough to make me hate my very powers of hearing! When your strenuous gentleman, for example, is exercising himself by flourishing leaden weights; when he is working hard, or else pretends to be working hard, I can hear him grunt; and whenever he releases his imprisoned breath, I can hear him panting in wheezy and high-pitched tones. Or perhaps I notice some lazy fellow, content with a cheap rubdown, and hear the crack of the pummelling hand on his shoulder, varying in sound according as the hand is laid on flat or hollow. Then, perhaps, a professional comes along, shouting out the score; that is the finishing touch. Add to this the arresting of an occasional roisterer or pickpocket, the racket of the man who always likes to hear his own voice in the bathroom, or the enthusiast who plunges into the swimming-tank with unconscionable noise and splashing. Besides all those whose voices, if nothing else, are good, imagine the hair-plucker with his penetrating, shrill voice—for purposes of advertisement—continually giving it vent and never holding his tongue except when he is plucking the armpits and making his victim yell instead. Then the cakeseller with his varied cries, the sausageman, the confectioner, and all the vendors of food hawking their wares, each with his own distinctive intonation.

So you say: "What iron nerves or deadened ears, you must have, if your mind can hold out amid so many noises, so various and so discordant, when our friend Chrysippus* is brought to his death by the continual good-morrows that greet him!" But I assure you that this racket means no more to me than the sound of waves or falling water; although you will remind me that a certain tribe once moved their city merely because they could not endure the din of a Nile cataract. Words seem to distract me more than noises; for words demand attention, but noises merely fill the ears and beat upon them. Among the sounds that din round me without distracting, I include passing carriages, a machinist in the same block, a saw-sharpener nearby, or some fellow who is demonstrating with little pipes and flutes at the Trickling Fountain, shouting rather than singing.

Furthermore, an intermittent noise upsets me more than a steady one. But by this time I have toughened my nerves against all that sort of thing, so that I can endure even a boatswain marking the time in high-pitched tones for his

---

* It is nowhere else related of the famous Stoic philosopher Chrysippus that he objected to the salutations of his friends; and, besides, the morning salutation was a Roman, not a Greek, custom.

crew. For I force my mind to concentrate, and keep it from straying to things outside itself; all outdoors may be bedlam, provided that there is no disturbance within, provided that fear is not wrangling with desire in my breast, provided that meanness and lavishness are not at odds, one harassing the other. For of what benefit is a quiet neighbourhood, if our emotions are in an uproar?

'Twas night, and all the world was lulled to rest.

This is not true; for no real rest can be found when reason has not done the lulling. Night brings our troubles to the light, rather than banishes them; it merely changes the form of our worries. For even when we seek slumber, our sleepless moments are as harassing as the daytime. Real tranquillity is the state reached by an unperverted mind when it is relaxed. Think of the unfortunate man who courts sleep by surrendering his spacious mansion to silence, who, that his ear may be disturbed by no sound, bids the whole retinue of his slaves be quiet and that whoever approaches him shall walk on tiptoe; he tosses from this side to that and seeks a fitful slumber amid his frettings! He complains that he has heard sounds, when he has not heard them at all. The reason, you ask? His soul's in an uproar; it must be soothed, and its rebellious murmuring checked. You need not suppose that the soul is at peace when the body is still. Sometimes quiet means disquiet.

We must therefore rouse ourselves to action and busy ourselves with interests that are good, as often as we are in the grasp of an uncontrollable sluggishness. Great generals, when they see that their men are mutinous, check them by some sort of labour or keep them busy with small forays. The much occupied man has no time for wantonness, and it is an obvious commonplace that the evils of leisure can be shaken off by hard work. Although people may often have thought that I sought seclusion because I was disgusted with politics and regretted my hapless and thankless position, yet, in the retreat to which apprehension and weariness have driven me, my ambition sometimes develops afresh. For it is not because my ambition was rooted out that it has abated, but because it was wearied or perhaps even put out of temper by the failure of its plans. And so with luxury, also, which sometimes seems to have departed, and then when we have made a profession of frugality, begins to fret us and, amid our economies, seeks the pleasures which we have merely left but not condemned. Indeed, the more stealthily it comes, the greater is its force. For all unconcealed vices are less serious; a disease also is farther on the road to being cured when it breaks forth from concealment and manifests its power. So with greed, ambition, and the other evils of the mind—you may be sure that they do most harm when they are hidden behind a pretence of soundness.

Men think that we are in retirement, and yet we are not. For if we have sincerely retired, and have sounded the signal for retreat, and have scorned outward attractions, then, as I remarked above, no outward thing will distract us; no music of men or of birds can interrupt good thoughts, when they have once become steadfast and sure. The mind which starts at words or at chance sounds is unstable and has not yet withdrawn into itself; it contains within itself an element of anxiety and rooted fear, and this makes one a prey to care, as our Vergil says:

I, whom of yore no dart could cause to flee,
Nor Greeks, with crowded lines of infantry,
Now shake at every sound, and fear the air,
Both for my child and for the load I bear.

This man in his first state is wise; he blenches neither at the brandished spear, nor at the clashing armour of the serried foe, nor at the din of the stricken city. This man in his second state lacks knowledge fearing for his own concerns, he pales at every sound; any cry is taken for the battle-shout and overthrows him; the slightest disturbance renders him breathless with fear. It is the load that makes him afraid. Select anyone you please from among your favourites of Fortune, trailing their many responsibilities, carrying their many burdens, and you will behold a picture of Vergil's hero, "fearing both for his child and for the load he bears."

You may therefore be sure that you are at peace with yourself, when no noise readies you, when no word shakes you out of yourself, whether it be of flattery or of threat, or merely an empty sound buzzing about you with unmeaning din. "What then?" you say; "is it not sometimes a simpler matter just to avoid the uproar?" I admit this. Accordingly, I shall change from my present quarters. I merely wished to test myself and to give myself practise. Why need I be tormented any longer, when Ulysses found so simple a cure for his comrades even against the songs of the Sirens? Farewell.

57. ON THE TRIALS OF TRAVEL

When it was time for me to return to Naples from Baiae, I easily persuaded myself that a storm was raging, that I might avoid another trip by sea; and yet the road was so deep in mud, all the way, that I may be thought none the less to have made a voyage. On that day I had to endure the full fate of an athlete; the anointing* with which we began was followed by the sand-sprinkle in the Naples tunnel.† No place could be longer than that prison; nothing could be dimmer than those torches, which enabled us, not to see amid the darkness, but to see the darkness. But, even supposing that there was light in the place, the dust, which is an oppressive and disagreeable thing even in the open air, would destroy the light; how much worse the dust is there, where it rolls back upon itself, and, being shut in without ventilation, blows back in the faces of those who set it going! So we endured two inconveniences at the same time, and they were diametrically different: we struggled both with mud and with dust on the same road and on the same day.

The gloom, however, furnished me with some food for thought; I felt a certain mental thrill, and a transformation unaccompanied by fear, due to the novelty and the unpleasantness of an unusual occurrence. Of course I am not speaking to you of myself at this point, because I am far from being a perfect person, or even a man of middling qualities; I refer to one over whom Fortune has lost her control. Even such a man's mind will be smitten with a thrill and he will change colour. For there are certain emotions, my dear Lucilius, which no courage can avoid; nature reminds courage how perishable a thing it is. And so he will contract his brow when the prospect is forbidding, will shudder at sudden apparitions, and will become dizzy when he stands at the edge of a high precipice and looks down. This is not fear; it is a natural feeling which reason cannot rout. That is why certain brave men, most willing to shed their own blood, cannot bear to see the blood of others. Some persons collapse and faint at the sight of a freshly inflicted wound; others are affected similarly on

---

* *i.e.*, an "anointing" with mud.

† A characteristic figure. After anointing, the wrestler was sprinkled with sand, so that the opponent's hand might not slip. The Naples tunnel furnished a shortcut to those who, like Seneca in this letter, did not wish to take the time to travel by the shore route along the promontory of Pausilipum.

handling or viewing an old wound which is festering. And others meet the sword-stroke more readily than they see it dealt.

Accordingly, as I said, I experienced a certain transformation, though it could not be called confusion. Then at the first glimpse of restored daylight my good spirits returned without forethought or command. And I began to muse and think how foolish we are to fear certain objects to a greater or less degree, since all of them end in the same way. For what difference does it make whether a watchtower or a mountain crashes down upon us? No difference at all, you will find. Nevertheless, there will be some men who fear the latter mishap to a greater degree, though both accidents are equally deadly; so true it is that fear looks not to the effect, but to the cause of the effect. Do you suppose that I am now referring to the Stoics, who hold that the soul of a man crushed by a great weight cannot abide, and is scattered forthwith, because it has not had a free opportunity to depart? That is not what I am doing; those who think thus are, in my opinion, wrong. Just as fire cannot be crushed out, since it will escape round the edges of the body which overwhelms it; just as the air cannot be damaged by lashes and blows, or even cut into, but flows back about the object to which it gives place; similarly the soul, which consists of the subtlest particles, cannot be arrested or destroyed inside the body, but, by virtue of its delicate substance, it will rather escape through the very object by which it is being crushed. Just as lightning, no matter how widely it strikes and flashes, makes its return through a narrow opening, so the soul, which is still subtler than fire, has a way of escape through any part of the body. We therefore come to this question—whether the soul can be immortal. But be sure of this: if the soul survives the body after the body is crushed, the soul can in no wise be crushed out, precisely because it does not perish; for the rule of immortality never admits of exceptions, and nothing can harm that which is everlasting. Farewell.

58. ON BEING

How scant of words our language is, nay, how poverty-stricken, I have not fully understood until today. We happened to be speaking of Plato, and a thousand subjects came up for discussion, which needed names and yet possessed none; and there were certain others which once possessed, but have since lost, their words because we were too nice about their use. But who can endure to be nice in the midst of poverty? There is an insect, called by the Greeks *oestrus,* which drives cattle wild and scatters them all over their pasturing grounds; it used to be called *asilus* in our language, as you may believe on the authority of Vergil:

Near Silarus groves, and eke Alburnus' shades
Of green-clad oak-trees flits an insect, named
Asilus *by the Romans; in the Greek*
The word is rendered oestrus. *With a rough*
And strident sound it buzzes and drives wild
The terror-stricken herds throughout the woods.

By which I infer that the word has gone out of use. And, not to keep you waiting too long, there were certain uncompounded words current, like *cernere ferro inter se,* as will be proved again by Vergil:

Great heroes, born in various lands, had come
To settle matters mutually with the sword.

This "settling matters" we now express by *decernere.* The plain word has become obsolete. The ancients used to say *iusso,* instead of *iussero,* in conditional clauses. You need not take my word, but you may turn again to Vergil:

The other soldiers shall conduct the fight
With me, where I shall bid.

It is not in my purpose to show, by this array of examples, how much time I have wasted on the study of language; I merely wish you to understand how many words, that were current in the works of Ennius and Accius, have become mouldy with age; while even in the case of Vergil, whose works are explored daily, some of his words have been filched away from us.

You will say, I suppose: "What is the purpose and meaning of this preamble?" I shall not keep you in the dark; I desire, if possible, to say the word *essentia* to you and obtain a favourable hearing. If I cannot do this, I shall risk it even though it put you out of humour. I have Cicero, as authority for the use of this word, and I regard him as a powerful authority. If you desire testimony of a later date, I shall cite Fabianus, careful of speech, cultivated, and so polished in style that he will suit even our nice tastes. For what can we do, my dear Lucilius? How otherwise can we find a word for that which the Greeks call οὐσία, something that is indispensable, something that is the natural substratum of everything? I beg you accordingly to allow me to use this word *essentia.* I shall nevertheless take pains to exercise the privilege, which you have granted me, with as sparing a hand as possible; perhaps I shall be content with the mere right. Yet what good will your indulgence do me, if, lo and behold, I can in no wise express in Latin the meaning of the word which gave me the opportunity to rail at the poverty of our language? And you will condemn our narrow Roman limits even more, when you find out that there is a word of one syllable which I cannot translate. "What is this?" you ask. It is the word ὄν. You think me lacking in facility; you believe that the word is ready to hand, that it might be translated by *quod est.* I notice, however, a great difference; you are forcing me to render a noun by a verb. But if I must do so, I shall render it by *quod est.* There are six ways in which Plato expresses this idea, according to a friend of ours, a man of great learning, who mentioned the fact today. And I shall explain all of them to you, if I may first point out that there is something called *genus* and something called *species.*

For the present, however, we are seeking the primary idea of *genus,* on which the others, the different *species,* depend, which is the source of all classification, the term under which universal ideas are embraced. And the idea of *genus* will be reached if we begin to reckon back from particulars; for in this way we shall be conducted back to the primary notion. Now "man" is a *species,* as Aristotle says; so is "horse," or "dog." We must therefore discover some common bond for all these terms, one which embraces them and holds them subordinate to itself. And what is this? It is "animal." And so there begins to be a *genus* "animal," including all these terms, "man," "horse," and "dog." But there are certain things which have life (*anima*) and yet are not "animals." For it is agreed that plants and trees possess life, and that is why we speak of them as living and dying. Therefore the term "living things" will occupy a still higher place, because both animals and plants are included in this category. Certain objects, however, lack life—such as rocks. There will therefore be another term to take precedence over "living things," and that is "substance." I shall classify "substance" by saying that all substances are either animate or inanimate. But there is still something superior to "substance"; for we speak of certain things as possessing substance, and certain things as lacking substance. What, then, will be the term from which these things are derived? It is that to which we lately gave an inappropriate name, "that which exists." For by using this term they will be divided into *species,* so that we can say: that which exists either possesses, or lacks, substance.

This, therefore, is what *genus* is—the primary, original, and (to play upon the word) "general." Of course there are the other *genera:* but they are "special" *genera:* "man" being, for example, a *genus.* For "man" comprises species: by nations—Greek, Roman, Parthian; by colours—white, black, yellow. The term comprises individuals also: Cato, Cicero, Lucretius. So "man" falls into the category *genus,* in so far as it includes many kinds; but in so far as it is subordinate to another term, it falls into the category *species.* But the *genus* "that which exists" is general, and has no term superior to it. It is the first term in the classification of things, and all things are included under it.

The Stoics would set ahead of this still another *genus,* even more primary; concerning which I shall immediately speak, after proving that the *genus* which has been discussed above, has rightly been placed first, being, as it is, capable of including everything. I therefore distribute "that which exists" into these two species—things with, and things without, substance. There is no third class. And how do I distribute "substance"? By saying that it is either animate or inanimate. And how do I distribute the "animate"? By saying: "Certain things have mind, while others have only life." Or the idea may be expressed as follows: "Certain things have the power of movement, of progress, of change of position, while others are rooted in the ground; they are fed and they grow only through their roots." Again, into what species do I divide "animals"? They are either perishable or imperishable. Certain of the Stoics regard the primary *genus* as the "something." I shall add the reasons they give for their belief; they say: "in the order of nature some things exist, and other things do not exist. And even the things that do not exist are really part of the order of nature. What these are will readily occur to the mind, for example centaurs, giants, and all other figments of unsound reasoning, which have begun to have a definite shape, although they have no bodily consistency."

But I now return to the subject which I promised to discuss for you, namely, how it is that Plato divides all existing things in six different ways. The first class of "that which exists" cannot be grasped by the sight or by the touch, or by any of the senses; but it can be grasped by the thought. Any generic conception, such as the generic idea "man," does not come within the range of the eyes; but "man" in particular does; as, for example, Cicero, Cato. The term "animal" is not seen; it is grasped by thought alone. A particular animal, however, is seen, for example, a horse, a dog.

The second class of "things which exist," according to Plato, is that which is prominent and stands out above everything else; this, he says, exists in a pre-eminent degree. The word "poet" is used indiscriminately, for this term is applied to all writers of verse; but among the Greeks it has come to be the distinguishing mark of a single individual. You know that Homer is meant when you hear men say "the poet." What, then, is this pre-eminent Being? God, surely, one who is greater and more powerful than anyone else.

The third class is made up of those things which exist in the proper sense of the term; they are countless in number, but are situated beyond our sight. "What are these?" you ask. They are Plato's own furniture, so to speak; he calls them "ideas," and from them all visible things are created, and according to their pattern all things are fashioned. They are immortal, unchangeable, inviolable. And this "idea," or rather, Plato's conception of it, is as follows: "The 'idea' is the everlasting pattern of those things which are created by nature." I shall explain this definition, in order to set the subject before you in a clearer light: Suppose that I wish to make a likeness of you; I possess in your own person the pattern of this picture, wherefrom my mind receives a certain outline, which it is to embody in its own handiwork. That outward appearance, then, which gives me instruction and guidance, this pattern for me to imitate, is the "idea." Such patterns, therefore, nature possesses in infinite number—of men, fish, trees, according to whose model everything that nature has to create is worked out.

In the fourth place we shall put "form." And if you would know what "form" means, you must pay close attention, calling Plato, and not me, to account for the difficulty of the subject. However, we cannot make fine distinctions without encountering difficulties. A moment ago I made use of the artist as an illustration. When the artist desired to reproduce Vergil in colours he would gaze upon Vergil himself. The "idea" was Vergil's outward appearance, and this was the pattern of the intended work. That which the artist draws from this "idea" and has embodied in his own work is the "form." Do you ask me where the difference lies? The former is the pattern; while the latter is the shape taken from the pattern and embodied in the work. Our artist follows the one, but the other he creates. A statue has a certain external appearance; this external appearance of the statue is the "form." And the pattern itself has a certain external appearance, by gazing upon which the sculptor has fashioned his statue; this is the "idea." If you desire a further distinction, I will say that the "form" is in the artist's work, the "idea" outside his work, and not only outside it, but prior to it.

The fifth class is made up of the things which exist in the usual sense of the term. These things are the first that have to do with us; here we have all such things as men, cattle, and things. In the sixth class goes all that which has a fictitious existence, like void, or time.

Whatever is concrete to the sight or touch, Plato does not include among the things which he believes to be existent in the strict sense of the term. These things are the first that have to do with us: here we have all such things as men, cattle, and things. For they are in a state of flux, constantly diminishing or increasing. None of us is the same man in old age that he was in youth; nor the same on the morrow as on the day preceding. Our bodies are hurried along like flowing waters; every visible object accompanies time in its flight; of the things which we see, nothing is fixed. Even I myself as I comment on this change, am changed myself. This is just what Heraclitus says: "We go down twice into the same river, and yet into a different river." For the stream still keeps the same name, but the water has already flowed past. Of course this is much more evident in rivers than in human beings. Still, we mortals are also carried past in no less speedy a course; and this prompts me to marvel at our madness in cleaving with great affection to such a fleeting thing as the body, and in fearing lest some day we may die, when every instant means the death of our previous condition. Will you not stop fearing lest that may happen once which really happens every day? So much for man—a substance that flows away and falls, exposed to every influence; but the universe, too, immortal and enduring as it is, changes and never remains the same. For though it has within itself all that it has had, it has it in a different way from that in which it has had it; it keeps changing its arrangement.

"Very well," say you, "what good shall I get from all this fine reasoning?" None, if you wish me to answer your question. Nevertheless, just as an engraver rests his eyes when they have long been under a strain and are weary, and calls them from their work, and "feasts" them, as the saying is; so we at times should slacken our minds and refresh them with some sort of entertainment. But let even your entertainment be work; and even from these various forms of entertainment you will select, if you have been watchful, something that may prove wholesome. That is my habit, Lucilius: I try to extract and render useful some element from every field of thought, no matter how far removed it may be from philosophy. Now what could be less likely to reform character than the subjects which we have been discussing? And how can I be made a better man by the "ideas" of Plato? What can I draw from them that will put a check on my appetites? Perhaps the very thought, that all these things which minister to our senses, which arouse and excite us, are by Plato denied a place among the things that really exist. Such things are therefore imaginary, and though they for the moment present a certain external appearance, yet they are in no case permanent or substantial; none the less, we crave them as if they were always to exist, or as if we were always to possess them.

We are weak, watery beings standing in the midst of unrealities; therefore let us turn our minds to the things that are everlasting. Let us look up to the ideal outlines of all things, that flit about on high, and to the God who moves among them and plans how he may defend from death that which he could not make imperishable because its substance forbade, and so by reason may overcome the defects of the body. For all things abide, not because they are everlasting, but because they are protected by the care of him who governs all things; but that which was imperishable would need no guardian. The Master Builder keeps them safe, overcoming the weakness of their fabric by his own power. Let us despise everything that is so little an object of value that it makes us doubt whether it exists at all. Let us at the same time reflect, seeing that Providence rescues from its perils the world itself, which is no less mortal than we ourselves, that to some extent our petty bodies can be made to tarry longer upon earth by our own providence, if only we acquire the ability to control and check those pleasures whereby the greater portion of mankind perishes. Plato himself, by taking pains, advanced to old age. To be sure, he was the fortunate possessor of a strong and sound body (his very name was given him because of his broad chest); but his strength was much impaired by sea voyages and desperate adventures. Nevertheless, by frugal living, by setting a limit upon all that rouses the appetites, and by painstaking attention to himself, he reached that advanced age in spite of many hindrances. You know, I am sure, that Plato had the good fortune, thanks to his careful living, to die on his birthday, after exactly completing his eighty-first year. For this reason wise men of the East, who happened to be in Athens at that time, sacrificed to him after his death, believing that his length of days was too full for a mortal man, since he had rounded out the perfect number of nine times nine. I do not doubt that he would have been quite willing to forgo a few days from this total, as well as the sacrifice.

Frugal living can bring one to old age; and to my mind old age is not to be refused any more than is to be craved. There is a pleasure in being in one's own company as long as possible, when a man has made himself worth enjoying. The question, therefore, on which we have to record our judgment is, whether one should shrink from extreme old age and should hasten the end artificially, instead of waiting for it to come. A man who sluggishly awaits his fate is almost a coward, just as he is immoderately given to wine who drains the jar dry and sucks up even the dregs. But we shall ask this question also: "Is the extremity of life the dregs, or is it the clearest and purest part of all, provided only that the mind is unimpaired, and the senses, still sound, give their support to the spirit, and the body is not worn out and dead before its time?" For it makes a great deal of difference whether a man is lengthening his life or his death. But if the body is useless for service, why should one not free the struggling soul? Perhaps one ought to do this a little before the debt is due, lest, when it falls due, he may be unable to perform the act. And since the danger of living in wretchedness is greater than the danger of dying soon, he is a fool who refuses to stake a little time and win a hazard of great gain.

Few have lasted through extreme old age to death without impairment, and many have lain inert, making no use of themselves. How much more cruel, then, do you suppose it really is to have lost a portion of your life, than to have lost your right to end that life? Do not hear me with reluctance, as if my statement applied directly to you, but weigh what I have to say. It is this, that I shall not abandon old age, if old age preserves me intact for myself, and intact as regards the better part of myself; but if old age begins to shatter my mind, and to pull its various faculties to pieces, if it leaves me, not life, but only the breath of life, I shall rush out of a house that is crumbling and tottering. I shall not avoid illness by seeking death, as long as the illness is curable and does not impede my soul. I shall not lay violent hands upon myself just because I am in pain; for death under such circumstances is defeat. But if I find out that the pain must always be endured, I shall depart, not because of the pain but because it will be a hindrance to me as regards all my reasons for living. He who dies just because he is in pain is a weakling, a coward; but he who lives merely to brave out this pain, is a fool.

But I am running on too long; and, besides, there is matter here to fill a day. And how can a man end his life, if he cannot end a letter? So farewell. This last word you will read with greater pleasure than all my deadly talk about death. Farewell.

65. ON THE FIRST CAUSE

I shared my time yesterday with ill health; it claimed for itself all the period before noon; in the afternoon, however, it yielded to me. And so I first tested my spirit by reading; then, when reading was found to be possible, I dared to make more demands upon the spirit, or perhaps I should say, to make more concessions to it. I wrote a little, and indeed with more concentration than usual, for I am struggling with a difficult subject and do not wish to be downed. In the midst of this, some friends visited me, with the purpose of employing force and of restraining me, as if I were a sick man indulging in some excess. So conversation was substituted for writing; and from this conversation I shall communicate to you the topic which is still the subject of debate; for we have appointed you referee. You have more of a task on your hands than you suppose, for the argument is threefold.

Our Stoic philosophers, as you know, declare that there are two things in the universe which are the source of everything—namely, cause and matter. Matter lies sluggish, a substance ready for any use, but sure to remain unemployed if no one sets it in motion. Cause, however, by which we mean reason, moulds matter and turns it in whatever direction it will, producing thereby various concrete results. Accordingly, there must be, in the case of each thing, that from which it is made, and, next, an agent by which it is made. The former is its material, the latter its cause.

All art is but imitation of nature; therefore, let me apply these statements of general principles to the things which have to be made by man. A statue, for example, has afforded matter which was to undergo treatment at the hands of the artist, and has had an artist who was to give form to the matter. Hence, in the case of the statue, the material was bronze, the cause was the workman. And so it goes with all things—they consist of that which is made and of the maker. The Stoics believe in one cause only—the maker; but Aristotle thinks that the word "cause" can be used in three ways: "The first cause," he says, "is the actual matter, without which nothing can be created. The second is the workman. The third is the form, which is impressed upon every work—a statue, for example." This last is what Aristotle calls the *idos.* "There is, too," says he, "a fourth—the purpose of the work as a whole." Now I shall show you what this last means. Bronze is the "first cause" of the statue, for it could never have been made unless there had been something from which it could be cast and moulded. The "second cause" is the artist; for without the skilled hands of a workman that bronze could not have been shaped to the outlines of the statue. The "third cause" is the form, inasmuch as our statue could never be called The Lance-Bearer or The Boy Binding his Hair had not this special shape been stamped upon it. The "fourth cause" is the purpose of the work. For if this purpose had not existed, the statue would not have been made. Now what is this purpose? It is that which attracted the artist which he followed when he made the statue. It may have been money, if he has made it for sale; or renown, if he has worked for reputation; or religion, if he has wrought it as a gift for a temple. Therefore this also is a cause contributing towards the making of the statue; or do you think that we should avoid including, among the causes of a thing which has been made, that element without which the thing in question would not have been made?

To these four Plato adds a fifth cause—the pattern which he himself calls the "idea"; for it is this that the artist gazed upon when he created the work which he had decided to carry out. Now it makes no difference whether he has this pattern outside himself, that he may direct his glance to it, or within himself, conceived and placed there by himself. God has within himself these patterns of all things, and his mind comprehends the harmonies and the measures of the whole totality of things which are to be carried out; he is filled with these shapes which Plato calls the "ideas,"—imperishable, unchangeable, not subject to decay. And therefore, though men die, humanity itself, or the idea of man, according to which man is moulded, lasts on, and though men toil and perish, it suffers no change. Accordingly, there are five causes, as Plato says: the material, the agent, the make-up, the model, and the end in view. Last comes the result of all these. Just as in the case of the statue—to go back to the figure with which we began—the material is the bronze, the agent is the artist, the make-up is the form which is adapted to the material, the model is the pattern imitated by the agent, the end in view is the purpose in the maker's mind, and, finally, the result of all these is the statue itself. The universe also, in Plato's opinion, possesses all these elements. The agent is God; the source, matter; the form, the shape and the arrangement of the visible world. The pattern is doubtless the model according to which God has made this great and most beautiful creation. The purpose is his object in so doing. Do you ask what God's purpose is? It is goodness. Plato, at any rate, says: "What was God's reason for creating the world? God is good, and no good person is grudging of anything that is good. Therefore, God made it the best world possible." Hand down your opinion, then, O judge; state who seems to you to say what is truest, and not who says what is absolutely true. For to do that is as far beyond our ken as truth itself.

This throng of causes, defined by Aristotle and by Plato, embraces either too much or too little.* For if they regard as "causes" of an object that is to be made everything without which the object cannot be made, they have named too few. Time must be included among the causes; for nothing can be made without time. They must also include place; for if there be no place where a thing can be made, it will not be made. And motion too; nothing is either made or destroyed without motion. There is no art without motion, no change of any kind. Now, however, I am searching for the first, the general cause; this must be simple, inasmuch as matter, too, is simple. Do we ask what cause is? It is surely Creative Reason,†—in other words, God. For those elements to which you referred are not a great series of independent causes; they all hinge on one alone, and that will be the creative cause. Do you maintain that form is a cause? This is only what the artist stamps upon his work; it is part of a cause, but not the cause. Neither is the pattern a cause, but an indispensable tool of the cause. His pattern is as indispensable to the artist as the chisel or the file; without these, art can make no progress. But for all that, these things are neither parts of the art, nor causes of it. "Then," perhaps you will say, "the purpose of the artist, that which leads him to undertake to create something, is the cause." It may be a cause; it is not, however, the efficient cause, but only an accessory cause. But there are countless accessory causes; what we are discussing is the general cause. Now the statement of Plato and Aristotle is not in accord with their usual penetration, when they maintain that the whole universe, the perfectly wrought work, is a cause. For there is a great difference between a work and the cause of a work.

Either give your opinion, or, as is easier in cases of this kind, declare that the matter is not clear and call for another hearing. But you will reply: "What pleasure do you get from wasting your time on these problems, which relieve you of none of your emotions, rout none of your desires?" So far as I am concerned, I treat and discuss them as matters which contribute greatly toward calming the spirit, and I search myself first, and then the world about me. And not even now am I, as you think, wasting my time. For all these questions, provided that they be not chopped up and torn apart into such unprofitable refinements,

* The Stoic view, besides making the four categories of "substance," "form," "variety," and "variety of relation." regarded material things as the only things which possessed being. The Stoics thus differ from Aristotle and Plato in holding that nothing is real except matter; besides, they relate everything to one ultimate cause, the acting force or efficient cause.

† *i.e.,* the creative force in nature, that is, Providence, or the will of Zeus.

elevate and lighten the soul, which is weighted down by a heavy burden and desires to be freed and to return to the elements of which it was once a part. For this body of ours is a weight upon the soul and its penance; as the load presses down the soul is crushed and is in bondage, unless philosophy has come to its assistance and has bid it take fresh courage by contemplating the universe, and has turned it from things earthly to things divine. There it has its liberty, there it can roam abroad;* meantime it escapes the custody in which it is bound, and renews its life in heaven. Just as skilled workmen, who have been engaged upon some delicate piece of work which wearies their eyes with straining, if the light which they have is niggardly or uncertain, go forth into the open air and in some park devoted to the people's recreation delight their eyes in the generous light of day; so the soul, imprisoned as it has been in this gloomy and darkened house, seeks the open sky whenever it can, and in the contemplation of the universe finds rest.

The wise man, the seeker after wisdom, is bound closely, indeed, to his body, but he is an absentee so far as his better self is concerned, and he concentrates his thoughts upon lofty things. Bound, so to speak, to his oath of allegiance, he regards the period of life as his term of service. He is so trained that he neither loves nor hates life; he endures a mortal lot, although he knows that an ampler lot is in store for him. Do you forbid me to contemplate the universe? Do you compel me to withdraw from the whole and restrict me to a part? May I not ask what are the beginnings of all things, who moulded the universe, who took the confused and conglomerate mass of sluggish matter, and separated it into its parts? May I not inquire who is the Master-Builder of this universe, how the mighty bulk was brought under the control of law and order, who gathered together the scattered atoms, who separated the disordered elements and assigned an outward form to elements that lay in one vast shapelessness? Or whence came all the expanse of light? And whether is it fire, or even brighter than fire? Am I not to ask these questions? Must I be ignorant of the heights whence I have descended? Whether I am to see this world but once, or to be born many times? What is my destination afterwards? What abode awaits my soul on its release from the laws of slavery among men? Do you forbid me to

---

* According to the Stoics, the soul, which consisted of fire or breath and was a part of the divine essence, rose at death into the ether and became one with the stars. Seneca elsewhere states that the soul went through a sort of purifying process—a view which may have had some influence on Christian thought. The souls of the good, the Stoics maintained, were destined to last until the end of the world, the souls of the bad to be extinguished before that time.

have a share in heaven? In other words, do you bid me live with my head bowed down? No, I am above such an existence; I was born to a greater destiny than to be a mere chattel of my body, and I regard this body as nothing but a chain which manacles my freedom. Therefore, I offer it as a sort of buffer to Fortune, and shall allow no wound to penetrate through to my soul. For my body is the only part of me which can suffer injury. In this dwelling, which is exposed to peril, my soul lives free. Never shall this flesh drive me to feel fear or to assume any pretence that is unworthy of a good man. Never shall I lie in order to honour this petty body. When it seems proper, I shall sever my connexion with it. And at present, while we are bound together, our alliance shall nevertheless not be one of equality; the soul shall bring all quarrels before its own tribunal. To despise our bodies is sure freedom.

To return to our subject; this freedom will be greatly helped by the contemplation of which we were just speaking. All things are made up of matter and of God; God controls matter, which encompasses him and follows him as its guide and leader. And that which creates, in other words, God, is more powerful and precious than matter, which is acted upon by God. God's place in the universe corresponds to the soul's relation to man. World-matter corresponds to our mortal body; therefore let the lower serve the higher. Let us be brave in the face of hazards. Let us not fear wrongs, or wounds, or bonds, or poverty. And what is death? It is either the end, or a process of change. I have no fear of ceasing to exist; it is the same as not having begun. Nor do I shrink from changing into another state, because I shall, under no conditions, be as cramped as I am now. Farewell.

67. ON ILL-HEALTH AND THE ENDURANCE OF SUFFERING

If I may begin with a commonplace remark, spring is gradually disclosing itself; but though it is rounding into summer, when you would expect hot weather, it has kept rather cool, and one cannot yet be sure of it. For it often slides back into winter weather. Do you wish to know how uncertain it still is? I do not yet trust myself to a bath which is absolutely cold; even at this time I break its chill. You may say that this is no way to show the endurance either of heat or of cold; very true, dear Lucilius, but at my time of life one is at length contented with the natural chill of the body. I can scarcely thaw out in the middle of summer. Accordingly, I spend most of the time bundled up; and I thank old age for keeping me fastened to my bed. Why should I not thank old age on this account? That which I ought not to wish to do, I lack the ability to do. Most of my converse is with books. Whenever your letters arrive, I imagine that I am with you, and I have the feeling that I am about to speak my answer, instead of writing it. Therefore let us together investigate the nature of this problem of yours, just as if we were conversing with one another.

You ask me whether every good is desirable. You say: "If it is a good to be brave under torture, to go to the stake with a stout heart, to endure illness with resignation, it follows that these things are desirable. But I do not see that any of them is worth praying for. At any rate I have as yet known of no man who has paid a vow by reason of having been cut to pieces by the rod, or twisted out of shape by the gout, or made taller by the rack." My dear Lucilius, you must distinguish between these cases; you will then comprehend that there is something in them that is to be desired. I should prefer to be free from torture; but if the time comes when it must be endured, I shall desire that I may conduct myself therein with bravery, honour, and courage. Of course I prefer that war should not occur; but if war does occur, I shall desire that I may nobly endure the wounds, the starvation, and all that the exigency of war brings. Nor am I so mad as to crave illness; but if I must suffer illness, I shall desire that I may do nothing which shows lack of restraint, and nothing that is unmanly. The conclusion is, not that hardships are desirable, but that virtue is desirable, which enables us patiently to endure hardships.

Certain of our school think that, of all such qualities, a stout endurance is not desirable—though not to be deprecated either—because we ought to seek by prayer only the good which is unalloyed, peaceful, and beyond the reach of trouble. Personally, I do not agree with them. And why? First, because it is impossible for anything to be good without being also desirable. Because, again, if virtue is desirable, and if nothing that is good lacks virtue, then everything good is desirable. And, lastly, because a brave endurance even under torture is desirable. At this point I ask you: is not bravery desirable? And yet bravery despises and challenges danger. The most beautiful and most admirable part of bravery is that it does not shrink from the stake, advances to meet wounds, and sometimes does not even avoid the spear, but meets it with opposing breast. If bravery is desirable, so is patient endurance of torture; for this is a part of bravery. Only sift these things, as I have suggested; then there will be nothing which can lead you astray. For it is not mere endurance of torture, but brave endurance, that is desirable. I therefore desire that "brave" endurance; and this is virtue.

"But," you say, "whoever desired such a thing for himself?" Some prayers are open and outspoken, when the requests are offered specifically; other prayers are indirectly expressed, when they include many requests under one title. For example, I desire a life of honour. Now a life of honour includes various kinds of conduct; it may include the chest in which Regulus was confined, or the wound of Cato which was torn open by Cato's own hand, or the exile of Rutilius, or the cup of poison which removed Socrates from goal to heaven. Accordingly, in praying for a life of honour, I have prayed also for those things without which, on some occasions, life cannot be honourable,

O thrice and four times blest were they
Who underneath the lofty walls of Troy
Met happy death before their parents' eyes!

What does it matter whether you offer this prayer for some individual, or admit that it was desirable in the past? Decius sacrificed himself for the State; he set spurs to his horse and rushed into the midst of the foe, seeking death. The second Decius, rivalling his father's valour, reproducing the words which had become sacred and already household words, dashed into the thickest of the fight, anxious only that his sacrifice might bring omen of success, and regarding a noble death as a thing to be desired. Do you doubt, then, whether it is best to die glorious and performing some deed of valour? When one endures torture bravely, one is using all the virtues. Endurance may perhaps be the only virtue that is on view and most manifest; but bravery is there too, and endurance and resignation and long-suffering are its branches. There, too, is foresight; for without foresight no plan can be undertaken; it is foresight that advises one to bear as bravely as possible the things one cannot avoid. There also is steadfastness, which cannot be dislodged from its position, which the wrench of no force can cause to abandon its purpose. There is the whole inseparable company of virtues; every honourable act is the work of one single virtue, but it is in accordance with the judgment of the whole council. And that which is approved by all the virtues, even though it seems to be the work of one alone, is desirable.

What? Do you think that those things only are desirable which come to us amid pleasure and ease, and which we bedeck our doors to welcome? There are certain goods whose features are forbidding. There are certain prayers which are offered by a throng, not of men who rejoice, but of men who bow down reverently and worship. Was it not in this fashion, think you, that Regulus prayed that he might reach Carthage? Clothe yourself with a hero's courage, and withdraw for a little space from the opinions of the common man. Form a proper conception of the image of virtue, a thing of exceeding beauty and grandeur; this image is not to be worshipped by us with incense or garlands, but with sweat and blood. Behold Marcus Cato, laying upon that hallowed breast his unspotted hands, and tearing apart the wounds which had not gone deep enough to kill him! Which, pray, shall you say to him: "I hope all will be as you wish," and "I am grieved," or shall it be "Good Fortune in your undertaking!"?

In this connexion I think of our friend Demetrius, who calls an easy existence, untroubled by the attacks of Fortune, a "Dead Sea." If you have nothing to stir you up and rouse you to action, nothing which will test your resolution by its threats and hostilities; if you recline in unshaken comfort, it is not tranquillity; it is merely a flat calm. The Stoic Attalus was wont to say: "I should prefer that Fortune keep me in her camp rather than in the lap of luxury. If I am tortured, but bear it bravely, all is well; if I die, but die bravely, it is also well." Listen to Epicurus; he will tell you that it is actually pleasant. I myself shall never apply an effeminate word to an act so honourable and austere. If I go to the stake, I shall go unbeaten. Why should I not regard this as desirable—not because the fire burns me, but because it does not overcome me? Nothing is more excellent or more beautiful than virtue; whatever we do in obedience to her orders is both good and desirable. Farewell.

71. ON THE SUPREME GOOD

You are continually referring special questions to me, forgetting that a vast stretch of sea sunders us. Since, however, the value of advice depends mostly on the time when it is given, it must necessarily result that by the time my opinion on certain matters reaches you, the opposite opinion is the better. For advice conforms to circumstances; and our circumstances are carried along, or rather whirled along. Accordingly, advice should be produced at short notice; and even this is too late; it should "grow while we work," as the saying is. And I propose to show you how you may discover the method.

As often as you wish to know what is to be avoided or what is to be sought, consider its relation to the Supreme Good, to the purpose of your whole life. For whatever we do ought to be in harmony with this; no man can set in order the details unless he has already set before himself the chief purpose of his life. The artist may have his colours all prepared, but he cannot produce a likeness unless he has already made up his mind what he wishes to paint. The reason we make mistakes is because we all consider the parts of life, but never life as a whole. The archer must know what he is seeking to hit; then he must aim and control the weapon by his skill. Our plans miscarry because they have no aim. When a man does not know what harbour he is making for, no wind is the right wind. Chance must necessarily have great influence over our lives, because we live by chance. It is the case with certain men, however, that they do not know that they know certain things. Just as we often go searching for those who stand beside us, so we are apt to forget that the goal of the Supreme Good lies near us.

To infer the nature of this Supreme Good, one does not need many words or any round-about discussion; it should be pointed out with the forefinger, so to speak, and not be dissipated into many parts. For what good is there in breaking it up into tiny bits, when you can say: the Supreme Good is that which is honourable? Besides (and you may be still more surprised at this), that which is honourable is the only good; all other goods are alloyed and debased. If you once convince yourself of this, and if you come to love virtue devotedly (for mere loving is not enough), anything that has been touched by virtue will be fraught with blessing and prosperity for you, no matter how it shall be regarded by others. Torture, if only, as you lie suffering, you are more calm in mind than your very torturer; illness, if only you curse not Fortune and yield not to the disease—in short, all those things which others regard as ills will become manageable and will end in good, if you succeed in rising above them.

Let this once be clear, that there is nothing good except that which is honourable, and all hardships will have a just title to the name of "goods," when once virtue has made them honourable. Many think that we Stoics are holding out expectations greater than our human lot admits of; and they have a right to think so. For they have regard to the body only. But let them turn back to the soul, and they will soon measure man by the standard of God. Rouse yourself, most excellent Lucilius, and leave off all this word-play of the philosophers, who reduce a most glorious subject to a matter of syllables, and lower and wear out the soul by teaching fragments; then you will become like the men who discovered these precepts, instead of those who by their teaching do their best to make philosophy seem difficult rather than great.

Socrates, who recalled the whole of philosophy to rules of conduct, and asserted that the highest wisdom consisted in distinguishing between good and evil, said: "Follow these rules, if my words carry weight with you, in order that you may be happy; and let some men think you even a fool. Allow any man who so desires to insult you and work you wrong; but if only virtue dwells with you, you will suffer nothing. If you wish to be happy, if you would be in good faith a good man let one person or another despise you." No man can accomplish this unless he has come to regard all goods as equal, for the reason that no good exists without that which is honourable, and that which is honourable is in every case equal. You may say: "What then? Is there no difference between Cato's being elected praetor and his failure at the polls? Or whether Cato is conquered or conqueror in the battle-line of Pharsalia? And when Cato could not be defeated, though his party met defeat, was not this goodness of his equal to that which would have been his if he had returned victorious to his native land and arranged a peace?" Of course it was; for it is by the same virtue that evil Fortune is overcome and good Fortune is controlled. Virtue, however, cannot be increased or decreased; its stature is uniform. "But," you will object, "Gnaeus Pompey will lose his army; the patricians, those noblest patterns of the State's creation, and the front-rank men of Pompey's party, a Senate under arms, will be routed in a single engagement; the ruins of that great oligarchy will be scattered all over the world; one division will fall in Egypt, another in Africa, and another in Spain! And the poor State will not be allowed even the privilege of being ruined once for all!" Yes, all this may happen; Juba's familiarity with every position in his own kingdom may be of no avail to him, of no avail to the resolute bravery of his people when fighting for their king; even the men of Utica, crushed by their troubles, may waver in their allegiance; and the good Fortune which ever attended men of the name of Scipio may desert Scipio in Africa. But long ago destiny "saw to it that Cato should come to no harm."

"He was conquered in spite of it all!" Well, you may include this among Cato's "failures"; Cato will bear with an equally stout heart anything that thwarts him of his victory, as he bore that which thwarted him of his praetorship. The day whereon he failed of election, he spent in play; the night wherein he intended to die, he spent in reading. He regarded in the same light both the loss of his praetorship and the loss of his life; he had convinced himself that he ought to endure anything which might happen. Why should he not suffer, bravely and calmly, a change in the government? For what is free from the risk of change? Neither earth, nor sky, nor the whole fabric of our universe, though it be controlled by the hand of God. It will not always preserve its present order; it will be thrown from its course in days to come. All things move in accord with their appointed times; they are destined to be born, to grow, and to be destroyed. The stars which you see moving above us, and this seemingly immovable earth to which we cling and on which we are set, will be consumed and will cease to exist. There is nothing that does not have its old age; the intervals are merely unequal at which Nature sends forth all these things towards the same goal. Whatever is will cease to be, and yet it will not perish, but will be resolved into its elements. To our minds, this process means perishing, for we behold only that which is nearest; our sluggish mind, under allegiance to the body, does not penetrate to bournes beyond. Were it not so, the mind would endure with greater courage its own ending and that of its possessions, if only it could hope that life and death, like the whole universe about us, go by turns, that whatever has been put together is broken up again, that whatever has been broken up is put together again, and that the eternal craftsmanship of God, who controls all things is working at this task.

Therefore the wise man will say just what a Marcus Cato would say, after reviewing his past life: "The whole race of man, both that which is and that which is to be, is condemned to die. Of all the cities that at any time have held sway over the world, and of all that have been the splendid ornaments of empires not their own, men shall some day ask where they were, and they shall be swept away by destructions of various kinds; some shall be ruined by wars, others shall be wasted away by inactivity and by the kind of peace which ends in sloth, or by that vice which is fraught with destruction even for mighty dynasties—luxury. All these fertile plains shall be buried out of sight by a sudden overflowing of the sea, or a slipping of the soil, as it settles to lower levels, shall draw them suddenly into a yawning chasm. Why then should I be angry or feel sorrow, if I precede the general destruction by a tiny interval of time?" Let great souls comply with God's wishes, and suffer unhesitatingly whatever fate the law of the universe ordains; for the soul at death is either sent forth into a better life, destined to dwell with deity amid greater radiance and calm, or else, at least, without suffering any harm to itself, it will be mingled with nature again, and will return to the universe.

Therefore Cato's honourable death was no less a good than his honourable life, since virtue admits of no stretching. Socrates used to say that verity and virtue were the same. Just as truth does not grow, so neither does virtue grow; for it has its due proportions and is complete. You need not, therefore, wonder that goods are equal, both those which are to be deliberately chosen, and those which circumstances have imposed. For if you once adopt the view that they are unequal, deeming, for instance, a brave endurance of torture as among the lesser goods, you will be including it among the evils also; you will pronounce Socrates unhappy in his prison, Cato unhappy when he reopens his wounds with more courage than he allowed in inflicting them, and Regulus the most ill-starred of all when he pays the penalty for keeping his word even with his enemies. And yet no man, even the most effeminate person in the world, has ever dared to maintain such an opinion. For though such persons deny that a man like Regulus is happy, yet for all that they also deny that he is wretched. The earlier Academics do indeed admit that a man is happy even amid such tortures, but do not admit that he is completely or fully happy. With this view we cannot in any wise agree; for unless a man is happy, he has not attained the Supreme Good; and the good which is supreme admits of no higher degree, if only virtue exists within this man, and if adversity does not impair his virtue, and if, though the body be injured, the virtue abides unharmed. And it does abide. For I understand virtue to be high-spirited and exalted, so that it is aroused by anything that molests it. This spirit, which young men of noble breeding often assume, when they are so deeply stirred by the beauty of some honourable object that they despise all the gifts of chance, is assuredly infused in us and communicated to us by wisdom. Wisdom will bring the conviction that there is but one good—that which is honourable; that this can neither be shortened nor extended, any more than a carpenter's rule, with which straight lines are tested, can be bent. Any change in the rule means spoiling the straight line. Applying, therefore, this same figure to virtue, we shall say: virtue also is straight, and admits of no bending. What can be made more tense than a thing which is already rigid? Such is virtue, which passes judgment on everything, but nothing passes judgment on virtue. And if this rule, virtue, cannot itself be made more straight, neither can the things created by virtue be in one case straighter and in another less straight. For they must necessarily correspond to virtue; hence they are equal.

"What," you say, "do you call reclining at a banquet and submitting to torture equally good?" Does this seem surprising to you? You may be still more surprised at the following—that reclining at a banquet is an evil, while reclining on the rack is a good, if the former act is done in a shameful, and the latter in an honourable manner. It is not the material that makes these actions good or bad; it is the virtue. All acts in which virtue has disclosed itself are of the same measure and value. At this moment the man who measures the souls of all men by his own is shaking his fist in my face because I hold that there is a parity between the goods involved in the case of one who passes sentence honourably, and of one who suffers sentence honourably; or because I hold that there is a parity between the goods of one who celebrates a triumph, and of one who, unconquered in spirit, is carried before the victor's chariot. For such critics think that whatever they themselves cannot do, is not done; they pass judgment on virtue in the light of their own weaknesses. Why do you marvel if it helps a man, and on occasion even pleases him, to be burned, wounded, slain, or bound in prison? To a luxurious man, a simple life is a penalty; to a lazy man, work is punishment; the dandy pities the diligent man; to the slothful, studies are torture. Similarly, we regard those things with respect to which we are all infirm of disposition, as hard and beyond endurance, forgetting what a torment it is to many men to abstain from wine or to be routed from their beds at break of day. These actions are not essentially difficult; it is we ourselves that are soft and flabby. We must pass judgment concerning great matters with greatness of soul; otherwise, that which is really our fault will seem to be their fault. So it is that certain objects which are perfectly straight, when sunk in water appear to the onlooker as bent or broken off. It matters not only what you see, but with what eyes you see it; our souls are too dull of vision to perceive the truth. But give me an unspoiled and sturdy-minded young man; he will pronounce more fortunate one who sustains on unbending shoulders the whole weight of adversity, who stands out superior to Fortune. It is not a cause for wonder that one is not tossed about when the weather is calm; reserve your wonderment for cases where a man is lifted up when all others sink, and keeps his footing when all others are prostrate.

What element of evil is there in torture and in the other things which we call hardships? It seems to me that there is this evil—that the mind sags, and bends, and collapses. But none of these things can happen to the sage; he stands erect under any load. Nothing can subdue him; nothing that must be endured annoys him. For he does not complain that he has been struck by that which can strike any man. He knows his own strength; he knows that he was born to carry burdens. I do not withdraw the wise man from the category of man, nor do I deny to him the sense of pain as though he were a rock that has no feelings at all. I remember that he is made up of two parts: the one part is irrational—it is this that may be bitten, burned, or hurt; the other part is rational—it is this which holds resolutely to opinions, is courageous, and unconquerable. In the latter is situated man's Supreme Good. Before this is completely attained, the mind wavers in uncertainty; only when it is fully achieved is the mind fixed and steady. And so when one has just begun, or is on one's way to the heights and is cultivating virtue, or even if one is drawing near the perfect good but has not yet put the finishing touch upon it, one will retrograde at times and there will be a certain slackening of mental effort. For such a man has not yet traversed the doubtful ground; he is still standing in slippery places. But the happy man, whose virtue is complete, loves himself most of all when his bravery has been submitted to the severest test, and when he not only, endures but welcomes that which all other men regard with fear if it is the price which he must pay for the performance of a duty which honour imposes, and he greatly prefers to have men say of him: "how much more noble!" rather than "how much more lucky!"

And now I have reached the point to which your patient waiting summons me. You must not think that our human virtue transcends nature; the wise man will tremble, will feel pain, will turn pale. For all these are sensations of the body. Where, then, is the abode of utter distress, of that which is truly an evil? In the other part of us, no doubt, if it is the mind that these trials drag down, force to a confession of its servitude, and cause to regret its existence. The wise man, indeed, overcomes Fortune by his virtue, but many who profess wisdom are sometimes frightened by the most unsubstantial threats. And at this stage it is a mistake on our part to make the same demands upon the wise man and upon the learner. I still exhort myself to do that which I recommend; but my exhortations are not yet followed. And even if this were the case, I should not have these principles so ready for practise, or so well trained, that they would rush to my assistance in every crisis. Just as wool takes up certain colours at once, while there are others which it will not absorb unless it is soaked and steeped in them many times; so other systems of doctrine can be immediately applied by men's minds after once being accepted, but this system of which I speak, unless it has gone deep and has sunk in for a long time, and has not merely coloured but thoroughly permeated the soul, does not fulfil any of its promises. The matter can be imparted quickly and in very few words: "Virtue is the only good; at any rate there is no good without virtue; and virtue itself is situated in our nobler part, that is, the rational part." And what will this virtue be? A true and never-swerving judgment. For therefrom will spring all mental impulses, and by its agency every external appearance that stirs our impulses will be clarified. It will be in keeping with this judgment to judge all things that have been coloured by virtue as goods, and as equal goods.

Bodily goods are, to be sure, good for the body; but they are not absolutely good. There will indeed be some value in them; but they will possess no genuine merit, for they will differ greatly; some will be less, others greater. And we are constrained to acknowledge that there are great differences among the very followers of wisdom. One man has already made so much progress that he dares to raise his eyes and look Fortune in the face, but not persistently, for his eyes soon drop, dazzled by her overwhelming splendour; another has made so much progress that he is able to match glances with her—that is, unless he has already reached the summit and is full of confidence.* That which is short of perfection must necessarily be unsteady, at one time progressing, at another slipping or growing faint; and it will surely slip back unless it keeps struggling ahead; for if a man slackens at all in zeal and faithful application, he must retrograde. No one can resume his progress at the point where he left off. Therefore let us press on and persevere. There remains much more of the road than we have put behind us; but the greater part of progress is the desire to progress.

I fully understand what this task is. It is a thing which I desire, and I desire it with all my heart. I see that you also have been aroused and are hastening with great zeal towards infinite beauty. Let us, then, hasten; only on these terms will life be a boon to us; otherwise, there is delay, and indeed disgraceful delay, while we busy ourselves with revolting things. Let us see to it that all time belongs to us. This, however, cannot be unless first of all our own selves begin to belong to us. And when will it be our privilege to despise both kinds of fortune? When will it be our privilege, after all the passions have been subdued and brought under our own control, to utter the words "I have conquered!"? Do you ask me whom I have conquered? Neither the Persians, nor the far-off Medes, nor any warlike race that lies beyond the Dahae;† not these, but greed, ambition, and the fear of death that has conquered the conquerors of the world. Farewell.

---

* In which case, he would be completely superior to her.

† A nomad Scythian tribe east of the Caspian Sea.

77. ON TAKING ONE'S OWN LIFE

Suddenly there came into our view today the "Alexandrian" ships—I mean those which are usually sent ahead to announce the coming of the fleet; they are called "mail-boats." The Campanians are glad to see them; all the rabble of Puteoli stand on the docks and can recognize the "Alexandrian" boats, no matter how great the crowd of vessels, by the very trim of their sails. For they alone may keep spread their topsails, which all ships use when out at sea, because nothing sends a ship along so well as its upper canvas; that is where most of the speed is obtained. So when the breeze has stiffened and becomes stronger than is comfortable, they set their yards lower; for the wind has less force near the surface of the water. Accordingly, when they have made Capreae and the headland whence

Tall Pallas watches on the stormy peak,

all other vessels are bidden to be content with the mainsail, and the topsail stands out conspicuously on the "Alexandrian" mail-boats.

While everybody was bustling about and hurrying to the water-front, I felt great pleasure in my laziness, because, although I was soon to receive letters from my friends, I was in no hurry to know how my affairs were progressing abroad, or what news the letters were bringing; for some time now I have had no losses, nor gains either. Even if I were not an old man, I could not have helped feeling pleasure at this; but as it is, my pleasure was far greater. For, however small my possessions might be, I should still have left over more travelling-money than journey to travel, especially since this journey upon which we have set out is one which need not be followed to the end. An expedition will be incomplete if one stops half-way, or anywhere on this side of one's destination; but life is not incomplete if it is honourable. At whatever point you leave off living, provided you leave off nobly, your life is a whole. Often, however, one must leave off bravely, and our reasons therefore need not be momentous; for neither are the reasons momentous which hold us here.

Tullius Marcellinus, a man whom you knew very well, who in youth was a quiet soul and became old prematurely, fell ill of a disease which was by no means hopeless; but it was protracted and troublesome, and it demanded much attention; hence he began to think about dying. He called many of his friends together. Each one of them gave Marcellinus advice—the timid friend urging him to do what he had made up his mind to do; the flattering and wheedling friend giving counsel which he supposed would be more pleasing to Marcellinus when he came to think the matter over; but our Stoic friend, a rare man, and, to praise him in language which he deserves, a man of courage and vigour admonished him best of all, as it seems to me. For he began as follows: "Do not torment yourself, my dear Marcellinus, as if the question which you are weighing were a matter of importance. It is not an important matter to live; all your slaves live, and so do all animals; but it is important to die honourably, sensibly, bravely. Reflect how long you have been doing the same thing: food, sleep, lust—this is one's daily round. The desire to die may be felt, not only by the sensible man or the brave or unhappy man, but even by the man who is merely surfeited."

Marcellinus did not need someone to urge him, but rather someone to help him; his slaves refused to do his bidding. The Stoic therefore removed their fears, showing them that there was no risk involved for the household except when it was uncertain whether the master's death was self-sought or not; besides, it was as bad a practise to kill one's master as it was to prevent him forcibly from killing himself. Then he suggested to Marcellinus himself that it would be a kindly act to distribute gifts to those who had attended him throughout his whole life, when that life was finished, just as, when a banquet is finished, the remaining portion is divided among the attendants who stand about the table. Marcellinus was of a compliant and generous disposition, even when it was a question of his own property; so he distributed little sums among his sorrowing slaves, and comforted them besides. No need had he of sword or of bloodshed; for three days he fasted and had a tent put up in his very bedroom. Then a tub was brought in; he lay in it for a long time, and, as the hot water was continually poured over him, he gradually passed away, not without a feeling of pleasure, as he himself remarked—such a feeling as a slow dissolution is wont to give. Those of us who have ever fainted know from experience what this feeling is.

This little anecdote into which I have digressed will not be displeasing to you. For you will see that your friend departed neither with difficulty nor with suffering. Though he committed suicide, yet he withdrew most gently, gliding out of life. The anecdote may also be of some use; for often a crisis demands just such examples. There are times when we ought to die and are unwilling; sometimes we die and are unwilling. No one is so ignorant as not to know that we must at some time die; nevertheless, when one draws near death, one turns to flight, trembles, and laments. Would you not think him an utter fool who wept because he was not alive a thousand years ago? And is he not just as much of a fool who weeps because he will not be alive a thousand years from now? It is all the same; you will not be, and you were not. Neither of these periods of time belongs to you. You have been cast upon this point of time; if you would make it longer, how much longer shall you make it? Why weep? Why pray? You are taking pains to no purpose.

Give over thinking that your prayers can bend
Divine decrees from their predestined end.

These decrees are unalterable and fixed; they are governed by a mighty and everlasting compulsion. Your goal will be the goal of all things. What is there strange in this to you? You were born to be subject to this law; this fate befell your father, your mother, your ancestors, all who came before you; and it will befall all who shall come after you. A sequence which cannot be broken or altered by any power binds all things together and draws all things in its course. Think of the multitudes of men doomed to death who will come after you, of the multitudes who will go with you! You would die more bravely, I suppose, in the company of many thousands; and yet there are many thousands, both of men and of animals, who at this very moment, while you are irresolute about death, are breathing their last, in their several ways. But you—did you believe that you would not some day reach the goal towards which you have always been travelling? No journey but has its end.

You think, I suppose, that it is now in order for me to cite some examples of great men. No, I shall cite rather the case of a boy. The story of the Spartan lad has been preserved: taken captive while still a stripling, he kept crying in his Doric dialect, "I will not be a slave!" and he made good his word; for the very first time he was ordered to perform a menial and degrading service—and the command was to fetch a chamber-pot—he dashed out his brains against the wall. So near at hand is freedom, and is anyone still a slave? Would you not rather have your own son die thus than reach old age by weakly yielding? Why therefore are you distressed, when even a boy can die so bravely? Suppose that you refuse to follow him; you will be led. Take into your own control that which is now under the control of another. Will you not borrow that boy's courage, and say: "I am no slave!"? Unhappy fellow, you are a slave to men, you are a slave to your business, you are a slave to life. For life, if courage to die be lacking, is slavery.

Have you anything worth waiting for? Your very pleasures, which cause you to tarry and hold you back, have already been exhausted by you. None of them is a novelty to you, and there is none that has not already become hateful because you are cloyed with it. You know the taste of wine and cordials. It makes no difference whether a hundred or a thousand measures pass through your bladder; you are nothing but a wine-strainer. You are a connoisseur in the flavour of the oyster and of the mullet; your luxury has not left you anything untasted for the years that are to come; and yet these are the things from which you are torn away unwillingly. What else is there which you would regret to have taken from you? Friends? But who can be a friend to you? Country? What? Do you think enough of your country to be late to dinner? The light of the sun? You would extinguish it, if you could; for what have you ever done that was fit to be seen in the light? Confess the truth; it is not because you long for the Senate chamber or the forum, or even for the world of nature, that you would fain put off dying; it is because you are loth to leave the fish-market, though you have exhausted its stores.*

You are afraid of death; but how can you scorn it in the midst of a mushroom supper?† You wish to live; well, do you know how to live? You are afraid to die. But come now: is this life of yours anything but death? Gaius Caesar was passing along the Via Latina, when a man stepped out from the ranks of the prisoners, his grey beard hanging down even to his breast, and begged to be put to death. "What!" said Caesar, "are you alive now?" That is the answer which should be given to men to whom death would come as a relief. "You are afraid to die; what! are you alive now?" "But," says one, "I wish to live, for I am engaged in many honourable pursuits. I am loth to leave life's duties, which I am fulfilling with loyalty and zeal." Surely you are aware that dying is also one of life's duties? You are deserting no duty; for there is no definite number established which you are bound to complete. There is no life that is not short. Compared with the world of nature, even Nestor's life was a short one, or Sattia's, the woman who bade carve on her tombstone that she had lived ninety and nine years. Some persons, you see, boast of their long lives; but who could

---

* Probably the strong tone of disapproval used in this paragraph is directed against the Roman in general rather than against the industrious Lucilius. It is characteristic of the diatribe.

† Seneca may be recalling the death of the Emperor Claudius.

have endured the old lady if she had had the luck to complete her hundredth year? It is with life as it is with a play: it matters not how long the action is spun out, but how good the acting is. It makes no difference at what point you stop. Stop whenever you choose; only see to it that the closing period is well turned. Farewell.

78. ON THE HEALING POWER OF THE MIND

That you are frequently troubled by the snuffling of catarrh and by short attacks of fever which follow after long and chronic catarrhal seizures, I am sorry to hear; particularly because I have experienced this sort of illness myself, and scorned it in its early stages. For when I was still young, I could put up with hardships and show a bold front to illness. But I finally succumbed, and arrived at such a state that I could do nothing but snuffle, reduced as I was to the extremity of thinness.* I often entertained the impulse of ending my life then and there; but the thought of my kind old father kept me back. For I reflected, not how bravely I had the power to die, but how little power he had to bear bravely the loss of me. And so I commanded myself to live. For sometimes it is an act of bravery even to live.

Now I shall tell you what consoled me during those days, stating at the outset that these very aids to my peace of mind were as efficacious as medicine. Honourable consolation results in a cure; and whatever has uplifted the soul helps the body also. My studies were my salvation. I place it to the credit of philosophy that I recovered and regained my strength. I owe my life to philosophy, and that is the least of my obligations! My friends, too, helped me greatly toward good health; I used to be comforted by their cheering words, by the hours they spent at my bedside, and by their conversation. Nothing, my excellent Lucilius, refreshes and aids a sick man so much as the affection of his friends; nothing so steals away the expectation and the fear of death. In fact, I could not believe that, if they survived me, I should be dying at all. Yes, I repeat, it seemed to me that I should continue to live, not with them, but through them. I imagined myself not to be yielding up my soul, but to be making it over to them.

All these things gave me the inclination to succour myself and to endure

---

* To such a degree that Seneca's enemy Caligula refrained from executing him, on the ground that he would soon die.

any torture; besides, it is a most miserable state to have lost one's zest for dying, and to have no zest in living. These, then, are the remedies to which you should have recourse. The physician will prescribe your walks and your exercise; he will warn you not to become addicted to idleness, as is the tendency of the inactive invalid; he will order you to read in a louder voice and to exercise your lungs the passages and cavity of which are affected; or to sail and shake up your bowels by a little mild motion; he will recommend the proper food, and the suitable time for aiding your strength with wine or refraining from it in order to keep your cough from being irritated and hacking. But as for me, my counsel to you is this—and it is a cure, not merely of this disease of yours, but of your whole life—"Despise death." There is no sorrow in the world, when we have escaped from the fear of death. There are these three serious elements in every disease: fear of death, bodily pain, and interruption of pleasures. Concerning death enough has been said, and I shall add only a word: this fear is not a fear of disease, but a fear of nature. Disease has often postponed death, and a vision of dying has been many a man's salvation. You will die, not because you are ill, but because you are alive; even when you have been cured, the same end awaits you; when you have recovered, it will be not death, but ill-health, that you have escaped.

Let us now return to the consideration of the characteristic disadvantage of disease: it is accompanied by great suffering. The suffering, however, is rendered endurable by interruptions; for the strain of extreme pain must come to an end. No man can suffer both severely and for a long time; Nature, who loves us most tenderly, has so constituted us as to make pain either endurable or short. The severest pains have their seat in the most slender parts of our body; nerves, joints, and any other of the narrow passages, hurt most cruelly when they have developed trouble within their contracted spaces. But these parts soon become numb, and by reason of the pain itself lose the sensation of pain, whether because the life-force, when checked in its natural course and changed for the worse, loses the peculiar power through which it thrives and through which it warns us, or because the diseased humours of the body, when they cease to have a place into which they may flow, are thrown back upon themselves, and deprive of sensation the parts where they have caused congestion. So gout, both in the feet and in the hands, and all pain in the vertebrae and in the nerves, have their intervals of rest at the times when they have dulled the parts which they before had tortured; the first twinges, in all such cases, are what cause the distress, and their onset is checked by lapse of time, so that there is an end of pain when numbness has set in. Pain in the teeth, eyes, and ears is most acute for the very reason that it begins among the narrow spaces of the body—no less acute, indeed, than in the head itself. But if it is more violent than usual, it turns to delirium and stupor. This is, accordingly, a consolation for excessive pain—that you cannot help ceasing to feel it if you feel it to excess. The reason, however, why the inexperienced are impatient when their bodies suffer is, that they have not accustomed themselves to be contented in spirit. They have been closely associated with the body. Therefore a high-minded and sensible man divorces soul from body, and dwells much with the better or divine part, and only as far as he must with this complaining and frail portion.

"But it is a hardship," men say, "to do without our customary pleasures—to fast, to feel thirst and hunger." These are indeed serious when one first abstains from them. Later the desire dies down, because the appetites themselves which lead to desire are wearied and forsake us; then the stomach becomes petulant, then the food which we craved before becomes hateful. Our very wants die away. But there is no bitterness in doing without that which you have ceased to desire. Moreover, every pain sometimes stops, or at any rate slackens; moreover, one may take precautions against its return, and, when it threatens, may check it by means of remedies. Every variety of pain has its premonitory symptoms; this is true, at any rate, of pain that is habitual and recurrent. One can endure the suffering which disease entails, if one has come to regard its results with scorn. But do not of your own accord make your troubles heavier to bear and burden yourself with complaining. Pain is slight if opinion has added nothing to it; but if, on the other hand, you begin to encourage yourself and say, "It is nothing—a trifling matter at most; keep a stout heart and it will soon cease"; then in thinking it slight, you will make it slight. Everything depends on opinion; ambition, luxury, greed, hark back to opinion. It is according to opinion that we suffer. A man is as wretched as he has convinced himself that he is. I hold that we should do away with complaint about past sufferings and with all language like this: "None has ever been worse off than I. What sufferings, what evils have I endured! No one has thought that I shall recover. How often have my family bewailed me, and the physicians given me over! Men who are placed on the rack are not torn asunder with such agony!" However, even if all this is true, it is over and gone. What benefit is there in reviewing past sufferings, and in being unhappy, just because once you were unhappy? Besides, every one adds much to his own ills, and tells lies to himself. And that which was bitter to bear is pleasant to have borne; it is natural to rejoice at the ending of one's ills.

Two elements must therefore be rooted out once for all—the fear of future suffering, and the recollection of past suffering; since the latter no longer concerns me, and the former concerns me not yet. But when set in the very midst of troubles one should say:

Perchance some day the memory of this sorrow
Will even bring delight.

Let such a man fight against them with all his might: if he once gives way, he will be vanquished; but if he strives against his sufferings, he will conquer. As it is, however, what most men do is to drag down upon their own heads a falling ruin which they ought to try to support. If you begin to withdraw your support from that which thrusts toward you and totters and is ready to plunge, it will follow you and lean more heavily upon you; but if you hold your ground and make up your mind to push against it, it will be forced back. What blows do athletes receive on their faces and all over their bodies! Nevertheless, through their desire for fame they endure every torture, and they undergo these things not only because they are fighting but in order to be able to fight. Their very training means torture. So let us also win the way to victory in all our struggles—for the reward is not a garland or a palm or a trumpeter who calls for silence at the proclamation of our names, but rather virtue, steadfastness of soul, and a peace that is won for all time, if Fortune has once been utterly vanquished in any combat. You say, "I feel severe pain." What then; are you relieved from feeling it, if you endure it like a woman? Just as an enemy is more dangerous to a retreating army, so every trouble that Fortune brings attacks us all the harder if we yield and turn our backs. "But the trouble is serious." What? Is it for this purpose that we are strong—that we may have light burdens to bear? Would you have your illness long-drawn-out, or would you have it quick and short? If it is long, it means a respite, allows you a period for resting yourself, bestows upon you the boon of time in plenty; as it arises, so it must also subside. A short and rapid illness will do one of two things: it will quench or be quenched. And what difference does it make whether it is not or I am not? In either case there is an end of pain.

This, too, will help—to turn the mind aside to thoughts of other things and thus to depart from pain. Call to mind what honourable or brave deeds you have done; consider the good side of your own life. Run over in your memory those things which you have particularly admired. Then think of all the brave men who have conquered pain: of him who continued to read his book as he allowed the cutting out of varicose veins; of him who did not cease to smile, though that very smile so enraged his torturers that they tried upon him every instrument of their cruelty. If pain can be conquered by a smile, will it not be conquered by reason? You may tell me now of whatever you like—of colds, bad coughing-spells that bring up parts of our entrails, fever that parches our very vitals, thirst, limbs so twisted that the joints protrude in different directions; yet worse than these are the stake, the rack, the red-hot plates, the instrument that reopens wounds while the wounds themselves are still swollen and that drives their imprint still deeper. Nevertheless there have been men who have not uttered a moan amid these tortures. "More yet!" says the torturer; but the victim has not begged for release. "More yet!" he says again; but no answer has come. "More yet!" the victim has smiled, and heartily, too. Can you not bring yourself, after an example like this, to make a mock at pain?

"But," you object, "my illness does not allow me to be doing anything; it has withdrawn me from all my duties." It is your body that is hampered by ill-health, and not your soul as well. It is for this reason that it clogs the feet of the runner and will hinder the handiwork of the cobbler or the artisan; but if your soul be habitually in practise, you will plead and teach, listen and learn, investigate and meditate. What more is necessary? Do you think that you are doing nothing if you possess self-control in your illness? You will be showing that a disease can be overcome, or at any rate endured. There is, I assure you, a place for virtue even upon a bed of sickness. It is not only the sword and the battle-line that prove the soul alert and unconquered by fear; a man can display bravery even when wrapped in his bed-clothes. You have something to do: wrestle bravely with disease. If it shall compel you to nothing, beguile you to nothing, it is a notable example that you display. O what ample matter were there for renown, if we could have spectators of our sickness! Be your own spectator; seek your own applause.

Again, there are two kinds of pleasures. Disease checks the pleasures of the body, but does not do away with them. Nay, if the truth is to be considered, it serves to excite them; for the thirstier a man is, the more he enjoys a drink; the hungrier he is, the more pleasure he takes in food. Whatever falls to one's lot after a period of abstinence is welcomed with greater zest. The other kind, however, the pleasures of the mind, which are higher and less uncertain, no physician can refuse to the sick man. Whoever seeks these and knows well what they are scorns all the blandishments of the senses. Men say, "Poor sick fellow!"

But why? Is it because he does not mix snow with his wine, or because he does not revive the chill of his drink—mixed as it is in a good-sized bowl—by chipping ice into it? Or because he does not have Lucrine oysters opened fresh at his table? Or because there is no din of cooks about his dining-hall, as they bring in their very cooking apparatus along with their viands? For luxury has already devised this fashion—of having the kitchen accompany the dinner, so that the food may not grow luke-warm, or fail to be hot enough for a palate which has already become hardened. "Poor sick fellow!"—he will eat as much as he can digest. There will be no boar lying before his eyes, banished from the table as if it were a common meat; and on his sideboard there will be heaped together no breast-meat of birds, because it sickens him to see birds served whole. But what evil has been done to you? You will dine like a sick man, nay, sometimes like a sound man.

All these things, however, can be easily endured—gruel, warm water, and anything else that seems insupportable to a fastidious man, to one who is wallowing in luxury, sick in soul rather than in body—if only we cease to shudder at death. And we shall cease, if once we have gained a knowledge of the limits of good and evil; then, and then only, life will not weary us, neither will death make us afraid. For surfeit of self can never seize upon a life that surveys all the things which are manifold, great, divine; only idle leisure is wont to make men hate their lives. To one who roams through the universe, the truth can never pall; it will be the untruths that will cloy. And, on the other hand, if death comes near with its summons, even though it be untimely in its arrival, though it cut one off in one's prime, a man has had a taste of all that the longest life can give. Such a man has in great measure come to understand the universe. He knows that honourable things do not depend on time for their growth; but any life must seem short to those who measure its length by pleasures which are empty and for that reason unbounded.

Refresh yourself with such thoughts as these, and meanwhile reserve some hours for our letters. There will come a time when we shall be united again and brought together; however short this time may be, we shall make it long by knowing how to employ it. For, as Posidonius says: "A single day among the learned lasts longer than the longest life of the ignorant." Meanwhile, hold fast to this thought, and grip it close: yield not to adversity; trust not to prosperity; keep before your eyes the full scope of Fortune's power, as if she would surely do whatever is in her power to do. That which has been long expected comes more gently. Farewell.

86. ON SCIPIO'S VILLA

I am resting at the country-house which once belonged to Scipio Africanus himself; and I write to you after doing reverence to his spirit and to an altar which I am inclined to think is the tomb of that great warrior. That his soul has indeed returned to the skies, whence it came, I am convinced, not because he commanded mighty armies—for Cambyses also had mighty armies, and Cambyses was a madman who made successful use of his madness—but because he showed moderation and a sense of duty to a marvellous extent. I regard this trait in him as more admirable after his withdrawal from his native land than while he was defending her; for there was the alternative: Scipio should remain in Rome, or Rome should remain free. "It is my wish," said he, "not to infringe in the least upon our laws, or upon our customs; let all Roman citizens have equal rights. O my country, make the most of the good that I have done, but without me. I have been the cause of your freedom, and I shall also be its proof; I go into exile, if it is true that I have grown beyond what is to your advantage!"

What can I do but admire this magnanimity, which led him to withdraw into voluntary exile and to relieve the state of its burden? Matters had gone so far that either liberty must work harm to Scipio, or Scipio to liberty. Either of these things was wrong in the sight of heaven. So he gave way to the laws and withdrew to Liternum, thinking to make the state a debtor for his own exile no less than for the exile of Hannibal.

I have inspected the house, which is constructed of hewn stone; the wall which encloses a forest; the towers also, buttressed out on both sides for the purpose of defending the house; the well, concealed among buildings and shrubbery, large enough to keep a whole army supplied; and the small bath, buried in darkness according to the old style, for our ancestors did not think that one could have a hot bath except in darkness. It was therefore a great pleasure to me to contrast Scipio's ways with our own. Think, in this tiny recess the "terror of Carthage," to whom Rome should offer thanks because she was not captured more than once, used to bathe a body wearied with work in the fields! For he was accustomed to keep himself busy and to cultivate the soil with his own hands, as the good old Romans were wont to do. Beneath this dingy roof he stood; and this floor, mean as it is, bore his weight.

But who in these days could bear to bathe in such a fashion? We think ourselves poor and mean if our walls are not resplendent with large and costly mirrors; if our marbles from Alexandria are not set off by mosaics of Numidian stone, if their borders are not faced over on all sides with difficult patterns, arranged in many colours like paintings; if our vaulted ceilings are not buried in glass; if our swimming-pools are not lined with Thasian marble, once a rare and wonderful sight in any temple pools into which we let down our bodies after they have been drained weak by abundant perspiration; and finally, if the water has not poured from silver spigots. I have so far been speaking of the ordinary bathing-establishments; what shall I say when I come to those of the freedmen? What a vast number of statues, of columns that support nothing, but are built for decoration, merely in order to spend money! And what masses of water that fall crashing from level to level! We have become so luxurious that we will have nothing but precious stones to walk upon.

In this bath of Scipio's there are tiny chinks—you cannot call them windows—cut out of the stone wall in such a way as to admit light without weakening the fortifications; nowadays, however, people regard baths as fit only for moths if they have not been so arranged that they receive the sun all day long through the widest of windows, if men cannot bathe and get a coat of tan at the same time, and if they cannot look out from their bath-tubs over stretches of land and sea. So it goes; the establishments which had drawn crowds and had won admiration when they were first opened are avoided and put back in the category of venerable antiques as soon as luxury has worked out some new device, to her own ultimate undoing. In the early days, however, there were few baths, and they were not fitted out with any display. For why should men elaborately fit out that which costs a penny only, and was invented for use, not merely for delight? The bathers of those day did not have water poured over them, nor did it always run fresh as if from a hot spring; and they did not believe that it mattered at all how perfectly pure was the water into which they were to leave their dirt. Ye gods, what a pleasure it is to enter that dark bath, covered with a common sort of roof, knowing that therein your hero Cato, as aedile, or Fabius Maximus, or one of the Cornelia, has warmed the water with his own hands! For this also used to be the duty of the noblest aediles—to enter these places to which the populace resorted, and to demand that they be cleaned and warmed to a heat required by considerations of use and health, not the heat that men have recently made fashionable, as great as a conflagration—so much so, indeed, that a slave condemned for some criminal offence now ought to be *bathed* alive! It seems to me that nowadays there is no difference between "the bath is on fire" and "the bath is warm."

How some persons nowadays condemn Scipio as a boor because he did not let daylight into his perspiring-room through wide windows, or because he did not roast in the strong sunlight and dawdle about until he could stew in the hot water! "Poor fool," they say, "he did not know how to live! He did not bathe in filtered water; it was often turbid, and after heavy rains almost muddy!" But it did not matter much to Scipio if he had to bathe in that way; he went there to wash off sweat, not ointment. And how do you suppose certain persons will answer me? They will say: "I don't envy Scipio; that was truly an exile's life—to put up with baths like those!" Friend, if you were wiser, you would know that Scipio did not bathe every day. It is stated by those who have reported to us the old-time ways of Rome that the Romans washed only their arms and legs daily—because those were the members which gathered dirt in their daily toil—and bathed all over only once a week. Here someone will retort: "Yes; pretty dirty fellows they evidently were! How they must have smelled!" But they smelled of the camp, the farm, and heroism. Now that spick-and-span bathing establishments have been devised, men are really fouler than of yore. What says Horatius Flaccus, when he wishes to describe a scoundrel, one who is notorious for his extreme luxury? He says: "Buccillus smells of perfume." Show me a Buccillus in these days; his smell would be the veritable goat-smell—he would take the place of the Gargonius with whom Horace in the same passage contrasted him. It is nowadays not enough to use ointment, unless you put on a fresh coat two or three times a day, to keep it from evaporating on the body. But why should a man boast of this perfume as if it were his own?

If what I am saying shall seem to you too pessimistic, charge it up against Scipio's country-house, where I have learned a lesson from Aegialus, a most careful householder and now the owner of this estate; he taught me that a tree can be transplanted, no matter how far gone in years. We old men must learn this precept; for there is none of us who is not planting an olive-yard for his successor. I have seen them bearing fruit in due season after three or four years of unproductiveness. And you too shall be shaded by the tree which

Is slow to grow, but bringeth shade to cheer
Your grandsons in the far-off years,

as our poet Vergil says. Vergil sought, however, not what was nearest to the truth, but what was most appropriate, and aimed, not to teach the farmer, but to please the reader. For example, omitting all other errors of his, I will quote the passage in which it was incumbent upon me today to detect a fault:

In spring sow beans then, too, O clover plant,
Thou'rt welcomed by the crumbling furrows; and
The millet calls for yearly care.

You may judge by the following incident whether those plants should be set out at the same time, or whether both should be sowed in the spring. It is June at the present writing, and we are well on towards July; and I have seen on this very day farmers harvesting beans and sowing millet.

But to return to our olive-yard again. I saw it planted in two ways. If the trees were large, Aegialus took their trunks and cut off the branches to the length of one foot each; he then transplanted along with the ball, after cutting off the roots, leaving only the thick part from which the roots hang. He smeared this with manure and inserted it in the hole, not only heaping up the earth about it, but stamping and pressing it down. There is nothing, he says, more effective than this packing process; in other words, it keeps out the cold and the wind. Besides, the trunk is not shaken so much, and for this reason the packing makes it possible for the young roots to come out and get a hold in the soil. These are of necessity still soft; they have but a slight hold, and a very little shaking uproots them. This ball, moreover, Aegialus lops clean before he covers it up. For he maintains that new roots spring from all the parts which have been shorn. Moreover, the trunk itself should not stand more than three or four feet out of the ground. For there will thus be at once a thick growth from the bottom, nor will there be a large stump, all dry and withered, as is the case with old olive-yards. The second way of setting them out was the following: he set out in similar fashion branches that were strong and of soft bark, as those of young saplings are wont to be. These grow a little more slowly, but, since they spring from what is practically a cutting, there is no roughness or ugliness in them.

This too I have seen recently—an aged vine transplanted from its own plantation. In this case, the fibres also should be gathered together, if possible, and then you should cover up the vine-stem more generously, so that roots may spring up even from the stock. I have seen such plantings made not only in February, but at the very end of March; the plants take hold of and embrace alien elms. But all trees, he declares, which are, so to speak, "thick-stemmed,"* should be assisted with tank-water; if we have this help, we are our own rain-makers.

I do not intend to tell you any more of these precepts, lest, as Aegialus did with me, I may be training you up to be my competitor. Farewell.

87. SOME ARGUMENTS IN FAVOUR OF THE SIMPLE LIFE

"I was shipwrecked before I got aboard."† I shall not add how that happened, lest you may reckon this also as another of the Stoic paradoxes; and yet I shall, whenever you are willing to listen, nay, even though you be unwilling, prove to you that these words are by no means untrue, nor so surprising as one at first sight would think. Meantime, the journey showed me this: how much we possess that is superfluous; and how easily we can make up our minds to do away with things whose loss, whenever it is necessary to part with them, we do not feel.

My friend Maximus and I have been spending a most happy period of two days, taking with us very few slaves—one carriage-load—and no paraphernalia except what we wore on our persons. The mattress lies on the ground, and I upon the mattress. There are two rugs—one to spread beneath us and one to cover us. Nothing could have been subtracted from our luncheon; it took not more than an hour to prepare, and we were nowhere without dried figs, never without writing tablets. If I have bread, I use figs as a relish; if not, I regard figs as a substitute for bread. Hence they bring me a New Year feast every day, and I make the New Year happy and prosperous by good thoughts and greatness of soul; for the soul is never greater than when it has laid aside all extraneous things, and has secured peace for itself by fearing nothing, and riches by craving no riches. The vehicle in which I have taken my seat is a farmer's cart. Only by walking do the mules show that they are alive. The driver is barefoot, and not because it is summer either. I can scarcely force myself to wish that others shall think this cart mine. My false embarrassment about the truth still holds out, you see; and whenever we meet a more sumptuous party I blush in spite

* An agricultural term not elsewhere found.

† *i.e.,* on my journey I travelled with almost as meagre an equipment as a shipwrecked man.

of myself—proof that this conduct which I approve and applaud has not yet gained a firm and steadfast dwelling-place within me. He who blushes at riding in a rattle-trap will boast when he rides in style.

So my progress is still insufficient. I have not yet the courage openly to acknowledge my thriftiness. Even yet I am bothered by what other travellers think of me. But instead of this, I should really have uttered an opinion counter to that in which mankind believe, saying, "You are mad, you are misled, your admiration devotes itself to superfluous things! You estimate no man at his real worth. When property is concerned, you reckon up in this way with most scrupulous calculation those to whom you shall lend either money or benefits; for by now you enter benefits also as payments in your ledger. You say, 'His estates are wide, but his debts are large.' 'He has a fine house, but he has built it on borrowed capital.' 'No man will display a more brilliant retinue on short notice, but he cannot meet his debts.' 'If he pays off his creditors, he will have nothing left.'" So you will feel bound to do in all other cases as well—to find out by elimination the amount of every man's actual possessions.

I suppose you call a man rich just because his gold plate goes with him even on his travels, because he farms land in all the provinces, because he unrolls a large account-book, because he owns estates near the city so great that men would grudge his holding them in the waste lands of Apulia. But after you have mentioned all these facts, he is poor. And why? He is in debt. "To what extent?" you ask. For all that he has. Or perchance you think it matters whether one has borrowed from another man or from Fortune. What good is there in mules caparisoned in uniform livery? Or in decorated chariots and

Steeds decked with purple and with tapestry,
With golden harness hanging from their necks,
Champing their yellow bits, all clothed in gold?

Neither master nor mule is improved by such trappings.

Marcus Cato the Censor, whose existence helped the state as much as did Scipio's—for while Scipio fought against our enemies, Cato fought against our bad morals—used to ride a donkey, and a donkey, at that, which carried saddle-bags containing the master's necessaries. O how I should love to see him meet today on the road one of our coxcombs, with his outriders and Numidians, and a great cloud of dust before him! Your dandy would no doubt seem refined and well-attended in comparison with Marcus Cato—your dandy, who, in the midst of all his luxurious paraphernalia, is chiefly concerned whether to turn his hand to the sword or to the hunting-knife. O what a glory to the times in which he lived, for a general who had celebrated a triumph, a censor, and what is most noteworthy of all, a Cato, to be content with a single nag, and with less than a whole nag at that! For part of the animal was pre-empted by the baggage that hung down on either flank. Would you not therefore prefer Cato's steed, that single steed, saddle-worn by Cato himself, to the coxcomb's whole retinue of plump ponies, Spanish cobs, and trotters? I see that there will be no end in dealing with such a theme unless I make an end myself. So I shall now become silent, at least with reference to superfluous things like these; doubtless the man who first called them "hindrances" had a prophetic inkling that they would be the very sort of thing they now are. At present I should like to deliver to you the syllogisms, as yet very few, belonging to our school and bearing upon the question of virtue, which, in our opinion, is sufficient for the happy life.

"That which is good makes men good. For example, that which is good in the art of music makes the musician. But chance events do not make a good man; therefore, chance events are not goods." The Peripatetics reply to this by saying that the premise is false; that men do not in every case become good by means of that which is good; that in music there is something good, like a flute, a harp, or an organ suited to accompany singing; but that none of these instruments makes the musician. We shall then reply: "You do not understand in what sense we have used the phrase 'that which is good in music.' For we do not mean that which equips the musician, but that which makes the musician; you, however, are referring to the instruments of the art, and not to the art itself. If, however, anything in the art of music is good, that will in every case make the musician." And I should like to put this idea still more clearly. We define the good in the art of music in two ways: first, that by which the performance of the musician is assisted, and second, that by which his art is assisted. Now the musical instruments have to do with his performance—such as flutes and organs and harps; but they do not have to do with the musician's art itself. For he is an artist even without them; he may perhaps be lacking in the ability to practise his art. But the good in man is not in the same way twofold; for the good of man and the good of life are the same.

"That which can fall to the lot of any man, no matter how base or despised he may be, is not a good. But wealth falls to the lot of the pander and the trainer of gladiators; therefore wealth is not a good." "Another wrong premise," they say, "for we notice that goods fall to the lot of the very lowest sort of men, not only in the scholar's art, but also in the art of healing or in the art of navigating." These arts, however, make no profession of greatness of soul; they do not rise to any heights nor do they frown upon what Fortune may bring. It is virtue that uplifts man and places him superior to what mortals hold dear; virtue neither craves overmuch nor fears to excess that which is called good or that which is called bad. Chelidon, one of Cleopatra's eunuchs, possessed great wealth; and recently Natalis—a man whose tongue was as shameless as it was dirty, a man whose mouth used to perform the vilest offices—was the heir of many, and also made many his heirs. What then? Was it his money that made him unclean, or did he himself besmirch his money? Money tumbles into the hands of certain men as a coin tumbles down a sewer. Virtue stands above all such things. It is appraised in coin of its own minting; and it deems none of these random windfalls to be good. But medicine and navigation do not forbid themselves and their followers to marvel at such things. One who is not a good man can nevertheless be a physician, or a pilot or a scholar—yes just as well as he can be a cook! He to whose lot it falls to possess something which is not of a random sort, cannot be called a random sort of man: a person is of the same sort as that which he possesses. A strong-box is worth just what it holds; or rather, it is a mere accessory of that which it holds. Whoever sets any price upon a full purse except the price established by the count of the money deposited therein? This also applies to the owners of great estates: they are only accessories and incidentals to their possessions.

Why, then, is the wise man great? Because he has a great soul. Accordingly, it is true that that which falls to the lot even of the most despicable person is not a good. Thus, I should never regard inactivity as a good; for even the tree-frog and the flea possess this quality. Nor should I regard rest and freedom from trouble as a good; for what is more at leisure than a worm? Do you ask what it is that produces the wise man? That which produces a god. You must grant that the wise man has an element of godliness, heavenliness, grandeur. The good does not come to every one, nor does it allow any random person to possess it. Behold:

What fruits each country bears, or will not bear;
Here grain, and there the vine, grow richlier.
And elsewhere still the tender tree and grass
Unbidden clothe themselves in green. Seest thou
How Tmolus ships its saffron perfumes forth,

And ivory comes from Ind; soft Sheba sends
Its incense, and the unclad Chalybes
Their iron.

These products are apportioned to separate countries in order that human beings may be constrained to traffic among themselves, each seeking something from his neighbour in his turn. So the Supreme Good has also its own abode. It does not grow where ivory grows, or iron. Do you ask where the Supreme Good dwells? In the soul. And unless the soul be pure and holy, there is no room in it for God.

"Good does not result from evil. But riches result from greed; therefore, riches are not a good." "It is not true," they say, "that good does not result from evil. For money comes from sacrilege and theft. Accordingly, although sacrilege and theft are evil, yet they are evil only because they work more evil than good. For they bring gain; but the gain is accompanied by fear, anxiety, and torture of mind and body." Whoever says this must perforce admit that sacrilege, though it be an evil because it works much evil, is yet partly good because it accomplishes a certain amount of good. What can be more monstrous than this? We have, to be sure, actually convinced the world that sacrilege, theft, and adultery are to be regarded as among the goods. How many men there are who do not blush at theft, how many who boast of having committed adultery! For petty sacrilege is punished, but sacrilege on a grand scale is honoured by a triumphal procession. Besides, sacrilege, if it is wholly good in some respect, will also be honourable and will be called right conduct; for it is conduct which concerns ourselves. But no human being, on serious consideration, admits this idea.

Therefore, goods cannot spring from evil. For if, as you object, sacrilege is an evil for the single reason that it brings on much evil, if you but absolve sacrilege of its punishment and pledge it immunity, sacrilege will be wholly good. And yet the worst punishment for crime lies in the crime itself. You are mistaken, I maintain, if you propose to reserve your punishments for the hangman or the prison; the crime is punished immediately after it is committed; nay, rather, at the moment when it is committed. Hence, good does not spring from evil, any more than figs grow from olive-trees. Things which grow correspond to their seed; and goods cannot depart from their class. As that which is honourable does not grow from that which is base, so neither does good grow from evil. For the honourable and the good are identical.

Certain of our school oppose this statement as follows: "Let us suppose that money taken from any source whatsoever is a good; even though it is taken by an act of sacrilege, the money does not on that account derive its origin from sacrilege. You may get my meaning through the following illustration: In the same jar there is a piece of gold and there is a serpent. If you take the gold from the jar, it is not just because the serpent is there too, I say, that the jar yields me the gold—because it contains the serpent as well—but it yields the gold in spite of containing the serpent also. Similarly, gain results from sacrilege, not just because sacrilege is a base and accursed act, but because it contains gain also. As the serpent in the jar is an evil, and not the gold which lies there, beside the serpent: so in an act of sacrilege it is the crime, not the profit, that is evil." But I differ from these men; for the conditions in each case are not at all the same. In the one instance I can take the gold without the serpent, in the other I cannot make the profit without committing the sacrilege. The gain in the latter case does not lie side by side with the crime; it is blended with the crime.

"That which, while we are desiring to attain it, involves us in many evils, is not a good. But while we are desiring to attain riches, we become involved in many evils; therefore, riches are not a good." "Your first premise," they say, "contains two meanings; one is: we become involved in many evils while we are desiring to attain riches. But we also become involved in many evils while we are desiring to attain virtue. One man, while travelling in order to prosecute his studies, suffers shipwreck, and another is taken captive. The second meaning is as follows: that through which we become involved in evils is not a good. And it will not logically follow from our proposition that we become involved in evils through riches or through pleasure; otherwise, if it is through riches that we become involved in many evils, riches are not only not a good, but they are positively an evil. You, however, maintain merely that they are not a good. Moreover," the objector says, "you grant that riches are of some use. You reckon them among the advantages; and yet on this basis they cannot even be an advantage, for it is through the pursuit of riches that we suffer much disadvantage." Certain men answer this objection as follows: "You are mistaken if you ascribe disadvantages to riches. Riches injure no one; it is a man's own folly, or his neighbour's wickedness, that harms him in each case, just as a sword by itself does not slay; it is merely the weapon used by the slayer. Riches themselves do not harm you, just because it is on account of riches that you suffer harm."

I think that the reasoning of Posidonius is better: he holds that riches are a cause of evil, not because, of themselves, they do any evil, but because they goad men on so that they are ready to do evil. For the efficient cause, which necessarily produces harm at once, is one thing, and the antecedent cause is another. It is this antecedent cause which inheres in riches; they puff up the spirit and beget pride, they bring on unpopularity and unsettle the mind to such an extent that the mere reputation of having wealth, though it is bound to harm us, nevertheless affords delight. All goods, however, ought properly to be free from blame; they are pure, they do not corrupt the spirit, and they do not tempt us. They do, indeed, uplift and broaden the spirit, but without puffing it up. Those things which are goods produce confidence, but riches produce shamelessness. The things which are goods give us greatness of soul, but riches give us arrogance. And arrogance is nothing else than a false show of greatness.

"According to that argument," the objector says, "riches are not only not a good, but are a positive evil." Now they would be an evil if they did harm of themselves, and if, as I remarked, it were the efficient cause which inheres in them; in fact, however, it is the antecedent cause which inheres in riches, and indeed it is that cause which, so far from merely arousing the spirit, actually drags it along by force. Yes, riches shower upon us a semblance of the good, which is like the reality and wins credence in the eyes of many men. The antecedent cause inheres in virtue also; it is this which brings on envy—for many men become unpopular because of their wisdom, and many men because of their justice. But this cause, though it inheres in virtue, is not the result of virtue itself, nor is it a mere semblance of the reality; nay, on the contrary, far more like the reality is that vision which is flashed by virtue upon the spirits of men, summoning them to love it and marvel thereat.

Posidonius thinks that the syllogism should be framed as follows: "Things which bestow upon the soul no greatness or confidence or freedom from care are not goods. But riches and health and similar conditions do none of these things; therefore, riches and health are not goods." This syllogism he then goes on to extend still farther in the following way: "Things which bestow upon the soul no greatness or confidence or freedom from care, but on the other hand create in it arrogance, vanity, and insolence, are evils. But things which are the gift of Fortune drive us into these evil ways. Therefore these things are not goods." "But," says the objector, "by such reasoning, things which are the gift of Fortune will not even be advantages." No, advantages and goods stand each in a different situation. An advantage is that which contains more of usefulness than of annoyance. But a good ought to be unmixed and with no element in it of harmfulness. A thing is not good if it contains more benefit than injury, but only if it contains nothing but benefit. Besides, advantages may be predicated of animals, of men who are less than perfect, and of fools. Hence the advantageous may have an element of disadvantage mingled with it, but the word "advantageous" is used of the compound because it is judged by its predominant element. The good, however, can be predicated of the wise man alone; it is bound to be without alloy.

Be of good cheer; there is only one knot left for you to untangle, though it is a knot for a Hercules: "Good does not result from evil. But riches result from numerous cases of poverty; therefore, riches are not a good." This syllogism is not recognized by our school, but the Peripatetics both concoct it and give its solution. Posidonius, however, remarks that this fallacy, which has been bandied about among all the schools of dialectic, is refuted by Antipater as follows: "The word 'poverty' is used to denote, not the possession of something, but the non-possession or, as the ancients have put it, deprivation (for the Greeks use the phrase 'by deprivation,' meaning 'negatively'). 'Poverty' states, not what a man has, but what he has not. Consequently there can be no fullness resulting from a multitude of voids; many positive things, and not many deficiencies, make up riches. "You have," says he, "a wrong notion of the meaning of what poverty is. For poverty does not mean the possession of little, but the non-possession of much; it is used, therefore, not of what a man has, but of what he lacks." I could express my meaning more easily if there were a Latin word which could translate the Greek word which means "not-possessing." Antipater assigns this quality to poverty, but for my part I cannot see what else poverty is than the possession of little. If ever we have plenty of leisure, we shall investigate the question: what is the essence of riches, and what the essence of poverty; but when the time comes, we shall also consider whether it is not better to try to mitigate poverty, and to relieve wealth of its arrogance, than to quibble about the words as if the question of the things were already decided.

Let us suppose that we have been summoned to an assembly; an act dealing with the abolition of riches has been brought before the meeting. Shall we be supporting it, or opposing it, if we use these syllogisms? Will these syllogisms help us to bring it about that the Roman people shall demand poverty and praise it—poverty, the foundation and cause of their empire—and, on the other hand, shall shrink in fear from their present wealth, reflecting that they have found it among the victims of their conquests, that wealth is the source from which office-seeking and bribery and disorder* have burst into a city once characterized by the utmost scrupulousness and sobriety, and that because of wealth an exhibition all too lavish is made of the spoils of conquered nations; reflecting, finally, that whatever one people has snatched away from all the rest may still more easily be snatched by all away from one? Nay, it were better to support this law by our conduct and to subdue our desires by direct assault rather than to circumvent them by logic. If we can, let us speak more boldly; if not, let us speak more frankly. Farewell.

90. ON THE PART PLAYED BY PHILOSOPHY IN THE PROGRESS OF MAN

Who can doubt, my dear Lucilius, that life is the gift of the immortal gods, but that living well is the gift of philosophy? Hence the idea that our debt to philosophy is greater than our debt to the gods, in proportion as a good life is more of a benefit than mere life, would be regarded as correct, were not philosophy itself a boon which the gods have bestowed upon us. They have given the knowledge thereof to none, but the faculty of acquiring it they have given to all. For if they had made philosophy also a general good, and if we were gifted with understanding at our birth, wisdom would have lost her best attribute—that she is not one of the gifts of Fortune. For as it is, the precious and noble characteristic of wisdom is that she does not advance to meet us, that each man is indebted to himself for her, and that we do not seek her at the hands of others.

What would there be in philosophy worthy of your respect, if she were a thing that came by bounty? Her sole function is to discover the truth about things divine and things human. From her side religion never departs, nor duty, nor justice, nor any of the whole company of virtues which cling together in close-united fellowship. Philosophy has taught us to worship that which is divine, to love that which is human; she has told us that with the gods lies dominion, and among men, fellowship. This fellowship remained unspoiled for a long time, until avarice tore the community asunder and became the cause

* Seneca here bursts into a diatribe on the corruption of Rome, a habit that may be found in many other of his writings.

of poverty, even in the case of those whom she herself had most enriched. For men cease to possess all things the moment they desire all things for their own.

But the first men and those who sprang from them, still unspoiled, followed nature, having one man as both their leader and their law, entrusting themselves to the control of one better than themselves. For nature has the habit of subjecting the weaker to the stronger. Even among the dumb animals those which are either biggest or fiercest hold sway. It is no weakling bull that leads the herd; it is one that has beaten the other males by his might and his muscle. In the case of elephants, the tallest goes first; among men, the best is regarded as the highest. That is why it was to the mind that a ruler was assigned; and for that reason the greatest happiness rested with those peoples among whom a man could not be the more powerful unless he were the better. For that man can safely accomplish what he will who thinks he can do nothing except what he ought to do.

Accordingly, in that age which is maintained to be the golden age, Posidonius holds that the government was under the jurisdiction of the wise. They kept their hands under control, and protected the weaker from the stronger. They gave advice, both to do and not to do; they showed what was useful and what was useless. Their forethought provided that their subjects should lack nothing; their bravery warded off dangers; their kindness enriched and adorned their subjects. For them, ruling was a service, not an exercise of royalty. No ruler tried his power against those to whom he owed the beginnings of his power; and no one had the inclination, or the excuse, to do wrong, since the ruler ruled well and the subject obeyed well, and the king could utter no greater threat against disobedient subjects than that they should depart from the kingdom.

But when once vice stole in and kingdoms were transformed into tyrannies, a need arose for laws and these very laws were in turn framed by the wise. Solon, who established Athens upon a firm basis by just laws, was one of the seven men renowned for their wisdom. Had Lycurgus lived in the same period, an eighth would have been added to that hallowed number seven. The laws of Zaleucus and Charondas are praised; it was not in the forum or in the offices of skilled counsellors, but in the silent and holy retreat of Pythagoras, that these two men learned the principles of justice which they were to establish in Sicily (which at that time was prosperous) and throughout Grecian Italy.

Up to this point I agree with Posidonius; but that philosophy discovered the arts of which life makes use in its daily round I refuse to admit. Nor will I ascribe to it an artisan's glory. Posidonius says: "When men were scattered over the earth, protected by eaves or by the dug-out shelter of a cliff or by the trunk of a hollow tree, it was philosophy that taught them to build houses." But I, for my part, do not hold that philosophy devised these shrewdly-contrived dwellings of ours which rise story upon story, where city crowds against city, any more than that she invented the fish-preserves, which are enclosed for the purpose of saving men's gluttony from having to run the risk of storms, and in order that, no matter how wildly the sea is raging, luxury may have its safe harbours in which to fatten fancy breeds of fish. What! Was it philosophy that taught the use of keys and bolts? Nay, what was that except giving a hint to avarice? Was it philosophy that erected all these towering tenements, so dangerous to the persons who dwell in them? Was it not enough for man to provide himself a roof of any chance covering, and to contrive for himself some natural retreat without the help of art and without trouble? Believe me, that was a happy age, before the days of architects, before the days of builders! All this sort of thing was born when luxury was being born—this matter of cutting timbers square and cleaving a beam with unerring hand as the saw made its way over the marked-out line.

The primal man with wedges split his wood.

For they were not preparing a roof for a future banquet-ball; for no such use did they carry the pine trees or the firs along the trembling streets with a long row of drays—merely to fasten thereon panelled ceilings heavy with gold. Forked poles erected at either end propped up their houses. With close-packed branches and with leaves heaped up and laid sloping they contrived a drainage for even the heaviest rains. Beneath such dwellings, they lived, but they lived in peace. A thatched roof once covered free men; under marble and gold dwells slavery.

On another point also I differ from Posidonius, when he holds that mechanical tools were the invention of wise men. For on that basis one might maintain that those were wise who taught the arts

Of setting traps for game, and liming twigs
For birds, and girdling mighty woods with dogs.

It was man's ingenuity, not his wisdom, that discovered all these devices. And I also differ from him when he says that wise men discovered our mines of iron and copper, "when the earth, scorched by forest fires, melted the veins of ore which lay near the surface and caused the metal to gush forth." Nay, the sort of men who discover such things are the sort of men who are busied with them. Nor do I consider this question so subtle as Posidonius thinks, namely, whether the hammer or the tongs came first into use. They were both invented by some man whose mind was nimble and keen, but not great or exalted; and the same holds true of any other discovery which can only be made by means of a bent body and of a mind whose gaze is upon the ground.

The wise man was easy-going in his way of living. And why not? Even in our own times he would prefer to be as little cumbered as possible. How, I ask, can you consistently admire both Diogenes and Daedalus? Which of these two seems to you a wise man—the one who devised the saw, or the one who, on seeing a boy drink water from the hollow of his hand, forthwith took his cup from his wallet and broke it, upbraiding himself with these words: "Fool that I am, to have been carrying superfluous baggage all this time!" and then curled himself up in his tub and lay down to sleep? In these our own times, which man, pray, do you deem the wiser—the one who invents a process for spraying saffron perfumes to a tremendous height from hidden pipes, who fills or empties canals by a sudden rush of waters, who so cleverly constructs a dining-room with a ceiling of movable panels that it presents one pattern after another, the roof changing as often as the courses—or the one who proves to others, as well as to himself, that nature has laid upon us no stern and difficult law when she tells us that we can live without the marble-cutter and the engineer, that we can clothe ourselves without traffic in silk fabrics, that we can have everything that is indispensable to our use, provided only that we are content with what the earth has placed on its surface? If mankind were willing to listen to this sage, they would know that the cook is as superfluous to them as the soldier. Those were wise men, or at any rate like the wise, who found the care of the body a problem easy to solve. The things that are indispensable require no elaborate pains for their acquisition; it is only the luxuries that call for labour. Follow nature, and you will need no skilled craftsmen.

Nature did not wish us to be harassed. For whatever she forced upon us, she equipped us. "But cold cannot be endured by the naked body." What then? Are there not the skins of wild beasts and other animals, which can protect us well enough, and more than enough, from the cold? Do not many tribes cover their bodies with the bark of trees? Are not the feathers of birds sewn together to serve for clothing? Even at the present day does not a large portion of the

Scythian tribe garb itself in the skins of foxes and mice, soft to the touch and impervious to the winds? "For all that, men must have some thicker protection than the skin, in order to keep off the heat of the sun in summer." What then? Has not antiquity produced many retreats which, hollowed out either by the damage wrought by time or by any other occurrence you will, have opened into caverns? What then? Did not the very first-comers take twigs and weave them by hand into wicker mats, smear them with common mud, and then with stubble and other wild grasses construct a roof, and thus pass their winters secure, the rains carried off by means of the sloping gables? What then? Do not the peoples on the edge of the Syrtes dwell in dug-out houses and indeed all the tribes who, because of the too fierce blaze of the sun, possess no protection sufficient to keep off the heat except the parched soil itself?

Nature was not so hostile to man that, when she gave all the other animals an easy rôle in life, she made it impossible for him alone to live without all these artifices. None of these was imposed upon us by her; none of them had to be painfully sought out that our lives might be prolonged. All things were ready for us at our birth; it is we that have made everything difficult for ourselves, through our disdain for what is easy. Houses, shelter, creature comforts, food, and all that has now become the source of vast trouble, were ready at hand, free to all, and obtainable for trifling pains. For the limit everywhere corresponded to the need; it is we that have made all those things valuable, we that have made them admired, we that have caused them to be sought for by extensive and manifold devices. Nature suffices for what she demands. Luxury has turned her back upon nature; each day she expands herself, in all the ages she has been gathering strength, and by her wit promoting the vices. At first, luxury began to lust for what nature regarded as superfluous, then for that which was contrary to nature; and finally she made the soul a bondsman to the body, and bade it be an utter slave to the body's lusts. All these crafts by which the city is patrolled—or shall I say kept in uproar—are but engaged in the body's business; time was when all things were offered to the body as to a slave, but now they are made ready for it as for a master. Accordingly, hence have come the workshops of the weavers and the carpenters; hence the savoury smells of the professional cooks; hence the wantonness of those who teach wanton postures, and wanton and affected singing. For that moderation which nature prescribes, which limits our desires by resources restricted to our needs, has abandoned the field; it has now come to this—that to want only what is enough is a sign both of boorishness and of utter destitution.

It is hard to believe, my dear Lucilius, how easily the charm of eloquence wins even great men away from the truth. Take, for example, Posidonius—who, in my estimation, is of the number of those who have contributed most to philosophy—when he wishes to describe the art of weaving. He tells how, first, some threads are twisted and some drawn out from the soft, loose mass of wool; next, how the upright warp keeps the threads stretched by means of hanging weights; then, how the inserted thread of the woof, which softens the hard texture of the web which holds it fast on either side, is forced by the batten to make a compact union with the warp. He maintains that even the weaver's art was discovered by wise men, forgetting that the more complicated art which he describes was invented in later days—the art wherein

The web is bound to frame; asunder now
The reed doth part the warp. Between the threads
Is shot the woof by pointed shuttles borne;
The broad comb's well-notched teeth then drive it home.

Suppose he had had the opportunity of seeing the weaving of our own day, which produces the clothing that will conceal nothing, the clothing which affords—I will not say no protection to the body, but none even to modesty!

Posidonius then passes on to the farmer. With no less eloquence he describes the ground which is broken up and crossed again by the plough, so that the earth, thus loosened, may allow freer play to the roots; then the seed is sown, and the weeds plucked out by hand, lest any chance growth or wild plant spring up and spoil the crop. This trade also, he declares, is the creation of the wise—just as if cultivators of the soil were not even at the present day discovering countless new methods of increasing the soil's fertility! Furthermore, not confining his attention to these arts, he even degrades the wise man by sending him to the mill. For he tells us how the sage, by imitating the processes of nature, began to make bread. "The grain," he says, "once taken into the mouth, is crushed by the flinty teeth, which meet in hostile encounter, and whatever grain slips out the tongue turns back to the selfsame teeth. Then it is blended into a mass, that it may the more easily pass down the slippery throat. When this has readied the stomach, it is digested by the stomach's equable heat; then, and not till then, it is assimilated with the body. Following this pattern," he goes on, "someone placed two rough stones, the one above the other, in imitation of the teeth, one set of which is stationary and awaits the motion of the other set. Then by the rubbing of the one stone against the other, the grain is crushed and brought back again and again, until by frequent rubbing it is reduced to powder. Then this man sprinkled the meal with water, and by continued manipulation subdued the mass and moulded the loaf. This loaf was, at first, baked by hot ashes or by an earthen vessel glowing hot; later on ovens were gradually discovered and the other devices whose heat will render obedience to the sage's will." Posidonius came very near declaring that even the cobbler's trade was the discovery of the wise man.

Reason did indeed devise all these things, but it was not right reason. It was man, but not the wise man, that discovered them; just as they invented ships, in which we cross rivers and seas—ships fitted with sails for the purpose of catching the force of the winds, ships with rudders added at the stern in order to turn the vessel's course in one direction or another. The model followed was the fish, which steers itself by its tail, and by its slightest motion on this side or on that bends its swift course. "But," says Posidonius, "the wise man did indeed discover all these things; they were, however, too petty for him to deal with himself and so he entrusted them to his meaner assistants." Not so; these early inventions were thought out by no other class of men than those who have them in charge today. We know that certain devices have come to light only within our own memory—such as the use of windows which admit the clear light through transparent tiles, and such as the vaulted baths, with pipes let into their walls for the purpose of diffusing the heat which maintains an even temperature in their lowest as well as in their highest spaces. Why need I mention the marble with which our temples and our private houses are resplendent? Or the rounded and polished masses of stone by means of which we erect colonnades and buildings roomy enough for nations? Or our signs for whole words, which enable us to take down a speech, however rapidly uttered, matching speed of tongue by speed of hand? All this sort of thing has been devised by the lowest grade of slaves. Wisdom's seat is higher; she trains not the hands, but is mistress of our minds.

Would you know what wisdom has brought forth to light, what she has accomplished? It is not the graceful poses of the body, or the varied notes produced by horn and flute, whereby the breath is received and, as it passes out or through, is transformed into voice. It is not wisdom that contrives arms, or walls, or instruments useful in war; nay, her voice is for peace, and she summons all mankind to concord. It is not she, I maintain, who is the artisan of our indispensable implements of daily use. Why do you assign to her such petty things? You see in her the skilled artisan of life. The other arts, it is true, wisdom has under her control; for he whom life serves is also served by the things which equip life. But wisdom's course is toward the state of happiness; thither she guides us, thither she opens the way for us. She shows us what things are evil and what things are seemingly evil; she strips our minds of vain illusion. She bestows upon us a greatness which is substantial, but she represses the greatness which is inflated and showy but filled with emptiness; and she does not permit us to be ignorant of the difference between what is great and what is but swollen; nay, she delivers to us the knowledge of the whole of nature and of her own nature. She discloses to us what the gods are and of what sort they are; what are the nether gods, the household deities, and the protecting spirits; what are the souls which have been endowed with lasting life and have been admitted to the second class of divinities, where is their abode and what their activities, powers, and will.

Such are wisdom's rites of initiation, by means of which is unlocked, not a village shrine, but the vast temple of all the gods—the universe itself, whose true apparitions and true aspects she offers to the gaze of our minds. For the vision of our eyes is too dull for sights so great. Then she goes back to the beginnings of things, to the eternal Reason which was imparted to the whole, and to the force which inheres in all the seeds of things, giving them the power to fashion each thing according to its kind. Then wisdom begins to inquire about the soul, whence it comes, where it dwells, how long it abides, into how many divisions it falls. Finally, she has turned her attention from the corporeal to the incorporeal, and has closely examined truth and the marks whereby truth is known, inquiring next how that which is equivocal can be distinguished from the truth, whether in life or in language; for in both are elements of the false mingled with the true.

It is my opinion that the wise man has not withdrawn himself, as Posidonius thinks, from those arts which we were discussing, but that he never took them up at all. For he would have judged that nothing was worth discovering that he would not afterwards judge to be worth using always. He would not take up things which would have to be laid aside.

"But Anacharsis," says Posidonius, "invented the potter's wheel, whose whirling gives shape to vessels." Then because the potter's wheel is mentioned in Homer, people prefer to believe that Homer's verses are false rather than the story of Posidonius! But I maintain that Anacharsis was not the creator of this wheel; and even if he was, although he was a wise man when he invented it, yet he did not invent it *qua* "wise man"—just as there are a great many things which wise men do as men, not as wise men. Suppose, for example, that a wise man is exceedingly fleet of foot; he will outstrip all the runners in the race by virtue of being fleet, not by virtue of his wisdom. I should like to show Posidonius some glass-blower who by his breath moulds the glass into manifold shapes which could scarcely be fashioned by the most skilful hand. Nay, these discoveries have been made since we men have ceased to discover wisdom.

But Posidonius again remarks, "Democritus is said to have discovered the arch, whose effect was that the curving line of stones, which gradually lean toward each other, is bound together by the keystone." I am inclined to pronounce this statement false. For there must have been, before Democritus, bridges and gateways in which the curvature did not begin until about the top. It seems to have quite slipped your memory that this same Democritus discovered how ivory could be softened, how, by boiling, a pebble could be transformed into an emerald—the same process used even today for colouring stones which are found to be amenable to this treatment! It may have been a wise man who discovered all such things, but he did not discover them by virtue of being a wise man; for he does many things which we see done just as well, or even more skilfully and dexterously, by men who are utterly lacking in sagacity.

Do you ask what, then, the wise man has found out and what he has brought to light? First of all there is truth, and nature; and nature he has not followed as the other animals do, with eyes too dull to perceive the divine in it. In the second place, there is the law of life, and life he has made to conform to universal principles; and he has taught us, not merely to know the gods, but to follow them, and to welcome the gifts of chance precisely as if they were divine commands. He has forbidden us to give heed to false opinions, and has weighed the value of each thing by a true standard of appraisement. He has condemned those pleasures with which remorse is intermingled, and has praised those goods which will always satisfy; and he has published the truth abroad that he is most happy who has no need of happiness, and that he is most powerful who has power over himself.

I am not speaking of that philosophy which has placed the citizen outside his country and the gods outside the universe, and which has bestowed virtue upon pleasure, but rather of that philosophy which counts nothing good except what is honourable—one which cannot be cajoled by the gifts either of man or Fortune, one whose value is that it cannot be bought for any value. That this philosophy existed in such a rude age, when the arts and crafts were still unknown and when useful things could only be learned by use—this I refuse to believe.

Next there came the fortune-favoured period when the bounties of nature lay open to all, for men's indiscriminate use, before avarice and luxury had broken the bonds which held mortals together, and they, abandoning their communal existence, had separated and turned to plunder. The men of the second age were not wise men, even though they did what wise men should do. Indeed, there is no other condition of the human race that anyone would regard more highly; and if God should commission a man to fashion earthly creatures and to bestow institutions upon peoples, this man would approve of no other system than that which obtained among the men of that age, when

No ploughman tilled the soil, nor was it right
To portion off or bound one's property.
Men shared their gains, and earth more freely gave
Her riches to her sons who sought them not.

What race of men was ever more blest than that race? They enjoyed all nature in partnership. Nature sufficed for them, now the guardian, as before she was the parent, of all; and this her gift consisted of the assured possession by each man of the common resources. Why should I not even call that race the richest among mortals, since you could not find a poor person among them?

But avarice broke in upon a condition so happily ordained, and, by its eagerness to lay something away and to turn it to its own private use, made all things the property of others, and reduced itself from boundless wealth to straitened need. It was avarice that introduced poverty and, by craving much, lost all. And so, although she now tries to make good her loss, although she adds one estate to another, evicting a neighbour either by buying him out or by wronging him, although she extends her country-seats to the size of provinces and defines ownership as meaning extensive travel through one's own property—in spite of all these efforts of hers no enlargement of our boundaries will bring us back to the condition from which we have departed.

When there is no more that we can do, we shall possess much; but we once possessed the whole world! The very soil was more productive when untilled, and yielded more than enough for peoples who refrained from despoiling one another. Whatever gift nature had produced, men found as much pleasure in revealing it to another as in having discovered it. It was possible for no man either to surpass another or to fall short of him; what there was, was divided among unquarrelling friends. Not yet had the stronger begun to lay hands upon the weaker; not yet had the miser, by hiding away what lay before him, begun to shut off his neighbour from even the necessities of life; each cared as much for his neighbour as for himself. Armour lay unused, and the hand, unstained by human blood, had turned all its hatred against wild beasts. The men of that day, who had found in some dense grove protection against the sun, and security against the severity of winter or of rain in their mean hiding-places, spent their lives under the branches of the trees and passed tranquil nights without a sigh. Care vexes us in our purple, and routs us from our beds with the sharpest of goads; but how soft was the sleep the hard earth bestowed upon the men of that day! No fretted and panelled ceilings hung over them, but as they lay beneath the open sky the stars glided quietly above them, and the firmament, night's noble pageant, marched swiftly by, conducting its mighty task in silence. For them by day, as well as by night, the visions of this most glorious abode were free and open. It was their joy to watch the constellations as they sank from mid-heaven and others, again, as they rose from their hidden abodes. What else but joy could it be to wander among the marvels which dotted the heavens far and wide? But you of the present day shudder at every sound your houses make, and as you sit among your frescoes the slightest creak makes you shrink in terror. *They* had no houses as big as cities. The air, the breezes blowing free through the open spaces, the flitting shade of crag or tree, springs crystal-clear and streams not spoiled by man's work, whether by water-pipe or by any confinement of the channel, but running at will, and meadows beautiful without the use of art—amid such scenes were their rude homes, adorned with rustic hand. Such a dwelling was in accordance with nature; therein it was a joy to live, fearing neither the dwelling itself nor for its safety. In these days, however, our houses constitute a large portion of our dread.

But no matter how excellent and guileless was the life of the men of that age, they were not wise men; for that title is reserved for the highest achievement. Still, I would not deny that they were men of lofty spirit and—I may use the phrase—fresh from the gods. For there is no doubt that the world produced a better progeny before it was yet worn out. However, not all were endowed with mental faculties of highest perfection, though in all cases their native powers were more sturdy than ours and more fitted for toil. For nature does not bestow virtue; it is an art to become good. They, at least, searched not in the lowest dregs of the earth for gold, nor yet for silver or transparent stones;

and they still were merciful even to the dumb animals—so far removed was that epoch from the custom of slaying man by man, not in anger or through fear, but just to make a show! They had as yet no embroidered garments nor did they weave cloth of gold; gold was not yet even mined.

What, then, is the conclusion of the matter? It was by reason of their ignorance of things that the men of those days were innocent; and it makes a great deal of difference whether one wills not to sin or has not the knowledge to sin. Justice was unknown to them, unknown prudence, unknown also self-control and bravery; but their rude life possessed certain qualities akin to all these virtues. Virtue is not vouchsafed to a soul unless that soul has been trained and taught, and by unremitting practise brought to perfection. For the attainment of this boon, but not in the possession of it, were we born; and even in the best of men, before you refine them by instruction, there is but the stuff of virtue, not virtue itself. Farewell.

91. ON THE LESSON TO BE DRAWN FROM THE BURNING OF LYONS

Our friend Liberalis is now downcast; for he has just heard of the fire which has wiped out the colony of Lyons. Such a calamity might upset anyone at all, not to speak of a man who dearly loves his country. But this incident has served to make him inquire about the strength of his own character, which he has trained, I suppose, just to meet situations that he thought might cause him fear. I do not wonder, however, that he was free from apprehension touching an evil so unexpected and practically unheard of as this, since it is without precedent. For fire has damaged many a city, but has annihilated none. Even when fire has been hurled against the walls by the hand of a foe, the flame dies out in many places, and although continually renewed, rarely devours so wholly as to leave nothing for the sword. Even an earthquake has scarcely ever been so violent and destructive as to overthrow whole cities. Finally, no conflagration has ever before blazed forth so savagely in any town that nothing was left for a second. So many beautiful buildings, any single one of which would make a single town famous, were wrecked in one night. In time of such deep peace an event has taken place worse than men can possibly fear even in time of war. Who can believe it? When weapons are everywhere at rest and when peace prevails throughout the world, Lyons, the pride of Gaul, is missing!

Fortune has usually allowed all men, when she has assailed them collectively, to have a foreboding of that which they were destined to suffer. Every great creation has had granted to it a period of reprieve before its fall; but in this case, only a single night elapsed between the city at its greatest and the city non-existent. In short, it takes me longer to tell you it has perished than it took for the city to perish.

All this has affected our friend Liberalis, bending his will, which is usually so steadfast and erect in the face of his own trials. And not without reason has he been shaken; for it is the unexpected that puts the heaviest load upon us. Strangeness adds to the weight of calamities, and every mortal feels the greater pain as a result of that which also brings surprise.

Therefore, nothing ought to be unexpected by us. Our minds should be sent forward in advance to meet all problems, and we should consider, not what is wont to happen, but what can happen. For what is there in existence that Fortune, when she has so willed, does not drag down from the very height of its prosperity? And what is there that she does not the more violently assail the more brilliantly it shines? What is laborious or difficult for her? She does not always attack in one way or even with her full strength; at one time she summons our own hands against us; at another time, content with her own powers, she makes use of no agent in devising perils for us. No time is exempt; in the midst of our very pleasures there spring up causes of suffering. War arises in the midst of peace, and that which we depended upon for protection is transformed into a cause of fear; friend becomes enemy, ally becomes foeman, The summer calm is stirred into sudden storms, wilder than the storms of winter. With no foe in sight we are victims of such fates as foes inflict, and if other causes of disaster fail, excessive good Fortune finds them for itself. The most temperate are assailed by illness, the strongest by wasting disease, the most innocent by chastisement, the most secluded by the noisy mob.

Chance chooses some new weapon by which to bring her strength to bear against us, thinking we have forgotten her. Whatever structure has been reared by a long sequence of years, at the cost of great toil and through the great kindness of the gods, is scattered and dispersed by a single day. Nay, he who has said "a day" has granted too long a postponement to swift-coming misfortune; an hour, an instant of time, suffices for the overthrow of empires! It would be some consolation for the feebleness of ourselves and our works, if all things should perish as slowly as they come into being; but as it is, increases are of sluggish growth, but the way to ruin is rapid. Nothing, whether public or private, is stable; the destinies of men, no less than those of cities, are in a whirl. Amid the greatest calm terror arises, and though no external agencies stir up commotion, yet evils burst forth from sources whence they were least expected. Thrones which have stood the shock of civil and foreign wars crash to the ground though no one sets them tottering. How few the states which have carried their good Fortune through to the end!

We should therefore reflect upon all contingencies, and should fortify our minds against the evils which may possibly come. Exile, the torture of disease, wars, shipwreck—we must think on these. Chance may tear you from your country or your country from you, or may banish you to the desert; this very place, where throngs are stifling, may become a desert. Let us place before our eyes in its entirety the nature of man's lot, and if we would not be overwhelmed, or even dazed, by those unwonted evils, as if they were novel, let us summon to our minds beforehand, not as great an evil as oftentimes happens, but the very greatest evil that possibly can happen. We must reflect upon Fortune fully and completely.

How often have cities in Asia, how often in Achaia, been laid low by a single shock of earthquake! How many towns in Syria, how many in Macedonia, have been swallowed up! How often has this kind of devastation laid Cyprus in ruins! How often has Paphos collapsed! Not infrequently are tidings brought to us of the utter destruction of entire cities; yet how small a part of the world are we, to whom such tidings often come!

Let us rise, therefore, to confront the operations of Fortune, and whatever happens, let us have the assurance that it is not so great as rumour advertises it to be. A rich city has been laid in ashes, the jewel of the provinces, counted as one of them and yet not included with them; rich though it was, nevertheless it was set upon a single hill, and that not very large in extent. But of all those cities, of whose magnificence and grandeur you hear today, the very traces will be blotted out by time. Do you not see how, in Achaia, the foundations of the most famous cities have already crumbled to nothing, so that no trace is left to show that they ever even existed? Not only does that which has been made with hands totter to the ground, not only is that which has been set in place by man's art and man's efforts overthrown by the passing days; nay, the peaks of mountains dissolve, whole tracts have settled, and places which once stood far from the sight of the sea are now covered by the waves. The mighty power of fires has eaten away the hills through whose sides they used to glow, and has levelled to the ground peaks which were once most lofty—the sailor's solace and his beacon. The works of nature herself are harassed; hence we ought to bear with untroubled minds the destruction of cities. They stand but to fall! This doom awaits them, one and all; it may be that some internal force, and blasts of violence which are tremendous because their way is blocked, will throw off the weight which holds them down; or that a whirlpool of raging currents, mightier because they are hidden in the bosom of the earth, will break through that which resists its power; or that the vehemence of flames will burst asunder the framework of the earth's crust; or that time, from which nothing is safe, will reduce them little by little; or that a pestilential climate will drive their inhabitants away and the mould will corrode their deserted walls. It would be tedious to recount all the ways by which fate may come; but this one thing I know: all the works of mortal man have been doomed to mortality, and in the midst of things which have been destined to die, we live!

Hence it is thoughts like these, and of this kind, which I am offering as consolation to our friend Liberalis, who burns with a love for his country that is beyond belief. Perhaps its destruction has been brought about only that it may be raised up again to a better destiny. Oftentimes a reverse has but made room for more prosperous fortune. Many structures have fallen only to rise to a greater height. Timagenes, who had a grudge against Rome and her prosperity, used to say that the only reason he was grieved when conflagrations occurred in Rome was his knowledge that better buildings would arise than those which had gone down in the flames. And probably in this city of Lyons, too, all its citizens will earnestly strive that everything shall be rebuilt better in size and security than what they have lost. May it be built to endure and, under happier auspices, for a longer existence! This is indeed but the hundredth year since this colony was founded—not the limit even of a man's lifetime. Led forth by Plancus, the natural advantages of its site have caused it to wax strong and reach the numbers which it contains today; and yet how many calamities of the greatest severity has it endured within the space of an old man's life!

Therefore let the mind be disciplined to understand and to endure its own lot, and let it have the knowledge that there is nothing which Fortune does not dare—that she has the same jurisdiction over empires as over emperors, the same power over cities as over the citizens who dwell therein. We must not cry out at any of these calamities. Into such a world have we entered, and under such laws do we live. If you like it, obey; if not, depart whithersoever you wish. Cry out in anger if any unfair measures are taken with reference to you individually; but if this inevitable law is binding upon the highest and the lowest alike, be reconciled to fate, by which all things are dissolved. You should not estimate our worth by our funeral mounds or by these monuments of unequal size which line the road; their ashes level all men! We are unequal at birth, but are equal in death. What I say about cities I say also about their inhabitants. Ardea was captured as well as Rome. The great founder of human law has not made distinctions between us on the basis of high lineage or of illustrious names, except while we live. When, however, we come to the end which awaits mortals, he says: "Depart, ambition! To all creatures that burden the earth let one and the same law apply!" For enduring all things, we are equal; no one is more frail than another, no one more certain of his own life on the morrow.

Alexander, king of Macedon, began to study geometry; unhappy man, because he would thereby learn how puny was that earth of which he had seized but a fraction! Unhappy man, I repeat, because he was bound to understand that he was bearing a false title. For who can be "great" in that which is puny? The lessons which were being taught him were intricate and could be learned only by assiduous application; they were not the kind to be comprehended by a madman, who let his thoughts range beyond the ocean. "Teach me something easy!" he cries; but his teacher answers: "These things are the same for all, as hard for one as for another." Imagine that nature is saying to us: "Those things of which you complain are the same for all. I cannot give anything easier to any man, but whoever wishes will make things easier for himself." In what way? By equanimity. You must suffer pain, and thirst, and hunger, and old age too, if a longer stay among men shall be granted you; you must be sick, and you must suffer loss and death. Nevertheless, you should not believe those whose noisy clamour surrounds you; none of these things is an evil, none is beyond your power to bear, or is burdensome. It is only by common opinion that there is anything formidable in them. Your fearing death is therefore like your fear of gossip. But what is more foolish than a man afraid of words? Our friend Demetrius is wont to put it cleverly when he says: "For me the talk of ignorant men is like the rumblings which issue from the belly. For," he adds, "what difference does it make to me whether such rumblings come from above or from below?" What madness it is to be afraid of disrepute in the judgment of the disreputable! Just as you have had no cause for shrinking in terror from the talk of men, so you have no cause now to shrink from these things, which you would never fear had not their talk forced fear upon you. Does it do any harm to a good man to be besmirched by unjust gossip? Then let not this sort of thing damage death, either, in our estimation; death also is in bad odour. But no one of those who malign death has made trial of it.

Meanwhile it is foolhardy to condemn that of which you are ignorant. This one thing, however, you do know—that death is helpful to many, that it sets many free from tortures, want, ailments, sufferings, and weariness. We are in the power of nothing when once we have death in our own power! Farewell.

93. ON THE QUALITY, AS CONTRASTED WITH THE LENGTH, OF LIFE

While reading the letter in which you were lamenting the death of the philosopher Metronax as if he might have, and indeed ought to have, lived longer, I missed the spirit of fairness which abounds in all your discussions concerning men and things, but is lacking when you approach one single subject—as is indeed the case with us all. In other words, I have noticed many who deal fairly with their fellow-men, but none who deals fairly with the gods. We rail every day at Fate, saying, "Why has A been carried off in the very middle of his career? Why is not B carried off instead? Why should he prolong his old age, which is a burden to himself as well as to others?"

But tell me, pray, do you consider it fairer that you should obey Nature, or that Nature should obey you? And what difference does it make how soon you depart from a place which you must depart from sooner or later? We should strive, not to live long, but to live rightly; for to achieve long life you have need of Fate only, but for right living you need the soul. A life is really long if it is a full life; but fullness is not attained until the soul has rendered to itself its proper Good, that is, until it has assumed control over itself. What benefit does this older man derive from the eighty years he has spent in idleness? A person like him has not lived; he has merely tarried awhile in life. Nor has he died late in life; he has simply been a long time dying. He has lived eighty years, has he? That depends upon the date from which you reckon his death! Your other friend, however, departed in the bloom of his manhood. But he had fulfilled all the duties of a good citizen, a good friend, a good son; in no respect had he fallen short. His age may have been incomplete, but his life was complete. The other man has lived eighty years, has he? Nay, he has existed eighty years, unless perchance you mean by "he has lived" what we mean when we say that a tree "lives."

Pray, let us see to it, my dear Lucilius, that our lives, like jewels of great price, be noteworthy not because of their width but because of their weight. Let us measure them by their performance, not by their duration. Would you know wherein lies the difference between this hardy man who, despising Fortune, has served through every campaign of life and has attained to life's Supreme Good, and that other person over whose head many years have passed? The former exists even after his death; the latter has died even before he was dead.

We should therefore praise, and number in the company of the blest, that man who has invested well the portion of time, however little, that has been allotted to him; for such a one has seen the true light. He has not been one of the common herd. He has not only lived, but flourished. Sometimes he enjoyed fair skies; sometimes, as often happens, it was only through the clouds that there flashed to him the radiance of the mighty star.* Why do you ask: "How long did he live?" He still lives! At one bound he has passed over into posterity and has consigned himself to the guardianship of memory.

And yet I would not on that account decline for myself a few additional years; although, if my life's space be shortened, I shall not say that I have lacked aught that is essential to a happy life. For I have not planned to live up to the very last day that my greedy hopes had promised me; nay, I have looked upon every day as if it were my last. Why ask the date of my birth, or whether I am still enrolled on the register of the younger men?† What I have is my own. Just as one of small stature can be a perfect man, so a life of small compass can be a perfect life. Age ranks among the external things.‡ How long I am to exist is not mine to decide, but how long I shall go on existing in my present way is in my own control. This is the only thing you have the right to require of me—that I shall cease to measure out an inglorious age as it were in darkness, and devote myself to living instead of being carried along past life.

And what, you ask, is the fullest span of life? It is living until you possess wisdom. He who has attained wisdom has reached, not the furthermost, but the most important, goal. Such a one may indeed exult boldly and give thanks to the gods—aye, and to himself also—and he may count himself Nature's creditor for having lived. He will indeed have the right to do so, for he has paid

---

* *i.e.*, the Sun.

† Men between the ages of seventeen and forty-six.

‡ As riches, health, etc.

her back a better life than he has received. He has set up the pattern of a good man, showing the quality and the greatness of a good man. Had another year been added, it would merely have been like the past.

And yet how long are we to keep living? We have had the joy of learning the truth about the universe. We know from what beginnings Nature arises; how she orders the course of the heavens; by what successive changes she summons back the year; how she has brought to an end all things that ever have been, and has established herself as the only end of her own being. We know that the stars move by their own motion, and that nothing except the earth stands still, while all the other bodies run on with uninterrupted swiftness. We know how the moon outstrips the sun; why it is that the slower leaves the swifter behind; in what manner she receives her light, or loses it again; what brings on the night, and what brings back the day. To that place you must go where you are to have a closer view of all these things. "And yet," says the wise man, "I do not depart more valiantly because of this hope—because I judge the path lies clear before me to my own gods. I have indeed earned admission to their presence, and in fact have already been in their company; I have sent my soul to them as they had previously sent theirs to me. But suppose that I am utterly annihilated, and that after death nothing mortal remains; I have no less courage, even if, when I depart, my course leads—nowhere."

"But," you say, "he has not lived as many years as he might have lived." There are books which contain very few lines, admirable and useful in spite of their size; and there are also the *Annals of Tanusius*—you know how bulky the book is, and what men say of it. This is the case with the long life of certain persons—a state which resembles the *Annals of Tanusius*! Do you regard as more fortunate the fighter who is slain on the last day of the games than one who goes to his death in the middle of the festivities? Do you believe that anyone is so foolishly covetous of life that he would rather have his throat cut in the dressing-room than in the amphitheatre? It is by no longer an interval than this that we precede one another. Death visits each and all; the slayer soon follows the slain. It is an insignificant trifle, after all, that people discuss with so much concern. And anyhow, what does it matter for how long a time you avoid that which you cannot escape? Farewell.

96. ON FACING HARDSHIPS

Spite of all do you still chafe and complain, not understanding that, in all the evils to which you refer, there is really only one—the fact that you *do* chafe and complain? If you ask me, I think that for a *man* there is no misery unless there be something in the universe which he thinks miserable. I shall not endure myself on that day when I find anything unendurable.

I am ill; but that is a part of my lot. My slaves have fallen sick, my income has gone off, my house is rickety, I have been assailed by losses, accidents, toil, and fear; this is a common thing. Nay, that was an understatement; it was an inevitable thing. Such affairs come by order, and not by accident. If you will believe me, it is my inmost emotions that I am just now disclosing to you: when everything seems to go hard and uphill, I have trained myself not merely to obey God, but to agree with His decisions. I follow Him because my soul wills it, and not because I must. Nothing will ever happen to me that I shall receive with ill humour or with a wry face. I shall pay up all my taxes willingly. Now all the things which cause us to groan or recoil are part of the tax of life—things, my dear Lucilius, which you should never hope and never seek to escape.

It was disease of the bladder that made you apprehensive; downcast letters came from you; you were continually getting worse; I will touch the truth more closely, and say that you feared for your life. But come, did you not know, when you prayed for long life, that this was what you were praying for? A long life includes all these troubles, just as a long journey includes dust and mud and rain. "But," you cry, "I wished to live, and at the same time to be immune from all ills." Such a womanish cry does no credit to a man. Consider in what attitude you shall receive this prayer of mine (I offer it not only in a good, but in a noble spirit): "May gods and goddesses alike forbid that Fortune keep you in luxury!" Ask yourself voluntarily which you would choose if some god gave you the choice—a life in a café or life in a camp.

And yet life, Lucilius, is really a battle. For this reason those who are tossed about at sea, who proceed uphill and downhill over toilsome crags and heights, who go on campaigns that bring the greatest danger, are heroes and front-rank fighters; but persons who live in rotten luxury and ease while others toil are mere turtle-doves safe only because men despise them. Farewell.

101. ON THE FUTILITY OF PLANNING AHEAD

Every day AND every hour reveal to us what a nothing we are, and remind us with some fresh evidence that we have forgotten our weakness; then, as we plan for eternity, they compel us to look over our shoulders at Death.

Do you ask me what this preamble means? It refers to Cornelius Senecio, a distinguished and capable Roman knight, whom you knew: from humble beginnings he had advanced himself to fortune, and the rest of the path already lay downhill before him. For it is easier to grow in dignity than to make a start; and money is very slow to come where there is poverty; until it can creep out of that, it goes halting. Senecio was already bordering upon wealth, helped in that direction by two very powerful assets—knowing how to make money and how to keep it also; either one of these gifts might have made him a rich man. Here was a person who lived most simply, careful of health and wealth alike. He had, as usual, called upon me early in the morning, and had then spent the whole day, even up to nightfall, at the bedside of a friend who was seriously and hopelessly ill. After a comfortable dinner, he was suddenly seized with an acute attack of quinsy, and, with the breath clogged tightly in his swollen throat, barely lived until daybreak. So within a very few hours after the time when he had been performing all the duties of a sound and healthy man, he passed away. He who was venturing investments by land and sea, who had also entered public life and left no type of business untried, during the very realization of financial success and during the very onrush of the money that flowed into his coffers, was snatched from the world!

Graft now thy pears, Meliboeus, and set out
thy vines in their order!

But how foolish it is to set out one's life, when one is not even owner of the morrow! O what madness it is to plot out far-reaching hopes! To say: "I will buy and build, loan and call in money, win titles of honour, and then, old and full of years, I will surrender myself to a life of ease." Believe me when I say that everything is doubtful, even for those who are prosperous. No one has any right to draw for himself upon the future. The very thing that we grasp slips through our hands, and chance cuts into the actual hour which we are crowding so full.

Time does indeed roll along by fixed law, but as in darkness; and what is it to me whether Nature's course is sure, when my own is unsure?

We plan distant voyages and long-postponed home-comings after roaming over foreign shores, we plan for military service and the slow rewards of hard campaigns, we canvass for governorships and the promotions of one office after another and all the while death stands at our side; but since we never think of it except as it affects our neighbour, instances of mortality press upon us day by day, to remain in our minds only as long as they stir our wonder.

Yet what is more foolish than to wonder that something which may happen every day has happened on any one day? There is indeed a limit fixed for us, just where the remorseless law of Fate has fixed it; but none of us knows how near he is to this limit. Therefore, let us so order our minds as if we had come to the very end. Let us postpone nothing. Let us balance life's account every day. The greatest flaw in life is that it is always imperfect, and that a certain part of it is postponed. One who daily puts the finishing touches to his life is never in want of time. And yet, from this want arise fear and a craving for the future which eats away the mind. There is nothing more wretched than worry over the outcome of future events; as to the amount or the nature of that which remains, our troubled minds are set aflutter with unaccountable fear.

How, then, shall we avoid this vacillation? In one way only—if there be no reaching forward in our life, if it is withdrawn into itself. For he only is anxious about the future, to whom the present is unprofitable. But when I have paid my soul its due, when a soundly-balanced mind knows that a day differs not a whit from eternity—whatever days or problems the future may bring—then the soul looks forth from lofty heights and laughs heartily to itself when it thinks upon the ceaseless succession of the ages. For what disturbance can result from the changes and the instability of Chance, if you are sure in the face of that which is unsure?

Therefore, my dear Lucilius, begin at once to live, and count each separate day as a separate life. He who has thus prepared himself, he whose daily life has been a rounded whole, is easy in his mind; but those who live for hope alone find that the immediate future always slips from their grasp and that greed steals along in its place, and the fear of death, a curse which lays a curse upon everything else. Thence came that most debased of prayers, in which Maecenas does not refuse to suffer weakness, deformity, and as a climax the pain of crucifixion provided only that he may prolong the breath of life amid these sufferings:

Fashion me with a palsied hand,
Weak of foot, and a cripple;
Build upon me a crook-backed hump;
Shake my teeth till they rattle;
All is well, if my life remains.
Save, oh, save it, I pray you,
Though I sit on the piercing cross!

There he is, praying for that which, if it had befallen him, would be the most pitiable thing in the world! And seeking a postponement of suffering, as if he were asking for life! I should deem him most despicable had he wished to live up to the very time of crucifixion: "Nay," he cries, "you may weaken my body if you will only leave the breath of life in my battered and ineffective carcass! Maim me if you will, but allow me, misshapen and deformed as I may be, just a little more time in the world! You may nail me up and set my seat upon the piercing cross!" Is it worth while to weigh down upon one's own wound, and hang impaled upon a gibbet, that one may but postpone something which is the balm of troubles, the end of punishment? Is it worth all this to possess the breath of life only to give it up? What would you ask for Maecenas but the indulgence of Heaven? What does he mean by such womanish and indecent verse? What does he fear by making such an agreement? What does he mean by begging so vilely for life? He cannot ever have heard Vergil say:

Tell me, is Death so wretched as that?

He asks for the climax of suffering, and—what is still harder to bear—prolongation and extension of suffering; and what does he gain thereby? Merely the boon of a longer existence. But what sort of life is a lingering death? Can anyone be found who would prefer wasting away in pain, dying limb by limb, or letting out his life drop by drop, rather than expiring once for all? Can any man be found willing to be fastened to the accursed tree, long sickly, already deformed, swelling with ugly tumours on chest and shoulders, and draw the breath of life amid long-drawn-out agony? I think he would have many excuses for dying even before mounting the cross!

Deny, now, if you can, that Nature is very generous in making death inevitable. Many men have been prepared to enter upon still more shameful bargains: to betray friends in order to live longer themselves, or voluntarily to debase their children and so enjoy the light of day which is witness of all their sins. We must get rid of this craving for life, and learn that it makes no difference when your suffering comes, because at some time you are bound to suffer. The point is, not how long you live, but how nobly you live. And often this living nobly means that you cannot live long. Farewell.

107. ON OBEDIENCE TO THE UNIVERSAL WILL

Where is that common-sense of yours? Where that deftness in examining things? That greatness of soul? Have you come to be tormented by a trifle? Your slaves regarded your absorption in business as an opportunity for them to run away. Well, if your friends deceived you (for by all means let them have the name which we mistakenly bestowed upon them, and so call them, that they may incur more shame by not being such friends)—if your friends, I repeat, deceived you, all your affairs would lack something; as it is, you merely lack men who damaged your own endeavours and considered you burdensome to your neighbours. None of these things is unusual or unexpected. It is as nonsensical to be put out by such events as to complain of being spattered in the street or at getting befouled in the mud. The programme of life is the same as that of a bathing establishment, a crowd, or a journey: sometimes things will be thrown at you, and sometimes they will strike you by accident. Life is not a dainty business. You have started on a long journey; you are bound to slip, collide, fall, become weary, and cry out: "O for Death!"—or in other words, tell lies. At one stage you will leave a comrade behind you, at another you will bury someone, at another you will be apprehensive. It is amid stumblings of this sort that you must travel out this rugged journey.

Does one wish to die? Let the mind be prepared to meet everything; let it know that it has reached the heights round which the thunder plays. Let it know that it has arrived where—

Grief and avenging Care have set their couch,
And pallid sickness dwells, and drear Old Age.

With such messmates must you spend your days. Avoid them you cannot, but despise them you can. And you will despise them, if you often take thought and anticipate the future. Everyone approaches courageously a danger which he has prepared himself to meet long before, and withstands even hardships if he has previously practised how to meet them. But, contrariwise, the unprepared are panic-stricken even at the most trifling things. We must see to it that nothing shall come upon us unforeseen. And since things are all the more serious when they are unfamiliar, continual reflection will give you the power, no matter what the evil may be, not to play the unschooled boy.

"My slaves have run away from me!" Yes, other men have been robbed, blackmailed, slain, betrayed, stamped under foot, attacked by poison or by slander; no matter what trouble you mention, it has happened to many. Again, there are manifold kinds of missiles which are hurled at us. Some are planted in us, some are being brandished and at this very moment are on the way, some which were destined for other men graze us instead. We should not manifest surprise at any sort of condition into which we are born, and which should be lamented by no one, simply because it is equally ordained for all. Yes, I say, equally ordained; for a man might have experienced even that which he has escaped. And an equal law consists, not of that which all have experienced, but of that which is laid down for all. Be sure to prescribe for your mind this sense of equity; we should pay without complaint the tax of our mortality.

Winter brings on cold weather; and we must shiver. Summer returns, with its heat; and we must sweat. Unseasonable weather upsets the health; and we must fall ill. In certain places we may meet with wild beasts, or with men who are more destructive than any beasts. Floods, or fires, will cause us loss. And we cannot change this order of things; but what we can do is to acquire stout hearts, worthy of good men, thereby courageously enduring chance and placing ourselves in harmony with Nature. And Nature moderates this world-kingdom which you see, by her changing seasons: clear weather follows cloudy; after a calm, comes the storm; the winds blow by turns; day succeeds night; some of the heavenly bodies rise, and some set. Eternity consists of opposites.

It is to this law that our souls must adjust themselves, this they should follow, this they should obey. Whatever happens, assume that it was bound to happen, and do not be willing to rail at Nature. That which you cannot reform, it is best to endure, and to attend uncomplainingly upon the God under whose guidance everything progresses; for it is a bad soldier who grumbles when following his commander. For this reason we should welcome our orders with energy and vigour, nor should we cease to follow the natural course of this most beautiful universe, into which all our future sufferings are woven.

Let us address Jupiter, the pilot of this world-mass, as did our great Cleanthes in those most eloquent lines—lines which I shall allow myself to render in Latin, after the example of the eloquent Cicero. If you like them, make the most of them; if they displease you, you will understand that I have simply been following the practise of Cicero:

Lead me, O Master of the lofty heavens,
My Father, whithersoever thou shalt wish.
I shall not falter, but obey with speed.
And though I would not, I shall go, and suffer,
In sin and sorrow what I might have done
In noble virtue. Aye, the willing soul
Fate leads, but the unwilling drags along.

Let us live thus, and speak thus; let Fate find us ready and alert. Here is your great soul—the man who has given himself over to Fate; on the other hand, that man is a weakling and a degenerate who struggles and maligns the order of the universe and would rather reform the gods than reform himself. Farewell.

108. ON THE APPROACHES TO PHILOSOPHY

The topic about which you ask me is one of those where our only concern with knowledge is to have the knowledge. Nevertheless, because it does so far concern us, you are in a hurry; you are not willing to wait for the books which I am at this moment arranging for you, and which embrace the whole department of moral philosophy. I shall send you the books at once; but I shall, before doing that, write and tell you how this eagerness to learn, with which I see you are aflame, should be regulated, so that it may not get in its own way. Things are not to be gathered at random; nor should they be greedily attacked in the mass; one will arrive at a knowledge of the whole by studying the parts. The burden should be suited to your strength, nor should you tackle more than you can adequately handle. Absorb not all that you wish, but all that you can hold. Only be of a sound mind, and then you will be able to hold all that you wish. For the more the mind receives, the more does it expand.

This was the advice, I remember, which Attalus* gave me in the days when I practically laid siege to his class-room, the first to arrive and the last to leave. Even as he paced up and down, I would challenge him to various discussions; for he not only kept himself accessible to his pupils, but met them half-way. His words were: "The same purpose should possess both master and scholar—an ambition in the one case to promote, and in the other to progress." He who studies with a philosopher should take away with him some one good thing every day: he should daily return home a sounder man, or in the way to become sounder. And he will thus return; for it is one of the functions of philosophy to help not only those who study her, but those also who associate with her. He that walks in the sun, though he walks not for that purpose, must needs become sunburned. He who frequents the perfumer's shop and lingers even for a short time, will carry with him the scent of the place. And he who follows a philosopher is bound to derive some benefit therefrom, which will help him even though he be remiss. Mark what I say: "remiss," not "recalcitrant."

"What then?" you say; "do we not know certain men who have sat for many years at the feet of a philosopher and yet have not acquired the slightest tinge of wisdom?" Of course I know such men. There are indeed persevering gentlemen who stick at it; I do not call them pupils of the wise, but merely "squatters." Certain of them come to hear and not to learn, just as we are attracted to the theatre to satisfy the pleasures of the ear, whether by a speech, or by a song, or by a play. This class, as you will see, constitutes a large part of the listeners, who regard the philosopher's lecture-room merely as a sort of lounging-place for their leisure. They do not set about to lay aside any faults there, or to receive a rule of life, by which they may test their characters; they merely wish to enjoy to the full the delights of the ear. And yet some arrive even with notebooks, not to take down the matter, but only the words, that they may presently repeat them to others with as little profit to these as they themselves received when they heard them. A certain number are stirred by high-sounding phrases, and adapt themselves to the emotions of the speaker with lively change of face and mind—just

---

* Seneca's first and most convincing teacher of Stoicism, to whom this letter is a tribute. The ablest of contemporary philosophers, he was banished during the reign of Tiberius.

like the emasculated Phrygian priests who are wont to be roused by the sound of the flute and go mad to order. But the true hearer is ravished and stirred by the beauty of the subject matter, not by the jingle of empty words. When a bold word has been uttered in defiance of death, or a saucy fling in defiance of Fortune, we take delight in acting straightway upon that which we have heard. Men are impressed by such words, and become what they are bidden to be, should but the impression abide in the mind, and should the populace, who discourage honourable things, not immediately lie in wait to rob them of this noble impulse; only a few can carry home the mental attitude with which they were inspired. It is easy to rouse a listener so that he will crave righteousness; for Nature has laid the foundations and planted the seeds of virtue in us all. And we are all born to these general privileges; hence, when the stimulus is added, the good spirit is stirred as if it were freed from bonds. Have you not noticed how the theatre re-echoes whenever any words are spoken whose truth we appreciate generally and confirm unanimously.

The poor lack much; the greedy man lacks all.
A greedy man does good to none; he does
Most evil to himself.

At such verses as these, your meanest miser claps applause and rejoices to hear his own sins reviled. How much more do you think this holds true, when such things are uttered by a philosopher, when he introduces verses among his wholesome precepts, that he may thus make those verses sink more effectively into the mind of the neophyte! Cleanthes used to say: "As our breath produces a louder sound when it passes through the long and narrow opening of the trumpet and escapes by a hole which widens at the end, even so the fettering rules of poetry clarify our meaning." The very same words are more carelessly received and make less impression upon us, when they are spoken in prose; but when metre is added and when regular prosody has compressed a noble idea, then the selfsame thought comes, as it were, hurtling with a fuller fling. We talk much about despising money, and we give advice on this subject in the lengthiest of speeches, that mankind may believe true riches to exist in the mind and not in one's bank account, and that the man who adapts himself to his slender means and makes himself wealthy on a little sum is the truly rich man; but our minds are struck more effectively when a verse like this is repeated:

He needs but little who desires but little.

Or,

He hath his wish, whose wish includeth naught.
Save that which is enough.

When we hear such words as these, we are led towards a confession of the truth.

Even men in whose opinion nothing is enough, wonder and applaud when they hear such words, and swear eternal hatred against money. When you see them thus disposed, strike home, keep at them, and charge them with this duty, dropping all double meanings, syllogisms, hair-splitting, and the other side-shows of ineffective smartness. Preach against greed, preach against high living; and when you notice that you have made progress and impressed the minds of your hearers, lay on still harder. You cannot imagine how much progress can be brought about by an address of that nature, when you are bent on curing your hearers and are absolutely devoted to their best interests. For when the mind is young, it may most easily be won over to desire what is honourable and upright; truth, if she can obtain a suitable pleader, will lay strong hands upon those who can still be taught, those who have been but superficially spoiled.

At any rate, when I used to hear Attalus denouncing sin, error, and the evils of life, I often felt sorry for mankind and regarded Attalus as a noble and majestic being—above our mortal heights. He called himself a king, but I thought him more than a king, because he was entitled to pass judgment on kings. And in truth, when he began to uphold poverty, and to show what a useless and dangerous burden was everything that passed the measure of our need, I often desired to leave his lecture-room a poor man. Whenever he castigated our pleasure-seeking lives, and extolled personal purity, moderation in diet, and a mind free from unnecessary, not to speak of unlawful, pleasures, the desire came upon me to limit my food and drink. And that is why some of these habits have stayed with me, Lucilius. For I had planned my whole life with great resolve. And later, when I returned to the duties of a citizen, I did indeed keep a few of these good resolutions. That is why I have forsaken oysters and mushrooms for ever: since they are not really food, but are relishes to bully the sated stomach into further eating, as is the fancy of gourmands and those who stuff themselves beyond their powers of digestion: down with it quickly, and up with it quickly! That is why I have also throughout my life avoided perfumes; because the best scent for the person is no scent at all. That is why my stomach is unacquainted with wine. That is why throughout my life I have shunned the bath, and have believed that to emaciate the body and sweat it into thinness is at once unprofitable and effeminate. Other resolutions have been broken, but after all in such a way that, in cases where I ceased to practise abstinence, I have observed a limit which is indeed next door to abstinence; perhaps it is even a little more difficult, because it is easier for the will to cut off certain things utterly than to use them with restraint.

Inasmuch as I have begun to explain to you how much greater was my impulse to approach philosophy in my youth than to continue it in my old age, I shall not be ashamed to tell you what ardent zeal Pythagoras inspired in me. Sotion* used to tell me why Pythagoras abstained from animal food, and why, in later times, Sextius did also. In each case, the reason was different, but it was in each case a noble reason. Sextius believed that man had enough sustenance without resorting to blood, and that a habit of cruelty is formed whenever butchery is practised for pleasure. Moreover, he thought we should curtail the sources of our luxury; he argued that a varied diet was contrary to the laws of health, and was unsuited to our constitutions. Pythagoras, on the other hand, held that all beings were inter-related, and that there was a system of exchange between souls which transmigrated from one bodily shape into another. If one may believe him, no soul perishes or ceases from its functions at all, except for a tiny interval—when it is being poured from one body into another. We may question at what time and after what seasons of change the soul returns to man, when it has wandered through many a dwelling-place; but meantime, he made men fearful of guilt and parricide, since they might be, without knowing it, attacking the soul of a parent and injuring it with knife or with teeth—if, as is possible, the related spirit be dwelling temporarily in this bit of flesh! When Sotion had set forth this doctrine, supplementing it with his own proofs, he would say: "You do not believe that souls are assigned, first to one body and then to another, and that our so-called death is merely a change of abode? You do not believe that in cattle, or in wild beasts, or in creatures of the deep, the soul of him who was once a man may linger? You do not believe that nothing on this earth is annihilated, but only changes its haunts? And that animals also have cycles of progress and, so to speak, an orbit for

* Pythagorean philosopher of the Augustine age, and one of Seneca's early teachers.

their souls, no less than the heavenly bodies, which revolve in fixed circuits? Great men have put faith in this idea; therefore, while holding to your own view, keep the whole question in abeyance in your mind. If the theory is true, it is a mark of purity to refrain from eating flesh; if it be false, it is economy. And what harm does it do to you to give such credence? I am merely depriving you of food which sustains lions and vultures."

I was imbued with this teaching and began to abstain from animal food; at the end of a year the habit was as pleasant as it was easy. I was beginning to feel that my mind was more active; though I would not today positively state whether it really was or not. Do you ask how I came to abandon the practise? It was this way: The days of my youth coincided with the early part of the reign of Tiberius Caesar. Some foreign rites were at that time being inaugurated, and abstinence from certain kinds of animal food was set down as a proof of interest in the strange cult. So at the request of my father, who did not fear prosecution, but who detested philosophy, I returned to my previous habits; and it was no very hard matter to induce me to dine more comfortably.

Attalus used to recommend a pillow which did not give in to the body; and now, old as I am, I use one so hard that it leaves no trace after pressure. I have mentioned all this in order to show you how zealous neophytes are with regard to their first impulses towards the highest ideals, provided that some one does his part in exhorting them and in kindling their ardour. There are indeed mistakes made, through the fault of our advisers, who teach us how to debate and not how to live; there are also mistakes made by the pupils, who come to their teachers to develop, not their souls, but their wits. Thus the study of wisdom has become the study of words.

Now it makes a great deal of difference what you have in mind when you approach a given subject. If a man is to be a scholar, and is examining the works of Vergil, he does not interpret the noble passage

Time flies away, and cannot be restored

in the following sense: "We must wake up; unless we hasten, we shall be left behind. Time rolls swiftly ahead, and rolls us with it. We are hurried along ignorant of our destiny; we arrange all our plans for the future, and on the edge of a precipice are at our ease." Instead of this, he brings to our attention how often Vergil, in speaking of the rapidity of time, uses the word "flies" (*fugit*).

The choicest days of hapless human life
Fly first; disease and bitter eld succeed,
And toil, till harsh death rudely snatches all.

He who considers these lines in the spirit of a philosopher comments on the words in their proper sense: "Vergil never says, 'Time goes,' but 'Time flies,' because the latter is the quickest kind of movement, and in every case our best days are the first to be snatched away; why, then, do we hesitate to bestir ourselves so that we may be able to keep pace with this swiftest of all swift things?" The good flies past and the bad takes its place. Just as the purest wine flows from the top of the jar and the thickest dregs settle at the bottom; so in our human life, that which is best comes first. Shall we allow other men to quaff the best, and keep the dregs for ourselves? Let this phrase cleave to your soul; you should be satisfied thereby as if it were uttered by an oracle:

Each choicest day of hapless human life
Flies first.

Why "choicest day?" Because what's to come is unsure. Why "choicest day"? Because in our youth we are able to learn; we can bend to nobler purposes minds that are ready and still pliable; because this is the time for work, the time for keeping our minds busied in study and in exercising our bodies with useful effort; for that which remains is more sluggish and lacking in spirit—nearer the end.

Let us therefore strive with all courage, omitting attractions by the way; let us struggle with a single purpose, lest, when we are left behind, we comprehend too late the speed of quick-flying time, whose course we cannot stay. Let every day, as soon as it comes, be welcome as being the choicest, and let it be made our own possession. We must catch that which flees. Now he who scans with a scholar's eye the lines I have just quoted, does not reflect that our first days are the best because disease is approaching and old age weighs upon us and hangs over our heads while we are still thinking about our youth. He thinks rather of Vergil's usual collocation of disease and eld; and indeed rightly. For old age is a disease which we cannot cure. "Besides," he says to himself, "think of the epithet that accompanies *eld*; Vergil calls it *bitter*,"—

Disease and bitter eld succeed.

And elsewhere Vergil says:

There dwelleth pale disease and bitter eld.

There is no reason why you should marvel that each man can collect from the same source suitable matter for his own studies; for in the same meadow the cow grazes, the dog hunts the hare, and the stork the lizard. When Cicero's book *On the State* is opened by a philologist, a scholar, or a follower of philosophy, each man pursues his investigation in his own way. The philosopher wonders that so much could have been said therein against justice. The philologist takes up the same book and comments on the text as follows: "There were two Roman kings—one without a father and one without a mother. For we cannot settle who was Servius's mother, and Ancus, the grandson of Numa, has no father on record." The philologist also notes that the officer whom we call dictator, and about whom we read in our histories under that title, was named in old times the *magister populi*; such is the name existing today in the augural records, proved by the fact that he whom the dictator chose as second in command was called *magister equitum*. He will remark, too, that Romulus met his end during an eclipse; that there was an appeal to the people even from the kings (this is so stated in the pontiffs' register and is the opinion of others, including Fenestella). When the scholar unrolls this same volume, he puts down in his notebook the forms of words, noting that *reapse*, equivalent to *re ipsa*, is used by Cicero, and *sepse* just as frequently, which means *se ipse*. Then he turns his attention to changes in current usage. Cicero, for example, says: "Inasmuch as we are summoned back from the very calx by his interruption." Now the line in the circus which we call the *creta* was called the *calx* by men of old time. Again, he puts together some verses by Ennius, especially those which referred to Africanus:

A man to whom nor friend nor foe could give
Due meed for all his efforts and his deed.

From this passage the scholar declares that he infers the word *opem* to have meant formerly not merely *assistance*, but *efforts*. For Ennius must mean that neither friend nor foe could pay Scipio a reward worthy of his efforts. Next, he congratulates himself on finding the source of Vergil's words:

Over whose head the mighty gate of Heaven
Thunders,

remarking that Ennius stole the idea from Homer, and Vergil from Ennius. For there is a couplet by Ennius, preserved in this same book of Cicero's, *On the State*:

If it be right for a mortal to scale the regions of Heaven,
Then the huge gate of the sky opens in glory to me.

But that I, too, while engaged upon another task, may not slip into the department of the philologist or the scholar, my advice is this—that all study of philosophy and all reading should be applied to the idea of living the happy life, that we should not hunt out archaic or far-fetched words and eccentric metaphors and figures of speech, but that we should seek precepts which will help us, utterances of courage and spirit which may at once be turned into facts. We should so learn them that words may become deeds. And I hold that no man has treated mankind worse than he who has studied philosophy as if it were some marketable trade, who lives in a different manner from that which he advises. For those who are liable to every fault which they castigate advertise themselves as patterns of useless training. A teacher like that can help me no more than a sea-sick pilot can be efficient in a storm. He must hold the tiller when the waves are tossing him; he must wrestle, as it were, with the sea; he must furl his sails when the storm rages; what good is a frightened and vomiting steersman to *me*? And how much greater, think you, is the storm of life than that which tosses any ship! One must steer, not talk.

All the words that these men utter and juggle before a listening crowd belong to others. They have been spoken by Plato, spoken by Zeno, spoken by Chrysippus or by Posidonius, and by a whole host of Stoics as numerous as excellent. I shall show you how men can prove their words to be their own: it is by doing what they have been talking about. Since therefore I have given you the message I wished to pass on to you, I shall now satisfy your craving and shall reserve for a new letter a complete answer to your summons; so that you may not approach in a condition of weariness a subject which is thorny and which should be followed with an attentive and painstaking ear. Farewell.

109. ON THE FELLOWSHIP OF WISE MEN

You expressed a wish to know whether a wise man can help a wise man. For we say that the wise man is completely endowed with every good, and has attained perfection; accordingly, the question arises how it is possible for anyone to help a person who possesses the Supreme Good.

Good men are mutually helpful; for each gives practise to the other's virtues and thus maintains wisdom at its proper level. Each needs someone with whom he may make comparisons and investigations. Skilled wrestlers are kept up to the mark by practise; a musician is stirred to action by one of equal proficiency. The wise man also needs to have his virtues kept in action; and as he prompts himself to do things, so is he prompted by another wise man. How can a wise man help another wise man? He can quicken his impulses, and point out to him opportunities for honourable action. Besides, he can develop some of his own ideas; he can impart what he has discovered. For even in the case of the wise man something will always remain to discover, something towards which his mind may make new ventures.

Evil men harm evil men; each debases the other by rousing his wrath, by approving his churlishness, and praising his pleasures; bad men are at their worst stage when their faults are most thoroughly intermingled, and their wickedness has been, so to speak, pooled in partnership. Conversely, therefore, a good man will help another good man. "How?" you ask. Because he will bring joy to the other, he will strengthen his faith, and from the contemplation of their mutual tranquillity the delight of both will be increased. Moreover they will communicate to each other a knowledge of certain facts; for the wise man is not all-knowing. And even if he were all-knowing, someone might be able to devise and point out short cuts, by which the whole matter is more readily disseminated. The wise will help the wise, not, mark you, because of his own strength merely, but because of the strength of the man whom he assists. The latter, it is true, can by himself develop his own parts; nevertheless, even one who is running well is helped by one who cheers him on.

"But the wise man does not really help the wise; he helps himself. Let me tell you this: strip the one of his special powers, and the other will accomplish nothing." You might as well, on that basis, say that sweetness is not in the honey: for it is the person himself who is to eat it, that is so equipped, as to tongue and palate, for tasting this kind of food that the special flavour appeals to him, and anything else displeases. For there are certain men so affected by disease that they regard honey as bitter. Both men should be in good health, that the one may be helpful and the other a proper subject for help. Again they say: "When the highest degree of heat has been attained, it is superfluous to apply more heat; and when the Supreme Good has been attained, it is superfluous to have a helper. Does a completely stocked farmer ask for further supplies from his neighbours? Does a soldier who is sufficiently armed for going well-equipped into action need any more weapons? Very well, neither does the wise man; for he is sufficiently equipped and sufficiently armed for life." My answer to this is, that when one is heated to the highest degree, one must have continued heat to maintain the highest temperature. And if it be objected that heat is self-maintaining, I say that there are great distinctions among the things that you are comparing; for heat is a single thing, but helpfulness is of many kinds. Again, heat is not helped by the addition of further heat, in order to be hot; but the wise man cannot maintain his mental standard without intercourse with friends of his own kind—with whom he may share his goodness. Moreover, there is a sort of mutual friendship among all the virtues.* Thus, he who loves the virtues of certain among his peers, and in turn exhibits his own to be loved, is helpful. Like things give pleasure, especially when they are honourable and when men know that there is mutual approval. And besides, none but a wise man can prompt another wise man's soul in an intelligent way, just as man can be prompted in a rational way by man only. As, therefore, reason is necessary for the prompting of reason, so, in order to prompt perfect reason, there is need of perfect reason.

Some say that we are helped even by those† who bestow on us the so-called "indifferent" benefits, such as money, influence, security, and all the other valued or essential aids to living. If we argue in this way, the veriest fool will be said to help a wise man. Helping, however, really means prompting the soul in accordance with Nature, both by the prompter's excellence and

* In other words, Wisdom, Justice, Courage, and Self-Restraint, together with other qualities of simplicity, kindness, etc., being "avatars" of Virtue herself, are interrelated.
† *i.e.*, certain of the Peripatetic school.

by the excellence of him who is thus prompted. And this cannot take place without advantage to the helper also. For in training the excellence of another, a man must necessarily train his own. But, to omit from discussion supreme goods or the things which produce them, wise men can none the less be mutually helpful. For the mere discovery of a sage by a sage is in itself a desirable event; since everything good is naturally dear to the good man, and for this reason one feels congenial with a good man as one feels congenial with oneself.

It is necessary for me to pass from this topic to another, in order to prove my point. For the question is asked, whether the wise man will weigh his opinions, or whether he will apply to others for advice. Now he is compelled to do this when he approaches state and home duties—everything, so to speak, that is mortal. He needs outside advice on such matters, as does the physician, the pilot, the attorney, or the pleader of cases. Hence, the wise will sometimes help the wise; for they will persuade each other. But in these matters of great import also—aye, of divine import, as I have termed them—the wise man can also be useful by discussing honourable things in common, and by contributing his thoughts and ideas. Moreover, it is in accordance with Nature to show affection for our friends and to rejoice in their advancement as if it were absolutely our own. For if we have not done this, even virtue, which grows strong only through exercising our perceptions, will not abide with us. Now virtue advises us to arrange the present well, to take thought regarding the future, to deliberate and apply our minds; and one who takes a friend into council with him can more easily apply his mind and think out his problem.

Therefore he will seek either the perfect wise man or one who has progressed to a point bordering on perfection. The perfect wise man, moreover, will help us if he aids our counsels with ordinary good sense. They say that men see farther in the affairs of others than in their own. A defect of character causes this in those who are blinded by self-love, and whose fear in the hour of peril takes away their clear view of that which is useful; it is when a man is more at ease and freed from fear that he will begin to be wise. Nevertheless, there are certain matters where even wise men see the facts more clearly in the case of others than in their own. Moreover, the wise man will, in company with his fellow sage, confirm the truth of that most sweet and honourable proverb—"always desiring and always refusing the same things": it will be a noble result when they draw the load "with equal yoke."

I have thus answered your demand, although it came under the head of subjects which I include in my volumes *On Moral Philosophy*. Reflect, as I am often wont to tell you, that there is nothing in such topics for us except mental gymnastics. For I return again and again to the thought: "What good does this do me? Make me more brave now, more just, more restrained! I have not yet the opportunity to make use of my training; for I still need the physician. Why do you ask of me a useless knowledge? You have promised great things; test me, watch me! You assured me that I should be unterrified though swords were flashing round me, though the point of the blade were grazing my throat; you assured me that I should be at ease though fires were blazing round me, or though a sudden whirlwind should snatch up my ship and carry it over all the sea. Now make good for me such a course of treatment that I may despise pleasure and glory. Thereafter you shall teach me to work out complicated problems, to settle doubtful points, to see through that which is not clear; teach me now what it is necessary for me to know!" Farewell.

111. ON THE VANITY OF MENTAL GYMNASTICS

You have asked me to give you a Latin word for the Greek *sophismata*. Many have tried to define the term, but no name has stuck. This is natural, inasmuch as the thing itself has not been admitted to general use by us; the name, too, has met with opposition. But the word which Cicero used seems to me most suitable: he calls them *cavillationes*. If a man has surrendered himself to them, he weaves many a tricky subtlety, but makes no progress toward real living; he does not thereby become braver, or more restrained, or loftier of spirit.

He, however, who has practised philosophy to effect his own cure becomes high-souled, full of confidence, invincible, and greater as you draw near him. This phenomenon is seen in the case of high mountains, which appear less lofty when beheld from afar, but which prove clearly how high the peaks are when you come near them; such, my dear Lucilius, is our true philosopher, true by his acts and not by his tricks. He stands in a high place, worthy of admiration, lofty, and really great. He does not stretch himself or walk on tiptoe like those who seek to improve their height by deceit, wishing to seem taller than they really are; he is content with his own greatness. And why should he not be content with having grown to such a height that Fortune cannot reach her hands to it? He is therefore above earthly things, equal to himself under all conditions—whether the current of life runs free, or whether he is tossed and travels on troubled and desperate seas; but this steadfastness cannot be gained through such hair-splittings as I have just mentioned. The mind plays with them, but profits not a whit; the mind in such cases is simply dragging philosophy down from her heights to the level ground.

I would not forbid you to practise such exercises occasionally; but let it be at a time when you wish to do nothing. The worst feature, however, that these indulgences present is that they acquire a sort of self-made charm, occupying and holding the soul by a show of subtlety; although such weighty matters claim our attention, and a whole life seems scarcely sufficient to learn the single principle of despising life. "What? Did you not mean 'control' instead of 'despise'?" No; "controlling" is the second task; for no one has controlled his life aright unless he has first learned to despise it. Farewell.

123. ON THE CONFLICT BETWEEN PLEASURE AND VIRTUE

Wearied with the discomfort rather than with the length of my journey, I have reached my Alban villa late at night, and I find nothing in readiness except myself, So I am getting rid of fatigue at my writing-table: I derive some good from this tardiness on the part of my cook and my baker. For I am communing with myself on this very topic—that nothing is heavy if one accepts it with a light heart, and that nothing need provoke one's anger if one does not add to one's pile of troubles by getting angry. My baker is out of bread; but the overseer, or the house-steward, or one of my tenants can supply me therewith. "Bad bread!" you say. But just wait for it; it will become good. Hunger will make even such bread delicate and of the finest flavour. For that reason I must not eat until hunger bids me; so I shall wait and shall not eat until I can either get good bread or else cease to be squeamish about it. It is necessary that one grow accustomed to slender fare: because there are many problems of time and place which will cross the path even of the rich man and one equipped for pleasure, and bring him up with a round turn. To have whatsoever he wishes is in no man's power; it is in his power not to wish for what he has not, but cheerfully to employ what comes to him. A great step towards independence is a good-humoured stomach, one that is willing to endure rough treatment.

You cannot imagine how much pleasure I derive from the fact that my weariness is becoming reconciled to itself; I am asking for no slaves to rub me down, no bath, and no other restorative except time. For that which toil has accumulated, rest can lighten. This repast, whatever it may be, will give me more pleasure than an inaugural banquet.* For I have made trial of my spirit on a sudden—a simpler and a truer test. Indeed, when a man has made preparations and given himself a formal summons to be patient, it is not equally clear just how much real strength of mind he possesses; the surest proofs are those which one exhibits off-hand, viewing one's own troubles not only fairly but calmly, not flying into fits of temper or wordy wranglings, supplying one's own needs by not craving something which was really due, and reflecting that our habits may be unsatisfied, but never our own real selves. How many things are superfluous we fail to realize until they begin to be wanting; we merely used them not because we needed them but because we had them. And how much do we acquire simply because our neighbours have acquired such things, or because most men possess them! Many of our troubles may be explained from the fact that we live according to a pattern, and, instead of arranging our lives according to reason, are led astray by convention.

There are things which, if done by the few, we should refuse to imitate; yet when the majority have begun to do them, we follow along—just as if anything were more honourable because it is more frequent! Furthermore, wrong views, when they have become prevalent, reach, in our eyes, the standard of righteousness. Everyone now travels with Numidian outriders preceding him, with a troop of slave-runners to clear the way; we deem it disgraceful to have no attendants who will elbow crowds from the road, or will prove, by a great cloud of dust, that a high dignitary is approaching! Everyone now possesses mules that are laden with crystal and murrine cups carved by skilled artists of great renown; it is disgraceful for all your baggage to be made up of that which can be rattled along without danger. Everyone has pages who ride along with ointment-covered faces so that the heat or the cold will not harm their tender complexions; it is disgraceful that none of your attendant slave-boys should show a healthy cheek, not covered with cosmetics.

You should avoid conversation with all such persons: they are the sort that communicate and engraft their bad habits from one to another. We used to think that the very worst variety of these men were those who vaunted their words: but there are certain men who vaunt their wickedness. Their talk is very harmful; for

---

* *i.e.*, a dinner given by an official when he entered upon his office.

even though it is not at once convincing, yet they leave the seeds of trouble in the soul, and the evil which is sure to spring into new strength follows us about even when we have parted from them. Just as those who have attended a concert carry about in their heads the melodies and the charm of the songs they have heard—a proceeding which interferes with their thinking and does not allow them to concentrate upon serious subjects—even so the speech of flatterers and enthusiasts over that which is depraved sticks in our minds long after we have heard them talk. It is not easy to rid the memory of a catching tune; it stays with us, lasts on, and comes back from time to time. Accordingly, you should close your ears against evil talk, and right at the outset, too; for when such talk has gained an entrance and the words are admitted and are in our minds, they become more shameless. And then we begin to speak as follows: "Virtue, Philosophy, Justice—this is a jargon of empty words. The only way to be happy is to do yourself well. To eat, drink, and spend your money is the only real life, the only way to remind yourself that you are mortal. Our days flow on, and life—which we cannot restore—hastens away from us. Why hesitate to come to our senses? This life of ours will not always admit pleasures; meantime, while it can do so, while it clamours for them, what profit lies in imposing thereupon frugality? Therefore get ahead of death, and let anything that death will filch from you be squandered now upon yourself. You have no mistress, no favourite slave to make your mistress envious; you are sober when you make your daily appearance in public; you dine as if you had to show your account-book to 'Papa'; but *that* is not living, it is merely going shares in someone else's existence. And what madness it is to be looking out for the interests of your heir, and to deny yourself everything, with the result that you turn friends into enemies by the vast amount of the Fortune you intend to leave! For the more the heir is to get from you, the more he will rejoice in your taking-off! All those sour fellows who criticize other men's lives in a spirit of priggishness and are real enemies to their own lives, playing schoolmaster to the world—you should not consider them as worth a farthing, nor should you hesitate to prefer good living to a good reputation."

These are voices which you ought to shun just as Ulysses did; he would not sail past them until he was lashed to the mast. They are no less potent; they lure men from country, parents, friends, and virtuous ways; and by a hope that, if not base, is ill-starred, they wreck them upon a life of baseness. How much better to follow a straight course and attain a goal where the words "pleasant" and "honourable" have the same meaning! This end will be possible for us if we understand that there are two classes of objects which either attract us or repel us. We are attracted by such things as riches, pleasures, beauty, ambition, and other such coaxing and pleasing objects; we are repelled by toil, death, pain, disgrace, or lives of greater frugality. We ought therefore to train ourselves so that we may avoid a fear of the one or a desire for the other. Let us fight in the opposite fashion: let us retreat from the objects that allure, and rouse ourselves to meet the objects that attack.

Do you not see how different is the method of descending a mountain from that employed in climbing upwards? Men coming down a slope bend backwards; men ascending a steep place lean forward. For, my dear Lucilius, to allow yourself to put your body's weight ahead when coming down, or, when climbing up, to throw it backward is to comply with vice. The pleasures take one down hill but one must work upwards toward that which is rough and hard to climb; in the one case let us throw our bodies forward, in the others let us put the check-rein on them.

Do you believe me to be stating now that only those men bring ruin to our ears, who praise pleasure, who inspire us with fear of pain—that element which is in itself provocative of fear? I believe that we are also injured by those who masquerade under the disguise of the Stoic school and at the same time urge us on into vice. They boast that only the wise man and the learned is a lover.* "He alone has wisdom in this art; the wise man too is best skilled in drinking and feasting. Our study ought to be this alone: up to what age the bloom of love can endure!" All this may be regarded as a concession to the ways of Greece; we ourselves should preferably turn our attention to words like these: "No man is good by chance. Virtue is something which must be learned. Pleasure is low, petty, to be deemed worthless, shared even by dumb animals—the tiniest and meanest of whom fly towards pleasure. Glory is an empty and fleeting thing, lighter than air. Poverty is an evil to no man unless he kick against the goads. Death is not an evil; why need you ask? Death alone is the equal privilege of mankind. Superstition is the misguided idea of a lunatic; it fears those whom it ought to love; it is an outrage upon those whom it worships. For what difference is there between denying the gods and dishonouring them?"

You should learn such principles as these, nay, rather you should learn them by heart; philosophy ought not to try to explain away vice. For a sick man, when his physician bids him live recklessly, is doomed beyond recall. Farewell.

* Meaning, in line with the Stoic paradoxes, that only the sage knows how to be rightly in love.

124. ON THE TRUE GOOD AS ATTAINED BY REASON

Full many an ancient precept could I give,
Didst thou not shrink, and feel it shame to learn
Such lowly duties.

But you do not shrink, nor are you deterred by any subtleties of study. For your cultivated mind is not wont to investigate such important subjects in a free-and-easy manner. I approve your method in that you make everything count towards a certain degree of progress, and in that you are disgruntled only when nothing can be accomplished by the greatest degree of subtlety. And I shall take pains to show that this is the case now also. Our question is, whether the Good is grasped by the senses or by the understanding; and the corollary thereto is that it does not exist in dumb animals or little children.

Those who rate pleasure as the supreme ideal hold that the Good is a matter of the senses; but we Stoics maintain that it is a matter of the understanding, and we assign it to the mind. If the senses were to pass judgment on what is good, we should never reject any pleasure; for there is no pleasure that does not attract, no pleasure that does not please. Conversely, we should undergo no pain voluntarily; for there is no pain that does not clash with the senses. Besides, those who are too fond of pleasure and those who fear pain to the greatest degree would in that case not deserve reproof. But we condemn men who are slaves to their appetites and their lusts, and we scorn men who, through fear of pain, will dare no manly deed. But what wrong could such men be committing if they looked merely to the senses as arbiters of good and evil? For it is to the senses that you and yours have entrusted the test of things to be sought and things to be avoided!

Reason, however, is surely the governing element in such a matter as this; as reason has made the decision concerning the happy life, and concerning virtue and honour also, so she has made the decision with regard to good and evil. For with them* the vilest part is allowed to give sentence about the better, so that the senses—dense as they are, and dull, and even more sluggish in man than in the other animals—pass judgment on the Good. Just suppose that one

* *i.e.*, the Epicureans.

should desire to distinguish tiny objects by the touch rather than by the eyesight! There is no special faculty more subtle and acute than the eye that would enable us to distinguish between good and evil. You see, therefore, in what ignorance of truth a man spends his days and how abjectly he has overthrown lofty and divine ideals, if he thinks that the sense of touch can pass judgment upon the nature of the Supreme Good and the Supreme Evil! He* says: "Just as every science and every art should possess an element that is palpable and capable of being grasped by the senses (their source of origin and growth), even so the happy life derives its foundation and its beginnings from things that are palpable, and from that which falls within the scope of the senses. Surely you admit that the happy life takes its beginnings from things palpable to the senses." But we define as "happy" those things that are in accord with Nature. And that which is in accord with Nature is obvious and can be seen at once—just as easily as that which is complete. That which is according to Nature, that which is given us as a gift immediately at our birth, is, I maintain, not a Good, but the beginning of a Good. You, however, assign the Supreme Good, pleasure, to mere babies, so that the child at its birth begins at the point whither the perfected man arrives. You are placing the tree-top where the root ought to be. If anyone should say that the child, hidden in its mother's womb, of unknown sex too, delicate, unformed, and shapeless—if one should say that this child is already in a state of goodness, he would clearly seem to be astray in his ideas. And yet how little difference is there between one who has just lately received the gift of life, and one who is still a hidden burden in the bowels of the mother! They are equally developed, as far as their understanding of good or evil is concerned; and a child is as yet no more capable of comprehending the Good than is a tree or any dumb beast.

But why is the Good non-existent in a tree or in a dumb beast? Because there is no reason there, either. For the same cause, then, the Good is non-existent in a child, for the child also has no reason; the child will reach the Good only when he reaches reason.† There are animals without reason, there are animals not yet endowed with reason, and there are animals who possess reason, but only incompletely;‡ in none of these does the Good exist, for it is reason that

* *i.e.*, the advocate of the "touch" theory.

† According to the Stoics (and other schools also), the "innate notions," or groundwork of knowledge, begin to be subject to reason after the attainment of a child's seventh year.

‡ *i.e.*, they are limited to "practical judgment."

brings the Good in its company. What, then, is the distinction between the classes which I have mentioned? In that which does not possess reason, the Good will never exist. In that which is not yet endowed with reason, the Good cannot be existent at the time. And in that which possesses reason but only incompletely, the Good is capable of existing, but does not yet exist. This is what I mean, Lucilius: the Good cannot be discovered in any random person, or at any random age; and it is as far removed from infancy as last is from first, or as that which is complete from that which has just sprung into being. Therefore, it cannot exist in the delicate body, when the little frame has only just begun to knit together. Of course not—no more than in the seed. Granting the truth of this, we understand that there is a certain kind of Good in a tree or a plant; but this is not true of its first growth, when the plant has just begun to spring forth out of the ground. There is a certain Good of wheat: it is not yet existent, however, in the swelling stalk, nor when the soft ear is pushing itself out of the husk, but only when summer days and its appointed maturity have ripened the wheat. Just as Nature in general does not produce her Good until she is brought to perfection, even so man's Good does not exist in man until both reason and man are perfected. And what is this Good? I shall tell you: it is a free mind, an upright mind, subjecting other things to itself and itself to nothing. So far is infancy from admitting this Good that boyhood has no hope of it, and even young manhood cherishes the hope without justification; even our old age is very fortunate if it has reached this Good after long and concentrated study. If this, then, is the Good, the good is a matter of the understanding.

"But," comes the retort, "you admitted that there is a certain Good of trees and of grass; then surely there can be a certain Good of a child also." But the true Good is not found in trees or in dumb animals; the Good which exists in them is called good only by courtesy. "Then what is it?" you say. Simply that which is in accord with the nature of each. The real Good cannot find a place in dumb animals—not by any means; its nature is more blest and is of a higher class. And where there is no place for reason, the Good does not exist. There are four natures which we should mention here: of the tree, animal, man, and God. The last two, having reasoning power, are of the same nature, distinct only by virtue of the immortality of the one and the mortality of the other. Of one of these, then—to wit God—it is Nature that perfects the Good; of the other—to wit man—pains and study do so. All other things are perfect only in their particular nature, and not truly perfect, since they lack reason.

Indeed, to sum up, that alone is perfect which is perfect according to nature as a whole, and nature as a whole is possessed of reason. Other things can be perfect according to their kind. That which cannot contain the happy life cannot contain that which produces the happy life; and the happy life is produced by Goods alone. In dumb animals there is not a trace of the happy life, nor of the means whereby the happy life is produced; in dumb animals the Good does not exist. The dumb animal comprehends the present world about him through his senses alone. He remembers the past only by meeting with something which reminds his senses; a horse, for example, remembers the right road only when he is placed at the starting-point. In his stall, however, he has no memory of the road, no matter how often he may have stepped along it. The third state—the future—does not come within the ken of dumb beasts.

How, then, can we regard as perfect the nature of those who have no experience of time in its perfection? For time is three-fold—past, present, and future. Animals perceive only the time which is of greatest moment to them within the limits of their coming and going—the present. Rarely do they recollect the past—and that only when they are confronted with present reminders. Therefore the Good of a perfect nature cannot exist in an imperfect nature; for if the latter sort of nature should possess the Good, so also would mere vegetation. I do not indeed deny that dumb animals have strong and swift impulses toward actions which seem according to nature, but such impulses are confused and disordered. The Good, however, is never confused or disordered.

"What!" you say, "do dumb animals move in disturbed and ill-ordered fashion?" I should say that they moved in disturbed and ill-ordered fashion, if their nature admitted of order; as it is, they move in accordance with their nature. For that is said to be "disturbed" which can also at some other time be "not disturbed"; so, too, that is said to be in a state of trouble which can be in a state of peace. No man is vicious except one who has the capacity of virtue; in the case of dumb animals their motion is such as results from their nature. But, not to weary you, a certain sort of good will be found in a dumb animal, and a certain sort of virtue, and a certain sort of perfection—but neither the Good, nor virtue, nor perfection in the absolute sense. For this is the privilege of reasoning beings alone, who are permitted to know the cause, the degree, and the means. Therefore, good can exist only in that which possesses reason.

Do you ask now whither our argument is tending, and of what benefit it will be to your mind? I will tell you: it exercises and sharpens the mind, and ensures, by occupying it honourably, that it will accomplish some sort of good. And even that is beneficial which holds men back when they are hurrying into wickedness. However, I will say this also: I can be of no greater benefit to you than by revealing the Good that is rightly yours, by taking you out of the class of dumb animals, and by placing you on a level with God. Why, pray, do you foster and practise your bodily strength? Nature has granted strength in greater degree to cattle and wild beasts. Why cultivate your beauty? After all your efforts, dumb animals surpass you in comeliness. Why dress your hair with such unending attention? Though you let it down in Parthian fashion, or tie it up in the German style, or, as the Scythians do, let it flow wild—yet you will see a mane of greater thickness tossing upon any horse you choose, and a mane of greater beauty bristling upon the neck of any lion. And even after training yourself for speed, you will be no match for the hare. Are you not willing to abandon all these details—wherein you must acknowledge defeat, striving as you are for something that is not your own and come back to the Good that is really yours?

And what is this Good? It is a clear and flawless mind, which rivals that of God,* raised far above mortal concerns, and counting nothing of its own to be outside itself. You are a reasoning animal. What Good, then, lies within you? Perfect reason. Are you willing to develop this to its farthest limits—to its greatest degree of increase? Only consider yourself happy when all your joys are born of reason, and when—having marked all the objects which men clutch at, or pray for, or watch over—you find nothing which you will desire; mind, I do not say *prefer*. Here is a short rule by which to measure yourself, and by the test of which you may feel that you have reached perfection: "You will come to your own when you shall understand that those whom the world calls fortunate are really the most unfortunate of all." Farewell.

* One of the most conspicuous Stoic paradoxes maintained that "the wise man is God."

About the Authors

MARCUS AURELIUS was born in 121 CE. He is believed to have been a bookish young boy who studied with a number of Stoic philosophers. He had a reputation for virtue from a young age and was adopted into the imperial family. This led to him becoming Emperor of Rome, a post he held from 161 until his death in 180.

EPICTETUS was born into slavery in ancient Greece in 50 CE. He founded his own school of philosophy and became one of the foundational thinkers of Stoic philosophy. His discourses were transcribed and shared by his student Arrian, and his work has influenced countless readers over the centuries, from Marcus Aurelius to Tom Wolfe.

SENECA was born in 1 BCE in Cordoba and educated in Rome, where he became an advisor for Emperor Nero and had a dramatic political career. However, he is best known for his contributions to Stoic philosophy, and his works played a central role in the renewed interest in Stoicism during the Renaissance.